Prentice-Hall International Series in Management

ATHOS AND COFFEY	*Behavior in Organizations: A Multidimensional View*
BAUMOL	*Economic Theory and Operations Analysis, 2nd ed.*
BOOT	*Mathematical Reasoning in Economics and Management Science*
BROWN	*Smoothing, Forecasting, and Prediction of Discrete Time Series*
CHAMBERS	*Accounting, Evaluation and Economic Behavior*
CHURCHMAN	*Prediction and Optimal Decision: Philosophical Issues of a Science of Values*
CLARKSON	*The Theory of Consumer Demand: A Critical Appraisal*
COHEN AND CYERT	*Theory of the Firm: Resource Allocation in a Market Economy*
CULLMAN AND KNUDSON	*Management Problems in International Environments*
CYERT AND MARCH	*A Behavioral Theory of the Firm*
FABRYCKY AND TORGERSEN	*Operations Economy: Industrial Applications of Operations Research*
FRANK, MASSY, AND WIND	*Market Segmentation*
GREEN AND TULL	*Research for Marketing Decisions, 2nd ed.*
GREENLAW, HERRON, AND RAWDON	*Business Simulation in Industrial and University Education*
HADLEY AND WHITIN	*Analysis of Inventory Systems*
HOLT, MODIGLIANI, MUTH, AND SIMON	*Planning Production, Inventories, and Work Force*
HYMANS	*Probability Theory with Applications to Econometrics and Decision-Making*
IJIRI	*The Foundations of Accounting Measurement: A Mathematical, Economic, and Behavioral Inquiry*
KAUFMANN	*Methods and Models of Operations Research*
LESOURNE	*Economic Analysis and Industrial Management*
MANTEL	*Cases in Managerial Decisions*
MASSÉ	*Optimal Investment Decisions: Rules for Action and Criteria for Choice*
McGUIRE	*Theories of Business Behavior*
MILLER AND STARR	*Executive Decisions and Operations Research, 2nd ed.*
MONTGOMERY AND URBAN	*Management Science in Marketing*
MONTGOMERY AND URBAN	*Applications of Management Science in Marketing*
MORRIS	*Management Science: A Bayesian Introduction*
MUTH AND THOMPSON	*Industrial Scheduling*
NELSON (ED.)	*Marginal Cost Pricing in Practice*
NICOSIA	*Consumer Decision Processes: Marketing and Advertising Decisions*
PETERS AND SUMMERS	*Statistical Analysis for Business Decisions*
PFIFFNER AND SHERWOOD	*Administrative Organization*
SIMONNARD	*Linear Programming*
SINGER	*Antitrust Economics: Selected Legal Cases and Economic Models*
VERNON	*Manager in the International Economy*
WAGNER	*Principles of Operations Research with Applications to Managerial Decisions*
ZANGWILL	*Nonlinear Programming: A Unified Approach*
ZENOFF AND ZWICK	*International Financial Management*

Prentice-Hall, Inc.
Prentice-Hall International, Inc., *United Kingdom and Eire*
Prentice-Hall of Canada, Ltd., *Canada*
J. H. DeBussy, Ltd., *Holland and Flemish-Speaking Belgium*
Dunod Press, *France*
Maruzen Company, Ltd., *Far East*
Herrero Hermanos, Sucs., *Spain and Latin America*
R. Oldenbourg, Verlag, *Germany*
Ulrico Hoepli Editore, *Italy*

MANAGEMENT PROBLEMS

IN

INTERNATIONAL

ENVIRONMENTS

EDITED BY

W. Arthur Cullman
OHIO STATE UNIVERSITY

Harry R. Knudson
UNIVERSITY OF WASHINGTON

Prentice-Hall, Inc., ENGLEWOOD CLIFFS, NEW JERSEY

ISBN: 0-13-548958-X

Library of Congress Catalog Card Number: 70-151042

Printed in the United States of America

10 9 8 7 6 5 4 3 2 1

The cases included in this book are not intended to
represent either correct or incorrect, desirable or undesirable,
administrative philosophy or behavior. They have been
included solely because of their intrinsic interest for purposes
of discussion. In many of the cases, names of people, places,
and figures have been disguised.

Prentice-Hall International, Inc., LONDON
Prentice-Hall of Australia, Pty. Ltd., SYDNEY
Prentice-Hall of Canada, Ltd., TORONTO
Prentice-Hall of India Private Limited, NEW DELHI
Prentice-Hall of Japan, Inc., TOKYO

Contents

Preface

One of the pioneering meetings to discuss the international dimensions of a professional education for career managers was held at Tulane University in December, 1967. Interest in this meeting, primarily organized by Dr. C. Jackson Grayson, was impressive, as was the attention that the meeting received in the press. It was clear that the better business schools in the United States and Canada had become aware of the growing importance of international economic relations and were prepared to make the necessary provisions to accommodate this growing field in their curriculum plans.

For those schools and educators who have been involved in international business, the challenge of providing a quality curriculum is significant. For those who are entering the field for the first time, the challenge is of even greater proportions. Apart from the sheer magnitude of the overall task, even a modest effort at conjuring up an image of the environment overseas presents a problem. As George Lombard of the Harvard Business School noted at the meeting, business may be "already facing most of these problems today. . . . We need to prepare a man to cope with a new combination of things." Dr. Grayson observed that "most of the descriptions of the ideal international business graduate are also descriptions of the ideal man."[1]

---

[1] See "How Business Schools Welcome the World," *Business Week* (December 9, 1967), p. 122.

It is not surprising, therefore, that there should be a great interest among educators in cases depicting business problems that are situated outside the North American continent. This interest has become even more pronounced as more and more organizations become multi-national in the scope of their operations, increasing the demand for business-school graduates with significant exposure to international business concepts and practices. In this context, IMEDE's research and case-gathering efforts have attracted attention, and the materials are much in demand as good examples of concrete, real-life business situations faced by active managers in a European environment. A number of these cases already have appeared in printed form, notably in *Business Policy—Text and Cases*, by Learned, Christensen, Andrews, and Guth,[2] *European Problems in General Management*, by Learned, Aguilar, and Valtz,[3] and in David Leighton's *International Marketing—Text and Cases*.[4]

These are all books devoted to major fields of study, and, ideally, some day there will be one or more such collections for every major field or specific area. Until that day, however, the only alternative available to the uninitiated looking for international cases is to plow through lists of cases written abroad and hope to find something that will suit his particular pedagogical needs. From this undesirable alternative grew the idea of composing a casebook cutting across subject areas in an international context—the gathering together between the covers of a single book of an anthology of cases that would be of significant value to the many international departments that are developing in many business schools throughout the world. Drawing from the vast IMEDE experience, a book containing this kind of information could be done by asking the widely recognized and acknowledged professors who have taught here in recent times to name those cases that they considered most appropriate and useful in their classroom activities. All major functional areas thus would be covered, and the frequency of suggestions would be a further guarantee of the quality and interrelatedness of the materials eventually selected.

It was an appealing idea, considered and discussed by several IMEDE faculty members in recent years. Unfortunately, the press of time and a wide variety of activities made it impossible to bring it to fruition.

---

[2]E. P. Learned, C. R. Christensen, K. R. Andrews, and W. D. Guth, *Business Policy—Text and Cases*, rev.ed. (Homewood, Ill.: Richard D. Irwin, Inc., 1969).

[3]E. P. Learned, F. J. Aguilar, and R. C. K. Valtz, *European Problems in General Management* (Homewood, Ill.: Richard D. Irwin, Inc., 1963).

[4]David Leighton, *International Marketing—Text and Cases* (New York: McGraw-Hill Book Co., Inc., 1966).

Similar thoughts occurred to the authors of this book, and they reacted promptly and enthusiastically to the challenge, devising a plan that would permit such a volume to be completed. Characteristically, they received the encouragement and support that the endeavor required from the Trustees of IMEDE. The faculty from earlier years responded with great enthusiasm and advice, which proved to be most valuable. The professional competence of Professors Cullman and Knudson required no further assistance to insure that the job would be done expertly and within the available time.

This book is a unique and highly useful volume since it brings together a wide variety of situations with their roots in several functional areas cutting across several cultural environments. It thus provides a highly relevant perspective for the student or executive interested in the study of business activities in an international environment. One of its most unique features is that it stresses the manager and managerial action in an international context.

I personally am convinced that it will prove to be a most valuable addition to any library of case material and an effective cornerstone in the building of any new collection with an emphasis on business problems gathered from different subject fields in many different lands.

L. DUSMET DE SMOURS
Director of IMEDE

Lausanne, Switzerland

Introduction

The prosperity of any business depends essentially on the performance of its managers of tomorrow. In an age of increasing complexity and advancing specialization in a truly international environment, companies will have to have available at the appropriate time men who have the ability to discern corporate purpose, to analyze the activities of the organization in their entirety, and to make recommendations for its future role and development. In order to have this kind of manager available at the right time, an organization needs to devote particular attention and effort to selecting, relatively early in their careers, young managers who have the inherent ability to lead the organization. The next step is to assure that they have the proper opportunity, environment, and educational facilities to develop the knowledge, skills, and attitudes necessary for positions of major responsibility.

Some years ago, Nestlé Alimentana S.A., one of the first-ranked corporations of the world with headquarters in Vevey, Switzerland, felt this need and created a Management Development Institute for the training of its managers as well as for executives from other companies who wished to specialize in the field of business. Thus in 1957, IMEDE (acronym for the formal French name of the Management Development Institute: Institut pour l'Etude des Méthodes de Direction de l'Entreprise) was founded, in cooperation with and under the patronage of the University of Lausanne. This educational institution was established specifically to serve international organizations in their efforts to accelerate and deepen the development of talented managers into professional career executives prepared by experience and training to meet effectively the challenges of change. A pioneer in the field of management education in Europe, IMEDE is widely recognized today as a leader in the art of developing experienced personnel for upper-echelon managerial positions in business and government.

The objectives of IMEDE are: to broaden the outlook and business understanding of managers whose previous experience has necessarily been concentrated in specialized functional areas; to heighten their sensitivity to the human and organizational problems of large international enterprises with roots in several different cultures; to inculcate in them analytical approaches to problems and systematic planning habits; and to provide knowledge of modern tools and techniques useful in the management of international companies.

IMEDE's primary course is the Annual Program, which lasts nine months and welcomes each year managers from all over the world. In the thirteenth Annual Program, held from September 1969 through May 1970, sixty-one executives from twenty-three different countries were enrolled. These managers, between the ages of twenty-eight and forty-five, possess many years of meaningful experience in a particular field of management. Building on this basis of experience and in most instances a university background, the annual course develops basic skill in the analysis of business problems and in decision-making, as well as provides essential substantive knowledge in the field of business administration. The program is composed of eight major courses: Management Control, Financial Management, Quantitative Methods, Marketing Management, Production and Operations Management, Organizational Behavior, General Management, and International Business. It is roughly patterned after the middle-management program of the Harvard Business School with which IMEDE maintains a close working relationship. Courses and discussions are in English. Professors are chosen from leading North American and European business schools, and they usually spend one full year on the IMEDE faculty, during which time they devote their efforts exclusively to IMEDE activities.

Apart from the Annual Program, IMEDE offers each year a number of shorter executive seminars, with the primary objective of improving the performance of managers and executives in a specialized area of business management. The longest of these special programs is the Seminar for Senior Executives. This seminar is intended for men at or about to enter the highest levels of management. For this group, the seminar has a twofold objective. First, it provides study and practical application of up-to-date concepts and analytical tools for dealing with business opportunities and problems. The second objective, of equal importance, is to strengthen each participant's general approach in dealing with the problem-solving and leadership demands of a top-level job. The international character of the program stems from the range of backgrounds of the faculty and participants and especially from the substantial time given to the study of international business operations.

Other shorter seminars given in 1969–1970 were: The Computer—Knowledge for Managers; Marketing Management Seminar; Growth through Acquisitions—Opportunities and Pitfalls; Seminar on Capital Budgeting; and Building Effective Organizations for the Seventies.

The methods of instruction used at IMEDE are designed to prepare the participant to grasp the complexities of business situations. A variety of approaches to learning are included, such as simulation exercises, films, discussion groups, report writing, research projects, field trips, and especially the analysis and discussion of cases—descriptions of events that have occurred in real business situations.

IMEDE supports an extensive research program in the form of case writing, course development, and project research. Since 1957 about six hundred cases, technical notes, monographs, or books on various aspects of business administration have been published under the auspices of the Institute. Most of this material has been placed at the disposal of other educational institutions as a contribution to the advancement of management education.

Research and case writing are done primarily by the IMEDE faculty, often with the assistance of research associates. IMEDE research associates are mature young men, graduates of leading business schools, who are usually in the early stages of an academic career.

The Case Method

At this point in time, a great deal of good explanatory material is available about the case method as a teaching device, the role of the discussion leader, and the role of the student. Thus, an elaborate description of the case method and the ways in which the materials in this book might be used would not be appropriate. However, it is useful to provide some comments about the case method, especially for those who might not have had a great deal of experience with this kind of teaching philosophy.

The case method is a form of instruction, more and more widely used both in universities and in business, in which the main reliance is upon the discussion of concrete incidents or situations. It is intended to provide practice in dealing effectively and responsibly with administrative problems.

A case is a written statement of an actual situation secured from a going business concern. It may be a situation at the worker or at the presidential level; it may be related to one or to several operating functions; or it may embrace the situation of an entire organization. It represents a normal day-to-day operating problem about which someone had to make a decision. The same information, insofar as practical, is furnished to the student as that which was available to the executive who had to make the original decision. In addition to presenting a problem for analysis and decision, cases also provide an opportunity to acquire some information about operations in different fields of business.

The members of the group or class are expected to read, study, evaluate, and informally discuss the assigned case in advance of the formal class meeting. The members participate in working out the problems and in reaching a group decision on a suggested course or courses of action. The group's decision must come from its own analysis and creative effort, subject to questions, criticism, and suggestions from all members. The results of the group decision should reflect the judgment and experience of each member who also seeks out and brings to the meeting any additional knowledge he thinks pertinent. The conclusions of the separate groups are then brought to a meeting where they are further discussed and analyzed.

In the discussion of a case, it may be found that members differ, often substantially, in their interpretation of events and issues as well as in ideas for action. This may result from differences in experience or viewpoints that, if properly analyzed and evaluated, should point toward a course of action based upon a broad view of the problem, going beyond departmental or functional aspects of an individual's interests and beyond existing practices and policies, to consider what is best for the entire operation.

The burden of thinking and carrying on the discussion may rest squarely upon the members. The discussion leader is frequently present essentially as a moderator and plays a relatively passive part during the discussion; he does not attempt to lead the group to a predetermined "answer" or "solution." On the other hand, many successful teachers provide effective case leadership by setting up the major parameters of the problem for discussion and guiding the members of the class to alternative conclusions. This type of instruction is often characterized by summarization of the major findings and potential decisions by the instructor at the conclusion of the discussions.

Development of This Book

The cases included in this book were chosen only after former IMEDE faculty members had been asked to nominate those cases that they felt had been the most useful and effective during the time they were teaching in a particular area. As the usual pattern is for a faculty member to spend one year at IMEDE, each course has been developed over the years by several leading teachers, and the cases in this book were screened by these individuals. In a sense, these materials represent the best of IMEDE.

After nominations of cases had been made, final selections were made—with a great deal of help from our colleagues on the 1969–70 IMEDE faculty. The few cases in each section cannot give comprehensive coverage of the issues in an area. Many very good cases could not be included because of space limitations, but the cases that were included represent typical kinds of problems that arise in international and multinational environments. All the cases, too, have a strong thread of general management issues in them and often specifically focus on decisions that an administrator must make in particular circumstances. For this reason, it is our expectation that those interested in international management will find here stimulating materials upon which to sharpen their analytical and decision-making abilities, without regard for any very specialized sphere of interest or concentration.

All the cases are the result of the IMEDE research program described above. They contain real problems that have actually occurred in business organizations, and, through the cooperation of the management of these organizations and the IMEDE researchers they are now available for use in management education programs.

Organization

The cases have been placed into sections corresponding to six of the courses in the IMEDE Annual Program. While two other courses, Quantitative Methods and International Business are also an integral part of the Annual Program, the teaching approach used in these courses has not resulted in a great deal of case research, and case materials in these areas have not been included. At the beginning of each section are some introductory remarks that represent the kind of remarks that the respective faculty members made at the start of each course during the Thirteenth Annual Program. These remarks are intended to give an overview and provide a perspective for each section although it should be recognized that each course was much more comprehensive than the number of cases in the section suggests. The typical course at IMEDE meets for fifty-five to sixty sessions in addition to some special elective sessions, thus a great deal of material can be covered. Also, because of the experience and general level of excellence of the executives participating in IMEDE programs, the pace is rapid and the performance level high. Each class session represents a significant amount of accomplishment.

In the first section of this text, Financial Management, the cases include a major case on acquisitions as well as cases on debt financing alternatives, equity and convertible financing and the market values of shares, and maintaining control during a period of expansion. Portugal, Switzerland, and the United Kingdom are the headquarters of the firms whose financial management is under consideration.

The second section of the book contains cases with a focus on Management Control. Companies under consideration are Danish, Italian, British, and a disguised location, and serve as an introduction to some of the more common problems of costing, transfer pricing, and handling of potentially obsolete inventory.

The cases in the section on Marketing Management present some especially challenging problems. The first case series involves determining price schedules for a new kind of venture in Italy. Next follows a case dealing with the problems a Dutch firm faced in creating a successful brand image for a consumer product new to the European market. In the third case series, a French company is presented with a proposal that would give it exclusive European rights to manufacture a new line of products. And finally a Swiss company deals with the question of introducing private brands into a market in which many manufacturers attempted to control the retail price of their products.

The cases in the Production and Operations Management section deal with a variety of problems. The first case in this section deals with the necessity of recommending a policy regarding the sales effort directed toward prime contractors in the United States aerospace industry by a German firm. The next case is concerned with the desirability of constructing a piece of automated equipment for the body assembly division of a European automobile manufacturer. The introduction of some new production scheduling techniques in a manufacturer of heavy industrial machinery is the problem covered in the third case in this section, while the final case involves the production problems a Benelux company has in trying to move into the market in another country.

The section on Organizational Behavior contains cases that describe problems involving the behavior of people in organizations and the ways the management of these organizations attempted to resolve these problems. One of the cases involves a Swiss subsidiary of a multinational company that becomes involved in policy decisions regarding the treatment of individuals when working in different parts of the world. Because of lack of uniformity in policies, the company has some potentially serious problems. The second case in this section involves the problems of developing an effective working relationship between two departments in a small Swiss company. Problems between staff specialists and operating executives are a basic part of this situation. The next case deals with the difficulties growing from a headquarters-field office relationship between two executives in an English firm. After a merger, these relationships will have much to do with the ultimate direction of the company. And the final case is concerned with the problems a bright young executive has in introducing new ideas into operations of a rather traditional multinational organization.

The last section of the book includes five cases based upon four organizations located in Germany, Austria, Switzerland, and the United Kingdom. A family dominated firm undergoing major changes is described in Zerssen (A) and (B). General management problems are capsulized in the Compagnie Chillon Electronique case, which describes the changing personal and company objectives and policies of the owner of a fast-growing Swiss technically based company. Planning and organizational approaches are subject to analysis in examining the Solartron Electronic case. Some problems of general management in multinational companies are highlighted in the case of an Austrian technically based company, the final case in this section.

Acknowledgements

We wish to acknowledge the efforts and contributions of the IMEDE professors and research associates who were engaged in the development and writing of the cases included in this book.

AGUILAR, F. J.	*Compagnie Chillon Electronique*
ANDREWS, K. R.	*Solartron Electronic (A)*
ANTHONY, R. N.	*Merz Chocolate Company*
BLACK, H. A.	*A/S Dansk Minox*
BRENGEL, P.	*Helveticus Company (A-B)*
	Solartron Electronic (A)
CULLMAN, W. A.	*Instrumental Controls Inc.*
DAVIS, R. T.	*Au Bon Marché*
DENNING, B. W.	*Frassati Company (A-E)*
DIETZ, A. T.	*Landis & Gyr (C)*
FAVILLE, D. E.	*Tinta N.V.*
FRY, J. N.	*Chambrey Céramiques (A-D)*
FULLER, S. H.	*Frassati Company (A-E)*
HOHL, E.	*Landis & Gyr (A-B)*
	Stardust Grinder
HUTCHINSON, D. S.	*Merz Chocolate Company*

JOLIVET, V.	*Sunderland Steel Products (A)*
KEEGAN, W. J.	*Laundrowash S.p.A. (A-C)*
KNUDSON, H. R.	*Pointe/Holland S. A.*
LANGER, L. C. R.	*Sunderland Steel Products (A)*
LEARNED, E. P.	*Compagnie Chillon Electronique*
	Solartron Electronic (C-D)
LEIGHTON, D. S. R.	*Laundrowash S.p.A. (A-B)*
MASSEY, E.	*Zerssen & Co. (A-B)*
NILAND, P.	*Cresta Automobile Co.*
	König Machine Works GmbH (A-B)
ROBICHECK, A. A.	*Companhia União Fabril*
SCHRIEBER, A. N.	*Bayerische Maschinen Werke*
SHEARON, W. T.	*Brook Bond & Company, Ltd.*
SHILLINGLAW, G.	*AB Thorsten (A-D)*
	Stardust Grinder
	Tipografia Stanca
SPIEGEL, J. W.	*Landis & Gyr (C)*
SUMMER, C. E.	*AB Thorsten (A-D)*
	Construction Equipment International (A-C)
	Harrogate Asphalt Products, Ltd.
TAYLOR, J.	*Stardust Grinder*
THOMPSON, L.	*Landis & Gyr (A-B)*
TOSDAL, H. R.	*Au Bon Marché*
URBAN, R. F.	*Companhia União Fabril*
UYTERHOEVEN, H.	*Zerssen & Co. (A-B)*
VANDELL, R. F.	*Brook Bond & Company, Ltd.*
WALLACE, D. L.	*Bayerische Maschinen Werke*
	United Food Products (A)

The managements of the various companies from which these researchers gathered the basic data for the cases also deserve to be recognized. Without their cooperation and willingness to share knowledge of their company's activities with the researchers—usually a demanding and time-consuming process—none of these cases could have been written. Through their efforts a significant contribution to international management education has been made.

We wish to acknowledge the contributions and encouragement of Luigi Dusmet de Smours, Director of IMEDE since 1967. This book was completed with his cooperation and understanding, and we appreciate his willingness to make necessary facilities and materials available to us.

In a larger sense, we owe special thanks to the leadership of the

Nestlé Alimentana Company and the Board of Trustees of IMEDE, who over the years have made a truly significant impact upon international management education and who have contributed directly to this book through support of IMEDE and its research program.

Many members of the staff at IMEDE helped us with various activities and problems involved in preparing this manuscript. In particular, Mr. Pierre Matras, Secretary General of IMEDE, was very helpful in finding appropriate and skilled secretarial help for us. Miss Paula Halter very efficiently did most of the secretarial work. Miss Jocelyne Zurn did an exceptional job of organizing the manuscript and editing the cases, and her attention to detail made our job much less difficult.

Finally, we would like to thank John Fayerweather, Professor at the Graduate School of Business of New York University, and Richard N. Farmer, Chairman of the International Business Department at the Graduate School of Business of Indiana University, for their helpful comments.

W. ARTHUR CULLMAN
HARRY R. KNUDSON

Lausanne, Switzerland

1

Financial Management

The course in Financial Management focuses on thirteen aspects of this field. The cases selected for inclusion in this book represent four companies, all of which offer the opportunity of analyzing more than one issue of importance to the company. The descriptions of the aspects under consideration during 1969–70 may be used as a guideline for examination of many areas of financial management that are receiving increasing attention.

A. *Introduction to Financial Management*
   This section of the course is designed to introduce some of the central issues of financial management and to show how they interrelate. Students should emerge with a rough concept of the territory that they will study in Financial Management—a vista to which subsequently more focused problems can be related.

B. *Financial Analysis*
   Students are introduced to the forces that increase or decrease the amount of capital required to operate a business, and the factors considered by lenders in deciding when and how capital will be advanced. The basic tools of financial analysis—ratios; funds flows—are introduced and must be used productively in a variety of credit circumstances.

C. *Capital Budgeting*
   Students are first asked to study the process of allocating capital among

investment alternatives. Once they have grasped the complexity of the
process, and are aware of the variety of factors that must be considered,
they are exposed to the various tools of analysis that provide insights at
various stages of the decision continuum. These include payback, simple
return on investment, discounted cash flow, net present value, expected
value, utility theory, linear programming, and simulation. Relevant costs
and investment flows and appropriate return criteria are given considerable emphasis, particularly as they relate to international investments.
Theory is set in practical contexts, so that students can gauge the value
and limitations of these tools in their own business activities.

D. *The Capital Rationing Process*
The capital budgeting cases to date have largely focused upon project
evaluation—that is, relevant analytical frameworks, appropriate data,
and interpretation of results. This next section of the course deals with
equally critical issues: generating a bountiful set of attractive ideas;
facilitating their flow through the organization; organizing data collection activities; evaluating the technical soundness of the project;
and reviewing performance. These are the practical problems that students at IMEDE are more likely to encounter regularly, and yet most
participants probably only have partially formulated approaches to the
resolution of these problems.

E. *Financial Forecasting*
Here, students are introduced to the basic tools of financial forecasting:
cash budgeting, pro forma statements, and the like. Considerable emphasis is placed on how the forecasts can be used to facilitate decision-
making and control. The problems of estimating, and coping efficiently
with uncertainties are also highlighted.

F. *Financing Operations through Short-Term Credit Sources*
By this point, students should have a good working grasp of the sources
of funds available to finance corporate operations and of what firms
must do to merit credit extension. This section of the course has two
objectives: to review and consolidate information and skills already
developed; and to expose students to some of the special problems
associated with effective use of short-term credit supplies.

G. *Working Capital Management*
In this section of the course, students are exposed to both the theory
of efficient working capital management and to the art of adapting
the general to fit the circumstances of the specific. Five topics are
covered: trade credit management; inventory management; cash management within a national banking system; international cash management; and marketable securities investments. Treatment of these
subjects—particularly inventory management—cannot be very comprehensive, and the materials focus on the financial considerations.

H. *Valuation*
The concept of maximizing the current market value of equity funds

is well-established as a desirable economic objective for a firm. The forces that create value are more open to sophisticated debate in both theory and practice even under American circumstances of comparatively perfect capital market conditions. In this section, I have chosen to emphasize the techniques of valuation in practical circumstances and the basic underlying theories only. These are all keystones to the materials on long-term financing that follow.

I.   *Basic Issues of Long-Term Financing*
      Students study the effects of long-term financing (debt, preferred, and common stock) upon shareholders' income, corporate risk, flexibility, control, timing, and similar financial matters. They are introduced to important concepts of dilution, coverage, cost, financial exposure, debt capacity, and valuation. Emphasis remains on decision-making, nevertheless. Students must learn to use their new analytical techniques and concepts realistically in situations where judgment is not easy.

J.   *Cost of Capital*
      In the previous few cases, students have been alerted to the fact that capital has a cost and that this cost is more than simply a function of the initial dilution. They now turn to measuring the overall cost of capital and to exploring its applications in capital budgeting activities.

K.   *Debt Policy*
      This section focuses upon the prevalent methods for measuring debt capacity, but it raises issues relating to some of the new approaches developed recently in the literature. The bridge from the literature to the practice is a particularly difficult one to cross in this area, and the practical considerations are especially hard to cover effectively in two class periods. This section, more than others in the course, is introductory.

L.   *Special Financial Problems*
      This section covers briefly some important financial subjects about which international businessmen should have a passing familiarity.

M.   *Mergers and Acquisitions*
      The merger cases provide both a review of material covered to date and a capstone to the course. Materials emphasize both the strategic aspects of growth through merger and the financial aspects of negotiation and valuation.

BROOKE BOND & CO. LTD.

In late February 1968, Mr. J. M. Thomson, Finance Director of Brooke Bond & Company Ltd., the largest of the world's tea enterprises with sales of £130 million, was preparing for a meeting of the firm's Diversification Committee, during which the potential attractiveness of acquiring Liebig's Extract of Meat Company Ltd. (LEMCO) would be considered further. LEMCO, with a turnover of £40 million, dominated certain segments of the United Kingdom packaged meat market and had operations and markets abroad. LEMCO was by far the largest acquisition prospect reviewed seriously by the Diversification Committee during its three-year history, and no doubt it would receive careful scrutiny. Mr. Thomson, who had raised the issue initially, would be expected to lead the discussion.

There were a number of issues relating to LEMCO on the agenda for the meeting. Among the more critical questions were: Does LEMCO's business constitute a sensible diversification move for Brooke Bond? Is the size of the acquisition an advantage or a disadvantage? How much should Brooke Bond be willing to pay, at the maximum, for the opportunities inherent in LEMCO? What form should an acquisition proposal take? And, assuming the acquisition looked promising and feasible, how should LEMCO management be approached?

Brooke Bond & Company Ltd.

Brooke Bond grew, blended and marketed more than a fourth of all tea consumed in the noncommunist world. Their operations were vertically integrated from the plantation through the distribution of branded products to retail outlets. Over the firm's history, which spanned nearly a century, management had carved out a commanding market position (38 percent of the market) in Great Britain, where 30 percent of the world's tea was consumed, and in several other countries, notably India, where tea consumption was growing rapidly. Brooke Bond had virtually no manufacturing facilities and very limited distribution in continental Europe (excluding the Soviet bloc) where 4½ percent of world tea sales took place, and it had only recently introduced a "Red Rose" brand into the metropolitan New York sector of the American market (8 percent of the total world sales). Unfortunately, growth in the firm's established markets was slowing down or stagnating, while certain underpenetrated markets were developing briskly. The ways and means of exploiting new markets were continuously under study.

At the end of World War II, management decided it had the resources to strike for a bigger share of the United Kingdom market or to enter into the European markets but not both. Their decision to concentrate on the larger British market proved rewarding at first as the market share increased noticeably, and consumption improved. In recent years, per capita consumption had leveled off. Outside the younger generation, who were not taking to tea with the same enthusiasm as their elders, population growth was small. Finally, Brooke Bond was finding it increasingly difficult to increase its market penetration further.

In the meanwhile, exchange regulations necessary to protect the pound made it extremely difficult to penetrate foreign markets. Foreign currencies requisite for investments in plant and marketing could only be acquired at a premium above the free exchange rate, currently 50 percent. Similar restraints existed in other sterling areas where the company operated. With all factors considered, a plant which might cost £3 million to construct in Britain, would probably cost Brooke Bond nearly £5 million to build in most other European countries. Brooke Bond, consequently, was at a marked disadvantage compared with companies not subject to exchange restrictions. The marketing disadvantages of late entry into established markets, the generally low rates of profitability on food items, and other uncertainties made these investment opportunities look unattractive relative to the resources required.

Brooke Bond offered a full line of tea products—twelve in all—catering to each of the important segments of the British tea markets. Nevertheless, Brooke Bond encountered stiff competition from specialty houses with more focused marketing objectives. Ty-phoo Tea Company, for example, sold only one tea blend for 1s 1d to 1s 6d ($\frac{1}{4}$ lb. packs) at the retail and had gained nearly 16.9 percent of the total British tea market. Unlike Brooke Bond, Ty-phoo distributed its products through brokers, not through their own distribution system; even so, Ty-phoo had achieved a comparable 94 percent market penetration and competed successfully with the comparable Brooke Bond product in the market place.[1] Brooke Bond also

---

1 According to the national marketing surveys in February/March 1968, Ty-phoo had 16.7 percent of the U.K. market and the two leading Brooke Bond brands, Dividend and P.G. Tips, had 14.5 percent and 19.4 percent of the market respectively. Dividend is the cheaper blend and Ty-phoo is much nearer to Dividend than to P.G. in *quality*. But in *price,* it is with P.G. that Ty-phoo competes, and the Brooke Bond product holds the competitive edge.

Exhibit 1

Brooke Bond. & Co. Ltd.
Financing & Operating Results 1959 to 1967
(Pound figures in thousands)

	1959	1960	1961	1962	1963	1964	1965	1966	1967
Distribution of world turnover									
Commodities & materials	£68,373	£77,539	£81,588	£83,673	£84,687	£87,074	£91,529	£85,174	£90,211
Production, selling and overhead expenses	8,507	9,604	10,452	12,307	13,445	14,670	14,878	14,603	16,731
Wages, salaries and employees' benefits	9,167	10,093	10,640	11,420	12,164	12,903	13,668	12,842	15,034
Depreciation	736	758	817	934	1,018	943	1,059	1,096	1,107
Group profit	4,323	4,395	4,062	5,231	6,068	7,212	7,242	6,642	7,564
Total world turnover	91,106	102,389	107,559	113,565	117,382	122,802	128,376	120,357	130,647
Appropriation of group profit									
Taxation on profits	2,023	1,998	1,851	3,085	3,529	4,129	3,536	3,112	3,454
Minority shareholders	87	80	37	73	63	76	120	95	157
Dividends: preference	36	37	37	37	37	37	36	47	60
ordinary	586	625	625	703	844	1,055	1,113	1,641	2,133
Retained profit	1,591	1,655	1,512	1,333	1,595	1,915	2,437	1,747	1,760
Group profit	4,323	4,395	4,062	5,231	6,068	7,212	7,242	6,642	7,564
Earnings per ordinary share	13.9s	14.7s	13.7s	10.9s	13.0s	12.7s	15.1s	12.4s	14.2s
Dividends per ordinary share	3.8s	4.0s	4.0s	3.7s	4.5s	4.5s	4.7s	6.0s	7.8s
Capital employed									
Net current assets	20,339	20,832	21,696	22,126	22,838	24,877	25,051	24,251	23,734
Fixed assets & investments	12,681	13,851	14,761	16,760	16,997	18,502	20,184	21,428	23,091
Goodwill	—	—	—	—	—	—	—	325	728
Total capital employed	33,020	34,683	36,457	38,886	39,835	43,379	45,235	46,004	47,553
Financed by									
Ordinary shareholders' capital 5/-	9,375	9,375	9,375	11,250	11,250	14,063	14,063	16,406	16,406
Reserves	16,266	18,035	19,509	19,681	21,293	21,569	23,882	21,957	23,784
Ordinary shareholders' capital employed	25,641	27,410	28,884	30,931	32,543	35,632	37,945	38,363	40,190
Pref. shareholders' capital	1,500	1,500	1,500	1,500	1,500	1,500	1,500	1,500	1,500
Shareholders' capital employed	27,141	28,910	30,384	32,431	34,043	37,132	39,445	39,863	41,690
Minority shareholders' interest	1,579	1,564	1,452	1,451	1,435	1,232	1,472	1,568	1,532
Deferred liabilities, etc.	4,300	4,209	4,621	5,004	4,357	5,015	4,318	4,573	4,331
Total capital employed	33,020	34,683	36,457	38,886	39,835	43,379	45,235	46,004	47,553

had stiff competition in the upper price ranges (2s or more per package at the retail) from companies, such as Twinings, that had built an image as specialists in high quality tea. This market was not expanding materially, however. Brooke Bond was more successful in the middle price ranges (60 percent of the market), but this sector, historically, had been exposed to frequent price promotion marketing inducements, and margins tended to be thinner. Although Brooke Bond management took pride in the fact that the taste of their tea products was superior to competition in each product class, the quality advantage did not always lead to market share advantages, despite the larger total marketing resources Brooke Bond had at its disposal.

British tea consumers tended to be quite discriminating in their tastes. They had not taken to convenience teas very readily. They complained that tea made from tea bags tasted "orangey". Although Brooke Bond had a good position in the tea bag market, it was a small but rapidly growing part of total sales. Similarly, instant tea products had not sold very well. Several large food companies, like Nestlé, had tried to enter the market some ten years ago but with very limited apparent success. Nevertheless, the British housewife was showing a marked preference for convenience food products, and Brooke Bond wanted to be prepared for the day it might affect tea sales. The firm had perfected an accelerated freeze dry process for making instant tea of unusually high taste quality in their laboratories a year ago, but they were still solving the problems required for marketable, mass production. This work was considered important in order to expand in world areas where convenience weighted equally with taste in the consumers' preference matrix and to protect Brooke Bond's current market position, particularly in the potentially vulnerable, middle-priced tea range.

Despite languishing markets, Brooke Bond had made steady progress in recent years. From 1959 to 1967, turnover had grown 43 percent at a relatively steady annual rate. Profits earned by ordinary shares had also risen by 83 percent during this period. The firm's financial position was strong; it had no long-term debts outstanding, and its liquid funds were more than ample for operating requirements. Results for key financial items from 1959 to 1967 are summarized in Exhibit 1.

Despite this progress management was not wholly complacent about the operating performance. Ty-phoo, for example, made higher profits, as a percentage of sales, despite their concentration in lower priced teas, which in fact gave rise to higher retail margins. Several members of management concluded from this that Brooke Bond's present distribution system was no longer economical. Costs of direct distribution had risen sharply in recent years. Petrol tax increases, more stringent maintenance requirements, sharp increases in labor costs, greater traffic congestion, and the like had all pushed local distribution costs up sharply, especially for a company making drops of low total value at many locations. Brooke Bond, for example, employed a fleet of seven hundred vans to service 132,000 outlets in the British Isles, and 65 percent of deliveries involved merchandise drops, valued at less than £50. Changing the distribution system would not be easy. Brooke Bond's red delivery vans were perhaps the most widely recongnized symbol of the company in the minds of the consumer Moreover, the direct personal selling contact with retail merchants had proved to be a historic strength. The company had recently acquired one of the two largest broker-distributors in England (although the brokerage/wholesaling of food was still a small part of the total distribution and tended to be quite splintered) in order to gain more experience in this field.

The market price of Brooke Bond's ordinary shares seemed to be depressed, given a profit growth rate of 8 percent, a good earnings record in relation to equity, and a comfortable dividend payment policy. The price earnings ratio in February 1968 was only 14.3 × earnings per share of 11.8d. The low market price of 14/- per share (ordinary "B" shares) was attributed, in part, to Brooke Bond's high concentration of assets in developing nations. Over 35 percent of assets were in marketing companies and tea plantations in Ceylon, India, Tanzania, and Kenya. In addition, the firm owned 1,000 acres of coffee producing land in Kenya. Both products tended to be in oversupply in the world markets, and prices for crops had trended steadily down in recent years. Finally, the company operated factories in India, Pakistan, South Africa, U.S., Canada, Kenya, Tanzania, Uganda, and Ceylon, as well as in the United Kingdom.

Three additional factors helped to explain the low price afforded Brooke Bond's shares in the market. Food stocks in general were not enjoying much favor in investing circles because consumption was not growing rapidly, and competition, especially from American firms, was growing. Second, the ownership of Brooke Bond was quite concentrated. The Brooke family owned most of the 2,625,000 shares of Class A stock, each with one vote. Although there were 63,000,000 shares of B stock in public hands, each B share held the right to 1/24th of one vote. The public consequently held no more than 50 percent of the voting power. In all other respects, the shares in the two classes shared equally in earnings and dividends. Family controlled companies tended, all other factors equal, to trade at lower price earnings ratios. The last, and perhaps most significant depressing force was the heavy dependence of the company on a single commodity-based product line. Branded tea sales constituted 90 percent of total revenues (40 percent in Britain alone). The company had introduced a coffee line in Britain, but this was only modestly successful, accounting for 5 percent of turnover. Miscellaneous other activities accounted for the balance. Tea accounted for an even larger share of profits.

Diversification

As British tea prospects diminished, management thought increasingly of diversification. There were several environmental forces affecting this thinking. Many other British food concerns were merging with British firms or selling out to foreign firms, mainly American. With this steady concentration of marketing power, Brooke Bond no longer had unique size advantages. In particular, Ty-phoo Tea had been acquired for £44 million by the Schweppes Group. This group had considerable marketing know-how and a strong marketing organization in the United States and in Western Europe, as well as England. Ty-phoo was now more likely to be a formidable competitor.

At the food retailing level, supermarkets and cooperatives were capturing an increasing share of the market. Brooke Bond was now selling to large customers, better able to use their power to achieve concessions from manufacturers. Private branding was a growing threat to market share as a result. In short, size was a more important factor in the struggle for shelf space and market acceptance.

The Diversification Committee of Brooke Bond had been meeting for three years. (In 1968, the committee consisted of Mr. Rutter, Deputy Chairman, Mr. Furber, Marketing Director, Mr. Sawdy, Tea Director, and Mr. Thomson). During this period, the committee had reached several conclusions: Diversification provided attractive opportunities to accelerate Brooke Bond's growth and to strengthen the firm's defensive position. Acquisition of a going concern was much more feasible than initiating a new business, given Brooke Bond's limited resources and experience outside the tea and coffee areas. The diversification would have to relate to activities in which Brooke Bond had experience to ease the digestive process. Hopefully, the acquisition would provide some synergistic benefits, although these would more likely affect the acquired firm than Brooke Bond. Growing enterprises were preferred to stagnating ones. Many of the better prospects had already been snapped up in the merger frenzy enveloping the British economy, and pressure for action was mounting. Indeed, there was a serious risk that Brooke Bond might find itself unwantingly an acquisition target under terms that would be difficult for management not to consider carefully.

The Diversification Committee had explored various industries that might be attractive and drawn up lists of candidates in these fields for consideration. Only a small number of these possibilities had evoked any enthusiasm, and they were mainly smaller firms in semirelated fields. These analyses were hampered at first by size considerations. Initially, the committee had explored firms with sales in the £2 to £3 million range; gradually their sights increased as they recognized the number of problems faced by small companies and the limited impact these firms would have on Brooke Bond's financial position. In 1967, most of their search was focused on firms with sales of £7 to £10 million—firms that could be purchased from cash resources available to the company, the preferred method of acquisition.

Along the way a number of small firms were purchased in such service areas as food brokering, travel, packaging, printing, insurance, and in the manufacture of plastics, toys, and hydrofoils. In several instances, these acquisitions bolstered staff capacities at Brooke Bond, as well as providing outside revenue. The cumulative impact of these activities on sales and profits was minor, but management had gained considerable experience in evaluating, negotiating, integrating, and living with an acquisition. They were now prepared for more meaty ventures.

Over time, a series of criteria had evolved to guide the Diversification Committee's thinking; these were:

1. Any company we buy must have good management. We do not have unlimited management resources, and our capabilities largely lie in handling problems in the unique tea business.
2. The products or services acquired must have significant growth potential.
3. The firm's profit to sales ratio must be better than the industry average.
4. The products must be branded and hold a reputation for high quality.
5. The firm must have suffecent size and strength to provide a springboard for becoming a significant market force in its industry.
6. The purchase price should probably not be less than £5 million or more than £10 million. We do not want to spread our management talents over a variety of ventures that are too small to be significant; yet we do not want to overly consume our financial strength on one acquisition.
7. The financial arrangements necessary for acquisition should not cause our shareholders serious earnings dilution or weaken their dividend safety.

This last point was the cause of serious concern. Many firms could be more readily acquired for stock than cash, although Brooke Bond with its strong financial resources preferred the latter. The modest price earnings ratio of the stock meant that Brooke Bond could not easily seek firms with high price earnings ratios, yet it was these firms that most often fitted the nonfinancial criteria. The committee eventually decided that Brooke Bond should be willing to accept some initial dilution of earnings per share for the right company.

This problem was worsened by the procedures used to acquire firms in England. The acquiring firm had to make a public tender offer for the shares of a company, with a significant public ownership. Often the tender was made after forewarning the management in question and with their cooperation; however, surprise and "unfriendly" tenders were also common. In any case, the acquiring firm had to make a bid substantially above the current market price of the securities before acceptance was assured. Although generalizations are difficult, the price premium was rarely less than 20 percent and often more than 25 percent above the value of the ordinary shares. In some cases, the value of the ordinary shares was already inflated by speculation that the firm was a "take-over" candidate. During the tender period, counterproposals by other firms interested in acquiring the company under bid could be and frequently were made. A bidding contest involving a troublesome proxy solicitation fight sometimes ensued. To avoid these difficulties, some firms preferred to bid high initially. Brooke Bond management personally felt more comfortable with the latter "more friendly" alternative, although they were open to any approach that seemed to fit the circumstances. A premium of 35 percent to 40 percent, of course, would not always assure success. The price value of the acquiring firm often fell in the market, occasionally quite substantially if the investing public did not find the acquisition sensible or the purchase price reasonable. A drastic decline in the price of the shares of the buyer would reduce the attractiveness of the exchange in the eyes of the seller. Making a sensible acquisition at a reasonable price was, therefore, quite important. In this environment, a share for share exchange with a firm with a price earnings ratio much above 10 X would probably involve a dilution of earnings for Brooke Bond shareholders. As the merger wave continued to grow in intensity, price premiums mounted. The year 1968 had started with a surge in mergers that appeared likely to grow worse before it grew better. This added to the pressures on the Diversification Committee; if they were going to recommend action, the sooner the decision was reached, the better would be the pricing prospects.

In January 1968, Mr. Thomson was reviewing some securities that had been recommended for addition to the company's pension portfolio. Among them was the Liebig's Extract of Meat Company. LEMCO had a good profit record but was selling at the modest price earnings ratio of 11.8 X. A healthy proportion of the firm's assets were located in South America and Rhodesia, and Mr. Thomson attributed the low price to this cause. In his mind, a firm with earnings concentrated in these regions probably deserved this sort of reception. He was about to pass over this prospect when the tax account caught his eye. He knew from the tax rates involved that the largest part of LEMCO's earnings must be concentrated in the British Isles. Risks suddenly took on a different meaning. The more he studied the company, the more attractive it looked, not only as an investment but as an acquisition candidate. Although the company was four times the size of companies currently under study, Mr. Thomson decided to raise the issue with the Diversification Committee. Their initial reaction, along with top management's, was surprisingly enthusiastic. Since Mr. Thomson had analyzed the company several years previously, when he was a merchant banker, he was given the task of spearheading the analysis.

LEMCO's operations were quite similar to Brooke Bond's except that the commodity base upon which it built its vertically integrated operations was meat.

In 1863, a Belgian engineer, Mr. Gilbert, established a manufacturing plant at Fray Bentos on the River Uruguay to convert meat into meat extract by a new process for shipments to Antwerp merchants who sold the products in meat-shy areas of Europe in jars bearing a distinctive Liebig trademark. The success of the company was immediate, and quickly capital became a problem. In 1865, Liebig's Extract of Meat Company was formed in London with capital of a half million pounds.

During the next ninety-five years, the company continued to expand steadily, although it encountered a number of crises. The basic product had to be modified when competitors found ways of increasing the nutritive value of their products. As refrigerated shipments of meat became increasingly possible throughout the world, manufacturing costs had to be reduced sharply to remain competitive. And the firm had weathered other serious crises.

The expansion of the firm took place on three continents. In South America, LEMCO had taken pains to increase its cattle raising and manufacturing facilities during its early years. By the turn of the century, LEMCO was tending enormous herds of cattle in Paraguay and Argentina and had two large manufacturing facilities. In Africa, LEMCO acquired large tracts of land in Southern Rhodesia, had stocked these with cattle during the World War I era, and had constructed a manufacturing facility there in 1932. Finally, LEMCO had greatly expanded its marketing business in Europe, particularly during the first three decades of the twentieth century.

By the late 1960s, LEMCO's sales still largely derived from processed meats. The line had been diversified to include soups, both canned and dehydrated, canned meats of various kinds, frozen convenience meat dishes, flavorings, potato chips, and canned fruits and vegetables. Exhibit 2 shows the proprietary products sold by LEMCO companies in the various countries that constituted their most important markets. LEMCO's main competition came from food companies, which were considerably larger in size. Competition was keenest in continental Europe. It was less severe in England, at least for the two main products. The Oxo cube held a virtual monopoly position in the bouillon cube field, and Fray Bentos corned beef and beef and kidney pie products had achieved a commanding market share.

Although the ownership of LEMCO had been fairly concentrated when the company was first formed, it was now very widely disbursed. No stockholder held more than a very small percentage of the stock and no group collectively held shares to assure working control. Despite this, LEMCO

Exhibit 2

Brooke Bond & Co. Ltd.

Product/Markets of Liebig's Extract of Meat Co. Ltd.

Products	Argentina	S. Africa	Rhodesia	U.K.	Belgium	Denmark	France	Germany	Holland	Italy	Norway	Spain	Switzerland	Canada
Meat extract	L			L	L	L	L	L	L	L	L		L	
Meat & veg. extract										Sapis				
Veg. extract										Vegedor			Vegedor	
Meat spread														
Corned beef	L	FB	FB	FB	FB			FB	FB				FB	FB
Canned meats	FB	FB	FB	FB					FB					FB
Bouillon cubes		Oxo	Oxo	Oxo	Oxo&L	Oxo	VX&L	L	Oxo&L	L	Oxo	L	L	Oxo
Beef tablets					L	L	L	L	L	L	L		L	
Chicken tablets							L	L		L		L		
Liquid bouillon		Oxo	Oxo	Oxo	Oxo	Oxo	VX	L	Oxo		Oxo		L	Oxo
Arome	L				L		L		L					
Tinned sauces							L							
Granulated broth								L						
Dehydrated soups		L&FB	L&FB		L		L	L	L	L	Oxo	L		
Tinned soups					L		L	L	L					
Prepared dishes					Bentos			Bentos	Bentos					
Canned veg.		LCV	LCV		L				L					
Dehydrated veg.		Sunrho	Sunrho											
Potato crisps				ChMunk										
Ham		Sunrho	Sunrho											
Tinned fruit		Sunrho	Sunrho & LCV											

Notes: L = Liebig; FB = Fray Bentos; VX = Viandox; LCV = Liebig Cashel Valley; ChMunk = Chipmunk

Some products, particularly bouillon cubes, beef tablets and chicken tablets, which are manufactured in different countries, vary somewhat in weight and composition from country to country.

retained the hallmark of a family concern. Two families, the Carlisles and Gunthers (related by marriage), had held positions in top management over the entire life of the company.

Mr. Thomson had drawn together all the public facts on LEMCO in a report to the Diversification Committee. Excerpts from this report are shown in Appendix A. These data indicated healthy profit margins and a profit growth rate of 11 percent over the past five years, despite serious developments in certain markets.

Mr. Thomson's Assessment

Mr. Thomson believed that Liebig was the most suitable potential partner that Brooke Bond had reviewed in the full course of the Diversification Committee's meetings. In his view, this alternative was particularly attractive because:

1. LEMCO operated in the rapidly growing convenience food markets. Specifically, it had at least seven products in its international line that could be categorized as convenience foods—canned meats, frozen meats, canned soups, dehydrated soups, fruit juices, canned beans, canned peaches, and canned vegetables.
2. In the United Kingdom, LEMCO had four universally known, well-established, first-class brand names (Oxo, Fray Bentos, Foster Clark, and LEMCO) with national distribution. Product quality was excellent.
3. LEMCO had strong marketing know-how. (J. Walter Thomson's Oxo campaign was an acknowledged classic.)
4. LEMCO had cleared the decks by a reconstruction of the board and by assigning specific areas of responsibility to three managing directors.
5. LEMCO had a new distributor organization and its own sales force. These men specialized by selling to certain classes of retail outlets. Brooke Bond would gain a concrete basis for comparing different distribution systems and finding the one that suited the whole best. Once the proper course was decided upon, changes could be implemented faster and move smoothly. In Mr. Thomson's view, ultimately savings, perhaps as large as £400,000 per year, would result.
6. Oxo would give Brooke Bond the opportunity to extend the range of products sold to the grocery trade and enhance its bargaining power.
7. LEMCO had a good R & D record, and Brooke Bond could dovetail their New Products Development Division with Brooke Bond's.
8. LEMCO had in-depth skill in factory operations for processing and packaging meat, soups, and allied products. It operated nineteen factories throughout the world of which seven were in the United Kingdom and Eire.

9. LEMCO had successfully computerized their paperwork associated with sales and distribution. In contrast, Brooke Bond's current clerical systems were a bottleneck and expensive.
10. LEMCO had laid a solid foundation for growth in hard currency areas (Western Europe) where Brooke Bond, too, wanted to expand quickly but lacked the currency.
11. LEMCO was long on United Kingdom generated profits (3.25 million) whereas Brooke Bond earned only half of its profits at home.
12. LEMCO was extremely cheap by current market standards, and the group had nearly £3½ million of cash in the kitty.

Altogether, Mr. Thomson foresaw savings from combined operations in the order of magnitude of £400,000 per year before taxes, although these benefits were not likely to be realized for several years.

Mr. Thomson thought that Brooke Bond offered LEMCO some important advantages also:

1. Membership of an enlarged food group that should be better able to resist the buying power of the supermarkets;
2. Cooperation in research and development;
3. Extended distribution in Canada, the United States, South Africa, East Africa; and possibly a tie-up in Australia; and
4. Association with a quality-oriented British operating company.

An acquisition of a company as large as LEMCO would put a severe strain on Brooke Bond's top management team. There would be a period of from three to five years before synergies apparent in the union could be realized in financial terms. During this interim, there would be little opportunity to seek out and acquire another major food organization because management and financial resources would be heavily committed.

Integrating two family-dominated companies, each with strong traditions, was also a concern. A successful merger would require much pruning and reorganization, if the combine were to become an organic whole, not two units stitched together with financial thread. Winning the interest of LEMCO's management might be difficult unless some concessions about employee security were offered. This sort of commitment would reduce flexibilities, create catch basins for discontent, and delay changes necessary to capitalize upon new found composite opportunities. There was also a risk that organizational problems might distract management's time unwarrantedly from the task of moving forward.

LEMCO's chairman had made the following statement of the Annual General Meeting on February 15:

> There is no question, as far as your Board and your company are concerned, of going out to amalgamate or merge with, or buy

any other company, or get involved in anything like that, other than if they thought it was going to be really beneficial to the stockholders. When that time comes, they might act. Meantime, we are pursuing our own way and let the sniping take place.

These remarks were, of course, capable of various interpretations. But they certainly did not amount to a categoric rejection of an approach from the right quarter. At this meeting, LEMCO's profits (before taxes) for fiscal 1968 had been forecast at £3.8 million.

Mr. Thomson believed he had gotten as good a picture of LEMCO from public sources as was possible in a short time. The major questions remained: Is this the right, first diversification move for us? And if so, how should we pursue it? With these questions before him, Mr. Thomson settled down to prepare for the forthcoming meeting of the Diversification Committee.

APPENDIX A

BROOKE BOND & CO. LTD.

Abstract of Business and Financial Information Available
on Liebig's Extract of Meat Co. Ltd.

1. *Geographical spread*

     The group's total resources totalled £24 million at August 31, 1967, (the date of the latest available published accounts) and were employed in the following geographical areas:

	£ million
U.K. and Eire	11.1
France, Italy Belgium Netherlands	3.6
Canada	.5
South Africa, Kenya Zambia, Tanzania Nigeria	1.2
Rhodesia	1.0
Argentina, Paraguay	6.6
	£24.0

     Liebig's owns and operates nineteen factories in different parts of the world, together with cattle ranches in Rhodesia, Argentina, and Paraguay.

     The group's position as a cattle producer as well as a meat processor gives it some hedge against fluctuations in raw material prices on the one hand and in consumer prices on the other. Liebig's, incidentally, is almost wholly unaffected by the current U.K. ban on meat imports from countries where hoof and mouth disease is endemic because group's frozen meat sales are made almost exclusively to countries outside the U.K.

2. *U.K. and Eire*

The principal operating company is Oxo Limited, which enjoyed record sales in 1967. Demand for Oxo cubes (including the new heavily promoted Golden Oxo product) increased as did also the demand for the wide range of canned meat products sold under the Fray Bentos label. Fray Bentos continues to dominate the corned beef market and its steak and kidney pies are now not only the brand leader but also outsell all competing brands put together.

Oxo's pretax profits surged forward impressively between 1963 and 1966 (£2.73 million in 1963, £2.88 million in 1964, £3.06 million in 1965 and £3.57 million in 1966). The 1967 figures for Oxo Limited are not yet separately available, but the indications in the chairman's statement accompanying the 1967 Report and Accounts are that they will be shown to represent a further advance. The really significant feature of Oxo's record is that, according to "The Grocer" of February 3 last, total consumer purchases of corned beef by weight had actually fallen by nearly 50 percent from 1958 to 1965. There has been only a slight recovery since then. Oxo as the market leader cannot fail to have been affected by this trend and the natural inference to be drawn is that the other newer Fray Bentos lines must have performed very well indeed.

Oxo's marketing and distribution methods came under fire some two years ago. Since then the sales organization has been completely reorganized on a specialist basis (see 4 below).

The group owns seven processing and packaging factories in the U.K. and Eire.

Another thriving company in the U.K. group is Oxoid Limited, which specializes in the manufacture and distribution of micro-biologic products (such as culture media and laboratory preparations). Oxoid is an active exporter and ships to 117 overseas countries, exports in fact accounting for 40 percent of its total turnover. Pretax profits have risen from £22,000 in 1965 and £81,000 in 1966 to £112,000 in 1967.

The group has a very active New Products Development Division, which has clearly made a significant contribution to the considerable expansion in Liebig's lines in recent years.

Liebig's distributes locally in all the above-mentioned territories. In being W. Melhuish, a Ranks Hovis subsidiary) one of whose main lines is potato chips. This has, on the face of it, proved a thoroughly bad investment with losses increasing from £72,000 in 1964 and £134,000 in 1965 to £219,000 in 1966. At the same time, one should recognize that Chipmunk is operating in what is undeniably a growth sector of the food business, with correspondingly rugged competition.

3. *U.K. Distribution System*

Oxo's distribution system was restyled in September 1967. The company's 239 representatives were split into specialized sections along the following lines.

Multiples and cooperatives	41
Cash and carry	27
Symbol groups	10
General—including merchandisers and six account executives	161
	239

The entire emphasis of the reorganization was on providing a more specialized service in depth to the different retail/wholesale outlets. It is of some interest to note that these changes were put into effect some five months or so in advance of what are likely to be some swinging price increases covering a wide range of Fray Bentos products. Devaluation no doubt played its part in these. All the same, the re-organization of the sales organization looks to have been well-timed.

4. *Europe*

Liebig's has now worked up a sizable (£3.6 million) investment in Europe with factories in France (Paris and Vaucluse), Belgium (Schoten) and Italy (Tortona). There is a marketing operation in each of these countries and also in the Netherlands. Profits from the European companies as a whole were said to have increased "substantially" in 1967. No further details are available.

5. *Canada*

The operating company here is Oxo Foods Limited, which runs a factory in Toronto and distributes both in Canada and the United States. The Canadian company in 1967 produced "the best financial results for several years" and is currently investigating ways and means of developing its interests in North America. The record for the previous six years is as follows:

1962	£24,000	(loss)
1963	10,000	
1964	9,000	(loss)
1965	7,000	
1966	4,000	(loss)
1967	30,000	

The U.S. company has returned small losses in the last few years (£2,000 in 1967).

6. *Africa*

There are subsidiary companies in South Africa, Rhodesia, Kenya, and Zambia and affiliated companies in Tanzania and Nigeria. There are factory operations in Johannesburg, Umtali, West Nicholson, Dar-es-Salaam, and Kano.

Liebig's distributes locally in all the above-mentioned territories. In Kenya it has a marketing arrangement with the Kenya Meat Commission. Tanzania is a (comfortable?) tandem operation with the state-owned National Development Corporation.

In Rhodesia, where the group owns cattle ranches and also operates a fruit and vegetable canning factory, conditions have clearly become difficult after the imposition of sanctions in 1966, but Liebig's (Rhodesia) Ltd. was in fact a highly successful company until U.D.I., as the following pretax figures illustrate

1962	£411,000	
1963	294,000	
1964	254,000	
1965	500,000	
1966	16,000	(loss)
1967	10,000	(loss)

Oxo (Zambia) Ltd. returned pretax profits of £10,000 in 1965, £17,000 in 1966, and £30,000 in 1967.

Oxo (South Africa) Ltd. has been quite a useful performer, with pretax profits rising as follows:

1963	£30,000
1964	36,000
1965	75,000
1966	47,000
1967	

Sharply increased overheads accounted for the fall in 1966. The 1967 figures are reported to have very nearly reached the 1965 level again.

7. *Latin America*

Liebig's owns ranches in Argentina and Paraguay and operates one factory in each of these countries. The Argentine factory—hitherto exclusively a corned beef producer—was recently converted to enable it to undertake the production of frozen beef.

While separate profit figures for the Latin American operations are not available, we may take it that they contributed next to nothing to consolidated profits in 1964, made a loss in 1965 of perhaps as much as £500,000, and a further loss in 1966 of about £200,000.

8. *Board of Directors*

The directors are as follows:

K. R. M. Carlisle, Chairman (aged 60)
H. P. T. Prideaux (53)
J. V. Cooper, F.C.A. (57)
C. M. Gaunt (57)

On February 15 last, a number of important changes were made at parent company board level. Three managing directors were named with direct responsibility for group activities within defined geographical areas. These managing directors are:

J. S. Hendrick   (to be responsible for the U.K. and Eire)
J. V. Cooper   (Continental Europe and Canada)
J. R. Stourton   (Africa and South America)

9. *Capital Structure*

The company has been fortunate in securing some pretty inexpensive gearing, as the following figures will show.

		Issued
a.	Loan capital	
	4% Debenture stock	£ 500,000
	$5\frac{3}{4}$% 2nd Debenture stock	3,000,000
		£3,500,000
b.	Preference capital	
	5% Cumulative Preference £1	£1,000,000
	$4\frac{1}{2}$% Cumulative Redeemable Preference	1,000,000
		£2,000,000
c.	Ordinary capital	
	27,000,000 5/- —ordinary	£6,750,000

The preference shares confer the usual restricted voting rights.

10. *Shareholdings (Ordinary)*

There were approximately 12,000 ordinary shareholders in all. The shares are widely held, with holdings of £50,000 stock (i.e., 200,000 shares) and over accounting for not more than 17 percent of the total 27,000,000 shares in issue. Financial or charitable institutions are among the thirteen holders with more than 200,000 shares. The directors hold in all £17,000 of stock, or 0.25 percent of the total.

11. *Market Capitalization*

The 5/- ordinary stock units are currently quoted at about 16/-, which puts a price tag on the total equity of £21.6 million. The shares at their present price are 4½d under their high for the year. Prices have ranged as follows over the last five years.

	1963	1964	1965	1966	1967/68
High	13/6	13/9	12/–	13/–	16/4½
Low	11/–	9/6	8/–	10/–	11/–

At their current price of 16/- the Liebig's ordinary are on a dividend yield of 5.0 percent based on a 16 percent dividend (covered 1.67 times) and a P/E basis of 11.8. Brooke Bond "B" currently stand at 14/- (having fallen from a price of 15/- at the beginning of February) to give a dividend yield of 4.0 percent (covered 1.85 times) and a P/E ratio of 14.3.

12. *Assets*

The consolidated balance sheet at August 31, 1967 showed the following position (the Brooke Bond figures at June 30, 1967 being added for comparison).

	Liebig's	(£000)		Brooke Bond	(£000)
Cash and equivalent	3,321			5,220	
Quoted investments	142			207	
Livestock, produce, stores, etc.	15,156			28,933 (stocks)	
Sundry debtors	6,771	25,390		8,946	43,306
Less: loans, overdrafts	2,378			6,093	
Sundry creditors	7,361	9,739		13,334	19,427
Net current assets		15,651			23,879
Freehold ranches and lands		2,080		(estates)	7,147
Freehold properties		3,075			5,799
Leasehold properties		620			1,168
Other fixed assets		3,537		(plant, etc.)	6,015
Goodwill		—			728
Unquoted investments		129			2,817
		25,092			47,553
Less: future tax		1,149			1,374
Total funds employed		23,943			46,179
Represented by:					
Loan capital		4,031		(o'seas cos.)	801
Preference capital		2,000			1,500
Minority interests		468			1,533
Tax equalisation		22			—
Pensions and deposits		—	—		2,157
Ordinary capital		6,750		16,406	
Reserves capital	3,987		12,578		
Revenue	6,685	10,672	17,422ª	11,205	23,782	40,188ª
		£23,943			£46,179

ª Total ordinary stockholders' book value per share are equivalent to 13/- a share for Liebig's (which compares with a current market price of 16/-) and 10/3 a share for Brooke Bond (which compares with a current market price of 14/-).

13. *Earnings*

The last ten years have seen a steady expansion of the business, with total funds employed nearly doubling (from £12.5 million in 1958 to £23.9 million in 1967). Over the same period sales turnover increased without a break, from £21.9 million to £40.5 million and profits before interests and tax from £2.1 million (9.6 percent of sales) to £3.8 million (8.4 percent of sales). These last percentage ratios represent a thoroughly commendable performance in a decade when:

1. Margins must have come under sustained pressure in the face of the buying power of the big multiples and supermarkets;
2. U.D.I. and sanctions knocked the Rhodesian earnings for six years;
3. The Aberdeen typhoid epidemic must have thumped the Fray Bentos corned beef profits severely; and
4. The Latin American operations have clearly been an unhappy drag on profits.

The record for the five years ended August 31, 1967 reads like this:

(in £000)	1963	1964	1965	1966	1967
1. Sales	32,400	33,700	34,300	37,700	40,452
2. Profit before					
interest and tax	3,263	3,179	3,395	3,822	3,803
(2) as % of (1)—(%)	10.1	9.4	9.9	10.1	9.4
(2) as % of total					
capital employed					
—(%)	12.2	11.7	12.3	13.7	13.5
3. Earned for ordinary					
(net)	1,218	963	1,552	1,947	1,801
(3) as % of equity					
capital employed					
—(%)	8.3	6.4	9.7	11.8	10.4
4. Earnings per ordinary					
share (4)	10.8	8.6	13.8	17.3	16.0
Dividends per					
ordinary share (4)	n.a.	n.a.	8.6	8.5	9.8

COMPANHIA UNIÂO FABRIL

In September 1966, Mr. João António Simôes de Almeida, chief executive officer of Companhia Uniâo Fabril (CUF), was drafting a final proposal for debt financing amounting to the equivalent of 273 million escudos. He planned to present a specific recommendation to his Board of Directors for their approval. He was still undecided about the denomination of the bonds, but he had narrowed his choice to three alternatives: Eurodollars, European units-of-account, or a multiple currency issue denominated in escudos, dollars, and Deutsche marks. (Eurodollar bonds are denominated in U.S. dollars but registered and sold only outside the United States. European unit-of-account bonds are expressed in terms of an artificial monetary equivalent and are payable to the holders on the basis of any one of seventeen European currencies. Multiple currency bonds are issued in fixed amounts of two or more specific currencies and are payable in any one of these currencies.) Mr. Simôes de Almeida felt that his decision would affect both the interest rate that the company would pay on the bonds and the company's future liability for repayment.

History of the Company

Companhia Uniâo Fabril was incorporated in 1865 as a producer of soaps and vegetable oil. After a merger with Companhia Aliança Fabril, the company's operations expanded, sometimes through subsidiary companies, into the chemical and fertilizer business, the spinning and weaving of jute, tobacco production and shipping. By 1966, CUF was the largest industrial organization in Portugal. (Exhibits 1 and 2 contain recent balance sheets and income statements.)

The operations of the CUF Group included banking and insurance, shipbuilding and repairing, pharmaceutical products, engineering services and nonferrous metals production, plus food and paint companies. In the past five years, aggregate sales had increased 56 percent, and total Group employment had grown to thirty thousand people. Estimated 1966 sales for

Exhibit 1

Companhia União Fabril

Condensed Comparative Balance Sheets

(in millions of escudos)

Assets

As of December 31	1964	1965	Provisional figures as of June 30, 1966
Current Assets			
Cash and banks	219	153	155
Notes receivable	25	12	55
Accounts receivable	830	827	860
Sundry debtors	30	50	53
Inventories	740	829	927
	1,844	1,871	2,050
Investment			
Participation in subsidiary companies and other investment	369	401	411
Fixed Assets (Note 1)			
Land, installations, plant, and equipment	1,798	1,943	1,943
Less: amortization	−123	−253	−318
Work in progress	382	471	560
	2,057	2,161	2,185
Other Assets	474	138	130
TOTAL	4,744	4,571	4,776

Liabilities and Capital

As of December 31	1964	1965	Provisional figures as of June 30, 1966
Current Liabilities			
Accounts payable	679	691	581
Loan installments payable in the following year	105	136	277
	784	827	854
Medium-Term Loans	523	325	294
Other Liabilities	560	455	622
Provisions for Taxes and Sundry Items	116	142	196
Capital and Reserves			
Share capital and appropriated reserve	1,500	1,500	1,500
Free reserves and unappropriated profits	268	329	313
Fixed assets revaluation reserve (See note)	993	993	993
	2,761	2,822	2,806
TOTAL	4,744	4,571	4,776

Note: All fixed assets were revalued by the company's technical staff as of January 1, 1964, in accordance with Decree no. 20258 of December 28, 1963, which permits enterprises whose fixed assets were undervalued to proceed to a revaluation.

This revaluation, together with the 1964 accounts, was submitted to the Governmental Tax Department and accepted.

As of December 31, 1963, the net book value of the company's fixed assets was 577 million escudos. After revaluation as of January 1, 1964, this net book value was increased to 1,570 million escudos. As a counterpart, the difference (993 million escudos) was appropriated to a special fixed asset revaluation reserve.

24

Exhibit 2   **Companhia União Fabril**
Condensed Comparative Profit and Loss Statement

	Year Ended December 31		Provisional Figures for Six Months Ended June 30, 1966
	1964	1965	
Sales	2,271	2,628	1,503
Less: cost of goods sold	1,828	2,105	1,217
selling and general commercial expenses	219	225	123
general and managerial expenses	31	30	13
Profit before amortization	193	268	150
Less: amortization	123	131	66
Net operating profit	70	137	84
Sundry profit	2	3	2
Total	72	140	86
Less: financing charges	36	42	37
Profit before taxation	36	98	49
Less: taxation	22	27	14
Net profit for the fiscal year	14	71	35

The CUF Group (including the scales of nonconsolidated subsidiaries) were expected to exceed 6 billion escudos (in excess of 200 million U.S. dollars).

Background Leading to the Bond Issue

During the first one hundred years of its development, CUF displayed a remarkable ability to generate funds internally. In the past, this source of capital was sufficient to support the company's growth; however, in recent years funds had also been raised from banks and suppliers in the form of short- or medium-term debt. On December 31, 1965, CUF's medium-term loans totaled 461 million escudos. Of this amount the equivalent of 273 million escudos (approximately 10 million U.S. dollars) represented loans that were contracted in currencies other than the escudo. Table 1 classifies these loans by foreign currency on the basis of December 1965 exchange rates. Because some of these loans had been negotiated under unfavorable circumstances, the Board of Directors had decided to consolidate them into

Table 1

Currency	Redemption Value (millions of escudos)
U.S. dollars	106
French francs	59
Deutsche marks	108
Total	273

a single long-term debt issue that would be less costly and burdensome for CUF.

Mr. Simôes de Almeida first considered the possibility of raising the necessary funds within Portugal. Even though the funds were required to repay foreign credits, there was freedom of capital movement in and out of Portugal. The problem was that allowable interest rates in Portugal had been held low through government control. The maximum allowable interest rate during most of the 1960s was 5 percent. Since this rate was available to savers on certain back deposits and on government bonds, there was little interest among investors in the corporate bond market. The result of such low yields was that much private capital was invested outside of Portugal, leaving revolving bank credit as the major source of funds available to business. Besides limiting interest rates, government policies in Portugal were aimed at keeping the limited capital of the country available for the small businesses and municipal projects that were forced to rely on local savings. This meant that larger companies were often requested by the government to seek capital in foreign markets even though they might have been able to raise the funds in Portugal.

Mr. Simôes de Almeida concluded that it would not be feasible to raise 273 million escudos in Portugal given the prevailing level of interest rates. A higher interest rate could not be used because of government considerations. Because of these factors, he turned his attention to the possibility of raising the funds in the international capital market.

Developments in European Capital Markets[1]

An international capital market had developed in the 1960s in Europe with the rebirth of Frankfurt, London, Amsterdam, and Brussels as financial centers. After World War II, only New York and Switzerland existed as financial centers of major significance, but changing economic and political situations caused each to give up its dominant position in the European

---

[1] The information in this section was compiled from several sources, the most important of which were *Weekly Bulletin,* Kredietbank, Brussels, and *Prospects,* Swiss Bank Corporation, Basel.

financial market. Adverse balance of payments problems caused the United States to limit its European activities in two ways. First, by means of the interest equalization tax in 1963, Americans were discouraged from investing funds outside the United States. Second, because of the "voluntary restraints" recommended by the federal government in 1965, U.S. corporations had been seeking capital in Europe for financing their foreign investments.

In the case of Switzerland, it had been the Swiss government's monetary policy that reduced the country's relative importance as a capital market. The central bank of Switzerland maintained a policy of restricting capital exports in the form of foreign loans. The Swiss did not wish their franc to be forced into the role of a reserve currency, and therefore limited the amount of their currency that was available in international markets. This was accomplished by restricting the number of foreign bond issues in Switzerland and creating a two- or three-year waiting period for registration of new issues. The result was that Switzerland's share of all international issues dropped from 90 percent in 1960 to 6 percent in 1965. In part this was due to a small absolute decline in the number of Swiss francs supplied to the capital markets, but mostly this reflected the tremendous growth of bond issues elsewhere.

At the same time, the demand for funds grew rapidly as more and more companies were seeking capital in Europe. Because of these factors, borrowers were forced to search for new sources of capital. Without easy access to Swiss francs, or dollars in the United States, they went to Germany, England, and other parts of Europe. Meanwhile, because of the U.S. balance of payment deficits there was a large pool of dollars held by institutions and individual investors outside the United States. This proved to be the most available capital source in Europe. The total value of new loans denominated in U.S. dollars and issued in Europe (Eurodollar loans) grew to 368 million dollars in 1965. The willingness of non-U.S. investors to hold dollars made this form of obligation very popular in European markets. Among the European centers handling Eurodollar issues, London was the largest, accounting for nearly 40 percent of the total bonds issued. The total outstanding amount of Eurodollar bonds by mid-1966 was approximately 11.0 billion. This amount represented 85 percent of all outstanding European foreign issues. For 1966, it was estimated that new Eurodollar issues would surpass 700 million.

Probably the second most favored denomination for foreign bonds was the Deutsche mark. Although it was 1957 before any foreign company issued a Deutsche mark loan in Germany, the volume soon increased. Between 1957 and 1963 loans to non-German companies totaling 774 million DM were floated. In the following two years more than 2.2 billion DM bonds were issued by foreign borrowers. This resulted in a severe shortage of marks. With Eurodollars and Deutsche marks accounting for the major portion of European foreign issues, other currencies did not gain as much popularity with international investors.

The rapid expansion of loan demand in Europe's capital markets during the first half of 1966 brought about a general rise in interest rates. Even countries such as Italy that traditionally followed a low-interest monetary policy were unable to counteract the trend. As demands for capital by governments, U.S. enterprises and European industry increased, interest rates continued to rise. This led to additional innovations for attracting capital into the markets. One new instrument was the European unit-of-account (EUA) bond, originally conceived by the Kredietbank of Brussels. (A more complete discussion of EUA bonds is presented in Appendix A.) Among the early issuers of EUA bonds were two Portuguese companies. The first was Sacor, a large petrochemical company, and the second was the Banco de Fomento, the Portuguese Development Bank. One advantage of this bond is that the borrower is able to draw funds from many European capital markets with a single issue. Another is that it attracts investors who may not normally purchase foreign bonds. For example, insurance companies usually hold their liabilities in just one currency with the result that they want their investments in the same currency. The unit-of-account bond is for these companies an alternative investment to local issues. Although the first EUA bond was issued in 1961, the use of EUA bonds through 1965 totaled only the equivalent of 68 million dollars. An apparent lack of understanding of this instrument existed among the investing public. In spite of this, an amount of EUA bonds surpassing 70 million dollars was expected to be issued during 1966.

In addition to the EUA, the search for new methods of attracting capital led to a revival of the multiple currency bond. In 1957, Petrofina, a large Belgian petrochemical company, issued a multiple currency bond denominated in Belgian francs, British pounds, and Deutsche marks. In the past few years this multiple denomination had become particularly popular for government issues. During recent months because of the weakness of the pound, many British issues had included multiple currency clauses.

Alternatives Open to the Company

Since CUF could not issue escudo bonds, Mr. Simôes de Almeida reviewed a number of foreign alternatives with the company's investment bankers. He paid particular attention to the current conditions in the European capital markets. He rejected bonds denominated in Deutsche marks because they appeared to be more difficult to issue than escudos due to the shortage of uninvested Deutsche marks. He also dismissed British pounds sterling because currency regulations restricted capital flows from England. He would have been interested in a Swiss franc loan because of low interest rates (5½ percent-5¾ percent), but the delay in issue time was between two and three years. Due to these factors he narrowed his choice of bond denomination to three alternatives: Eurodollars, European units-of-account, and a multiple currency issue in escudos, Deutsche marks, and U.S. dollars.

In the opinion of the company's investment bankers, CUF would find acceptance among investors for any of these issues. In each case the bonds would have a ten-year maturity and a similar schedule of amortization. Mr. Simôes de Almeida's main concern was the cost of the loan and the risk that the company assumed in connection with future payments of interest and principal. He had estimated the effective rate for issuing Eurodollar bonds to be 7¼ percent. For EUA bonds and for multiple currency bonds the effective rate would be about 6¾ percent.

Concerning CUF's future liability, Mr. Simôes de Almeida knew that dealing in any foreign currency bonds exposed the company to risks of changes in currency parity rates as defined by the International Monetary Fund (IMF). In addition, because of temporary differences in supply and demand for various currencies, exchange rates may fluctuate as much as three-quarters of 1 percent above or below IMF parity values in the course of normal trading. There are two European currencies that are allowed to fluctuate more widely—the Portuguese escudo and the Swiss franc. The escudo is permitted to rise or fall 1.15 percent from its IMF parity value before the central bank of Portugal will intervene, and the Swiss franc is allowed to move as much as 1.75 percent on either side of parity. The IMF parity rates for the escudo plus buy and sell rates for foreign currencies as of August 31, 1966 are shown in Exhibit 3.

Exchange fluctuations within normal trading limits may affect the amount that a company has to pay its bond holders even if no official revaluations take place. For example, suppose that market demand for escudos is rather low at the time of payment, dropping the prevailing ex-change rate to 29 escudos per U.S. dollar (from the IMF parity value of 28.749) and that Deutsche marks are in great demand driving their dollar equivalent to $3.97 (IMF parity = $4.00). In this case, CUF would have to pay 29,000 escudos in payment of a straight $1,000 Eurodollar bond. How-ever, the holder of an EUA bond or a multiple currency bond denominated in U.S. dollars and Deutsche marks would specify payment in Deutsche marks. At parity, the payment of 4,000 Deutsche marks or 1,000 U.S. dollars would cost the company 28,749 escudos. But in order to repay an EUA or multiple currency bond in marks, the effective cost would be 29,169 escudos.[2]

With all this in mind, Mr. Simôes de Almeida was attempting to dif-

---

[2] 29,000 escudos = 1,000 U.S. dollars = 3,970 Deutsche marks; therefore payment of 1,000 EUA = 4,000 DM requires 29,169 escudos.

Exhibit 3   **Companhia Uniâo Fabril**

International Value of the Escudo

Currency	IMF Parity	Current Exchange Rates	
		Buy Rate	Sell Rate
	1	2	3
Austria: Schilling	90.44	89.17	89.93
Belgium: Franc	173.92	172.66	173.27
Denmark: Krone	24.03	23.90	24.23
France: Franc	17.17	16.92	17.37
Germany: Deutsche mark	13.91	13.76	14.21
Greece: Drachma	104.35	103.45	104.75
Iceland: Krona	149.57	148.48	149.03
Ireland: Pound	1.24	1.23	1.25
Italy: Lira	2174.00	2149.67	2154.68
Luxemburg: Franc	173.92	172.66	173.27
Netherlands: Guilder	12.59	12.47	12.98
Norway: Krone	24.85	24.69	24.98
Sweden: Krona	17.99	17.86	18.15
Switzerland: Franc	15.21	14.92	15.08
Turkey: Pound	31.31	31.03	31.36
United Kingdom: Pound	1.24	1.23	1.25
United States: Dollar	3.48	3.45	3.47

On August 31, 1966, the IMF parity rate was 28.749 escudos to US $1.00; that is, at parity 100 escudos was equivalent to US $3.48. Column 1 in the table expresses the parity of 100 escudos in relation to seventeen different currencies. Column 2 shows the August 31, 1966 *buy* rate, i.e., the amount of foreign currency that could be bought for 100 escudos. Finally, column 3 gives the current *sell* rate or the amount of foreign currency needed to buy 100 escudos.

ferentiate the risks related to each type of bond. He had also received a staff report (Appendix B) discussion current monetary trends. Now he was prepared to reach his final recommendation.

APPENDIX A

European Unit-of-Account

The European unit-of-account (EUA) bond is an obligation whose principal and interest are fixed and payable in terms of "units-of-account." The *base* value of the unit-of-account in September 1966 was the IMF parity of the United States dollar (or the equivalent of .88867088 grams of fine gold). The holder of a unit-of-account bond may elect to be paid on the basis of any of seventeen currencies according to predefined rates of exchange. These exchange rates as of September 1966 are given in Table 1.

The base value of a "unit-of-account" changes only if *all* seventeen

Table 1

```
1 EUA =  26.000 Schilling (Austria)
1 EUA =  50.000 Franc (Belgium)
1 EUA =   6.907 Krone (Denmark)
1 EUA =   4.937 Franc (France)
1 EUA =   4.000 Mark (Germany)
1 EUA =   0.357 Pound (United Kingdom)
1 EUA =  30.000 Drachma (Greece)
1 EUA =  43.000 Krona (Iceland)
1 EUA = 625.001 Lira (Italy)
1 EUA =  50.000 Franc (Luxemburg)
1 EUA =   3.620 Guilder (Netherlands)
1 EUA =   7.143 Krone (Norway)
1 EUA =  28.749 Escudo (Portugal)
1 EUA =   5.173 Krona (Sweden)
1 EUA =   4.373 Franc (Switzerland)
1 EUA =   0.357 Pound (Ireland)
1 EUA =   9.000 Pound (Turkey)
```

currencies change their respective initial values *and* if at least two thirds change in one direction. If both conditions are met, the unit-of-account changes in the same direction as the majority. The amount of the change is equal to that of the *smallest* currency change in the same direction. Some examples may make this clearer:

1. Suppose that British pounds, Greek drachmas, and Turkish pounds all devalue 10 percent. There would be no change in the base value of the unit-of-account, but the relationship between the EUA and these three currencies would change in direct relation to the amount of the devaluation. Therefore, the "local currency" liability on EUA bonds of companies located in these countries would rise by 10 percent. Thus, a Turkish company would now have to use 9,900 Turkish pounds to repay a 1,000 EUA bond. Before devaluation it could have repaid the same bond with 9,000 Turkish pounds.

2. If Dutch guilders were revalued up 10 percent while Austrian schillings and Norwegian krona were devalued 15 percent, there would still be no change in the base value of the unit-of-account.

3. Suppose that all seventeen currencies devalue, as follows:

    4 currencies devalue 20%
    6 currencies devalue 15%
    3 currencies devalue 10%
    4 currencies devalue 5%

The base of the unit-of-account would decline in value by 5 percent, an amount equal to the smallest percentage devaluation. However, it is important to remember that if just one currency had not changed, the base value of the units-of-account would have remained unchanged.

The effect of this devaluation on a company's liability depends upon the relative change of that company's local currency. If the local currency also devalued by 5 percent, the company's liability in local-currency terms would remain unchanged. For companies located in other countries, the net effect would be to increase the effective cost of debt. For example, the effective liability of a company located in a country that devalued by 20 percent would be equal to 1.1428 times its previous local currency liability $[(1 + .20)/(1 + .05) = 1.1428]$.

4. As another example, suppose the following changes occurred:

> 3 currencies revalue upward 10%
> 4 currencies devalue   20%
> 2 currencies devalue   15%
> 6 currencies devalue   10%
> 2 currencies devalue   5%

The unit-of-account would then be devalued (it moves with the two-thirds majority) by 5 percent (the amount of the smallest change in that direction). In the three countries where a 10 percent revaluation upward occurred, a company's liability (in local terms) would be reduced by approximately 14 percent $[(1 - .10)/(1 + .05) = .858]$.

5. As a final example, if all seventeen currencies devalue by 20 percent, the base value of the EUA also declines by 20 percent. It is important to note that in this case neither the effective liability of any issuer nor the investment value to any holder would change.

The purpose of this complex sounding arrangement is the creation of a stable artificial monetary unit that will protect investors and borrowers from major changes in exchange rates. For the investor the principal attraction of unit-of-account bonds is their protection against devaluation. Since the holders of EUA bonds are allowed to specify payment at maturity in terms of any of the seventeen listed currencies[1], they avoid capital losses unless the unit-of-account itself is devalued. For example, assume that the Belgian franc is devalued 10 percent bringing 1 EUA = 55 Belgian francs. The holder of Belgian franc bonds would suffer a 10 percent capital loss

---

[1] Actual payment is never made in Swiss francs because of Swiss government intervention; however, payment in another currency can be specified on the basis of Swiss francs. This gives the investor a *de facto* Swiss franc bond.

in terms of "international purchasing power," but the holder of an **EUA** bond would now receive at maturity 55 Belgian francs for every 1 EUA. In this way the holder of a unit-of-account bond may protect the international value of his investment in spite of local devaluation.

The major risk that the investor is left to bear is that his own currency will be revalued upward in terms of the unit-of-account. In this case he will be worse off than if he had been holding fixed obligations in his own currency. For example, suppose only the Greek drachma revalued upward 10 percent, so that 1 EUA = 27 drachmas. In this case, Greek investors would receive 27,000 drachmas for each 1,000 EUA bonds whereas the investment required 30,000 drachmas. These investors would have been better off had they bought drachma-denominated bonds.

From the company's point of view the major risk is that its own currency will be devalued in relation to the EUA. To the extent that a company feels that its local currency is as strong as the EUA, the company limits its liability to the value of the original obligation.

APPENDIX B

Report on Monetary and Economic Outlook

This report presents a brief overall look at current monetary trends (September 1966) and economic indicators in Western Europe and the United States. The purpose is to present information pertaining to future currency stability in these areas. The first part of this report contains a short summary of our conclusions about global monetary developments for the remainder of 1966 and 1967. This summary is followed by separate sections on Portugal, Germany, and the United States. The last part of the report consists of tables and statistical information.

Summary of Principal Conclusions

In our opinion, current economic conditions indicate that the following trends will characterize monetary developments during the next few years.

1. Increasing demand for loans should force interest rates higher over the next few years.
2. The escudo will remain firm at its present IMF parity.
3. The Deutsche mark will strengthen in terms of other currencies.
4. Despite balance-of-payment pressures, the United States dollar will retain its international value in terms of gold and other currencies.
5. Some of the other principal currencies in the unit-of-account, notably the British pound, may come under considerable pressure.

Increased demand on the capital markets of Europe will come from expanding local business enterprises and continued government financing. Added to this demand will be large bond issues by European subsidiaries of American firms acting in accordance with their government's recommendation to raise capital outside the United States. The result of this combined activity is expected to be a shortage of funds available for investment. This will bring higher interest rates. Also, rapid economic expansion may bring inflationary pressures to bear on several countries of Europe. A recent measure of inflationary trends is given in Table 1, while Table 2 lists changes in official exchange rates of European currencies in relation to the U.S. dollar. This first index shows how the cost of living has risen in the various countries of Europe and the United States during the past seven years.

The escudo should remain strong as a result of steady economic growth within Portugal. This growth is largely the result of the success of the government's central development plans. As long as Portugal's trade deficit is offset by inflows from tourism, banking, insurance, and capital investment, the currency will be stable.

The Deutsche mark should grow even stronger as Germany adds to its trade surplus each year. German exports of automobiles, machine tools, and

Table 1   **Cost of Living Index**

Index Numbers: December 1958 = 100

Country	*Year*						
	1959	1960	1961	1962	1963	1964	1965
Austria	102	102	108	111	115	119	126
Belgium	102	101	108	104	108	112	117
Denmark	102	103	110	119	122	129	138
France	106	110	114	120	126	127	131
Germany	102	103	106	109	113	115	120
Greece	103	105	103	107	108	110	115
Iceland	91	95	105	115	133	151	165
Ireland	98	101	104	108	112	120	124
Italy	102	103	106	113	120	128	129
Netherlands	103	103	106	106	111	117	124
Norway	101	101	106	111	112	119	121
Portugal	103	104	106	108	111	116	120
Sweden	101	105	108	113	117	121	128
Switzerland	99	101	105	108	113	115	121
Turkey	111	114	121	127	132	134	142
United Kingdom	100	102	106	109	111	116	122
United States	101	103	104	105	107	108	110

Source: International Financial Statistics, IMF (September, 1966).

Table 2   **Changes in IMF Parity Rates**
1958—August 1966

		IMF Parity to $1 U.S.	
Date	*Country and Currency*	*Before*	*After*
February 22, 1960	Iceland: Krona	16.2857	38.00
August 20, 1960	Turkey: Pound	2.80	9.00
March 6, 1961	Germany: Deutsche Mark	4.20	4.00
March 7, 1961	Netherlands: Guilder	3.80	3.62
August 4, 1961	Iceland: Krona	38.00	43.00

Source: International Financial Statistics, IMF (September, 1966).

electrical machinery are increasing. Germany faces problems of inflation due to excessive economic expansion, but this will not undermine the basic strength of its economy. The Deutsche mark is expected to remain one of Europe's hardest currencies.

The U.S. economy, despite foreign payments imbalance, is fueled by the Vietnam War and other government spending and should support the strength of the dollar. The problems threatening the dollar's stability include potential domestic inflation, very high interest rates in Europe and a decline in foreign exchange reserves. As serious as these difficulties are, it does not appear that they will undermine basic confidence in the dollar..

The pound sterling will probably continue to be under pressure because of internal economic weaknesses, chronic external payment deficits, and a great deal of speculation. The Bank of England should be supported, as it has been in the past, by members of the IMF in its efforts to maintain the international value of the pound. For example, at the end of August the Federal Reserve Bank of the United States increased its short-term emergency credit lines with the Bank of England from 750 million dollars to 1.35 billion. Similar swap agreements exist between England and the other members of the Bank for International Settlements. Still, it seems likely that the pound and those currencies closely linked with the pound will come under pressure. These other currencies include the Irish pound, the Norwegian krone, the Danish krone, and the Austrian schilling. In the case that some change in the parity value of the British pound should take place, it is our opinion that these other currencies would follow. For this reason the weakness of the pound sterling appears to be the greatest threat to change the present international monetary relationships. However, we feel that because of external support devaluation of the British pound will not be necessary.

Portugal

Portugal's second six-year development plan was successfully concluded in 1964. During the final year the country's gross national product grew in real terms 7.3 percent. The increase was considerably better than the impressive 6.5 percent average rate for the whole six-year plan. Now the Transitional Investment Plan (1966–67) is being implemented. At this midpoint it appears that the program's goals for annual growth are being achieved. Starting in 1968 the government will launch a third six-year Social and Economic Development Plan.

In the area of foreign trade, Portugal consistently runs a deficit. This is due to the fact that Portuguese industry must import most of its raw materials. As business has expanded, this trade deficit has increased. Table 3 shows the growth of this unfavorable trade balance. While Portuguese export revenues grew faster than import expenditures during the first half of 1966, there is little hope of eliminating this unfavorable trade imbalance. But, as can be seen in Table 3, this trade deficit is almost entirely offset by income from tourist receipts, private transfers, and other income, such as shipping and insurance. Also, during the last few years, several European countries have granted large loans to Portugal for the development of both agriculture and industry. These loans have created a large surplus in the nation's capital account and resulted in substantial positive net balance of payments for Portugal during the last four years.

As with any nation that is dependent upon imports, foreign exchange reserves are especially important for Portugal. Table 3 also contains year-end totals of Portuguese gold and convertible currency reserves. As of July 31, 1966, Portugal's foreign exchange reserves reached an all-time high of 31,779 million escudos. This growth of monetary reserves has greatly strengthened the escudo in relation to other currencies.

Table 3   Summarized Balance of Payments and Foreign Exchange Reserves of Portugal

(millions of escudos)

Year	Balance of Trade	Net Flow from Tourism, Services, and Transfer	Capital Account	Errors or Omissions	Net Balance of Payments	Gold + Convertible Currency Reserves at Year End
1959						23,912
1960	−3,036	+2,657	+ 154	+ 51	− 174	23,738
1961	−5,277	+1,123	+1,625	−223	−2,752	20,972
1962	−4,272	+3,256	+4,274	− 35	+3,223	24,031
1963	−4,605	+3,976	+2,712	+ 54	+2,137	25,830
1964	−5,233	+5,715	+2,980	+ 40	+3,502	28,499
1965	−9,307	+8,316	+3,252	+ 62	+2,323	30,752

Source: International Financial Statistics, IMF (September, 1966).

In summary, because the economy is strengthening, the balance of payments is positive, and the foreign exchange reserves of Portugal are quite large, the outlook for the escudo is very good. In fact, on the basis of its twelve-year foreign exchange record, the escudo ranks internationally among the world's most stable currencies.

Germany

After periods of domestic stress and inflation, there seems to be some stability coming into the German economy. Industrial production is expanding, but the inflation has been checked. The cost of living index for the year ending July 31, 1966 rose only 2.9 percent as compared with a 5 percent rise during the 1965 calendar year. Exports are increasing as the sales of automobiles, machine tools, and electrical machinery outside Germany become larger. Export revenues for the first eight months of 1966 surpassed those for the same period in 1965 by 11.2 percent. It appears that Germany's trade surplus in 1966 will be four times the one in 1965. This will bring the trade surplus back to 1963-64 levels and have a strong favorable effect on Germany's balance of payments. These figures are summarized in Table 4.

Table 4   Summarized Balance of Payments and Foreign Exchange Reserves of Germany

(millions of DM)

Year	Balance of Trade	Net Flow from Tourism, Services, and Transfer	Capital Account	Errors or Omissions	Net Balance of Payments	Gold + Convertible Currency Reserves at Year End
1959						23,621
1960	+5,223	− 569	+1,788	+1,565	+8,007	31,628
1961	+6,615	−3,728	−5,227	+ 412	−1,928a	28,281a
1962	+3,477	−5,619	+ 509	+1,081	− 552	27,729
1963	+6,032	−5,119	+2,179	− 520	+2,572	30,301
1964	+6,081	−5,855	−2,022	+1,808	+ 12	30,313
1965	+1,203	−7,630	+2,421	+2,500	−1,506	28,807
June 1966	+2,222	−3,978	− 519	+1,268	−1,007	27,800

a The additional 1,419 million DM decrease in Deutsche Bundesbank's reserves is due to the DM revaluation.

Source: Monthly Report of the Deutsche Bundesbank (September, 1966).

Germany's foreign exchange reserves as of June 1966 equaled 27,800 million Deutsche marks or more than 7 billion dollars. Although this is not a record high level, it should be more than adequate support for the Deutsche mark. Although the net outflow of foreign exchange from Germany due to tourism and services is expected to increase, economists predict that Germany's trade surplus will more than offset this rise. This will improve further Germany's balance of payments and increase its foreign exchange reserves. Primarily for this reason the Deutsche mark is expected to remain one of Europe's hardest currencies.

United States

The United States is in the midst of an economic boom that is being spurred on by the production of war materials and large government spending programs. Disposable income has grown rapidly and created new demand for consumer products. Externally, the country's positive balance of trade stands between four and five billion dollars per year. In spite of this, there are some serious weaknesses facing the dollar. The relevant balance-of-payments figures and foreign currency reserve totals given in Table 5 reveal some of the problems.

In the first place, the U.S. positive balance of trade is somewhat misleading because many of the exports are financed through foreign aid programs and military assistance. Even if these programs were to be discontinued, the United States would still have a favorable balance of trade; however, the surplus would not be so great. In the second place, two factors cause large outflows of foreign exchange for the United States: military expenditures and overseas private capital investment. These expenditures have grown larger than the trade surplus and are primarily responsible for the negative balance-of-payments position. In 1966 it appears that President Johnson's "voluntary restrictions" on direct foreign investment are reducing capital outflows. At the same time it is clear that military expenditures are rising rapidly.

During the last six years the United States has suffered large losses of gold and convertible foreign currency reserves. The losses of gold alone have been equal to almost one billion dollars each year. Between the end of 1959 and June 30, 1966 total reserves have dropped from 21,202 billion dollars to 14,958 billion dollars. During the same period official foreign holdings of dollar liabilities have grown by more than six billion. Since these could have been converted into gold, the willingness of foreign governments to hold U.S. dollar deposits eased the strain on the U.S. balance of payments. Any cashing in of these holdings would have seriously depleted United States gold reserves.

It appears that the United States must take some corrective action to improve its balance-of-payments position. At the same time a move to liquidate dollar holdings by foreign governments seems very unlikely. In short, these problems are serious, but they should not be expected to alter the worldwide value and acceptance of the dollar. The basic strength of the U.S. economy, in our best estimation, will be sufficient to support the international value of the dollar.

Table 5

Summarized Balance of Payments and Foreign Exchange Reserves of the United States of America

(millions of U.S. dollars)

Year	Balance of Trade	Net Military Expenditures and Sales	Net Flow from Tourism, Services, and Transfer	Capital Account	Errors or Omissions	Foreign Official Liabilities	Net Balance of Payments	Gold Reserves	Gold + Convertible Currency Reserves at Year End
1959								19,506	21,202
1960	+4,757	−2,734	− 339	−3,845	− 941	+1,259	−1,843	17,804	19,359
1961	+5,444	−2,579	+ 170	−3,376	−1,006	+ 741	− 606	16,947	18,753
1962	+4,417	−2,427	+ 464	−4,001	−1,159	+1,173	−1,533	16,057	17,220
1963	+5,079	−2,279	+ 313	−4,805	− 351	+1,666	− 377	15,596	16,843
1964	+6,676	−2,087	+1,136	−6,056	−1,011	+1,171	− 171	15,471	16,672
1965	+4,788	−2,037	+1,412	−5,036	− 429	+ 80	−1,222	14,065	15,450
June 30 1966	+2,210	−1,311	+ 629	−1,565	+ 51	− 506	− 492	13,530	14,958

Source: International Financial Statistics, IMF (September, 1966).

LANDIS & GYR, AG (A)

Landis & Gyr Holding, AG, of Zug, Switzerland, published a prospectus on January 24, 1957, offering a 3¼ percent convertible bond issue of Sfr. 15,000,000 for subscription at par (plus 0.6 percent, half the federal stamp tax). The issue was the first one of its kind to be offered in Switzerland by a Swiss company. Individual bonds had a par value of Sfr. 1,000 and carried a maturity date of 1972; however, they were subject to redemption by lot under a sinking fund requirement beginning February 1, 1961. The convertibility feature gave bondholders the option of exchanging their bonds for Class B stock of Landis & Gyr, AG, also of Zug, after February 1, 1960, one bond being convertible into one B share.

Landis & Gyr, AG, until 1956 a family-held manufacturing company, was owned in large part by Landis & Gyr Holding, AG, through the medium of its Class A stock. The B stock named in the prospectus comprised only a small part of the company's total capitalization at the time, but this class of stock was destined to become the company's principal financing medium. Individual shares had a par value of Sfr. 200. The company's directors intended to list the issue on the Zürich Stock Exchange in the future, but a representative market price had not yet been established for the 20,000 B shares that were currently outstanding. As a result, it was difficult to estimate the value of the conversion privilege, a fact that complicated the problem of appraising the value of the convertible bonds.

Company Background Information

Landis & Gyr was founded in 1906 as a partnership by Messrs. Landis and Gyr. The company was incorporated in 1914, and most of its stock continued to be held by the founder families until 1956. From the company's inception, management had followed the policy of retaining a high percentage of earnings and financing expansion with these funds. On the average, retained earnings had increased at a rate of more than 8 percent per year, and hence the company's reserves by 1956 were many times as large as the paid-in capital of Sfr. 10 million.

Landis & Gyr's product line included a wide variety of meters and control devices used in measuring and regulating the transmission and distribution of electricity. The trend of the company's sales had been closely correlated with the growth of electricity consumption and had not been appreciably affected by changes in the nature of the prime source of power used in generating electricity. Consumption of electrical energy was expected to increase even more rapidly in the future, and therefore the directors of Landis & Gyr were optimistic about their company's continued long-range development.

By 1956, after repeated expansion and modernization, the main plant in Zug had become one of the major factories in Switzerland. Another Swiss plant was under construction in Einsiedeln, and other expansion projects had either just been completed or were being contemplated for the company's manufacturing subsidiaries in Switzerland and abroad (in England, Germany, France, Holland, and Austria). The labor force numbered more than 8,0000 workers and employees, approximately half employed in Zug and half in the subsidiaries.

Sales from the Zug plant in 1956 exceeded Sfr. 68 million and were divided in roughly a 2:3 ratio between the domestic market and foreign markets scattered all around the world. Combined sales of the subsidiaries were only slightly less than those of the Zug plant, but these companies individually tended to produce almost exclusively for their respective national markets. In the United States, Landis & Gyr products were sold through the company's own sales firm. Competition was keen in most important market areas, especially where German and American firms were active, but management was confident of the company's ability to hold its own against its competitors. In a field where technical know-how and skilled craftsmanship were at a premium, Landis & Gyr had already established a reputation for the general excellence of its products.

The Decision to Become a Public Company

The postwar growth of sales and physical facilities produced as impressive increase in the financial needs of Landis & Gyr, and in 1952 the Board of Directors—consisting at the time, with one exception, of nonfamily members—concluded that the company had already outgrown its capital base or would do so in the near future. More new investment opportunities, which the directors considered desirable in their own right, were at hand or in sight than could possibly be financed with retained earnings. Moreover, the company was not able to count on customer deposits as a major source of outside funds, as was true of many Swiss manufacturers of industrial equipment. Customers, unfortunately, were inclined to ignore the special design and engineering work that went into a large part of Landis & Gyr's production and demanded terms similar to those offered by standard-line producers.

In 1952, therefore, the Board advanced a proposal to sell an issue of stock to new shareholders. This proposal was rejected by the majority shareholders because it would have required them to relinquish roughly 25 percent of their equity interest in return for what was judged to be a wholly inadequate subcription of new capital. The proposed price of new shares was based upon the dividend payments of previous years, and it was argued that these had been maintained at too low a level, for understandable reasons, to provide a fair basis of basis of valuation. At the time, even the majority stockholders did not know that the proposed price was equal to less than one-third of the current book value of the stock and only about three times the actual per share earnings.[1]

A second proposal of the Board, to issue Sfr. 3.5 million of new shares to stockholders, was later accepted and put into effect in March, 1953. All the new shares were taken up by old stockholders, and Landis & Gyr's stated capital was raised as a result to Sfr. 10 million.

The capital problem was too big to be solved by that move alone, however, and consequently the question of how Landis & Gyr might gain access to the equity capital market became a topic of frequent discussion at company meetings. In May, 1956, the majority stockholders voted a sweeping change in the composition of the Board of Directors, and eight months later the first steps were taken to open the company to public investment.

At approximately the same time, to call attention to the company and gain public confidence, management instituted a dramatic change in the company's reporting practices. Before 1956 Landis & Gyr, like most similarly situated companies, had not made its financial statements or annual reports available to outsiders; even the majority shareholders, as mentioned above, did not have a clear picture of the actual situation. Henceforth, however, it was agreed that financial statements would be published publicly, and beyond this, that financial information would be included in the statements, which was not normally disclosed by Swiss companies. Current assets and current liabilities, for example, were to be reported at their true value to permit interested outside observers to form an accurate opinion of the company's liquidity and its working capital position. Management did not go so far as to disclose all hidden reserves by revaluing the depreciable as-

---

1 That such a situation could have arisen was later attributed to the fact that Swiss law confers discretionary authority upon a Board of Directors to withhold information from stockholders concerning actual earnings and book values.

sets carried as pro memoria items. This move was contemplated for the future, but in the meantime some indication of the size of these reserves was conveyed to investors by the balance sheet figures (required by Swiss law), which showed the insured value of such assets.

The first balance sheet (dated December 31, 1956) to be published under this policy was released in early 1957 and is shown here as Exhibit 1. To give investors a better indication of the financial developments that had taken place during 1956, management also released 1955 year-end figures, adjusted to reflect the new reporting policy. They too are reproduced in Exhibit 1, and the income statement for 1956 is shown in Exhibit 2.

Exhibit 1

Landis & Gyr, AG (A)

Balance Sheets, Jan. 1 and Dec. 31, 1956

(in 000 Sfr.)

	Jan. 1, 1956 after Profit Distribution		Dec. 31, 1956 before Profit Distribution and Capital Increase	
Assets				
Cash		2,846		6,360
Accounts receivable	10,098		13,123	
Provision for bad debts and transportation risk	1,300	8,798	1,300	11,823
Miscellaneous assets and accruals		1,332		985
Inventories	30,998		39,062	
Provision of 33¹/₃% allowed by tax laws	10,333		13,021	
Special provision	750	19,915	750	25,291
Current assets		32,891		44,459
Participations (at cost)		11,059		11,403
Apartment houses		1,768		1,718
Insured value—4,887				
Land		1,526		1,619
Buildings—factory and administration		p.m.		p.m.
Insured value—19,482				
Machinery and equipment		p.m.		p.m.
Insured value—39,862				
Patents, models and cost of research		p.m.		p.m.
Fixed assets		14,353		14,740
Total assets		47,244		59,199
Total valuation reserves on current assets	12,383		15,071	

Exhibit 1 (cont.)   **Landis & Gyr, AG (A)**

		Jan. 1, 1956 after Profit Distribution		Dec. 31, 1956 before Profit Distribution and Capital Increase
Liabilities and Equity				
Promissory notes		640		341
Banks		3,093		1,529
Representatives		421		836
Affiliated companies		9		72
Accounts payable		2,083		1,516
Accruals		2,087		1,990
Dividend payment		1,000		—
Current liabilities		9,334		6,285
Customers' deposits		417		318
Landis & Gyr Holding, AG		—		—
Guarantees, various creditors		2,852		3,726
Personal foundation		3,872		5,303
Long-term loans		1,677		1,689
Total liabilities		18,152		17,321
Stock capital		10,000		
Class A stock			16,000	
Class B stock			4,000	20,000
Legal reserve	1,915		1,915	
Reserve for periods of recession	1,250		1,250	
Reserve for leveling dividend				
payments	4,000		4,000	
Special reserve	76		48	
General free reserve	11,822		12,266	
Profit of the period and				
carry forward of profit	30	19,093	2,400	21,879
Capital and reserves		29,093		41,879
Total		47,245		59,200

The Financial Reorganization

The decision to open Landis & Gyr to investment by the general public did not imply that the owner families had decided to relinquish their majority interest in the enterprise. Understandably, they wished, if possible, to retain effective control, and this objective was in part responsible for the complexity of later financial transactions and the form of the ensuing recapitalization. The following paragraphs attempt to describe these events

Exhibit 2   **Landis & Gyr, AG (A)**

Income Statement, Year Ending Dec. 31, 1956

(in 000 Sfr.)

Gross margin	21,892
Income from subsidiaries	2,698
Carry forward of profit from 1955	30
Total	24,620
Administrative and selling expenses (including taxes and contributions to personnel foundation)	19,086
Loss on bad debts	2
Increase of provision on inventories	2,688
Increase of general free reserve	444
Profit (at the disposition of stockholders)	2,400

Proposal of the Board of Directors

for

Distribution of 1956 Profit

Dividend payment (10% net on par value of Sfr. 20,000,000 plus 5% federal coupon tax)	2,105
Increase of the legal reserve	240
Increase of the special reserve	35
Tax on 1957 capital increase of Sfr. 1,000,000	20
Total	2,400

in their logical sequence and not necessarily their chronological order since the actual change to a public corporation was carried out through a series of more or less simultaneous moves. The principal steps were the following:

1. Formation of Landis & Gyr Holding, AG;
2. Recapitalization of Landis & Gyr, AG; and
3. Issuance of convertible debentures by Landis & Gyr Holding, AG.

Formation of Landis & Gyr Holding, AG

In December, 1956, the majority stockholders of Landis & Gyr organized a new company, Landis & Gyr Holding, AG. This company was to play a major part in future financial transactions between the operating company and its original stockholders and also, in the first instance, between the company and the investing public.

Landis & Gyr Holding was established with an intial paid-in capital of Sfr. 15 million contributed by the majority stockholders of the operating company, i.e., members of the Gyr family. This sum was subscribed in the form of shares of Landis & Gyr stock, valued for purposes of this transaction at 400 percent of their par value. The capital of the holding company, on the other hand, was represented by 15,000 shares of Sfr. 1,000 par value, all registered and transferable only with consent of the company's Board of Directors.

One purpose of this step was to multiply the financial capacity of the original shareholders for the benefit of Landis & Gyr, AG. As individuals, they were in no position to borrow or raise the amount of money that was wanted as new equity capital for the operating company. The same could not be said, however, of a company that held a clear majority voting interest in the operating company. It would be able to offer guarantees to investors and creditors that stockholders individually could not hope to provide. The power of the holding company in this respect was later used, as explained below, to raise outside funds for the purchase of Sfr. 10 million of newly issued Landis & Gyr shares.

The creation of a holding company also appeared to present other advantages in that it would be able to serve as a reservior for dividends paid by the operating company and as a "financial agent" for the operating company when securities were to be offered to the general public.

As a reservoir for dividend and other distributions, the holding company would shield members of the family from the full impact of Switzerland's personal income and personal property taxes. Dividends paid to an individual shareholder were taxable, of course, as personal income, but dividends paid to a corporate holding company were not taxable under the federal law and the law of most cantons. With the holding company in existence, it would therefore be possible to reinvest dividends in excess of the annual income needs of the members of the family in Landis & Gyr, AG, without exposing them to personal taxation. The ensuing appreciation of holding company stock would have no immediate tax consequences for shareholders since capital gains were not taxable as personal income under federal and most cantonal tax laws. Finally, to complete the picture, it was anticipated that this arrangement would permit Landis & Gyr to increase its cash dividend from time to time without serious damage to its cash position, since funds paid to the holding company would be recovered by Landis & Gyr in exchange for the issuance of additional new shares.

The second advantage mentioned, that of serving as financial intermediary between the operating company and the public, was less evident. Under Swiss law, corporations were not permitted to deal in their own securities and hence to hold or sell "treasury stock." The operating company was barred, therefore, from selling its own stock in any other manner than through formally announced offerings to its own stockholders. Landis & Gyr Holding, however, would be an independent corporation under the law and, as such, would not be bound by these restrictions. It would be able to purchase new shares from the operating company, either periodic rights offerings or special issues tailored to the operating company's need for funds and financial position at the time, and resell them to investors, immediately or in stages depending on market conditions. As an independent entity, the holding company would also be able to underwrite the value of purchase warrants, which the operating company might issue at a later time. Any profits realized from such transactions would be reinvested in Landis & Gyr, AG, giving it another source of new capital.

Recapitalization of Landis & Gyr, AG

Simultaneously with the formation of the holding company, arrangements were concluded with Swiss banks for the holding company to borrow Sfr. 10 million at short term. These funds were to be used to increase the paid-in capital of Landis & Gyr from Sfr. 10 to 20 million.

Preparatory to this step, however, Landis & Gyr, AG, was recapitalized. The company's capital stock at the time consisted of 10,000 shares of common stock of Sfr. 1,000 par value. These shares were called in during December, 1956, and in their place were issued 100,000 shares of Sfr. 100 par value (a 10 to 1 stock split). The new shares were henceforth known as A shares.

The same stockholders' meeting, which approved this change, also voted to increase the capital of the company by Sfr. 10 million by issuing 60,000 additional Class A shares and 20,000 new Class B shares with a par value of Sfr. 200. The terms of the offering entitled all stockholders to purchase either two new A shares or one new B share at par for each two old A shares held. Both classes of stock were given one vote per share, but dividend and liquidation rights were allotted in relation to their respective par values.

The A shares with their greater voting power—par value ratio—were designed to provide a means of vesting effective control of Landis & Gyr for the indefinite future in the hands of the holding company and the majority stockholders. As noted, the shares were registered and transferable only with consent of the Board of Directors. The B shares, on the other hand, although registered, were not to be subject to any transfer restrictions. They were to become the company's vehicle for future equity financing, and the directors announced that it was their intention in time to list the shares on the Zürich Stock Exchange. Public ownership of B shares was to be initiated through sales of shares received by the holding company and its stockholders in the recapitalization.

The final decision on the par values and voting privileges of the two classes of stock was influenced both by Swiss law and fundamental policy considerations. Under the governing Code of Obligations the lowest par value that could be given to common shares was Sfr. 100, and it was generally not thought desirable to award more than one vote to one share. Given the control objective of the majority stockholders, these considerations in effect dictated the characteristics of the A shares.

The directors had more latitude, however, in fixing the characteristics of the B stock. While Swiss law required that every stockholder be given at least one vote for each share owned, it did not decree that all shares had to have the same par value. The relative voting power of the A shares could have been increased, therefore, by issuing B shares with a par value of Sfr. 500, 1,000, or even 5,000. While clearly desirable from a control standpoint, it was also anticipated that a high par value would produce a high market price and a corresponding restriction on the salability of the stock. A high par value therefore seemed to be contrary to the goal of establishing a wide public interest in the B stock. The compromise, as noted above, was to establish Sfr. 200 as the par value of the B shares; on this basis they received half the voting power of the A shares.

After the foregoing distinctions between the two classes of stock had been pointed out, most of the minority shareholders elected to subscribe for B shares only. The holding company used the proceeds of its short-term loans primarily to buy A shares, and it ended the year with the financial position shown in Exhibit 3. In general terms, the net result of all these transactions was to give the Gyr family effective control of well over 80 percent of the total 180,000 registered votes. Either directly or indirectly

Exhibit 3   **Landis & Gyr, AG (A)**

Landis & Gyr Holding, AG
Balance Sheet, December 31, 1956
(in 000 Sfr.)

Assets	
Participations (primarily A stock of Landis & Gyr, SA)	26,371
Land and buildings	874
Furniture and equipment	—
Machinery	3
Other assets	1
Total assets	27,249
Liabilities	
Banks and creditors	11,994
Mortgages	196
Tax liabilities	15
Stock capital	15,000
Reserves	44
Total liabilities	27,249

Note: These figures include the assets (land and buildings) and liabilities of a small subsidiary that was merged with the holding company in 1956.

through the holding company, they held most of the 160,000 A shares outstanding and a large part of the 20,000 B shares.

With the voting relationship that existed between A stock and B stock, this result meant that Landis & Gyr would be able to issue more than Sfr. 32 million par value of B stock without endangering the absolute voting majority of the owners of the holding company and privately held A stock. New stock would not be sold to new shareholders at par, of course but at a figure near its market price; and, therefore, the actual potential for new equity financing, while as then undetermined, was certain to be a sizable multiple of Sfr. 32 million.

In this connection it may be recalled that the holding company, acting as "financial agent" for the operating company, was slated to sell the latter's shares publicly and turn over the proceeds to the operating company. Initially, these transfers were to be made in the form of loans. Periodically, however, after the authorization of stockholders had been obtained, these loans were to be replaced by additional issues of Landis & Gyr B shares of equivalent value. This type of refunding would be advantageous to both companies: the financial position of the operating company would be strengthened by the addition of more equity capital; the holding company would receive marketable securities in place of nonmarketable notes and nontaxable dividends in place of taxable interest payments. Finally, if the need to avoid too great a loss of voting power were ever to arise, new A shares could be issued to the holding company in place of B shares.

Issuance of Convertible Debentures by Landis & Gyr Holding, AG

The final step to be undertaken by the directors was a consolidation of the short-term bank loan of Sfr. 10 million contracted by the holding company. Ordinary debentures could have been sold for this purpose, but a refunding of this kind was not considered desirable since it would not have advanced the ultimate objective of creating a public interest in the B stock of Landis & Gyr, AG. The solution to the problem was found in an issue of Landis & Gyr Holding, AG, convertible debentures, the end conversion security being the Landis & Gyr B stock. Although it was recognized that this would be the first public offering in Switzerland of the convertible debentures of a Swiss company, the directors were confident that the issue would be well received.

The offering, as finally settled, was for Sfr. 15 million of $3\frac{1}{4}$ percent bonds at par plus half the stamp tax, or Sfr. 1,006 per bond. The bonds were registered, but their transfer rights were not restricted in any way. Beginning February 1, 1961, Sfr. 1,250,000 of bonds would be retired annually, the last installment being redeemed in 1972. The holding company would have the option of meeting this sinking fund requirement by either purchasing bonds in the open market or drawing them by lot; however, the requirement would be waived to the extent of any voluntary conversion of bonds, which took place during the year. After February 1, 1967, and on every subsequent coupon date, Landis & Gyr Holding would have the right to call all outstanding bonds for retirement. The call price for this purpose—and also for the sinking fund—was fixed at par.

The amount of the issue, Sfr. 15 million, exceeded the holding company's short-term bank credit and other liabilities by about Sfr. 3 million. The latter amount, to be used for general corporate purposes, was less urgently needed than the funds for debt repayment, and accordingly only Sfr. 12 million of the issue was placed with underwriters, the Swiss Credit Bank, the Union Bank of Switzerland, and the investment banking firm of Rahn & Bodmer. For their services, the underwriters were to be paid their usual commission; on similar transactions this generally amounted to roughly 2 percent of the par value of the issue. The remainder of the issue, Sfr. 3 million, was to be offered to investors by the holding company through its own channels.

The coupon rate of $3\frac{1}{4}$ percent was somewhat lower than the prevailing market rate at the time. During the last two months of 1956 and the first two weeks of 1957, the rate on new bond issues varied between $3\frac{1}{4}$ percent and 4 percent, the bulk of the issues being offered at either $3\frac{1}{2}$ percent or $3\frac{3}{4}$ percent. Landis & Gyr Holding, AG, was one of the few firms to go as low as $3\frac{1}{4}$ percent. In doing so, the directors and the banks relied on the appeal of the conversion feature to interest new investors.

The conversion rate, as previously noted, was fixed at one bond of Sfr. 1,000 par value for one B share of Sfr. 200 par value. Conversion would be permitted at any time after February 1, 1960, except in the case of bonds that were called for retirement under the sinking fund provisions; these bonds would only be convertible for three months after their call date and not at all, of course, after their redemption for cash. A bondholder who intended to convert his bonds was required to notify one of the three underwriter banks of his intention and deposit his bonds and unused coupons with the bank; as trustee for the company, Swiss Credit Bank would hold 15,000 B shares against such conversion requests. Bonds deposited for conversion would not draw interest for the year in which they were deposited; however, the B stock issued in exchange would entitle the owner to the current year's dividend, or in the case of January deposits, to the preceding year's dividend. Subscription rights for new B shares arising from capital increases dated officially between February 1 and December 31 would not be issued to shareholders who converted their bonds during the same period.

One question that arose in connection with the mechanics of conversion concerned the source of B shares for Landis & Gyr Holding. If the entire issue of bonds were to be deposited for conversion, the holding company would be obliged to provide the trustees with 15,000 B shares. The holding company's investment in Landis & Gyr, AG, consisted almost exclusively of A shares, however, and therefore some arrangement had to be found to guarantee that B shares would be available to the holding company when they were needed. This problem was solved in a legal sense by giving the holding company an option to purchase 15,000 of the 20,000 B shares that had been issued to stockholders when Landis & Gyr was first recapitalized; under the agreement these shares were deposited in trust with the Swiss Credit Bank in Zürich. Actually however, it was not anticipated that the holding company would find it necessary to exercise this option because other sources of B shares would become available to the company before the conversion period was scheduled to begin in 1960. As owner of 50 percent of the manufacturing company's outstanding stock capital, Landis & Gyr Holding would have an opportunity to buy a substantial number of shares under the projected policy of increasing the B stock capital at regular intervals. The holding company would also be able to buy purchase warrants for B stock on the open market at such times and extraordinary issues if and when they should be authorized by Landis & Gyr stockholders.

The critical feature of the bonds, from the standpoint of the directors, was the conversion ratio, for it would determine the appeal of the issue to prospective investors and, on the other side, the exposure of old shareholders to later dilution of their equity interests. In setting the ratio at one B share of Sfr. 200 par value for one bond of Sfr. 1,000 par value, the directors reached what they thought was a fair compromise between the interests of both groups.

On the assumption of full conversion, stockholders were asked to surrender 7.2 percent (15,000/195,000) of their voting interest in exchange for Sfr. 15 million; this deal stood in sharp contrast to that proposed four years earlier by the former Board of Directors, a 20 percent interest for roughly Sfr. 4 million. From the investing public's point of view, on the other hand, the effective conversion price was based upon a price-earnings ratio (against current earnings, including those of the subsidiaries) of roughly 10:1, and the directors were confident that the market price of the B shares would be well above Sfr. 1,000 by early 1960 when the conversion privilege was scheduled to become effective. Basically, the company's expanding earning power was counted on to support this higher price. In addition, however, the directors projected dividend and capital distribution policies, which were expected to produce a strong, buoyant influence on the market's evaluation of the stock.

Landis & Gyr, it was announced, would henceforth plan to pay an annual cash dividend of 10 percent on the par value of its stock; in this connection, a reserve of Sfr. 4 million was already in existence to permit continuation of dividend payments in years of reduced earnings. The company also stated that it planned to increase its B stock capital at a rate of 4 or 5 percent per year through rights offerings priced at par. These two policy announcements meant that future B stockholders could expect a per share distribution of Sfr. 20 in cash and a purchase warrant of greater value, the exact worth of the warrant being dependent upon the prevailing market price of the B stock. Exhibit 4 shows the theoretical value of warrants or subscription rights for 4 and 5 percent capital increases at various B stock prices between Sfr. 800 and 1,800. Briefly, these figures suggest rights values in the range of Sfr. 24 to 80. Thus, the combined value of the distribution would fall somewhere between Sfr. 45 and 101.[2] In summary, then, the directors foresaw a minimum yield of 4.5 percent on the offering price of the convertible debentures, and price advances of the B stock above Sfr. 800 were expected to produce roughly proportionate percentage increases in this yield figure (Exhibit 5).

The policy of issuing new B stock at par at regular intervals was adopted not only to give shareholders a high yield on their investment, as shown above, but also to conserve funds for investment, within the manufacturing company. In the Landis & Gyr annual report for 1956, management pointed out that it was well within the company's capacity to distribute a cash dividend of Sfr. 50; such a payout policy, however, would lead to a serious loss of funds (Sfr. 5 million) and a corresponding loss of liquidity or retardation of the company's future rate of expansion. By way of contrast,

Exhibit 4   **Landis & Gyr, AG (A)**

Value of the Subscription Rights per B Share, for
Various Market Values of Class B Stock and
Capital Increases of 4 and 5 Percent

Market Price of Class B Stock	Annual Capital Increase	
	4 Percent	5 Percent
800	24	30
1,000	32	40
1,200	40	50
1,400	48	60
1,600	56	70
1,800	64	80

Note: Theoretical value of one right equals $M - S/N + 1$ where M is the market price prevailing before the issue, S is the subscription price, and N is the ratio of old shares to new shares.

---

2 The value of the cash dividend net of the 5 percent federal coupon tax was taken to be Sfr. 21, not Sfr. 20.

Exhibit 5

Landis & Gyr, AG (A)

Annual Yield of B Shares at Various Market Prices for
Capital Increases of 4 and 5 Percent

Market Price of Class B Stock	Capital Increase 4 Percent			Capital Increase 5 Percent		
	In Swiss Francs	Percentage of Sfr. 1,000 Purchase Price	Percentage of Market Price	In Swiss Francs	Percentage of Sfr. 1,000 Purchase Price	Percentage of Market Price
800	45	4.5	5.6	51	5.1	6.3
1,000	53	5.3	5.3	61	6.1	6.1
1,200	61	6.1	5.1	71	7.1	5.9
1,400	69	6.9	4.9	81	8.1	5.8
1,600	77	7.7	4.8	91	9.1	5.7
1,800	85	8.5	4.7	101	10.1	5.6

the announced cash dividend-rights offering policy promised an initial cash drain of only Sfr. 1 million.[3]

Management was fully aware that annual stock increases could not be continued indefinitely without seriously diluting the value of existing shares, and hence the value of the conversion privilege of the convertible debentures, if earnings failed to advance at a commensurate pace. As noted earlier, however, the company was thought to have a backlog of excellent investment projects, and management was confident that earnings would continue at a gratifying rate. Nevertheless, as reassurance for potential investors, a pledge was added to the prospectus for the convertible debentures to the effect that total issues of B stock prior to May 1, 1960 would not be allowed to exceed Sfr. 3 million par value. The directors also stated that no privileged claims would be granted in the interim to capital increases that might take place after that date and, otherwise, that no action would be taken that might injure the conversion privilege of holders of the convertible debentures.

As final evidence of their confidence that the market price of B shares would be above Sfr. 1,000 in early 1960, the directors undertook to guarantee the value of the B stock subscription rights, which bondholders would receive after 1960 if they exercised their option to convert bonds to B shares. The guarantee consisted of a standing offer by Landis & Gyr Holding to purchase subscription rights from former bondholders at a price corresponding to an exrights market price of Sfr. 1,000 for the B shares. If the rights corresponded to a capital increase of 5 percent, for example, the

---

3 A cash dividend of Sfr. 2 million, representing a 10 percent dividend on stock capital of Sfr. 20 million, less Sfr. 1 million, representing the proceeds of a 5 percent capital increase at par.

bid price would be fixed at Sfr. 40 per right; if the capital increase were 4 percent the bid would be Sfr. 32.

. . .

On January 24, 1957, the three banks offered the convertible debentures to the public. It was announced that allocations were to be made on a first come-first served basis until the issue was sold. Investors were required to pay for the bonds within ten days of the confirmation of their subscription orders; however, interest at $3\frac{1}{4}$ percent would be charged on balances due after February 1, 1957, the interest date of the bonds.

LANDIS & GYR, AG (B)

The Sfr. 15 million convertible debenture offering of Landis & Gyr Holding, AG [described in Landis & Gyr, AG (A)], was distributed without difficulty by the underwriters. Within a short time the over-the-counter price went to a premium, to 104 during the first week and then to much higher levels. During this initial conditioning period, a Basel investment firm took a particularly active interest in the bonds and at one point held as much as 15 percent of the issue for its clients and its own account. Regular over-the-counter quotations are available from August, 1957, by which time the bonds had reached a high point of 129 (Exhibit 1).

Major Developments in 1957 and 1958

The policy of periodical rights-offerings of B stock, announced first in the prospectus for the convertible debentures and explained further in the 1956 annual report, was put into practice in 1957. At the annual meeting of shareholders on June, 7, 1957, the Board proposed that the stock capital of Landis & Gyr, AG, be increased from Sfr. 20 to Sfr. 21 million through the issuance of 5,000 B shares. The proposal provided that the increase should be dated back to January 1, 1957 and that the new shares should participate in dividend and other distributions for 1957. The motion on this proposal was accepted without dissent.

During July a few small lots of B shares were sold to outside investors for the first time to test the market's valuation of the security. The initial price paid for the shares was Sfr. 1,400, and within a short time some shares were traded in the over-the-counter market at prices up to Sfr. 1,460. By November, however, after following the general trend of the stock market, the price had fallen back to Sfr. 1,400, and a few shares were subsequently traded slightly below this level.

Landis & Gyr's operations in 1957 were less satisfactory than in 1956 (Exhibits 2 and 3). Although production and sales of the Zug plant increased by 6.7 and 4.4 percent, respectively, net profit failed to increase commensurately. On the contrary, higher labor costs and strong price competition caused profit before depreciation to decline by Sfr. 700,000 (a drop of 2 percentage points in its ratio to sales). The foreign subsidiaries were reported to have had much the same experience. Nevertheless, they transferred Sfr. 2,845,000 to the parent company in Zug (in the form of dividends, interest payments, and royalties), slightly more than in 1956, and still managed to finance most of their new investments from internal sources.

Management's predictions for 1958, as set forth in the 1957 report to stockholders, were somewhat pessimistic. Unfilled orders at the end of 1957 were lower than the year before, Swiss orders by 10 percent and export orders (for the Zug plant) by 1 percent; with no marked pickup in sight, management predicted that sales volume for the year as a whole would be somewhat below 1957. Sales prices were expected to suffer from heavier competition and labor costs to continue their recent upward trend. On the other hand, the forecast was not all black. A number of recently completed investment projects were counted on to begin showing an effect on manufacturing costs, and the extensive research program promised to open several new, profitable investment possibilities.

At the stockholders' meeting in May, 1958, in accord with the company's announced policy, the Board again proposed a 5 percent capital increase. The issue was approved by shareholders, and the subsequent sale of 5,250 new B shares at par raised the company's total capital from Sfr. 21,000,000 to Sfr. 22,050,000. This issue was dated back to January 1, 1958.

A second proposal, to increase the par capital by an additional Sfr. 950,000, was also approved. In this case, however, the shareholders waived their preemptive right to the issue, and the entire bloc of 4,750 B shares was sold to Landis & Gyr Holding, AG, at a price of Sfr. 1,000 per share. The holding company paid in the par value of the shares in cash and the balance of Sfr. 800 per share (Sfr. 3,800,000 in total) in the form of a cancellation of credits which it had previously extended to the manufacturing company. Subsequently, the holding company reoffered these 4,750 B shares to stockholders and others at a price of Sfr. 1,450, including its commission of Sfr. 2.06 per share; each shareholder, if he desired, was permitted to purchase up to one share from the holding company for each 20 B shares or 40 A shares held. The holding company therefore made a "profit" of Sfr. 447.94 per share. Under the terms of the original authorization, however, it was obliged to distribute this profit in cash to Landis & Gyr's stockholders. On a per share basis, the profit amounted to Sfr. 20.26 for the B stock and Sfr. 10.13 for the A stock.[1]

---

[1] Actually, the holding company's "profit" was less than the figure stated above because the over-the-counter price of the stock at the time was somewhat less than Sfr. 1,450. If the holding company had been able to resell all shares at this price, however, it would have received Sfr. 6,877,715 from the sale, net of its commission of Sfr. 2.06 per share.

After the annual meeting had been adjourned, the directors forwarded a previously prepared listing application for Landis & Gyr Class B stock to the officials of the Zürich Stock Exchange. As a result of the actions which had just been taken, there were currently 35,000 B shares outstanding; of this total, 15,000 were held on deposit in the Swiss Credit Bank against future conversion of the convertible debentures, roughly 10,000 were held by Landis & Gyr Holding and its stockholders, and 10,000 were already in the hands of outside investors, including the original minority stockholders. The latter total was certain to be increased in the near future by sell-offs of many newly created shares, and listing, needless to say, was counted on to facilitate the secondary distribution of these shares.

The listing was completed on May 15. An active market interest in the stock developed almost immediately, and it was traded during the remainder of the month at prices between Sfr. 1,440 and 1,390. Later, during the summer and autumn, the price seemed to sag slightly in relation to the closest comparable price index of shares of Swiss companies, but in every month except November some trades were quoted at prices above Sfr. 1,400 (Exhibit 1).

When the market value of the B stock was seen to be firmly established in the neighborhood of Sfr. 1,400, the next logical decision was taken, namely, to advance the 1960 conversion date of the convertible debentures. In originally putting off the start of the conversion period to 1960, the directors had taken, as events proved, an unduly conservative view of the market's probable reception of the B stock and the time that would be required for its price to climb above the conversion price of Sfr. 1,000. The bondholders, when asked, gave their consent to the proposed new date, October 1, 1958. Thereafter, conversion occurred on a large scale, and the selling pressure created by those who wanted to realize their capital gain undoubtedly contributed to the somewhat lower year-end prices of the B stock. By February, 1959, almost 90 percent of the bonds had been exchanged for B stock. The remaining bonds were held primarily by insurance companies which, by law, were not allowed to hold common stock.

On September 30, the company's books were closed for 1958 in accord with a vote taken at the last stockholders' meeting to change the end of the company's accounting year from December to September. Subsequently, the publication of the annual report for this period revealed that Landis &

Of the funds actually received, however, Sfr. 950,000 was owed to the operating company for the par value of the shares, and Sfr. 2,127,715 to shareholders as a distribution of the holding company's "profit" on the transaction. The balance was available to the holding company as general funds.

The selling price of Sfr. 1,450 for this issue was one of three prices on which stockholders were asked to vote at the annual meeting. The other prices, Sfr. 1,405 and Sfr. 1,427.50 would have led to cash distributions of Sfr. 18.26 and 19.26 respectively, on each B share.

Exhibit 1   Landis & Gyr, AG (B)

Market Prices of Landis & Gyr Holding, AG, Convertible Debentures,
Landis & Gyr, AG, Class B Stock, and Stock Price Index

		Convertible Bond (in %)		B Shares (in Sfr.)		Price Index of Swiss Machinery and Metal Stocks (End of Month)
		high	low	high	low	
1957	February					391.1
	March					394.1
	April	N.A.	N.A.			403.9
	May					399.4
	June					381.2
	July					380.0
	August	129	126			370.0
	September	123	115			304.8
	October	112	110			282.9
	November	120	118			306.3
	December	118	115			312.1
1958	January	121	119			311.2
	February	130	127			299.2
	March	138	135			297.4
	April	140	136			298.4
	May	—	—	1440	1390	295.4
	June	138	137	1410	1380	299.8
	July	138	134	1420	1390	305.4
	August	$135\frac{1}{2}$	135	1420	1395	318.6
	September	138	137	1420	1400	336.9
	October	132	130	1420	1310[a]	334.8
	November	134	132	1375	1350	331.0
	December	139	135	1410	1365	334.1
1959	January	—	135	1420	1325[c]	337.9
	February	134[b]	132[b]	1420	1325	N.A.

[a] After conversion right became effective.
[b] No sales.
[c] After 5 percent capital issue at par. Rights were quoted at Sfr. 56.50–57.50, equivalent
to Sfr. 1330–1350 for the stock ex dividends and rights.

Gyr had taken one more major step in the direction of full disclosure of
financial data. Management had broken with precedent in the previous
year by releasing actual sales figures and expense data for both 1957 and
1956. The 1958 innovation, however, like that of 1956, affected the balance
sheet. Fixed assets were revalued to show their historical cost and the
depreciation reserves which had been created against them on the basis of
sound costing principles. This move revealed all hidden reserves except
those that existed on participations and possibly on patents. For comparative
purposes the 1957 year-end balance sheet was also adjusted to the same
basis and published in the 1958 report. These statements are presented in
Exhibit 2 and the accompanying income statements in Exhibit 3.

Exhibit 2

Landis & Gyr, AG (B)

Income Statements
Nine-Month Periods Ending Sept. 30, 1957, 1958

	1957			1958	
	Year	%	9 months = $\frac{3}{4}$	9 months	%
Gross sales	75,319,700.68		56,489,775.—	57,259,859.15	
Customs and freight expenses	- 4,453,301.28		- 3,339,976.—	- 3,584,142.92	
Net sales	70,866,399.40		53,149,799.—	53,675,716.23	
Increase inventories (excluding raw materials, tool production and research expenditure)	14,263,228.—		10,697,421.—	6,184,042.—	
Total Value of Production	85,129,627.40	100,00	63,847,220.—	59,859,758.23	100,00
Manufacturing expenses (not including depreciation)	-50,637,229.60	59,48	-37,977,922.—	-35,479,767.90	59,27
Sales and administrative expenses (including nonspecific costs and taxes)	-18,582,128.93	21,83	-13,936,597.—	-15,374,588.77	25,68
Bad debts	- 6,469.05	—	- 4,852.—	570.90	
Charge against special reserve	- 18,035.30	0,03	- 13,526.—	61,957.65	0,10
Royalties, dividends, interest from subsidiaries contributed to research and dividends payable	+ 2,845,665.55	3,34	+ 2,134,248.—	+ 3,085,384.93	5,15
Total cost **before depreciation**	66,398,197.33	78,00	49,798,649.—	-47,831,500.29	79,90
Gross earnings before depreciation	18,731,430.07	22,00	14,048,571.—	12,028,257.94	20,10
Profit from sale of land	-		-	22,555.—	0,04
Total gross earnings	18,731,430.07	22,00	14,048,571.—	12,050,812.94	20,14
Depreciation (including research expenditure)	7,328,871.—	8,61	5,496,652.—	5,783,827.48	9,66
Gross earnings	11,402,559.07	13,39	8,551,919.—	6,266,985.46	10,48
Employee benefits (retirement fund, bonus, etc.)	- 3,760,754.50	4,42	- 2,820,566.—	- 2,505,798.40	4,19
Net earnings	7,641,804.57	8,97	5,731,353.—	3,761,187.06	6,29
Increase valuation reserves	- 4,712,835.—	6,04	- 3,534,626.—	- 1,948,422.—	2,25
Increase (decrease) surplus	- 428,969.57		321,727.—	+ (602,234.94)	
Profit at disposal of the stockholders	2,500,000.—	2,93	1,875,000.—	2,415,000.—	4,04
Wages and salaries (excluding bonus and payments to retirement fund, etc.)	25,284,814.—	39,60		26,980,978.16	45,07

59

Exhibit 3

Landis & Gyr, AG (B)

Balance Sheets
Dec. 31, 1957; Jan. 1, 1958; Sept. 30, 1958

	December 31, 1957 (after Dividend Payment)		Change due to the decision of the Board of Directors concerning revaluation of fixed assets, etc.	January 1, 1958		September 30, 1958 (before Dividend Payment)	
A.1 Cash, banks		1,629,718.76			1,629,718.76		3,556,980.32
A.2 Accounts receivable	14,622,486.29			14,622,486.29		15,084,849.30	
Valuation reserve	1,300,000.—	13,322,486.29		1,300,000.—	13,322,486.29	1,300,000.—	13,784,849.30
A.3 Prepayments		2,056,483.22			2,056,483.22		2,305,464.68
A.4 Inventories (at cost or market)	47,786,545.—			47,786,545.—		49,284,634.—	
Valuation reserve	15,928,848.—			15,928,848.—		16,428,211.—	
Special reserve	750,000.—	31,107,697.—		750,000.—	31,107,697.—	750,000.—	32,106,423.—
Current Assets		48,116,385.27			48,116,385.27		51,753,717.30
(Valuation reserves A)	*(17,978,848.—)*			*(17,978,848.—)*		*(18,478,211.—)*	
B Investment in subsidiaries (at cost)	14,359,537.85	+ 429,312.—		14,788,849.85		18,816,411.35	
C Houses and auxiliary buildings	1,762,195.25	+ 259,727.75		2,021,923.—		1,966,141.—	
D.1 Land	1,514,590.—	+ 264,780.—		1,779,370.—		1,772,335.—	
D.2 Factory and office buildings							
Original cost				27,935,655.—		31,287,035.—	
Depreciation				7,914,981.—		8,575,414.—	
Subtotal				20,020,674.—		22,711,621.—	
Valuation reserve		*(+ 2,834,857.—)*		2,834,857.—		3,092,937.—	
Net	3,800,000.—	+13,385,817.—		17,185,817.—		19,618,684.—	
D.3 Equipment							
Original cost				51,841,032.—		57,686,768.—	
Depreciation				24,467,213.—		25,825,400.—	
Subtotal				27,373,819.—		31,861,368.—	
Valuation reserve		*(+12,493,815.—)*		12,493,815.—		13,684,794.—	
Net	p.m.	+14,880,004.—		14,880,004.—		18,176,574.—	
D.4 Research expenditures, Patents	p.m.			p.m.		p.m.	
B-D **Investments and Fixed Assets**	21,436,323.10	+29,219,640.75		50,655,963.85		60,350,145.35	
(Valuation reserves D)		*(+15,328,672.—)*	*(15,328,672.—)*			*(16,777,731.—)*	
Total Assets	69,552,708.37	+29,219,640.75		98,772,349.12		112,103,862.65	
(Valuation reserves A + D)	*(17,978,848.—)*	*(+15,328,672.—)*	*(33,307,520.—)*			*(35,255,942.—)*	

Exhibit 3 (cont.)

Landis & Gyr, AG (B)
Balance Sheets (cont.)
Dec. 31, 1957; Jan. 1, 1958; Sept. 30, 1958

	December 31, 1957 (after Dividend Payment)		Changes	January 1, 1958		September 30, 1958 (before Dividend Payment)	
A.1 Acceptances	59,776.85			59,776.85			83,941.20
A.2 Banks	4,331,205.80		Changes due to the decision	4,331,205.80			—
A.3 Selling commissions	1,121,562.25		of the Board of Directors	1,121,562.25			1,654,067.24
A.4 Subsidiaries	102,880.15		concerning revaluation	102,880.15			76,627.15
A.5 Suppliers	3,167,612.13		of fixed assets, etc.	3,167,612.13			1,986,590.45
A.6 Accrued items	2,930,198.42			2,930,198.42			3,483,397.61
A.7 Dividends	2,210,526.32			2,210,526.32			—
A.8 Uncashed dividends	—			—			501.02
A **Total Current Liabilities**		13,923,761.92			13,923,761.92		7,285,124.67
B **Prepayments**		738,264.26			738,264.26		1,549,186.77
C **Landis & Gyr Holding Corp.**		5,609,544.20			5,609,544.20		15,491,063.—
D **Noncurrent Accounts Payable**	2,937,451.63			2,937,451.63			3,949,449.59
E **Retirement Fund**	4,975,810.90			4,975,810.90			5,789,641.40
F **Mortgages, etc.**	2,405,219.75			2,405,219.75			2,244,335.70
		10,318,482.28			10,318,482.28		11,983,426.69
Total Liabilities		30,590,052.66			30,590,052.66		36,308.801.13
A.1 Common stock shares							
160 000 A at Fr. 100.—	16,000.000.—			16,000,000.—		16,000,000.—	
25 000 B at Fr. 200.—	5,000,000.—			5,000,000.—		5,000,000.—	
new:							
10 000 B at Fr. 200.—	—			—		2,000,000.—	
total						23,000,000.—	
A.2 Paid-in surplus	—			—		3,800,000.—	
A **Paid-in Capital** total		21,000,000.—			21,000,000.—		26,800,000.—
B.1 Legal reserve	2,405,000.—			2,405,000.—		2,405,000.—	
B.2 Reserve for full employment measures	1,250,000.—			1,250,000.—		1,250,000.—	
B.3 Reserve for dividend payments	4,000,000.—			4,000,000.—		4,000,000.—	
B.4 Special reserve	104,220.85			104,220.85		42,263.20	
B.5 Unrestricted earned surplus	10,203,434.86		+ 29,219,640.75	39,423,075.61		38,882,798.32	
B Earned surplus (excluding valuation reserve)		17,962,655.71	+ 29,219,640.75		47,182,296.46		46,580,061.52
C Profit placed at the disposal of stockholders	—			—			2,415,000.—
(Valuation reserves)	*(17,978,848.—)*		*(+ 15,328,672.—)* *(33,307,520.—)*			*(35,255,942.—)*	
(Earned income, gross amount, including valuation reserves and profit)	*(35,941,503.71)*		*(+ 44,548,312.75)* *(80,489,816.46)*			*(84,251,003.52)*	
Equity Capital		38,962,655.71	+ 29,219,640.75		68,182,296.46		75,795,061.52
(Valuation reserves)	*(17,978,848.—)*		*(+ 15,328,672.—)* *(33,307,520.—)*			*(35,255,942.—)*	
		69,552,708.37	*(+ 29,219,640.75)*		98,772,349.12		112,103,862.65
	(17,978,848.—)		*(+ 15,328,672.—)* *(33,307,520.—)*			*(35,255,942.—)*	
Guarantees	4,165,067.15			4,165.067.15		5,533,510.20	

Operations for 1958 (a nine-month "year") bore out the slightly pessimistic predictions voiced by management in its 1957 annual report. While sales held up in comparison to the same period for the preceding year (actually increasing by some Sfr. 770,000), net earnings decreased by almost Sfr. 2 million; as a percentage of the total value of production, earnings dropped from 9.0 to 6.3 percent. The change was attributable in large part to higher selling and administrative expenses; these increased by almost Sfr. 1.4 million as a result of higher salaries, an increase in the size of the sales force, increased research expenditures, and higher taxes. Management stated flatly in the 1958 report that net earnings of Sfr. 3.8 million, representing a 5 percent return on equity, were to be considered unsatisfactory.

Fortunately, the foreign subsidiaries were less affected by the 1958 recession than was the Swiss company. Their sales reached a total of Sfr. 69 million, 14 percent above the comparable nine-month period of 1957, and their earnings exceeded those of the parent company. Income realized by the Swiss parent concern from their operations was accordingly increased by almost Sfr. 1 million.

During the last quarter of 1958, while the report to stockholders was being prepared, operations in Zug showed signs of material improvement, and the directors stated that they were confident that 1959 would be a better year for the company. Plans were laid, therefore, to go ahead with the company's customary distributions, despite the fact that 1958 had only been a nine-month year.

Proposals to the Stockholders' Meeting of February 14, 1959

The proposals that the Board of Directors presented to the stockholders' meeting in Zug on February 14, 1959, were summarized as follows:

1. Payment of a dividend of 10 percent (Sfr. 20 per B share with a par value of Sfr. 200).
2. The issue of rights for one new share of each 20 shares held against payment of the par value of Sfr. 200 (5,750 additional B shares).
3. The issue of 4,250 additional B shares with a par value of Sfr. 200, for which the Landis & Gyr Holding Corporation is ready to pay approximately Sfr. 1,355 each. (This price is based on the quoted price at the Zürich Stock Exchange minus the approximate value of dividends and rights. Stockholders interested in buying additional shares at the price of Sfr. 1,355 are invited to send their subscriptions to Landis & Gyr Holding Corporation, Zug, until February 28, 1959.)

Approval of these proposals, it was pointed out, would increase the total stock capital of Landis & Gyr, AG, to Sfr. 25 million, represented by 160,000 A shares and 45,000 B shares. The par value of the company's stock capital would thus have been increased by Sfr. 15 million or 150 percent in the short space of three years. The company also would have received Sfr. 8.7 million of additional paid-in surplus from sales of stock to the holding company at premium prices.

Cost of Capital and Earnings Requirements

In considering how to vote on the proposals put forward by the Board of Directors, stockholders were confronted with the problem of again assessing the wisdom of the policy of combining a low cash dividend payment with the periodic issue of rights for new shares. The ultimate purpose of this policy, as the directors had announced in the 1956 annual report, was to conserve cash and permit Landis & Gyr, AG, to keep growing at the same rate as the consumption of electrical power was increasing.

The market price of the Class B stock had tended to fluctuate around Sfr. 1,400 (Exhibit 4) in spite of the diluting effects of successive rights

Exhibit 4   **Landis & Gyr, AG (B)**
Yield of B Shares at Selected Market Prices
(in Sfr.)

Market price	800	1,000	1,200	1,400	1,600	1,800
Dividend payment	21	21	21	21	21	21
Subscription rights—from 5% capital increase at par	30	40	50	60	70	80
Total yield	51	61	71	81	91	101
Yield in percent of market price	6.3	6.1	5.9	5.8	5.7	5.6

offerings priced at only Sfr. 200. Each year, B stockholders had received roughly Sfr. 80 in cash dividends and the value of subscription rights. This represented a yield of about 5.8 percent on the market price of Sfr. 1,400, a higher figure than was obtainable on almost any other well-known Swiss stock.

From the company's standpoint, however, the new capital could be said to have quite different costs. Judged in terms of the actual cash dividend drain, the cost was either high or low depending upon whether the dividend was compared with the capital received from shareholders or the holding company. A cash dividend of Sfr. 20 on an issue price of Sfr. 200 suggested a cost of 10 percent; on Sfr. 1,355, however, it was less than 1.5 percent. While the 10 percent figure was acknowledged to be high, the directors had stated in their 1956 report that they believed that this cost would be covered by earnings on the additional surplus reinvested in the business.

In the directors' view, the ratio of cash dividends to the price of new issues was not in itself an adequate measure of the company's cost of capital. Landis & Gyr, AG, possessed enormous retained earnings, and these clearly had some bearing on the question. After careful study it was concluded that the minimum rate of earnings required to support the established dividend-subscription rights policy was 6 percent on paid-in capital and surplus. This figure rested on the following line of reasoning.

Assuming a fair book value of Sfr. 1,000 compared to the market value of Sfr. 1,400, the par value of a B share equaled one-fifth of its book value. If the company were to earn 6 percent on the book value of its equity, earnings per share would amount to Sfr. 60. However, the cash dividend of 10 percent on par would cause a cash outflow of Sfr. 20 (2 percent on book value), leaving retained earnings of Sfr. 40 (4 percent on book value). The following period would therefore begin with a per share equity of Sfr. 1,040, 104 percent). If the company also decided to increase its stock capital by 5 percent through rights offering of new B shares priced at par (Sfr. 200), the paid-in par value per original share would increase to Sfr. 210. The new capital, Sfr. 10 per old share, would be available with the Sfr. 1,040 to increase the company's earning power during subsequent periods. The total, Sfr. 1,050, expressed in relation to the new par value of Sfr. 210, would therefore again equal the original 5 : 1 ratio.

From this point of view, earnings of 6 percent would suffice to support the combined dividend and rights offering policy indefinitely without diluting the initial equity of shareholders. The market price, to be sure, would not be expected to rise much because of the continued creation of new shares at Sfr. 200, but neither would it be expected to drop much below its original level of Sfr. 1,400.

Although the directors were convinced that the market value of the company's stock in the long run would depend on its yield rather than the book value of its underlying assets, they believed that its market price nevertheless would tend to at least approximate its "real" value, as represented by the book equity figure. This relationship was not thought to hold for all Swiss stocks, because most of them provided inadequate cash returns and therefore sold for less than their fair book values; in their case, the issuance of new stock at market prices would unquestionably have the effect of diluting the equity interest of the original shareholders. Even if a new issue took the form of a rights offering to old shareholders, some owners would be compelled to sell old shares at the unfavorable market price in order to obtain cash to purchase the new issue; other owners who might elect to sell their subscription rights would receive a low return, corresponding to the depressed market price of the stock. For this reason it was the announced objective of the directors of Landis & Gyr to keep the market price and "real" value of the company's stock and its earning power reasonably close together. The combination dividend-subscription rights policy was thought to do this by promoting a stable market price for the stock.

In normal years, the directors believed that the company's earnings would undoubtedly exceed its dividend requirement of only 2 percent on fair book value, even allowing for the growth of the requirement from regular capital increases. This would raise the problem of adjusting the yield of the stock to the increased earning power of the company. As long as an increase of cash dividends was not considered advisable, however, the best adjustment, in the directors' view, would be special additional capital increases.

LANDIS & GYR, AG (C)

Landis & Gyr, AG remained a family-owned and controlled enterprise from its founding at the end of the nineteenth century until 1956. At that time the directors of the Swiss manufacturer of electrical measuring and regulating devices determined that a new source of equity funds would have to be tapped if the firm's growth objectives were to be realized.[1] As a result, the legal organization of the enterprise was modified to allow the family to maintain effective control via a holding company owning A shares in the operating subsidiary. Then B shares were distributed to the general public, first via the device of a convertible debenture issue and later through additional convertible issues and rights issues of B shares.

Exhibit 1   **Landis & Gyr, AG**

Operating Results

	1960	1961	1962	1963	1964	1965
Sales (Sfr. million)	201.44	223.93	246.82	266.39	293.29	329.30
Total earnings (Sfr. million)	16.69	19.09	22.18	23.77	26.35	28.35
Total equity capital (Sfr. million)	186.79	205.22	259.80	324.47	376.25	402.78
Net profits as a percentage of equity capital	8.94	9.30	8.54	7.33	7.00	7.04
Net profits as a percentage of sales	8.29	8.52	8.99	8.92	8.98	8.61

The B shares, hereafter referred to as common shares, opened on the Zürich Exchange slightly above Sfr. 1,400 and then rose to a high of Sfr. 2,480 near the end of 1960. The price of the stock continued to rise during the booming stock market of 1961–62, reaching a high of Sfr. 4,700 in 1962. Then the market broke, and the price of the stock fell substantially, reaching a low of 1,600. The price history of Landis & Gyr common since is given in Exhibits 2 and 3.

---

[1] Recent Landis & Gyr operating results are shown in Exhibit 1.

Exhibit 2   **Landis & Gyr, AG**

Per Share Data   *Rights Data*

	Stock Price Range[a]		Cash Dividend[d] (Sfr.)	Earnings[d] (Sfr.)	Rights Ratios	Rights Issue Price (Sfr.)	Rights Values (Sfr.)
	Actual (Sfr.)	Adjusted (Sfr.)					
1958	1440–1310	899– 817	20	32.7[bc]	1:20	par 200	62.0
1959	1440–1260	936– 819	20	41.0[b]	1:20	par 200	57.5
1960	2480–1360	1679– 921	20	127.2	1:20	par 200	60.0
1961	4335–2320	3154–1571	20	136.4	1:15	par 200	210.0
1962	4700–2475	3418–1938	20	137.8	1:20	par 200	205.0
					1:10	2,500 Sfr.	165.0
1963	3620–2985	3026–2498	20	137.8	1:14	par 200	210.0
1964	3225–2050	2828–1962	20	119.0	1:10	par 200	255.0
1965	2195–1610	2101–1610	20	122.0	1:20	par 200	82.5

a Stock prices are for calendar years.
b Earnings figures for 1958 and 1959 do not include earnings of subsidiaries.
c Due to Landis & Gyr's change of fiscal years from—December to October—September,
1958 was a nine-month year.
d Cash dividends per share and earnings per share are not adjusted for rights issues.

Exhibit 3   **Landis & Gyr, AG**

Stock Prices Indices
(1958 low = 100)

	Swiss Industrial Shares[a]	Landis & Gyr	
	High Low	Actual High Low	Adjusted[b] High Low
1958	115.9–100.0	109.9–100.0	110.0–100.0
1959	146.9–104.9	109.9– 96.2	114.6– 96.2
1960	206.5–146.8	189.3–103.8	205.5–112.7
1961	295.6–229.3	330.9–177.1	386.0–192.3
1962	298.1–192.8	358.8–188.9	418.4–237.2
1963	213.8–194.8	276.3–227.9	370.4–305.8
1964	190.5–166.6	246.2–156.5	346.1–240.1
1965	169.3–137.6	167.6–122.9	257.2–197.1

a Based on Swiss National Bank Index.
b Adjusted for rights offerings.

In 1956, Landis & Gyr announced in the prospectus offering the first convertible issue and in its annual report that it would be the company's policy to pay out small cash dividends supplemented by annual rights issues at par. In 1957, management reported to stockholders that rights would, as a rule, be issued on a 1:20 or a 1:25 basis as long as such increases in outstanding common shares were justified by earnings in the sense that book value would not thereby be lowered below the book value of the shares at the beginning of the year. It was further reported to the stockholders that, should book value per share increase sufficiently, issues at ratios lower than 1 : 20 would be made time to time.

This policy has been reaffirmed in later annual reports to stockholders and orally at annual meetings. For example, the Summary of the Annual Report 1959–60 concludes as follows:

> As has been the case every year since 1953, the Board of Directors submits to the Stockholders' Meeting, to be held on March 25th, 1961, in Zug, the proposal to pay out a dividend of 10 percent (Sfr. 20—per B share with a nominal value of Sfr. 200.—).
>
> In addition, the Board of Directors again is proposing the issue of rights for new shares, payable at par value. Instead, however, of the customary issue of one share for 20 held, an issue of one share for 15 shares held is proposed; on the basis of the quotation for B Shares since the beginning of 1961, the value of rights should thus be considerably higher than Sfr. 100.—for each B share. This proposal is not to be considered as a change of policy, and it is planned to return next year to the policy followed since 1957 of issuing one new share for 20. This year's proposal is intended as a gesture of gratitude toward the new Stockholders, whose number since the last Stockholders' Meeting—due to the conversion of bonds—has increased from less than 900 to more than 2500.
>
> In finalizing this summary, we wish to emphasize that it is the policy of the Company to combine a low but steady dividend payment with the regular issue of rights for new shares. This policy reflects the aim of Landis & Gyr Corp. to keep growing at a rate comparable with that of the consumption of electric power, and it is abundantly evident that the demand for its products is increasing. The Board of Directors wishes to express to all Stockholders its appreciation of their valuable support in attaining this goal.

On the basis of this policy, stockholders who sell their rights receive in cash dividends plus the cash value of rights a total sum approximately equal to the per share earnings on the common shares. In fact, in years when the market value of the shares is high the cash return to shareholders who sell their rights exceeds the return they would receive if all earnings were paid out in dividends. Table 1 illustrates this relationship.

If earnings amount to Sfr. 120 per share, and a cash dividend of Sfr. 20 is paid, the total cash return to shareholders who sell their rights can be determined from this table. For example if the market price is 2400 and rights are issued on a 1 : 20 basis, the selling shareholder will receive in dividends and from rights Sfr. 125, Sfr. 5 more than earnings per share. Furthermore, rights proceeds are tax free.

Management feels that cash return is especially important to many stock-

Table 1

Market Price Sfr.	Subscription Price Sfr.	Value per Right (Sfr.)		
		1 : 25	1 : 20	1 : 15
1600	200	54	67	88
1800	200	52	76	100
2000	200	69	86	112
2200	200	77	95	125
2400	200	85	105	138

holders and to the public stockholders as a whole in view of the ownership composition. Approximately 80 percent of the shares are held in less than 100 share lots. Further details with regard to ownership composition are included in Exhibit 4, which provides a breakdown for 1963 that management still considers to be representative of the current situation.

Swiss firms as a whole had a good year in 1965, and some pressure for dividend increases began to be exerted. In January 4, 1966, a financial newspaper in Zürich, *Finanz und Wirtschaft,* published Open Letters from its editors to the Board of Directors of Swiss corporations and to stockholders in Swiss Corporations urging that dividends be increased. Dr. Andreas C. Brunner, Finance Director of Landis & Gyr, immediately answered in an open reply, to which the editors appended a rebuttal. Translations of this exchange of letters are included in Exhibits 5–7.

Against this background the Board of Directors of Landis & Gyr met to decide what action with regard to dividends and rights to propose to the stockholders meeting on March 12, 1966.

Exhibit 4

Landis & Gyr, AG
Stockholder Composition—B Shares[a]
(March, 1963)

Held by	1–10 Shares			11–30 Shares			31–100 Shares			100 + Shares			TOTAL		
	1	2	3	1	2	3	1	2	3	1	2	3	1	2	3
Individuals	2648	9399	3.5	440	7303	16.6	88	4362	49.5	8	1167	146	3184	22231	7.0
Swiss banks	1110	5520	5.0	443	7461	16.8	80	3715	46.5	23	5057	220	1656	21753	13.1
	3758	14919	4.0	883	14764	16.7	168	8077	48.0	31	6224	201	4840	43984	9.1
Foreign banks	7	24	3.5	6	115	19.2	3	175	52.3	2	228	114	18	524	29.1
Pension + insurance funds	31	156	5.0	17	328	19.3	20	1026	51.3	9	2161	240	77	3671	43.8
Other legal entities	76	388	5.1	42	790	18.8	21	1050	50.0	8	1483	185	147	3711	25.2
	3872	15487	—	948	15997	—	212	10328	—	50	10096	—	5082	51890	—
Percentage of total	76.2	29.9	—	18.6	30.8	—	4.2	20.3	—	1.0	19.5	—	100.0	100.0	—

1 = Number of shareholders; 2 = Number of shares; 3 = Average shares per holder
a B shares held by Landis & Gyr Holding not included.

Exhibit 5   **Landis & Gyr, AG**
Finanz und Wirtschaft, Zürich, Wednesday, January 5, 1966

<u>Open Letter</u>

To the Board of Directors
<u>of Swiss Corporations</u>

Zürich, January 4, 1966

Dear Sirs,

The year 1965 was the fourth in a row, during which the
market value of all stocks quoted on the Swiss stock market
fell. For the 25 leading securities, the decrease amounted
to 6.7 percent in 1965 and to 25.4 percent for the last 4
years. The decline would look even more unfavorable if
the special case of Hoffman-La-Roche were omitted. The
decreases would then be respectively 13 percent and 34
percent.

Maybe when you read those figures you will just shrug
your shoulders and as a member of a family who controls
a company or as a large shareholder, you will think of
taxes on income and private capital, which are lower when
stock prices decrease (and stay at a low level) than when
the opposite is the case. Maybe, however, you are also a
member of the circle of open-minded owners, who consider
the continuous decline in stock prices since 1961 on the
Swiss market as a very annoying phenomenon—annoying most
of all since the stock market is a tool of the capitalistic
economy and is an institution of considerable importance
for all the national economy. For a stock market which is
notoriously weak and which reacts to issues of new equity
with falling prices (latest example: Swissair), can no
longer perform correctly its most important function, an
organ of creation and distribution of capital. It is par-
alyzed by a continuous downward price trend.

If you further consider that your company sooner or
later will hope to or want to issue new equity, then you
will perhaps not remain indifferent to the trend in stock
prices. You have in your hand the power to influence in
a substantial way the development of stock prices, first
of all by an appropriate increase of dividend. However,
you must then decide to change your past financing and

income retention policies. Follow the American example: from the (true!) declared net earnings, about 45 percent are distributed as dividends to shareholders. The remainder is used for internal financing. The result of this policy is a stock market which functions well, which has been rising for years, and which shows no downward reactions to new issues of capital. In Switzerland companies declare only a small proportion of their true earnings and pay out only 15 to 25 percent in dividends. While the American shareholder trusts the companies' statements and the stock market, the Swiss shareholder over the last few years has become less and less trusting and is retiring from the Swiss stock market.

It seems to us that the time has come for you to do something really courageous. And it is not too late! But the policies of the past will no longer do. If something is not done the state could suddenly be obliged to intervene as has happened in other countries. And neither you nor we want this.

With best greetings,

Finanz und Wirtschaft
Editorship

To the Shareholders
of Swiss Corporations

Zürich, January 4, 1966

Dear Ladies and Gentlemen,

   In our letter to the Board of Directors of your companies
we have spoken for you. It is well-known that many share-
owners have already sold their shares because they were
disappointed with the policy of their company towards them
(insufficient publicity, inadequate dividends, and, therefore, too small yields). Most shareholders have lost all
interest in the proceedings of their company's general
assembly because it is controlled by the Board of Directors. Many shareholders give their voting rights to banks,
which according to tradition always support the proposals
of the Board.
   In your own interest, do not let your bank convince you
to surrender your voting rights in its favor. Also require
your companies to send regular letters to shareholders in
order to keep you informed about their problems. Require
further that the general assembly meetings take place on
a Saturday in order to make participation easier. Furthermore, you must not only go to the general assembly, but you
must also defend your own interests. You have the right,
like for example the American, British, or German shareholders, to be properly informed about the net earnings
and to receive an appropriate dividend. Only then will
your shares again have the character of a truly participating security, and only then will they be quoted at a
fair price.
   You should further consider whether it is appropriate for
the Swiss shareholders to organize some kind of association for the protection of securities, which of course
will not work against, but rather in cooperation with
company management.

With best greetings,

Finanz und Wirtschaft
Editorship

Exhibit 6   **Landis & Gyr, AG**
Finanz und Wirtschaft, Zürich, Wednesday, January 26, 1966

Answer to an "Open Letter"
To the editorial staff of <u>Finanz und Wirtschaft</u>
from Dr. A. Brunner-Gyr, Zug

Letters—even "Open Letters"—achieve their aim only if they reach addressees and when also the addressees answer. As I consider myself to be an addressee I am going to answer your letter.

The facts which you listed in your introduction are well known to me. As I completely agree with you—as you know—about the capitalistic economy and the role of the stock exchange, I am not just going to shrug my shoulders. Also for tax reasons I am not interested in low stock prices, since in order to pay my taxes I must in any case sell shares. I long ago figured out that the lower their prices the more shares I have to sell.

I also agree with you about the statement concerning the "American example," and I believe that you hit the nail on the head when you were writing about the suspicious Swiss shareholders; however, I would rather call them discouraged and I understand their attitude.

However, here are my "buts":

You are convinced that an "appropriate increase of dividends" should have a "substantial influence" on the development of stock prices and, therefore, you put forth demands according to this thought.

However, you did not define in your letter what one could consider to be an "appropriate increase of dividends." For my part I cannot imagine what influence an increase of the Landis & Gyr dividend from 10 percent (Sfr. 20) to, for example, 12 percent (Sfr. 24) could have even if I thought that you would make a friendly comment about this gesture of goodwill.

However, in an "up-to-date discussion about the stock exchange" you give a hint that one could expect the yield (in this case) to remain at its present level if the payout were doubled or tripled because "the price would increase."

Although I am sympathetic with "impossible" propositions I cannot agree with your belief that an unrealistic, "appropriate" increase of dividends is going to have this result. Experience shows that the theories of the finance press are not always in accordance with Stock Exchange practice. All the same, I am going to follow your thoughts and am supposing that Landis & Gyr were to increase its dividend, for example, to Sfr. 60, that is to say triple it. This increase would correspond approximately to an "American dividend" of about 50 percent of the profit per share and would also surpass your boldest expectations. However, it is obvious that such an increased payment of dividends would claim increased profits and would, therefore, prevent a par increase of capital.

Do you now believe that the Landis & Gyr shareholders would prefer to get a dividend of Sfr. 60 instead of a priority right on par issues? A 5 percent priority right on par issues would return Sfr. 90 at a stock price of Sfr. 1,700 (before the increase of capital) plus the dividend of Sfr. 20, and at a price of about Sfr. 1,000 it would still return Sfr. 60.

I have not tried to embarrass you with this question, as I believe that nowadays there are shareholders who would choose this "unfavorable" way for completely irrational reasons. (They would perhaps change their attitude once they realize that the dividends are taxable, while many Landis & Gyr shareholders who have held their shares for a long time are entitled to have priority rights free of taxes.)

However, if most of the Landis & Gyr shareholders (not according to the number of shares but to the number of persons) would take this position, I would realize that we are really in a bad state. We would be forced to the realization that the Stock Exchange has lost its functional capacity as there would not be enough capital to be invested, that is to say, not enough people who would take investment risks.

What should we do then? Would it be the right moment to encourage companies to increase their dividends? Just when they would have to pay higher dividends they might not be able to replace their money since they would perhaps not be allowed to have such rising expenditures when borrowing.

In order to save Swiss companies' honour, we must say that

since 1961 they have not changed their dividend policy.
The buyers at that time knew that it would not change,
since the companies gave them no basis for such hopes.

Although I agree with you that the companies could have
some more goodwill and imagination in shareholder relations, I think that the "Open Letter" to the Board of
Directors failed in its purpose because of several reasons
and mainly cherishes false hopes. Do you really want to
create "false hopes"?

Would it not be more important to look for the reasons
for the Stock Exchange's present situation? The dividend
policy of the Swiss companies has not changed since 1961,
as we have already said, but we cannot say the same for
the Stock Exchange's public. It has changed, showing that
the saying "Les extrêmes se touchent" ("the extremes come
together") is true. But since the Stock Exchange is still
the place where the relationship between supply and demand
is the only important factor, one should think how this
fact can be reinforced in the mind of the actual and
potential shareholders.

Exhibit 7   **Landis & Gyr, AG**
                Finanz und Wirtschaft, Zürich, Wednesday, January 26, 1966

The Editorial Staff's Postscript

We would not like to disapprove Dr. Brunner's statement
that "the theory of the financial press is not always in
accordance with the Stock Exchange's practice." We would
simply add that the theory of a financial manager of
Landis & Gyr "is not always in accordance with the Stock
Exchange's practice." Just remember the fall in price of
the participation securities and the bonds with variable
interest, after the puzzling financial transactions of
Landis & Gyr, which were not positively accepted by the
Stock Exchange.

Now let us take about the main point. We think that Dr.
Brunner sees our "Open Letter" too much through Landis &
Gyr glasses, glasses which surely do not fit the nose of
an average Swiss corporation. Where, except at Landis &
Gyr, is there a belief that the shareholder has the choice
between a regular priority right on par issues that has
existed until now and a (provisionally still hypothetic)
trebled dividend? However, Landis & Gyr does not need to
exaggerate. One can also imagine the yearly 5 percent
priority right on par issue continuing with an added
increase in dividends from 20 to 25 Sfr. that would not
harm Landis & Gyr's self-financing ability! We would
recommend such a "gesture of good will" which is much
friendlier than Dr. Brunner's "proposition of trebled
dividend and priority rights abolishment"....

In our mentioned "up-to-date topic discussion of the
Stock Exchange" (FuW No. 1/2 January 5) we "did not give
a hint" that we were "counting upon possibly doubling or
tripling dividends, but simply, with Bally as an example,
explained that compared with international businesses
many Swiss companies could pay much higher dividends
according to their actual yield. Although Bally, as shoe-
makers abroad, according to their turnover could pay
twice as much, we are not so simple as to count on it. It
is much more likely that a camel would go through the eye
of a needle....

And what about "the right moment" to encourage the companies to increase dividends? Hic Rhodus, hic salta!

Unfortunately in Switzerland one is far too often talking about the "right moment" and, therefore, misses the appropriate accomplishment. If the psychological moment for an increase of dividends has ever been, then surely it is today, i.e, not a double or treble increase, but 1-2 percent yearly increase (of the share capital). This has nothing to do with the bigger problems of the companies obtaining loans. One has waited so long for the increase of dividends, that the Stock Exchange has suffered. In the meantime shareholders have suffered a decline in capital of around 10 billion Sfr. We believe that Landis & Gyr also does not think that its "stabilization of dividend" is ideal and that it is looking for a more flexible policy for paying out dividends.

And at last if the shareholders should again have a "false and disappointed hope" about the increase of dividends, then it is of course our fault and not the Board of Directors'—horribile dictu—since the FuW is calling attention in "Open Letters" to the fact that the companies could pay higher dividends if they only wanted to.

SUNDERLAND STEEL
PRODUCTS LTD. (A)

In March 1960, the management of Sunderland Steel Products Ltd., in Hull, England, was planning to raise £300,000 in long-term funds. Four sources were being considered: (1) a permanent bank overdraft; (2) a mortgage loan from an insurance company; (3) the sale of preferred stock; and (4) the sale of common stock. Mr. Leonard Sunderland, assistant to the managing director, was assigned to study these alternatives and to submit his recommendations to management.

Sunderland Steel Products Ltd. began in 1850 as an ironmonger (a supplier of iron and steel) in the prosperous port city of Hull, England. In 1890, the company purchased a foundry to meet the increasing local demand for castings and ironwork from railroad construction companies and the steel industry. The business expanded gradually under successive generations of the Sunderland family, but by 1945 annual turnover still remained under £1,000,000. In contrast to this historical rate of growth, the company grew rapidly during the early 1950s; and in 1956 annual sales passed £3½ million, but sales declined in the succeeding three years. In 1960 the company was the largest private firm in Hull and had the largest steel stockyard in Northern England. The company's financial record from 1952 to 1959 is shown in Exhibits 1 and 2.

The company had three main divisions: a Metal Windows Division, a Foundry Division, and a Steel Service Center. The Metal Windows Division manufactured a standardized high-quality metal window frame under the trade name of Everlast, special-purpose window frames, steel curtain walling, and metal partitions. In 1959 this division was the company's major source of profit.

The Foundry Division manufactured a wide variety of iron castings for manufacturers of automobiles, diesel engines, aircraft, railway equipment, and agricultural equipment. Sunderland was a leader in the development of melting and casting processes and recently had developed a special process for making Spheroidal Graphite (S.G.) iron, which had qualities similar to steel. In spite of management's efforts to develop special skills and products, the Foundry Division had not always been profitable, due to

Exhibit 1   **Sunderland Steel Products Ltd. (A)**

Balance Sheets 1952–59, as of December 31

(£000 Sterling)

	1952	1953	1954	1955	1956	1957	1958	1959[a]
Assets:								
Cash	84	28	2	10	71	2	1	2
Accounts receivable	371	388	362	452	482	538	415	490
Inventory	204	264	248	211	267	414	493	419
Total current assets	659	680	612	673	820	954	909	911
Investments	39	39	39	39	39	6	6	2
Fixed assets (net)	154	180	171	223	294	323	341	348[b]
Total assets	852	899	822	935	1,153	1,283	1,256	1,261
Liabilities:								
Accounts payable	281	230	159	209	300	380	277	230
Taxes payable	—	82	65	47	108	99	99	47
Dividends payable	13	11	13	14	11	14	2	14
Bank overdraft	—	—	22	—	—	—	91	174
Total current liabilities	294	323	259	270	419	493	469	465
Future taxes	72	55	31	77	56	70	29	29
Preference shares—								
5% (3,300 Shares)	33	33	33	33	33	33	33	33
Common stock[c]	257	257	257	257	275	275	275	275
Capital surplus	—	—	—	—	18	18	18	18
Earned surplus	196	231	242	298	352	394	432	441
Total liabilities and								
net worth	852	899	822	935	1,153	1,283	1,256	1,261
Net working capital	365	357	353	403	402	461	440	446
Net worth	486	521	532	588	678	720	758	767

[a] 1959 figures do not reflect acquisition of new properties in November 1959.

[b] The insurance value of the fixed assets was approximately three times the book value.

[c] 1952–1954—257,000 shares; 1955–1959—275,000 shares.

severe competition and overcapacity in the industry. Management was confident, however, that the division would grow and prosper, especially in view of the recent recovery in the foundry trade, the increasing need for special-quality metals, and the development of the S.G. process. Several large companies had approached Sunderland in late 1959 to express interest in the S.G. process and, in one instance, had offered a contract for 80–100 tons of S.G. castings per week. The existing total capacity of the foundry was only 70 tons a week, of which 55 tons (including 25 tons of S.G. iron) were currently being used. Management believed that this and other contracts would bring substantial profits if more foundry capacity could be developed.

The Steel Service Center consisted of a steel stockyard with facilities for profile burning, shearing, welding, and fabrication, and a design department. The center's business often contributed the greatest share of the company's

Exhibit 2

Sunderland Steel Products Ltd. (A)

Annual Results for Years Ending December 31, 1952–1959

(£000 Sterling)

	1952	1953	1954	1955	1956	1957	1958	1959
Sales	2,434	2,324	2,131	2,743	3,595	3,364	2,805	2,442
Gross margin	487	399	349	493	517	551	490	504
Trading profit (Before depreciation)	191	149	85	190	173	196	120	117
Tax	100	69	40	92	74	89	41	39
Depreciation	20	20	13	18	22	39	33	33
Net profit after depreciation and taxes[a]	71	60	32	80	77	68	46	45
Dividends	28	24	21	25	23	26	7	36
Retained earnings	43	36	11	55	54	42	39	9
Dividends as a percent of par value of 20 shillings	10%	8.75%	7.5%	9%	8%	9%	3.5%[b]	12.5%[b]

[a] Profit tax was raised from 10 percent to 12½ percent in April 1960. Income tax in 1960 was expected to be 7/9d on the £. Total tax was thus expected to be about 51.25% of taxable income.

[b] Effectively 8 percent each year; dividend delayed for special tax reasons in 1958.

sales and profit, but its profits tended to fluctuate. Management expected the center to produce a reasonable profit in 1960, since 1959 had brought a recovery from the 1958 recession. During the first six months of 1960, the center's sales were 52 percent above those in the same period of 1959 (Exhibit 3).

Exhibit 3   **Sunderland Steel Products Ltd. (A)**

Sales to March 1960 (£000)

Division	6 months to 31–3–59	6 months to 31–3–60	% Change
Metal Windows	400	445	+11.2
Foundry	194	274	+41.5
Steel Service	608	925	+52.0
	1,202	1,644	+36.8

The company's main plant was located on a seven-acre site paralleling the docks and contained the foundry, steel stockyard, manufacturing plant for Everlast windows, and company offices. The assembly plant and storage facilities were located on a two-acre site about a mile from the main plant. The main plant had grown in piecemeal fashion over the years; space had become inadequate, and operations had become increasingly less efficient for the volume and type of work to be done.

In August 1959, management learned that a large foundry, the Roper Foundry, and an adjoining factory on a large piece of land near the company's main plant would soon be for sale. These facilities had been built by the Government during World War II for war production. From 1948 to 1959 they had been used by a large firm of engineers and tool-makers but then had been closed because of lack of work. Both of the properties seemed to fit well into Sunderland's expansion plans. The Roper Foundry, with 120,000 square feet of covered space, would permit the doubling of production of iron castings on a more efficient basis. The adjoining factory would provide space for combined production and assembly operations of the Metal Windows Division and adequate space for engineering and administrative offices, with enough land for a 40 percent expansion. Management estimated that use of the properties would save the company £18,000 annually in operating expenses and also £16,000 in alterations and repairs, which otherwise would have to be made on the existing plant.

It was learned that both properties would be for sale at £205,000. After careful examination of the properties and their prospective benefits to Sunderland's operations, the management decided to offer £50,000 for the foundry and £140,000 for the factory. Both offers were accepted quickly, and title to the properties was transferred in November 1959. It was estimated that as a result of the purchase, financial needs for the fiscal year ending September 30, 1960, would be as follows:

Item	*Amount*
Roper Foundry	£ 50,000
Roper Factory	140,000
Previously authorized contracts	70,000
Estimated moving costs	20,000
Total cash requirements	£280,000

In each of the five years following fiscal 1960, the company expected to make capital expenditures of about £100,000. Funds from within the company (depreciation and retained earnings) were expected to be at least £65,000 each year, thus leaving about £35,000 that would have to be raised from external sources. These estimates were subject to considerable variation, since business conditions could vary widely from year to year.

Purchase of the properties had been financed by an increase of £150,000 in the bank overdraft and an increase of £40,000 in trade credit. Although it would have been possible to continue these arrangements, management preferred to use long-term sources of capital. In March 1960, it was dicided that the company should raise £300,000 from one of the following sources: (1) a permanent bank overdraft; (2) a mortgage loan from an insurance company; (3) the sale of preferred stock; or (4) the sale of common stock.

The permanent bank overdraft appeared to be an easy and cheap form of financing. Sunderland had maintained an excellent relationship with its bank for over 50 years and had never used the full amount of its overdraft. Discussions with officers of the bank indicated that the maximum overdraft could be increased from £300,000 to £450,000 if the company would increase its equity capital by £150,000 in the near future. Bank interest on the overdraft would be 1 percent over the Bank of England rate but not less than 4 percent in any case. The Bank of England rate had fluctuated as follows during recent years:

	1957—7%
March	1958—6%
May	1958—5½%
June	1958—5%
Aug.	1958—4½%
Oct.	1959—4%
Jan.	1960—5%

Mr. Leonard Sunderland foresaw several disadvantages in financing by means of a permanent bank overdraft. First, although the overdraft normally was repayable at the company's volition, the bank could not guarantee that the new overdraft limit would be permanent; if the Bank of England or the bank's head office in London called for a reduction of credit, the bank would have to comply. Second, if the financial condition of Sunderland should become poor, the bank might ask to acquire a preferred position in relation to other creditors of the company. Third, in case the company defaulted in its payments of interest and principal on the loan, the bank would have the right to elect a new Board of Directors.

A mortgage loan for £300,000 might be obtained from an insurance company at an interest rate of about $1\frac{1}{2}$ percent above the Bank of England rate prevailing at the time of negotiation. Whether this interest rate would be more or less expensive than the overdraft rate would depend on future fluctuations of the Bank rate. An insurance company loan would probably have a maturity of 30 years and would likely be amortized in equal installments starting in the fifth year. It was expected that the lending insurance company would impose certain restrictions on Sunderland; for example, the total of the insurance company loan, the bank overdraft, and any future long-term borrowings would not be allowed to exceed Sunderland's equity. Such restrictions were not expected to be a burden. Under the existing scarcity of credit, however, the insurance companies were in a strong bargaining position; and it was feared that they might ask the right to acquire shares in the company as a condition to the loan, although no information was yet available on this score.

The sale of cumulative preferred stock appeared problematical, although Sunderland already had preference shares outstanding. The dividend rate on preferred stock would probably have to be from 2 percent to 4 percent above the bank rate at the time of sale. The dividend would be paid from the company's profits after profits and income taxes (whereas interest was a tax deductible expense). The cost of selling an issue of preferred stock was estimated to be about 3 percent of the amount sold.

The final alternative was to sell an issue of new common stock. This stock might be sold to existing stockholders or sold in a block to a merchant bank or sold to the general public. In the latter case, a commission of about 8 percent of the selling price would have to be paid to the investment bankers selling the stock. The price at which the common stock might be sold had not been established. The stock was rarely traded, but the prices of the occasional transactions are shown in Exhibit 4. The stock market in early 1960 was firm, and a good price for the stock was expected by some members of management.

Sunderland Steel's management was confident that the recent business recovery would continue and bring earnings at least as high as the 1955–57 level. Trading profits (before depreciation and taxes) were expected to reach £300,000 by 1965.

Different preliminary opinions were held by various members of manage-

Exhibit 4

Market Price, Earnings, and Dividends per Share, 1954–60
(in shillings)

Year	Price per Share	Earnings per Share	Dividends per Share
1954	25	2.48	1.50
1955a	40	6.23	1.80
1956	40	5.60	1.06
1957	38–40	4.96	1.40
1958	32	3.36	1.56
1959	b	3.28	1.56

a Outstanding common shares increased from 257,000 to 275,000 shares.
b Shares not traded in 1959 and 1960.

ment concerning the best way to finance Sunderland's needs. Some liked debt financing because the interest was tax deductible, family control of the firm would not be diluted (the Sunderland family controlled 70 percent of the common stock), and the anticipated higher earnings would not have to be shared with new stockholders. Others preferred common stock financing to strengthen the company's financial structure and provide greater bargaining power in future debt financing. Also, a new issue of common stock, if sold to the general public, would create a broader market for existing stock. One man leaned toward preferred stock as a good compromise.

Mr. Leonard Sunderland was therefore faced with the task of weighing the fundamental merits and disadvantages of the four alternatives in order to recommend one of them to the company's top management.

2

Management Control

In the Management Control area great emphasis is placed upon the use of information and quantitative data as a means of managerial decision-making rather than upon the examination of systems of accumulating accounting data. The primary objective is to help managers increase their awareness and understanding of the measurements, interpretations, and use of figure data within the firm and recognize the impact of the environment in which the firm exists.

The examination of this area may be divided into four approximately equal sections.

1. *Purpose and Structure of Accounting Information*
   a. The meaning of fundamental accounting terms and related concepts
   b. The major assumptions on which accounting measurements are based
   c. The general structure of accounting records, reports, and systems
   d. Financial statements and their analysis

2. *Internal Management Control*
   a. Basic concepts of managerial control
   b. Principles of cost accounting including "full cost" and "direct cost" systems

3. *Accounting Information for Decision-Making*
   a. Characteristics of cost
   b. Cost-volume-profit relationships
   c. Relevant costs for decision-making
   d. Capital acquisition planning and decision-making

4. *Management Control Systems*
   a. Characteristics of management control systems
   b. Responsibility centers within a control system
   c. Divisional profit centers and interdivisional pricing
   d. Overall systems for management control

MERZ CHOCOLATE COMPANY

In November 1957, Mr. Edwards, manager of the commercial department of the Merz Chocolate Company, presided over a conference with the general managers of the company's plants in Atlantis and Polaris. Merz was a large manufacturer of cocoa and chocolate with plants throughout the world. The conference had been called to decide the price at which cocoa powder would be sold by the Atlantis plant to the Polaris plant. Mr. Edwards felt that this problem had already taken up too much time and that a decision should be reached quickly.

Cocoa Processing

In the processing of cocoa, raw cocoa beans were sorted, roasted, winnowed, milled, and pressed. The milling process, due to the heat generated, converted the material into a fatty liquid, which when pressed produced cocoa butter. The butter was later filtered and molded for ease in handling.

The dry residue from the press was a hard cocoa cake, which was crushed and sifted to become cocoa powder. The press could be adjusted to vary the amount of butterfat left in the cake. This varied from a practicable minimum of 12 percent up to about 20 percent. Cocoa powder was sold for use in drinks and as a general flavoring. Cocoa butter was later used, together with additional milled cocoa beans, in the manufacture of chocolate.

Merz endeavored to balance the production and sale of cocoa powder and butter in the form of branded end products; but, depending on consumer preferences in each market area, surpluses of powder or butter resulted. These then had to be sold in bulk, often at reduced prices.

Prices of Cocoa Beans, Cocoa Butter, and Cocoa Powder

World prices for cocoa beans tended to follow the price set by the Ghana Cocoa Board in Accra, the center of the cocoa growing industry. Well-

Exhibit 1

Merz Chocolate Company

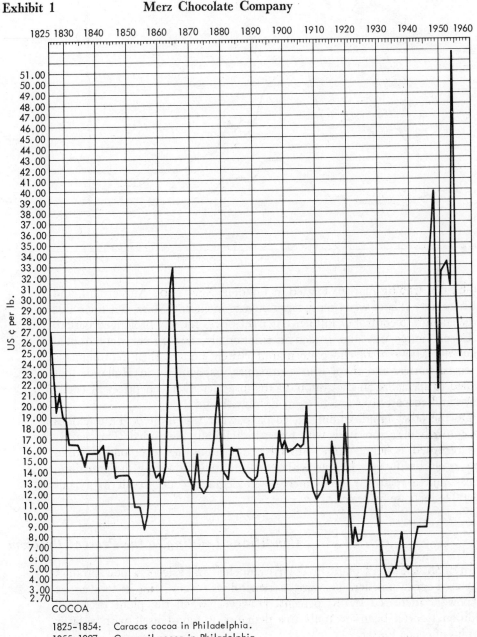

COCOA

1825-1854: Caracas cocoa in Philadelphia.
1855-1897: Guyaquil cocoa in Philadelphia.
1898-1906: Guyaquil cocoa in London.
1907-1912: Babia in New York.
1913-1950: Accra cocoa in New York.

Exhibit 2

Merz Chocolate Company

Quoted Prices of Cocoa Beans & Cocoa Butter
in Atlantis

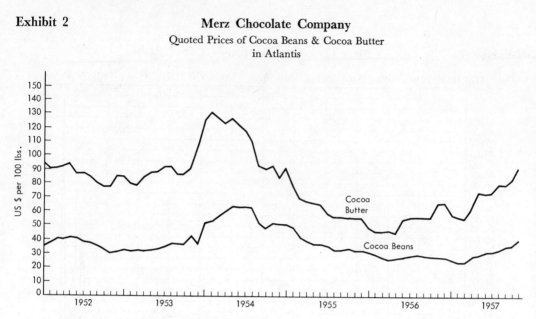

established trading markets existed in London, New York, Amsterdam, and other centers. There were many large buyers, including Merz, but none was large enough to control or influence market prices for any prolonged period.

Cocoa butter was also traded internationally, and prices were quoted regularly. Many small chocolate manufacturers bought their requirements of cocoa butter, and there were companies, particularly in Holland, that tended to specialize in the supply of this product. Data on prices of cocoa beans and cocoa butter are given in Exhibits 1 and 2.

On the other hand, trading in cocoa powder was limited. Transactions were usually on a spot basis with prices individually bargained. The market was regarded as being "thin"—that is, large quantities, over one hundred tons, could hardly ever be sold without substantially lowering the prevailing price—and a relatively small increase in demand could result in a considerable increase in price.

Conditions Leading to the Present Problem

In 1955, the Merz plant in Polaris launched the sale of a new product that used cocoa powder. This was a tremendous success, and its total usage of powder increased by 30 percent. However, when the plant processed additional cocoa beans to meet this demand, it found itself with a large surplus of cocoa butter.

It first attempted to sell this cocoa butter to other manufacturers in Polaris, but they too were selling more powder and likewise had surpluses of cocoa butter. When it then tried to sell cocoa butter abroad, it found that the butter had a flavor that foreign chocolate manufacturers did not like and to which they were unaccustomed. This flavor resulted from the type of beans used in Polaris and the processing techniques.

The only apparent alternative method of restoring the balance between powder and butter was for the Merz plant in Polaris to reduce the amount of beans it processed and to buy powder from other sources. The general manager of the Polaris plant, Mr. Dexter, knew that there were Merz plants in other countries that had a surplus of powder. He therefore asked Mr. Edwards to arrange shipments of powder from one of these plants as a solution to his problem. He estimated his annual needs at about 800 tons of cocoa powder.

Mr. Edwards selected the Atlantis plant because it appeared to have the greatest difficulty in selling powder and balancing its production of beans. That plant produced about 3,000 tons of cocoa powder a year, of which it used about 1,200 tons in its own branded end products and which were sold through regular sales channels. The balance of about 1,800 tons of powder was sold with difficulty, usually at prices considerably below prevailing market levels.

Mr. Edwards's approach originally was to allow the two plants to reach an agreement on prices between themselves. But although several shipments of powder were made, there were frequent disagreements over the price to be paid. The principal difficulties arose when the price of cocoa beans or cocoa butter fluctuated or when the market prices quoted for powder differed greatly from the agreed price, appearing to favor one or other of the plants.

These prolonged arguments finally came to the attention of Mr. Edwards. His view was that, if it were economical to ship powder from Atlantis to Polaris, then the actual price to be paid was somewhat irrelevant. It was, from the overall viewpoint of Merz, merely a transaction "from one pocket to another." Corporate taxes were almost identical in both countries, and there was no difficulty in the transfer of profits.

He decided that a contract should be signed by the two managers that would cover the additional powder requirements of the Polaris plant. If usage of powder greatly exceeded estimates, then a new contract would be negotiated for the excess requirements. This procedure would enable Mr. Cartwright, manager of the Atlantis plant, to buy immediately on futures all the beans needed for the next year. This appeared to avoid the problems created by fluctuating market prices. Moreover, it permitted greater stability in planning production schedules.

Mr. Edwards's Proposal for Determining Price

Mr. Edwards then proposed that the price of powder should be based on the price of cocoa beans and butter in Atlantis. He chose this method because there were no regular market quotations of powder prices, and transactions were carried out on an individual spot basis with considerable fluctuations in the prices. Cocoa bean and cocoa butter prices on the other hand were quoted regularly both in Polaris and Atlantis. Market prices in Polaris were occasionally different from those in Atlantis, but the gap did not remain for long.

Because of the close relationship between butter and bean prices, Mr. Edwards proposed that as all the beans needed for the coming year would

Exhibit 3   **Merz Chocolate Company**

Valuation of Cocoa Powder—Present Method

	Quantity in lbs.	Cents per lb.	Labor & Overhead	Total
Raw cocoa beans[a]	100.00	40.00		4,000.00
Warehousing and freight		.35		35.00
Handling shrinkage	1.40			
	98.60	40.92		4,035.00
Cleaning costs			16.20	16.20
Cleaning shrinkage	.85			
	97.75	41.44		4,051.20
Roasting costs			8.15	8.15
Roasting shrinkage	3.20			
	94.55	42.93		4,059.35
Winnowing costs			12.18	12.18
Winnowing shrinkage	10.80			
	83.75	48.62		4,071.53
Milling costs			21.49	21.49
Milling shrinkage	1.10			
	82.65	49.52		4,093.02
Pressing				
Input to press	189.55	49.52		9,386.52
Cocoa butter extracted[a]	88.80	90.70		8,054.16
(Market price 91.94¢ per lb. less filtering and molding costs at 1.24)				
Pressing costs		1.30	130.55	130.55
Cocoa cake output (12% fat)	100.75	14.52		1,462.91
Grinding and Packaging of Powder				
Labor and warehouse		1.15	115.00	115.00
Packing material		.35	35.00	35.00
Wastage	.75			
	100.00	16.13		1,612.91
General Overhead				
Commission of 8% includes depreciation and head office charges		1.29		
Freight charges to Polaris		1.25		
Cost of delivered cocoa powder		18.67		

a Price on day of purchasing annual requirement of beans.

be bought at the time the contract was signed the market price of butter in Atlantis on the day of signing the contract should also be taken as a basis for costing throughout the year. In the event butter prices for that particular day happened to be abnormal, an average of butter prices for several recent days would be used.

Based on these principles, Mr. Edwards's assistant calculated a cost price for the cocoa powder produced in Atlantis. These calculations are summarized in Exhibit 3. First, he developed the cost of the liquid produced in the milling process by adding to the cost of cocoa beans the labor and overhead involved up to this stage. Then he deducted the value of the butter produced; this he took as the market price less filtering and molding charges. To the value of the cocoa cake he then added the cost of further processing and packaging, general overhead commission, and freight. This resulted in a cost of powder at 18.67 cents per pound[1] delivered to the Polaris plant.

Other Possibilities

This calculation was in fact the same as those in the cost accounting system actually in use in the Atlantis plant. Mr. Edwards stated that he would not object to the proposal of an entirely different method of costing. However, he felt that any new method chosen should be one that was suitable for costing cocoa butter and powder throughout the plant and not one designed only for this particular problem of shipments to Polaris. The difficulty in coming to an agreement might perhaps indicate that there was a serious weakness in the present cost system. If that were the case, then he said the entire system should be given a most thorough investigation.

Prior to the adoption of the present method in 1952, several other systems of cost accounting had been tried. For the purpose of reviewing the results and making comparisons, Mr. Edwards had his assistant prepare calculations using these different methods, based on current prices and also on prices in effect in November 1956. These calculations are shown in Exhibits 4–7 and the results are summarized in Exhibit 8.

By-Product Costing Method

Before 1937, cocoa butter in Merz plants had been valued each day at the current market price, without regard to the actual cost of beans used. Cocoa powder was then costed as the sum of bean prices and processing costs, less butter prices. As a result, fluctuations in the price of cocoa beans, which were frequent, fell entirely on the cost of powder. Exhibit 4 shows

---

[1] All prices are given in U.S. dollars to disguise the currency of the actual countries involved.

Exhibit 4   **Merz Chocolate Company**

Valuation of Cocoa Powder—Based on Daily
Quoted Prices in November 1957

	Illustrating Method Used Generally before 1937				
Explanation					
1. Prices are beginning of week quotations in Atlantis					
2. Layout is an abbreviated form of Exhibit 3					
Quantity		1	2	3	4
—	Raw bean market price ¢/lb.	36.50¢	40.00¢	41.00¢	40.50¢
—	Cocoa butter market price ¢/lb.	84.00	91.94	94.50	94.15
100 lbs.	Raw beans	3,650.00	4,000.00	4,100.00	4,050.00
98.60	Warehousing & freight	35.00	35.00	35.00	35.00
97.75	Cleaning costs	16.20	16.20	16.20	16.20
94.55	Roasting costs	8.15	8.15	8.15	8.15
83.75	Winnowing costs	12.18	12.18	12.18	12.18
82.65	Milling costs	21.49	21.49	21.49	21.49
		3,743.02	4,093.02	4,193.02	4,143.02
—	Cost of Material per Pound	45.29	49.52	50.73	50.13
	Input to press				
189.55	Material as above	8,584.72	9,386.52	9,615.87	9,502.14
88.80	Cocoa butter extracted				
	(Market price less 1.24				
	further charges).	7.349.01	8,054.16	8,281.49	8,250.41
	Pressing costs	130.55	130.55	130.55	
100.75	Cost of cocoa cake out	1,366.26	1,462.91	1,464.93	1,382.55
100.00	Grinding & packing	115.00	115.00	115.00	115.00
100.00	Packing material	35.00	35.00	35.00	35.00
100.00	Total cost of processing	1,516.26	1,612.91	1,614.93	1,532.55
100.00	General overhead commission	121.30	129.03	129.19	130.60
100.00	Freight to Polaris	125.00	125.00	125.00	125.00
100.00	Cost of 100 lbs. of cocoa powder	1,762.56	1,866.94	1,869.12	1,788.15
1.00	Cost of 1 lb. delivered cocoa powder	17.63	18.67	18.69	17.88

the week-by-week cocoa powder prices that would have resulted had this method been used in November 1957.

During the 1930s prices of cocoa beans dropped while prices of butter remained relatively stable. This resulted in low or even zero costs for the cocoa powder. As such, the "cost" of cocoa powder was obviously artificial. Moreover, as the majority of cocoa processors used similar costing systems, the prices of cocoa powder remained at rock bottom, destroying market confidence and leading to dumping.

Butter-Bean Price Ratio Method

In 1937, Merz adopted a butter-bean price ratio method whereby one pound of butter was costed at 2.2 times the price of one pound of the beans actually used. This ratio was derived from the past average ratio of the market prices of cocoa beans and cocoa butter. The use of this method served to dampen the fluctuations in powder prices and remained generally in force in Merz plants until 1950. The cost price of butter thereby derived remained close to the market price. An example of this calculation is shown in Exhibit 5.

Exhibit 5   **Merz Chocolate Company**

Valuation of Cocoa Powder—Price Ratio Method

	Quantity in lbs.	Cents per lb.	Labor & Overhead	Total Costs
1. *Valuation of Cocoa Butter*				
Price of raw cocoa beans		40.00¢ per lb.		
Price of cocoa butter used (40.00 × 2.2)		88.00¢ per lb.		
Less further filtering and handling		1.24		
Value of cocoa butter		86.76¢ per lb.		
2. *Further Processing*				
Pressing				
Input to press as per Exhibit 3	189.55	49.52	—	9,386.52
Cocoa butter extracted	88.80	86.76	—	7,704.29
Pressing costs		1.30	130.55	130.55
Cocoa cake output	100.75	17.99	—	1,812.78
Grinding & packing powder				
Labor and warehouse		1.15	115.00	115.00
Packing material		.35	35.00	35.00
Shrinkage	.75			
	100.00	19.63		1,962.78
General overhead (commission 8%)		1.57		
Freight charges to Polaris		1.25		
Cost delivered cocoa powder		22.45		

Butter Fat Content Method

In 1950, a new method was introduced in many of the Merz plants to simplify the calculations required. As competition intensified, different blends and grades of beans were used in chocolate manufacturing. This new method attributed all the cost of the raw material obtained in the pressing stage to the butter fat content. As is shown in Exhibit 6 for current prices, the cost of 189.55 pounds of material output from the press was 9,517.07¢. This contained 100.89 pounds of fat, each pound of which was therefore worth 94.33¢. Thus a pound of cocoa cake, containing 12 percent of fat, was costed at 11.321¢ per pound.

This fat content method at first worked well, that is, the prices calculated for cocoa powder and butter closely followed actual market prices. In 1952 and following years, however, the market price structure again changed. As a result, other costing methods were again considered.

Exhibit 6   **Merz Chocolate Company**
Valuation of Cocoa Powder—Fat Content Method

Valuation of Fat		
Weight of material charged to press to provide		
100 lbs. of finished cocoa powder		189.55 lbs.
Cost of material charged at 49.52¢/lb.		
(based on bean price of 40¢/lb. See Exhibit 3.)	9,386.52	
Cost of pressing...	130.55	
Total cost of material output from press		9,517.07¢
Fat content of material output (53.226% fat)		100.89 lbs.
Basic cost of each pound of fat		94.33¢
Valuation of Cocoa Cake		
Output of cocoa cake from press		100.75 lbs.
Fat content of this cake (12%)		12.09 lbs.
Value of fat content of cocoa cake (at 94.33¢/lb.)		1,140.45
Value, i.e., of cocoa cake output (100.75 lbs. or 11.32¢ per lb.)		1,140.45

Further Processing	Quantity	Cents per lb.	Labor & Overhead	Total Costs
Grinding and Packing				
From press, as calculated above	100.75	—	—	1,140.45
Labor and warehouse		1.15	115.00	115.00
Packing material		.35	35.00	35.00
Shrinkage	.75			
	100.00	12.90		1,290.45
General overhead commission of 8%		1.03		
Freight charges to Polaris		1.25		
Cost delivered cocoa powder		15.18		

Adoption of Current Method

The Atlantis plant was one of the first Merz plants to drop the fat content method. It found that under this system the cost of cocoa butter it produced was well above prevailing market prices. According to Mr. Cartwright, general manager of the Atlantis plant, this placed his company at a serious competitive disadvantage. The majority of his competitors bought their butter on the open market and were thus able to produce chocolate at a significantly lower cost. He therefore revised the accounting system in 1953, adopting the method currently in use and which is summarized in Exhibit 3.

Other Merz plants gradually followed this lead, and by 1957 most of the plants were using the same system.

Weight Ratio Method

In 1953, the Polaris plant had considered the use of a weight ratio method. This costed each pound of butter taken from the press at five times that of each pound of powder. The 5:1 ratio was selected because it provided a cocoa butter price that was on the average 2.2 times the cost of the beans used. It was therefore a variation of the butter-bean ratio method. Exhibit 7 shows how the cost of cocoa powder was obtained by this method.

However, in 1953 the cocoa crop was very small, and prices of beans, butter, and powder rose sharply. The price of cocoa butter reached a level where many chocolate manufacturers started to use substitutes. This restrained further increases in the price of cocoa butter, and this in turn led butter producers to increase the price of their cocoa powder. The demand for cocoa powder remained high, especially as the use of cocoa butter substitutes required the use of more cocoa powder to maintain the "chocolate" flavor. As a result of these pressures, the ratio of cocoa butter to cocoa bean prices changed from an average of 2.2 to a figure of about 1.6. Theoretically a new weight ratio could have been calculated, which would have approximated this new price; but in view of the instability of the market

Exhibit 7   **Merz Chocolate Company**

Valuation of Cocoa Powder—Weight Ratio Method

Valuation of Cocoa Cake

Each pound of cocoa butter extracted is costed
  at five times the value of each pound of powder.)

Cost of material charged to press (from Exhibit 3)
  (189.55 lbs. × 49.52¢ per lb.) .... = 9,386.52
Cost of pressing............................... = 130.55
Total cost of material output (consisting of 88.80 lbs.
  of butter and 100.75 lbs. of cocoa cake........... =   9,517.07
Let y be the cost per lb. of butter extracted.

Then: $88.80y + \left(\dfrac{100.75y}{5}\right)$ .... =   9,517.07

$444.0y + 100.75y$ .... =   47,585.35

$544.75y$ .... =   47,585.35

y .... =   87.35

$\dfrac{y}{5}$ .... =   17.47

    i.e., cost of each pound of cocoa cake is 17.47¢

Further Processing Grinding and Polishing	Quantity	Cents per lb.	Labor & Overhead	Total Costs
From press as calculated above	100.75	17.47	—	1,760.10
Labor and warehousing.....................		1.15	115.00	115.00
Packing materials		.35	35.00	35.00
Shrinkage	.75			
	100.00	19.10		1,910.10
General overhead (commission 8%)		1.53		
Freight charges to Polaris		1.25		
Cost delivered cocoa powder		21.88		

structure, the weight ratio method was never actually used. Instead, the Polaris plant adopted the same system as the other plants, i.e., similar to that shown in Exhibit 3.

Exhibit 8   **Merz Chocolate Company**

Summary of Calculations of Cost of Cocoa Powder in November 1957
and Corresponding Figures for November 1956

	November 1957	November 1956ᵃ
Present method (Exhibit 3)	18.67¢	35.50¢
Price ratio method (Exhibit 5)	22.45	19.71
Fat content method (Exhibit 6)	15.18	12.96
Weight ratio method (Exhibit 7)	21.88	18.44
Market price of cocoa beans	40.00¢	32.50¢
Market price of cocoa butter	91.94	55.00
Valuation of cocoa butter (by price ratio method from Exhibit 6 plus filtering and molding charges of 1.24¢ per lb.	88.00¢	70.26¢
Valuation of cocoa butter (by fat content method from Exhibit 4 plus filtering and molding charges of 1.24¢ per lb.)	95.57	78.53
Valuation of cocoa butter (by weight ratio method from Exhibit 5 plus filtering and molding charges of 1.24¢ per lb.)	88.59	72.81

a Calculations in this column were made in the same manner as in the corresponding Exhibits 3-7.

Discussion of the Various Methods

Mr. Dexter, manager of the Polaris plant, thought that the fat content method should be used to cost the cocoa powder manufactured in Atlantis. The Atlantis plant was primarily interested in extracting butter. This was the most valuable product for them, and Mr. Dexter thought it logical that their cost system should be based on the butter fat content.

Furthermore, he said, this was apparently the only method that made allowance for the fact that the powder processed by Atlantis for Polaris had a fat content of only 12 percent, whereas the powder Atlantis regularly processed for its own use contained 20 percent fat. Atlantis would therefore extract more of the valuable fat from the powder it processed for Polaris, but, under by-product costing, that powder would be costed in the same manner as if it contained 20 percent fat.

Another advantage of the fat content method of costing, according to Mr. Dexter, was that it maintained a reasonable ratio between cocoa butter and cocoa powder prices, avoiding the extreme fluctuations that resulted when the market price of one was used to find the cost of the other.

Mr. Cartwright disagreed with these arguments. In the first place, he said, the by-product method did make allowance for the different butter fat contents of the cocoa powder. The differentiation was not directly obvious but nevertheless a differentiation did exist. Under the by-product method the offsetting credit from the cocoa butter obtained was considerably increased when the cocoa powder contained only 12 percent fat. This resulted in a marked reduction in the price of the cocoa powder.

To prove his point, Mr. Cartwright made a quick calculation, which is reproduced in Exhibit 9, showing how the price of cocoa powder varied according to its fat content. Going on further, Mr. Cartwright pointed out that the fat content method had only been introduced in other plants as a convenient and simple method for costing different grades of powder. It had only been used within each plant and had never been used for interplant shipments. More important, this method attached no significance to the real value of powder. To him the idea that cocoa powder should be valued on the basis of its fat content alone was unrealistic. The appeal of cocoa powder to the public depended entirely on its flavor and aroma; cocoa butter had little of either of these two qualities. It thus did not seem logical to him to value powder on its content of something that, to the public, was worthless.

Exhibit 9

Merz Chocolate Company
Comparison of Cost Price of Cocoa Powders
Containing 12% and 20% Fat

	Quantity	Cents per lb.	Labor & Overhead	Total
To produce 100 lbs. of cocoa powder containing 12% fat				
Pressing (see Exhibit 3)				
Input to press	189.55	49.52		9,386.32
Cocoa butter extracted	88.80	90.70		8,054.56
Pressing costs		1.30		130.55
Subtotal	100.75	14.52		1,462.91
Grinding and packaging	.75	1.50	150.00	150.00
Subtotal	100.00	16.13		1,612.91
General overhead and freight		2.54		
Total	100.00	18.67		
To produce 100 lbs. of cocoa powder containing 20% fat				
Pressing (see Exhibit 3)				
Input to press	172.32	49.52		8,533.29
Cocoa butter extracted	71.57	90.70		6,491.40
Pressing costs		1.30		130.55
Subtotal	100.75	21.56		2,172.44
Grinding and packaging	.75	1.50	150.00	150.00
Subtotal	100.00	23.22		2,322.44
General overhead and freight		3.11		
Total	100.00	26.33		

Note: The material input to the press contains 53.2 percent fat in total, in both cases.

In Mr. Cartwright's opinion the strongest argument of all against Mr. Dexter's proposal was that, because it was not based on market prices, the fat content system was no help in deciding how a plant should balance its production and sale of butter and powder.

Mr. Edwards noted these arguments carefully. In his mind the problem of shipping powder to Polaris was but one of the several problems with which a plant cost accounting system should be capable of dealing. He began to wonder what kind of system should be used.

AB THORSTEN (A)

This case deals with an investment proposal made by Anders Ekstrom, President of AB Thorsten, a firm engaged in the production and sale of chemicals, with headquarters in Stockholm, Sweden. This proposal was made to the management of Roget S.A., in Brussels, Belgium. AB Thorsten is a 100 percent owned subsidiary of Roget S.A.[1]

Summary of Operations: Roget S.A.

Roget S.A. is one of the largest industrial companies in Belgium. Founded forty years ago, the company originally produced a line of simple products for sale in Belgium. Today it has expanded to produce 208 complex chemical products in 21 factories.

Mr. André Juvet, President of Roget, states that the organization of the Company (Exhibit 1) is the result of careful planning:

> "Until five years ago, we were organized with one large manufacturing division here in Belgium, and one large sales division. One department of the sales division was devoted to export sales. However, exports grew so fast, and domestic markets became so complex, that we created three main product divisions, each with its own manufacturing plants and sales organizations. In addition, we have created foreign subsidiaries to take over the business in certain areas. For example, in Industrial Chemicals we have two subsidiaries—one in the U.K. and one in Sweden, which serves all Scandinavia. At the same time, the domestic department of the Industrial Chemicals Division exports to the rest of Europe. The U.K. and Sweden account for 9 percent and 5 percent of sales in that division, but 14 percent added to total sales is very important.
>
> "Another thing we achieve in the new organization is individual profit responsibility of all executives at all levels. Mr. Gillot is

---

[1] The letters "AB" and "S.A." are the equivalent designations in Sweden and Belgium of "Corp." or "Inc." in the U.S. and "Ltd." in the U.K.

Organization Chart Roget S.A.

Exhibit 1

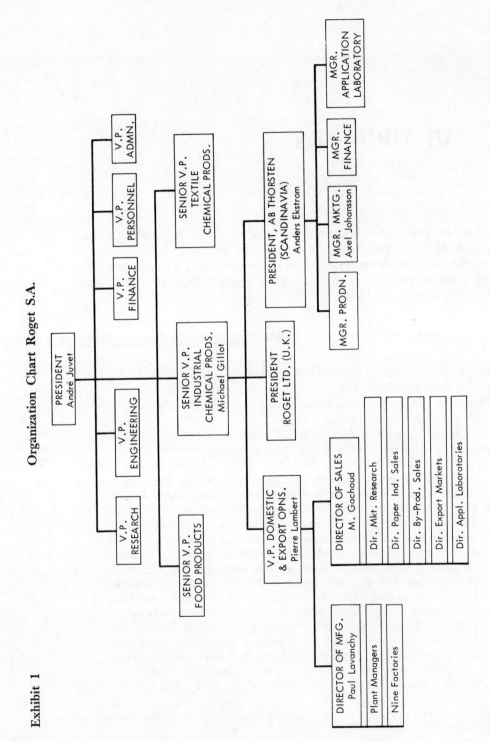

responsible for profits for all industrial chemicals, Mr. Lambert is responsible for profits from domestic operations (manufacturing and sales) and export sales to countries where we do not have subsidiaries or factories, and Mr. Ekstrom is responsible for profits in Scandinavia. We also utilize a rather liberal bonus system to reward executives at each level, based on the profits of their divisions.

"This, together with a policy of promotion from within, helps stimulate managers in Roget to a degree not enjoyed by some of our competitors. It also helps to keep men in an industry where experience is of great importance. Most of our executives have been in the starch chemicals business all of their lives. It is a complex business, and we feel that it takes many years to learn it.

"We have developed certain policies—rules of the game—that govern relationships with our subsidiary company presidents. These are intended to maintain efficiency of the whole Roget complex, while at the same time to give subsidiary managers autonomy to run their own businesses. For example a subsidiary manager can determine what existing Roget products he wants to sell in his part of the world market. Export sales will quote him the same price as they quote agents in all countries. He is free to bargain, and if he doesn't like the price he needn't sell the product. Second, we encourage subsidiaries to propose to division management in Brussels the development of new products. If these are judged feasible we manufacture them in Belgium for supply to world markets. Third, the subsidiary president can build his own manufacturing plants if he can justify the investment in his own market."

Company Background : AB Thorsten

AB Thorsten was purchased by Roget S.A. eight years ago. Since that time the same four men have constituted Thorsten's Board of Directors: Ekstrom; Mr. Michael Gillot, Senior Vice-President in charge of Roget's Industrial Chemical Products Division; Mr. Ingve Norgren, a Swedish banker; and Mr. Ove Svensen, a Stockholm industrialist. Swedish corporation law requires any company incorporated in Sweden to have Swedish directors, and the Roget management felt fortunate in finding two men as prominent as Norgren and Svensen to serve on the Thorsten Board.

During the first four years of Roget's ownership, Thorsten's sales fluctuated between Skr. 5 and 7 million but hit a low at the end of that period.[2] The Board of AB Thorsten decided at that time that the company was in serious trouble, and that the only alternative to selling the company was to

---

[2] In round numbers, the Skr. is approximately equivalent to U.S. $0.20, or ten Belgian francs (Bfr.). To avoid confusion, all monetary figures in this case series are stated in Swedish kroner, even though some of the actual transactions are made in Belgian francs.

hire a totally different management to overhaul and streamline the entire company operation.

On advice of the Swedish directors, Mr. Anders Ekstrom, a thirty-eight-year-old graduate of the Royal Institute of Technology, was hired. He had had sixteen years of experience in production engineering for a large machinery company, as marketing manager of a British subsidiary in Sweden, and as division manager responsible for profits in a large paper company.

Ekstrom has been president of AB Thorsten for the past four years. In that time, sales have increased to Skr. 20 million, and profits have reached levels that Roget's management finds highly satisfactory. Both Ekstrom and Norgren (a director) attribute this performance to: (a) an increase in industrial activity in Scandinavia; (b) changes in production methods, marketing strategy, and organization structure made by Ekstrom; (c) the hiring of competent staff; and (d) Ekstrom's own ambition and hard work. To these reasons the case writer also adds Ekstrom's knowledge of modern planning techniques—rather sophisticated market research methods, financial planning by use of discounted cash flows and incremental analysis, and, as Ekstrom puts it, "all those things my former company had learned from the American companies."

Ekstrom says that at the time he joined Thorsten, he knew it was a risk. "I like the challenge of building a company. If I do a good job here, I will have the confidence of Norgren and Svenson as well as of the Roget management in Brussels. Deep down inside, succeeding in this situation will teach me things that will make me more competent as a top executive. So I chose this job even though I had at the time (and still have) offers from other companies."

Initial Proposal for Manufacture of XL-4

Two years ago, Ekstrom informed the Thorsten Board of Directors that he proposed to study the feasibility of constructing a factory in Sweden for the manufacture of XL-4, a product used in paper converting. He explained that he and his customer engineers had discovered a new way of helping large paper mills convert their machines at little cost so that they could use XL-4 instead of competitors' products. Large paper mill customers would be able to realize dramatic savings in material handling and storage costs and to shorten drying time substantially. In his judgment, Thorsten could develop a market in Sweden almost as big as Roget's present worldwide market for XL-4. XL-4 was then being produced in Roget's Domestic Division at the rate of six hundred tons a year, but none of this was going to Sweden. Ekstrom states:

At that meeting, Mr. Gillot and the other directors seemed enthusiastic. Gillot said, "Of course—go ahead with your study and when you have a proposed plan, with the final return on investment, send it in and we will consider it thoroughly."

During the next six months, we did the analysis. My market research department estimated the total potential in Sweden at eight hundred tons of XL-4 per year. We interviewed important customers and conducted trials in the factories of three big companies, which proved that with the introduction of our machine designs the large cost saving would indeed materialize. We determined that if we could sell the product for Skr. 1,850 per ton, we could capture one-half of the market within a three-year period, or four hundred tons a year.

At the same time, I called the head of the Corporate Engineering Division in Brussels (see Exhibit 1) asking his help in designing a plant to produce four hundred tons per year, and in estimating the cost of the investment. This is a routine thing. The central staff divisions are advisory and always comply with requests for help. He assigned a project manager and four other engineers to work on the design of factory and machinery, and to estimate the cost. At the same time I assigned three men from my staff to work on the project. In three months this joint task group reported that the necessary plant could be built for Skr. 700,000.

All this we summarized in a pro forma calculation (Exhibits 2 through 5). This calculation, together with a complete written explanation, was mailed eighteen months ago to Mr. Gillot. I felt rather excited, as did most of my staff. We all know that introduction of new products is one of the keys to continued growth and profitability. The yield of this investment (15 percent) was well above the minimum 8 percent established as a guideline for new investment by the Roget Vice-President of Finance. We also knew that it was a *good* analysis, done by modern tools of management. In the covering letter, I asked that it be put on the agenda for the next Board meeting.

The minutes of the next Board meeting held in Stockholm three weeks later show on the agenda "A Proposal for Investment in Sweden" to be presented by Mr. Ekstrom, using a series of charts (Exhibits 2 through 5). The minutes also quote his remarks as he explained the proposal to other directors:

You will see from the summary table (Exhibit 2) that this project is profitable. On an initial outlay of Skr. 700,000 for equipment and Skr. 56,000 for working capital, we get a rate of return of 15 percent and a present value of Skr. 246,000.

Let me explain some of the figures underlying this summary

Exhibit 2

**AB Thorsten Proposal for Manufacture
of XL-4 in Sweden**

Financial Summary
(all figures in Skr.)

Year	Description	After-Tax Cash Flows[a]	Present Value at 8%
0	Equipment	−700,000	
	Working capital	− 56,000	
	Total	−756,000	−756,000
1	Cash operating profit	+105,000	
	Working capital	− 2,000	
	Total	+103,000	+ 95,000
2	Cash operating profit	+160,000	
	Working capital	− 7,000	
	Total	+153,000	+131,000
3	Cash operating profit	+215,000	+171,000
4	Cash operating profit	+215,000	+158,000
5	Cash operating profit	+215,000	+146,000
6	Cash operating profit	+145,000	+ 91,000
7	Cash operating profit	+145,000	
	Recovery value of equipment and working capital	+215,000	—
	Total	+360,000	+210,000
	Grand Total	+650,000	+246,000

Net present value	Skr. 246,000
Payback period (before tax)	4 years
Internal rate of return	15%

a From Exhibits 3, 4, and 5.

table. My second chart (Exhibit 3) summarizes the operating cash
flows that we expect to get from the XL-4 project. The sales
forecast for the first seven years is shown in column 2. The forecast was not extended beyond seven years because our engineers
estimate that the technology of starch manufacture will improve
gradually, so that major plant renovations will become economical
at about the end of the seventh year. Actually, we see no reason
why this particular product, XL-4, will decline in demand after
seven years.

The estimated variable cost of Skr. 1,000 per ton shown in
column 3 is our estimate of the full operating cost of manufacturing XL-4 in Sweden, including out-of-pocket fixed costs such as

Exhibit 3

AB Thorsten

Estimated Operating Cash Flows from
Manufacture and Sale of XL-4 in Sweden

1	2	3	4	5	6	7	8	9	10	11
Year	Sales (in Tons)	Var. Costs per Ton	Sales Price per Ton	Var. Profit Margin per Ton (4 − 3)	Total Var. Profit Margin (2 × 5)	Promotion Costs	Profit Contrib. (6 − 7)	Tax Depreciation	Tax 50% of (8 − 9)	Net Cash Flow After Tax (8 − 10)
		(Skr. per ton)			(figures in thousands of Skr.)					
1	200	1,000	2,000	1,000	200	130	70	140	(35)	105
2	300	1,000	1,850	850	255	75	180	140	20	160
3	400	1,000	1,850	850	340	50	290	140	75	215
4	400	1,000	1,850	850	340	50	290	140	75	215
5	400	1,000	1,850	850	340	50	290	140	75	215
6	400	1,000	1,850	850	340	50	290	—	145	145
7	400	1,000	1,850	850	340	50	290	—	145	145
Total	2,500				2,155	455	1,700	700	500	1,200

Exhibit 4

AB Thorsten

Estimated Working Capital Required for
Manufacture and Sale of XL-4 in Sweden[a]
(Skr. 000)

	1	*2*	*3*	*4*	*5*	*6*
				Change	*Tax Credit*	*Net*
		Other Curr.	*Working*	*from*	*(30% of*	*Funds*
	Inventory	*Assets less*	*Capital*	*Previous*	*Change*	*Required*
	at Cost	*Curr. Liab.*	*(1 + 2)*	*Year*	*in 1)*	*(4 − 5)*
Year 0	80	0	80	+80	24	56
Year 1	90	−5	85	+ 5	3	2
Year 2	100	−5	95	+10	3	7
Year 3 & later	100	−5	95	0	0	0
Total	100	−5	95	95	30	65

[a] These figures are in addition to the estimated equipment cost of Skr. 700,000.

Exhibit 5

AB Thorsten

Estimated End-of-Life Value of
Swedish Assets

Plant	Skr. 300,000	
Less tax on gain if sold at this price	150,000	
Net value of plant		Skr. 150,000
Working capital	Skr. 95,000	
Less payment of deferred tax on special inventory reserves.....................	30,000	
Net value of working capital		65,000
Net value of Swedish assets after 7 years		Skr. 215,000

plant management salaries but excluding depreciation. These fixed costs must of course be included because they are incremental to the decision.

As column 4 shows, we feel certain that we can enter the market initially with a selling price of Skr. 2,000 a ton, but full market penetration will require a price reduction to Skr. 1,850 at the beginning of the second year.

The variable profit resulting from these figures is shown in columns 5 and 6. Column 7 then lists the market development and promotion expenditures that are needed to launch the product and achieve the forecasted sales levels. Column 8 contains the net operating cash flows before tax, based on figures in the preceding columns.

The cost of the plant can be written off for tax purposes over a five-year period, at the rate of 20 percent of original cost each year. Subtracting this amount from the before-tax cash flow yields the taxable income figures summarized in column 9. The tax in column 10 is then subtracted from the before-tax cash flow to yield the after-tax cash flow in column 11.

A proposal of this kind also requires some investment in working capital. My third chart (Exhibit 4) summarizes our estimates on this element. We'll need about Skr. 80,000 to start with, but some of this can be deducted immediately from our income taxes. Swedish law permits us to deduct 60 percent of the cost of inventories from taxable income. For this reason, we can get an immediate reduction of Skr. 24,000 in the taxes we have to pay on our other income in Sweden. This is shown in column 5. The net investment in working capital is thus only Skr. 56,000, the figure we show in column 6.

We'll need small additional amounts of working capital in the next two years, and these amounts are also shown in column 6. Altogether, our working capital requirements will add up to Skr. 65,000 by the end of our second full year of operations.

Now let's look at one last chart (Exhibit 5). Seven years is a very conservative estimate of the life of the product. If we limit the analysis to seven years, we'll be overlooking the value of our assets at the end of that time. At the very worst, the plant itself should be worth Skr. 300,000 after seven years. We'd have to pay tax on that, of course, because the plant would be fully depreciated, but this would still leave us with Skr. 150,000 for the plant.

The working capital should be fully recoverable, too. After paying the deferred tax on inventories, we'd still get Skr. 65,000 back on that. The total value at the end of seven years would thus be Skr. 215,000.

Mr. Ekstrom ended this opening presentation by saying, "Gentlemen, it seems clear from these figures that we can justify this investment in Sweden on the basis of sales to the Swedish market. The group vice-president for finance has laid down the policy that any new investment should yield at least 8 percent. This particular proposal shows a return of 15 percent. My management and I strongly recommend this project." (The Thorsten vice-presidents for production, sales, and finance had been called into the Board meeting to be present when this proposal was made.)

Ekstrom told the case writer that while he was making this proposal he was sure that it would be accepted.

AB THORSTEN (B)

Mr. Ekstrom's proposal for the construction of a factory to manufacture XL-4 in Sweden was presented to Mr. Gillot, Roget S.A.'s Senior Vice-President in charge of Industrial Chemicals, eighteen months ago. The proposal was placed on the agenda for the next meeting of Roget's Board of Directors. Mr. Ekstrom recalled:

> When the Board met in Stockholm three weeks later, I presented the plan along with my directors of sales, finance, and production. We took only an hour, since I was sure Gillot had checked it thoroughly with various corporate staff departments (Finance, Engineering) as well as with the sales and manufacturing managers in the Domestic and Export Operations Department within his own division.
>
> Gillot said that it seemed to him to be a clear case. He asked interesting questions, mainly about the longer-term likelihood that we could see more than 400 tons a year, and about how we would get the money. I explained that we in Sweden were very firm in our judgment that we would reach four hundred tons a year even before one year, but felt constrained to show a conservative estimate of a three-year transition period. We also showed him how we could finance any expansion by borrowing in Sweden. That is, if Roget would furnish the initial capital, and if our four hundred tons were reached quickly, any further expansion would easily be lent by banks. The two Swedish directors confirmed this. The Board voted unanimously to construct the plant.

Disagreement between Parent and Subsidiary

About a week later, Gillot telephoned Ekstrom. "Since my return to Brussels I have been through some additional discussions with the production and marketing people here in the Domestic Department. They think the engineering design and plant cost is accurate but that you are too optimistic on your sales forecast. It looks like you will have to justify this more." Ekstrom related the following:

I pushed him to set up a meeting the following week. This meeting was attended by myself and my marketing and production directors, from Sweden, and four people from Belgium—Gillot, Lavanchy (Director of Manufacturing), Gachoud (Director of Sales), and Lambert (Vice-President for Domestic and Export).[1]

That was one of the worst meetings of my life. It lasted all day. Gachoud said that they had sales experience from other countries and that in his judgment the market potential and our share were too optimistic. I told him over and over how we arrived at this figure but he just kept repeating the overoptimism argument. Then Lavanchy said that the production of this product is complicated and that he had difficulties producing it in Belgium, even with trained workers who have long experience. I told him I only needed five trained production workers and that he could send me two men for two months to train Swedes to do the job. I impressed on him that "if you can manufacture it in Belgium you can manufacture it for us in Sweden until we learn if you don't have confidence in Swedish technology." He repeated that the difficulties in manufacturing were great. I stressed that we were prepared to learn and take the risk. Somehow I just couldn't get through to him.

Lavanchy then said that the whole world market for Roget was only six hundred tons a year, that it was being produced in Belgium at this level, and that it was inconceivable that Sweden alone could take four hundred tons.

At 6 P.M. everyone was tired. Lambert had backed up his two production and sales officials all day, repeating their arguments. Gillot seemed to me to just sit there and listen, occasionally asking questions. I cannot understand why he didn't back me up. He seemed so easy to get along with at the prior Board meeting in Stockholm—and he seemed decisive. Not so at this meeting. He seemed distant, indecisive, and an ineffective executive.

He stopped the meeting without a solution and said that he hoped all concerned would do more investigation of this subject. He vaguely referred to the fact that he would think about it himself and let us know when another meeting would be held.

Objection from a Swedish Director

Ekstrom states that he returned to Stockholm and reported the meeting to his own staff, and to the two Swedish members of his Board. "They, like I, were really disgusted. Here we were operating with initiative and with excellent financial techniques. Roget management had often made talks in which they emphasized the necessity for decentralized profit responsibilities, authority, and initiative on the part of foreign subsidiary Presidents. One of

---

[1] See the first case in this series, AB Thorsten (A), Exhibit 1, p. 102, for a chart of Roget's organization structure and roster of top executives.

my men told me that they seem to talk decentralization and act like tin gods at the same time."

Mr. Norgren, the Swedish banker on Thorsten's Board, expressed surprise. "I considered this carefully. It is sound business for AB Thorsten, and XL-4 will help to build one more growth company in the Swedish economy. Somehow, the management in Brussels has failed to study this, or they don't wish the Swedish subsidiary to produce it. I have today dictated a letter to Mr. Gillot telling him that I don't know why the project is rejected, that Roget has a right to its own reasons, but that I am prepared to resign as a director. It is not that I am angry, or that I have a right to dictate decisions for the whole world-wide Roget S.A. It is simply that, if I spend my time studying policy decisions, and those decisions do not serve the right function for the business, then it is a waste of time to continue."

Finally, Ekstrom states, "while I certainly wouldn't bring these matters out in a meeting, I think those Belgian production and sales people simply want to build the empire and make the money in Roget Belgium. They don't care about Thorsten and Sweden. That's a smooth way to operate. We have the ideas and initiative, and they take them and get the payoff."

Further Study

After Mr. Gillot received Norgren's letter, he contacted Messrs. Lavanchy, Gachoud, and Bols (V.P. Finance, Roget Corporate Staff). He told them that the Swedish XL-4 project had become a matter of key importance for the whole Roget Group, because of its implications for company profits, and for the morale and autonomy of the subsidiary management. He asked them to study the matter and report their recommendations in one month. Meanwhile, he wrote Ekstrom, "Various members of the Corporate Headquarters are studying the proposal. You will hear from me within about six weeks regarding my final decision."

AB THORSTEN (C)

Anders Ekstrom, Managing Director of AB Thorsten, spent a busy eight months after requesting and receiving permission from the management of his parent company in Belgium, Roget S.A., to study the feasibility of building a factory in Sweden to make XL-4, an industrial adhesive. Previous cases in this series have focused on the events of this eight-month period. This case picks up the story at that point and presents the reactions of Roget's headquarters staff during the ensuing month.

Summary of Previous Cases

1. During the first six months, Ekstrom and his staff studied the XL-4 project and prepared a report, recommending construction of the factory.
2. At the end of that time, Ekstrom mailed his report to Mr. Gillot, the head of Roget's Industrial Chemical Products Division.
3. Three weeks later, the proposal was approved unanimously by AB Thorsten's Board of Directors, meeting in Stockholm. Gillot attended this meeting in his capacity as one of Roget's representatives on the Thorsten Board.
4. One week later, Gillot telephoned Ekstrom to say that production and marketing officials in Belgium would not endorse the proposal unless Ekstrom could present a stronger case for it. Ekstrom requested a meeting to defend the proposal.
5. One week after that, Ekstrom and the Thorsten directors of marketing and production met in Brussels with Gillot and three other Roget executives: Mr. Lambert (Vice-President for Domestic and Export), Mr. Lavanchy (Director of Manufacturing), and Mr. Gachoud (Director of Sales). No decision was reached at this meeting.
6. One week after this meeting, Ekstrom reported back to his executives in Sweden that the project was being turned down. Mr. Norgren, a

Swedish director, wrote to Roget that he was prepared to resign from the Thorsten Board if the proposal were not approved.

7. A few days after receiving this letter, Gillot told the production and marketing executives in Belgium that the XL-4 project was of key importance and asked them to study it and report to him in one month.

Report of Roget's Director of Manufacturing

A month after he was asked to study the XL-4 project, Lavanchy gave Gillot a memorandum explaining his reasons for opposing the proposal:

At your request, I have reexamined thoroughly all of the cost figures that bear on the XL-4 proposal. I find that manufacture of this product in Sweden would be highly uneconomical, for two reasons: (1) overhead costs would be higher; and (2) variable costs would be greater.

As to the first, we can produce XL-4 in Belgium with less overhead cost. Suppose that Thorsten does sell four hundred tons a year so that our total worldwide sales rise to one thousand tons. We can produce the whole one thousand tons in Belgium with essentially the same capital investment we have now. If we produce one thousand tons, our fixed costs will decrease by Skr. 120 a ton.[1] That means Skr. 72,000 in savings on production for domestic and export to countries other than Sweden (six hundred tons a year), and Skr. 120,000 for worldwide production including Sweden (one thousand tons).

Second, we could save on variable costs. If we were to produce the extra four hundred tons in Belgium, the total production of one thousand tons a year would give us longer production runs, lower set-up costs, and larger raw material purchases, thus allowing mass purchasing and material handling and lower purchase prices. My accounting department has studied this and concludes that our average variable costs will decrease from Skr. 950 a ton to Skr. 930 (Exhibit 1). This Skr. 20 per ton difference means a saving of Skr. 12,000 on Belgian domestic production or Skr. 20,000 for total worldwide production, assuming that Sweden takes four hundred tons a year.

Taxes on these added profits are about the same in Belgium as in Sweden—about 50 percent of taxable income.

In conclusion, that plant should not be built. Ekstrom is a bright young man, but he does not know the adhesives business. He would be head over heels in costly production mistakes from the very

---

[1] Total fixed cost in Belgium is the equivalent of Skr. 180,000 a year. Divided by 600, this equals Skr. 300 a ton. If it were spread over one thousand tons, the average fixed cost would be Skr. 180.

Exhibit 1   **AB Thorsten**

Estimated Variable Cost of Manufacturing
XL-4 in Belgium for Shipment to Sweden

Variable costs per ton:		
Manufacturing..	Skr.	930
Shipping from Belgium to Sweden		50
Swedish import duty		400
Total Variable Cost per ton	Skr.	1,380
Total Variable Cost, 400 tons to Sweden	Skr.	552,000

beginning. I recommend that you inform the Thorsten management that it is in the company's interest, and therefore it is Roget policy, that he must buy from Belgium.

Report of Vice-President of Finance

The same day, Gillot received the following memorandum from Eric Bols, Roget's financial vice-president:

I am sending you herewith estimates of the working capital requirements if Roget increases its production of XL-4 in our Belgian plant from six hundred to one thousand tons a year (Exhibit 2). Initially, we will need Skr. 54,000, mostly for additional inventories. By the end of the second year, this will have increased to Skr. 74,000. Incidentally, the tax credits shown in column 5 of

Exhibit 2   **AB Thorsten**

Estimated Working Capital Required for Manufacture of
XL-4 in Belgium for Sale in Sweden
(Skr. 000)

	1	2	3	4	5	6
	Inventory at Cost	Other Curr. Assets less Curr. Liab.	Working Capital (1 + 2)	Change from Previous Year	Tax Credit (30% of Change in 1)	Net Funds Required (4 − 5)
Year 0	50	10	60	+60	6[a]	54
Year 1	55	15	70	+10	0	10
Year 2	60	20	80	+10	0	10
Year 3 & later	60	20	80	0	0	0
Total	60	20	80	80	6	74

a Based on finished goods inventory of Skr. 20,000 in Sweden.

the exhibit are based on a Swedish law, which permits businesses to deduct 60 percent of inventory costs from taxable income.

I have also looked at Lavanchy's calculations for the fixed and variable manufacturing costs and am in full agreement with them.

Ekstrom's Thoughts at This Time

In an interview about this same time, Ekstrom expressed some impatience with "the way things are going. I have other projects that need developing for Thorsten, and this kind of long-range planning takes much time and energy. Also, just keeping on top of the normal operating problems of the business we already have takes up a lot of my time. Sometimes I feel like telling them to go and sell XL-4 themselves."

AB THORSTEN (D)

Anders Ekstrom, Managing Director of Sweden's AB Thorsten, is apprehensive about the profit position of XL-4, an industrial adhesive product.[1] He is now selling XL-4 at a price of Skr. 1,850 a ton, which is Skr. 300 less than its delivered cost. At the same time, M. Gillot, Senior Vice-President of Roget S.A., and Ekstrom's immediate superior in Belgium, is wondering what decision he should take regarding Ekstrom's request that he lower the price at which the Belgian Company sells XL-4 to the Swedish Company.

AB Thorsten is a wholly-owned subsidiary of Roget S.A., one of the largest chemical companies in Belgium. Thorsten buys XL-4 from Roget's Industrial Chemical Products Division, at a transfer price of Skr. 1,700 a ton (Skr. 2,150 with transport costs and import duties). This case describes the problems faced by management as it tries to resolve a conflict arising from this transfer price. It covers a fourteen-month period, during which the following events tooks place:

1. Fourteen months ago, Ekstrom introduced XL-4 to Swedish customers at a price of Skr. 2,500.
2. Six months ago, after his request for a lower transfer price was turned down, he lowered the price to a more competitive Skr. 2,200.
3. Two months ago, his request for a lower transfer price again denied, he reduced his selling price a second time, to Skr. 1,850.

Ekstrom now says that he may withdraw XL-4 from the Swedish market if he cannot find a way to make it show a profit.

---

[1] The title of "Managing Director" in Sweden and in Britain is approximately the same as that of "President" in the United States.

Organization Structure: Roget S.A.[2]

Roget S.A. began operations forty years ago, manufacturing and selling chemicals in the domestic Belgian market. It has grown steadily, partly through growth and partly through purchase of companies such as Thorsten, so that it now produces 208 products in twenty-one factories. Its organization structure is shown in Exhibit 1, p. 00.

According to M. Juvet, Roget's Managing Director:

> We are organized on a divisional basis. For example, take the Industrial Chemicals Division, headed by M. Gillot. This is set up as a separate company, and Gillot is responsible for profits. This concept of decentralization is extended down to the departments under him—except that they are responsible for profits on a geographic basis instead of a product basis.
>
> One of these is the Domestic Department, under M. Lambert. This department sells industrial chemicals throughout Belgium and exports its products to countries in which we do not manufacture. It has its own factories to supply both of these markets, and its own sales force in Belgium. The Domestic Department, like our other Brussels-based departments, markets most of its export volume through our foreign subsidiaries and uses independent selling agents only in countries where we don't have our own personnel.
>
> M. Lambert runs this department on his own. He is responsible for its profits just as he would be if it were an independent company. In much the same way, Ekstrom is responsible for the profits made by AB Thorsten.
>
> A big company like Roget benefits from this kind of organization. We must divide the work of management. No man can do it all. Placing responsibility for profits enables us to measure the result of operations, and it is an important means of attracting and motivating top quality executives. Each head of a product division will have more initiative and will work harder if he is in effect head of his own company. Our bonus system, based on division profits, adds to this kind of motivation.

Company Background: AB Thorsten

AB Thorsten was purchased by Roget eight years ago. After a period of low profits and shrinking sales in Sweden, Roget employed Mr. Anders Ekstrom as the Managing Director. A thirty-eight-year-old graduate of the Royal Institute of Technology, with sixteen years' experience in production and marketing, Ekstrom appears to be an executive with a good deal of

---

2 Note: Those who have studied previous cases in this series should skip the next three sections of this case and jump to the section headed, "Rejection of the Swedish Proposal."

ambition and a wide acquaintance with modern financial and planning techniques.

When he joined the company, Ekstrom decided that the best way to restore Thorsten's profitability was to introduce new products, promote them aggressively, and back them up with a first-class technical services staff. In the four years since he became managing director, Thorsten's sales have increased from Skr. 7 million to Skr. 20 million, and profits have increased in even higher ratio.

Early History of the XL-4 Project

XL-4 is an adhesive product used in the paper converting industry, and one that Ekstrom and his management are sure will enjoy a large market in Sweden. Although total production in Roget's Belgian plant for all other markets is six hundred tons a year, Ekstrom's market studies have convinced him that four hundred tons a year can be sold to paper companies in Sweden, provided that his customer engineering staff helps customers to modify their own equipment, and that the price can be lowered. He has conclusive evidence that large paper companies can reap significant cost savings due to lower materials handling costs and faster drying times.

Ekstrom and his top manufacturing and sales executives spent six months preparing a feasibility study, which proposed building a plant in Sweden to manufacture XL-4, and presented this at a Thorsten Board meeting one month later. He states, "we did a complete market study, engineering study, and financial study, using discounted cash flows, which showed that we should build a factory in Sweden with a payback period of four years and a rate of return of 15 percent on invested capital. This was presented at a Thorsten Board meeting in Stockholm and approved unanimously.[3]

> During the next two months, several things happened. First, M. Gillot informed me that there were objections from Lambert (Vice-President, Domestic and Export Department), Lavanchy (Director of Manufacturing in the Industrial Chemical Products Division) and Gachoud (Director of Sales in the same division). I convinced him that we should hold a meeting with all these men in Brussels but that meeting ended in chaos, with me arguing over and over for the plant in Sweden and the others saying over and over that we would have too many problems in manufacturing and that we did not have the capabilities and experience in the adhesives industry that they possessed in Belgium. They also had no

3 Swedish law requires that all corporations have two Swedish directors for every foreign director. Thorsten's Board is composed of a Swedish banker, a Stockholm industrialist, Mr. Ekstrom, and M. Gillot, a Senior Vice-President of Roget S.A. Details of this proposal are reported in AB Thorsten (A).

confidence in my market projection, saying that they didn't think that we could sell four hundred tons a year.[4] Finally, M. Gillot asked the Belgian executives to study the matter further and give him a formal report on whether the plant should be built.[5]

Rejection of the Swedish Proposal

After studying all the reports on the XL-4 project, Gillot decided not to approve the proposal for a Swedish plant. He wrote to Ekstrom:

> I am sorry to inform you that your proposal to manufacture XL-4 in Sweden has been rejected. I know that you and your management have done an outstanding job of market research, engineering planning, and profit estimation, but two other factors worked against you. First, it seems more profitable for our Belgian plant to manufacture XL-4 and export it to Sweden. Second, executives in our Domestic Division here are convinced that the product should be made in Belgium where we have the experience and knowhow. They are also not sure that you can sell four hundred tons a year in Sweden.
>
> I want you to know, however, that we in headquarters are most appreciative of the kind of work you are doing in Sweden. This adverse decision in no way reflects a lack of confidence in you or a failure on our part to recognize your outstanding performance as the managing director of one of our most important daughter companies.

Introduction of XL-4 into Sweden

Immediately after this decision, Ekstrom decided to order XL-4 from Roget Domestic and Export Division.

> At this point, I decided to prove to them that the market is here. They quoted me a delivered price of Skr. 2,150 a ton (head office billing price of Skr. 1,700, plus Skr. 50 transportation and Skr. 400 import duty).[6] Because of heavy promotion and customer engineering costs (my engineers helping paper companies adapt their machinery), I had to have a gross margin of Skr. 350 a ton. This meant I had to sell it for Skr. 2,500.

---

4 Events during these two months are reported in AB Thorsten (B), 1969.

5 The reports of these executives are presented in AB Thorsten (C), 1969.

6 Some of these figures were actually expressed in Belgian francs. To avoid possible confusion, all figures have been expressed at their Swedish kroner equivalents.

He penciled the following table:

Head office billing price	Skr. 1,700
Shipping cost	50
Import duty	400
Delivered cost	Skr. 2,150
Allowance for promotion and engineering costs	350
Swedish selling price	Skr. 2,500

I knew I could never achieve sales of four hundred tons a year at this price. It was higher than the prices of other adhesives suitable for this market, and Swedish paper companies are very cost-conscious. I knew that we could do some business at this price, however, and this would give our engineers some practical experience in converting customers' equipment to take XL-4. Later on, we could reduce the price and try for the main market.

I wrote to M. Gachoud, Director of Sales for the Domestic and Export Department in Brussels, showing him the figures, saying that we could eventually reach four hundred tons a year in sales, and asking him to reduce the head office billing price. He declined.

For the next eight months sales were disappointing. At the end of this period, still having faith in our research over the last two years, I decided to lower the price to Skr. 2,200. I hoped that this would induce paper companies to try XL-4 and prove to themselves that it would lower their costs significantly. Of course, this was only Skr. 50 more than my cost, and I could hardly continue permanently on that basis. With me and my company being judged on profits, it is not worth our while to spend all of this time and resources on XL-4 for such a small mark-up.

Sales did increase during the next four months, to 150 tons, and I knew I could sell about two hundred tons regularly at this price. But I was still intent on proving the market at four hundred tons.

This time I went personally to see M. Gachoud in Brussels and practically demanded that he lower the price of XL-4 exported from Belgium to Sweden. He explained that with a sales volume of 150–200 tons a year in Sweden, sold at an export transfer price of Skr. 1,700, and with strong doubts in his mind that we could ever reach four hundred tons a year, he could not agree to the reduction.

At this point I decided to prove that I was right by executing a bold move, backed up by the use of modern financial planning methods. I lowered the price to Skr. 1,850 a ton. I figured that someone in Brussels had to understand my reasoning, if I explained it well enough and backed it up with forceful direct action.

Please don't get the idea that this was simply a political trick. I wouldn't have done it if I hadn't believed that it would bring in added profits for the group as a whole. I felt sure that volume would go up to four hundred tons, and at that rate we would produce a profit contribution of at least Skr. 113,000 a year for the Roget group. This is Skr. 24,000 more than I could hope for at the old price and a volume of two hundred tons.

I showed my calculations to M. Gillot after I had decided to go ahead. Here is a little table of figures that I sent to him then (all figures are in Swedish kroner) :

	At 200 tons		At 400 tons	
	Per Ton	*Total*	*Per Ton*	*Total*
Selling price	2,200	440,000	1,850	740,000
Variable costs:				
Manufacturing (Belgium)	930		930	
Shipping (Belgium-Sweden)	50		50	
Import duty (Sweden)	400		400	
Total variable costs	1,380	276,000	1,380	552,000
Factory margin		164,000		188,000
Promotional costs		75,000		75,000
Profit contribution to				
Roget group		89,000		113,000

Let me explain this table. I knew that the Belgian cost accountants used a figure equivalent to Skr. 1,250 a ton as the full cost of manufacturing XL-4. The production people told me, however, that the Belgian plant had enough capacity to supply me with four hundred tons of XL-4 a year without additional investment for expansion and that they could manufacture the additional four hundred tons at a variable cost of Skr. 930 a ton. This meant that the fixed costs were sunk costs and I could ignore them. This is why the manufacturing cost figure in the table is Skr. 930.

Adding in the transportation costs and import duties brings the total variable costs to Skr. 1,380 a ton. My own promotional and engineering costs amounted to about Skr. 130,000 during the first year, but we were already over that hump. They are budgeted for this year at Skr. 75,000 and will go down to Skr. 50,000 a year from now on, mostly for technical services to customers. To avoid an argument, though, I used Skr. 75,000 in the table I sent to M. Gillot.

This gives me the profit contribution of Skr. 113,000 a year that you see at the bottom of the table. This is Skr. 24,000 more than I could have expected at the old price. To me that's conclusive.

I tell you all this to emphasize that my main motive was to improve our group's profit performance. Even so, I must admit that I still hope to persuade M. Gillot to let me build an XL-4 factory in Sweden. That plant will be profitable at a volume of four hundred tons and a price of Skr. 1,850, and I suppose that this may have been at the back of my mind, too. If I can show him that the four hundred tons is not a Swedish dream, I think he'll go along. It's ridiculous to pay import duties that amount to more than 20 percent of the selling price if you don't have to, and if I could have convinced him on the size of the market fourteen months ago, I think that I would have had my plant.

In the two months since this last price reduction, sales of XL-4 have increased to a rate of 270 tons a year. Ekstrom feels certain that within another twelve months he will reach the 400-ton level. He also says, however, that he finds himself in a quandary.

> The Swedish company is losing Skr. 300 on every ton we sell, plus a great deal of selling and engineering time that could be switched to other products. This is bound to affect the profits of my company when I give my annual report to M. Gillot. This is why I quit trying to deal with Gachoud. Last week I wrote to M. Gillot, asking him to direct Gachoud to sell me the product at Skr. 1,100. I'm hoping for a reply this week.

The Parent Company's Transfer Pricing Policy

Gillot has not yet decided what to do with this request. As he says:

> Transfer pricing in this company is pretty unsystematic. Each of us division managers is expected to price his own products, and the top management executive committee doesn't interfere. I have the same kind of authority over transfer prices as I have over the prices we charge our independent agents. We've never thought of them as separate problems. I've never been in a situation like this, though, and I want to think it through carefully before I act.
>
> Our attitude toward transfer pricing is probably the result of the way we operated in foreign markets in the beginning. We developed our export trade for many years by selling our products to independent agents around the world. We still do a lot of business that way. These agents estimated the prices at which they could sell the product and then negotiated with the export sales manager in Brussels for the best price they could get.
>
> When we began setting up our own daughter companies in our bigger markets, we just continued the same practice. Of course, daughter companies like Thorsten cannot shift to a competing supplier, but they have great freedom otherwise. For example, they can try to negotiate prices with us here at headquarters. This healthy competition within the company keeps us all alert. If they think Belgium is too rigid, they can refuse to market that particular

product in their home country. Of, if they can justify building their own manufacturing plants, they can make the product themselves and not deal with the Belgian export department at all.

A Norwegian Example

Head office practices have resulted in head office billing prices that vary widely from market to market. In some cases, outside agents are able to obtain products at lower prices than Roget charges to its own subsidiaries. Ekstrom particularly wanted to tell the case writers about a Norwegian example. XL-4 is sold in Norway through an independent agent. This agent sells XL-4 to his customers at the equivalent of Skr. 1,290 plus Norwegian import duty. He persuaded Gachoud to sell him XL-4 at a price of Skr. 1,225, thus in effect giving him an agent's commission of Skr. 65 a ton. Roget also agreed to pay the shipping costs to Norway, amounting to Skr. 52 a ton. This meant that Roget received only Skr. 1,173 a ton to cover manufacturing and administrative costs and provide a profit margin. This was less than the average full cost of production in Belgium (Skr. 1,250) and Skr. 257 less than the Skr. 1,700 price at which Roget billed AB Thorsten.

"At one point," Ekstrom says, "I even thought of buying my XL-4 through the Norwegian agent. But then I realized that this would be destructive warfare against Belgium. The total profits of the Roget group of companies would be less by the amount of the Norwegian agent's commission. I would be blamed for this when Lambert or Gillot reported it to the Executive Committee."

Other Factors to Consider

Division managers' performance in Roget S.A. was judged largely on the basis of the amount of profit they were able to generate on product sales, including both sales to agents and sales to subsidiary companies. The managing board relied on this to induce the division managers to work for greater company profits.

The performance of the daughter company managers was appraised in much the same way. Ekstrom, for example, knew that group management in Brussels judged his performance on the basis of the amount of profit reported on AB Thorsten's income statement. Because of his success in the past four years, Roget's managing board gave him a good deal more freedom than the managers of any of the other subsidiaries enjoyed, but this happy state of affairs would come to an end if Thorsten's reported profits began to slide.

Gillot says that he must also consider three other factors before reaching a decision. First, Ekstrom's profit analysis must be evaluated. Second, Ekstrom's feelings of responsibility as head of the Swedish company must not be destroyed. Finally, he must review the points made by Lambert and Gachoud. Gillot says that Lambert told him, "If Ekstrom decides to take advantage of company rules and discontinues selling XL-4 in Sweden, we can certainly find an independent agent in Sweden to handle it. That's one bridge we'll never have to cross, though. Ekstrom will never push it that far. He believes in introducing new products as the key to his success. If we stand fast, he will simply raise the price back to a level that is profitable for both of us."

Taxes and foreign exchange regulations had no bearing on M. Gillot's decision. Income tax rates in Belgium were about the same as in Sweden, and no restrictions were placed on Thorsten's ability to obtain foreign exchange to pay for imported goods or pay dividends. In fact, Roget's top management insisted that each daughter company play the role of good citizen in its own country, by measuring taxable income on the same basis as that used by management in the evaluation of the subsidiary's pretax profit performance. No attempt was to be made to divert taxable income from one country to another.

*   *   *

As this case is written, both Ekstrom on the one hand and Lambert and Gachoud on the other are waiting for M. Gillot to settle the transfer pricing question and let them know his decision.

STARDUST GRINDER COMPANY

In May 1964, Mr. Sorrel, the general manager of the English plant of the Stardust Grinder Company, was considering what he should do at a meeting he was to attend that afternoon with his sales manager, accountant, and development engineer. The meeting was to discuss the introduction by Adolph Müller and Company, a German competitor, of a plastic ring to take the place of a steel ring presently used in certain machines sold by the company. The new ring, which had been put on the market only a few weeks previously, not only had a much longer life than the Stardust steel ring but also had a much lower cost. Mr. Sorrel's problem stemmed from the fact that his company had a large quantity of the steel rings on hand and had a substantial inventory of special steel for their manufacture, which, after a thorough survey, he had found could not be sold even for scrap. The total book value of these inventories was approximately £6,000.[1]

For over sixty years the Stardust Grinder Company had manufactured industrial machines that it sold in a number of countries. The company's head office was in Switzerland. In general, the separate plants were allowed considerable leeway in administering their own affairs. However, the executives in Switzerland could be approached easily for advice either by correspondence and telephone or during their visits to the individual plants.

The particular machine involved in Mr. Sorrel's decision was made only at the English plant situated in Manchester, which employed over 6,000 persons. The different models were priced between £250 and £400. Each machine contained a number of rings.

Parts, which in total accounted for a substantial part of the company's business, were sold separately sometimes, as in the case of the steel rings, for use on similar machines manufactured by competitors. Some of the rings produced by the Stardust Grinder Company were sold separately as parts;

---

[1] 1 pound = 20 shillings; 1 shilling = 12 pence; £1 = 240 pence; symbols: pound/shilling/pence = £/s./d. (1964)

126

the remainder were used in the assembly of machines in the Manchester plant.

Throughout its history, the company had followed the practice of providing the best quality it could at reasonable prices. As a result it had established a good reputation everywhere. In some countries competition hardly existed. In others, despite strong efforts by competitors, it had succeeded in keeping large shares of the available markets. However, in recent years, particularly since the Korean War, the competition had become much stronger. Japanese manufacturers had had more than a little success in entering the field with low-priced spare parts. Other companies had appeared with lower quality and lower priced machines. There was little doubt but that in the future competition would become more intense. Technological developments would come faster and have a much greater impact on competitive activities.

The sales manager, Mr. Matthews, had learned of the new plastic ring shortly after its appearance and had immediately asked when the Stardust Company would be able to supply them, particularly for sale to customers in Germany where Adolph Müller and Company was providing probably the strongest competition faced by the Stardust Company. Mr. Lanergan, the development engineer, said that no technical or design difficulties would arise to delay production of the plastic rings. He estimated that production of the plastic rings could begin in September and that inventories of the new part in quantities adequate to meet the Stardust Grinder Company's machine assembly requirements and also service customers in most market areas could be established by the latter part of September.

The company already had a plastics division that was not operating at full capacity. The additional tools and equipment necessary could be obtained for about £200.

At this point Mr. Lanergan had raised the question about the investment in steel ring inventories, which would not be used up by September. Mr. Matthews said that if the new ring could be produced at a substantially lower cost than the steel ones, the inventory problem was irrelevant. It should be sold for whatever could be obtained or even thrown away if it could not be sold. However, the size of the inventory, which he estimated might be equal to more than a year's supply, caused Mr. Sorrel to question this suggestion. He recalled that the size of the inventory was the result of having to order the highly specialized steel in large amounts in order to find a mill willing to handle the order.

The discussion then became very heated; Mr. Matthews insisted that the company could not hope to retain its position unless it provided its customers with the best quality of parts available. He furthermore emphasized that as Adolph Müller and Company were said to be selling the plastic ring at about the same price as the Stardust steel ring, and as the cost of the former would be much less than the latter, the company was refusing profits as well. Finally, it was decided that the company should prepare to manufacture the new ring as soon as possible but that they would only be sold in those markets where they were offered by competitors until the inventories of the old model and the steel were exhausted. No one expected that the new rings would be produced by any company other than Adoph Müller for some time. This meant that not more than 10 percent of the company's markets would be affected.

Shortly after this, Mr. Schmid of the parent company in Switzerland visited Manchester. During a review of company problems the plastic ring case was discussed. Mr. Schmid agreed that the company should proceed with plans for its production and try to find some other use for the steel. He then said "if this does not seem possible, I would, of course, expect you to use this material and produce the steel rings." But he added that as the additional revenue of the plastic ring might well offset the cost of carrying the inventory of the steel parts plus the cost of the raw material involved, it might be economically feasible to introduce the new ring much sooner than might be expected. He suggested that this possibility be explored without delay.

Within a few days after Mr. Schmid's visit, both Mr. Lanergan and Mr. Matthews came in to see Mr. Sorrel. The former came because he felt that the plastic ring would completely destroy demand for the steel ring as tests had indicated that it had at least four times the wearing properties. However, because he understood that the price of the competitive ring was very high (perhaps even higher than the Stardust steel ring) he felt that the dicision to sell the plastic ring only in the market areas where difficulties existed was a good one. "In this way we would probably be able to continue supplying the steel ring until stocks, at least of processed parts, were used up."

Mr. Matthews, the sales manager, was still strongly, even violently, against selling any steel rings after the new ones became available. The company had always prided itself on giving its customers the best products available. If steel rings were sold in some areas, while plastic rings were being sold elsewhere, customers in the former would eventually find out. The result would affect the sale of machines, the selling price of which was many times that of the rings. He produced figures to show that if the selling price of both rings remained at 860 s. per hundred, the additional profit from the plastic rings, which would cost 173 s. per hundred as contrasted with 768 s. per hundred for the steel, would more than cover the so-called investment in the steel inventory within less than a year at present volume levels. Mr. Sorrel refused to change his decision of the previous meeting but agreed to have another discussion within a week.

In anticipation of the meeting and also having in mind Mr. Schmid's suggestion, Mr. Sorrel obtained the following data from the cost department on the cost of plastic and steel rings:

	Plastic rings	Steel rings
Material	s. 8 9d.	s. 231 4d.
Direct labor	40 10	145 3
Overhead[a]		
Departmental	91 10	286 6
Administrative .	32 6	105 10
Total (per 100 rings)	s. 173 11d.	s. 768 11d.

[a] Overhead was allocated on the basis of direct labor. (Although no attempt had ever been made to separate variable and fixed overheads it was estimated that the variable portion of the overhead costs included in the above summary would range between twenty-five and thirty percent of the departmental amounts at the production volumes anticipated.)

Mr. Sorrel also learned that the inventory of special steel of 17,200 lbs. had cost £2,700 and was equal to about a seventy-week supply if sales continued at its current rate of 340 rings per week. If production of the rings were discontinued immediately, however, the supply of finished rings would be reduced to about 7,800 by the time the plastic rings could be produced, assuming that sales of the rings continued to average 340 per week.

It then occurred to Mr. Sorrel that during the next two or three months the plant would not be operating at capacity. As the company had a policy of employing its excess labor during slack periods at about 70 percent of regular wages on maintenance and repair projects rather than laying the men off, he wondered if it would be a good idea to convert the steel inventory into rings during this period and so save on the labor cost.

TIPOGRAFIA STANCA S.p.A.

Mr. Giulio Cattani, founder and President of Tipografia Stanca, S.p.A., was worried. The company was doing more business than ever before—sales were at an annual rate of about L.125,000,000 a year[1]—but net income had decreased slightly during recent months and the income/sales ratio had dropped sharply. Mr. Cattani wondered what had gone wrong and what he could do about it. He called in his chief (and only) accountant, Mr. Gaetano Pareto, and asked him to find out what was happening.

Tipografia Stanca was an Italian corporation, located in Milan and doing a general printing business on a customer order basis. Mr. Cattani set the price to be charged for each job. When possible, he waited until the work was done and then quoted a price equal to 140 percent of the cost of the paper stock used, plus L.2,500 for each labor hour. Straight-time wage rates in the past, adjusted for recent wage rate increases, had averaged about L.800 an hour, and this formula seemed to provide an adequate margin to cover overhead costs and provide a good profit.

Most of Tipografia Stanca's work was done on the basis of predetermined contract prices. In bidding on these jobs, Mr. Cattani applied his standard pricing formula to his own estimates of the amount of labor and paper stock the job would require. He prided himself on his ability to make these estimates, but he sometimes quoted a price that was higher or lower than the formula price, depending on his judgment of the market situation.

Stanca's production procedures were fairly simple. When a customer's order was received, it was assigned a production order number and a production order was issued. The material to be printed, known as the customer's "copy," was given to a copyeditor who indicated on the copy the sizes and styles of type that should be used. The editor sometimes made changes in the copy, usually after telephoning the customer to discuss the changes.

Once the customer's material had been copyedited, it was sent to the composing room, where it was set in type. A "proof" copy was printed by

---

1 In 1968 the Italian lira could be exchanged at the rate of approximately L.620 to the United States dollar or L.144 to the Swiss franc.

hand and returned to the copyeditor, who checked the printed copy against the original. Any errors in the proof were indicated in the margin, and the marked proof was sent to the customer for approval. At this point the customer might decide to make changes in the copy, and these changes, as well as corrections of typesetting errors, were made as soon as the corrected proof was returned to the composing room.

In some cases a second proof was sent to the customer for his approval, but at Tipografia Stanca most orders were sent to the pressroom as soon as the customer's corrections had been made and the second proof had been approved by the copy editor.

At this point, the order was ready for production on one of the presses in the pressroom. Printing instructions were contained in the production order, which specified the particular press to be used, the number of copies to be printed, the color, size, style, weight, and finish of the "stock" or paper to be used, and similar details. Copies were then printed, bound, and packaged for delivery to the customer.

An order could take as little as one day in the copyediting and composing room stages or as long as several weeks. Printing, binding, and packaging seldom took more than two days except on very large production runs of multipage booklets.

For many years the shop had had enough work to keep it busy steadily throughout the year, without serious seasonal slack. As a result, Tipografia Stanca's before-tax profit had fluctuated between 13 and 15 percent of net sales. The interim profit report for the first half of 1968 therefore came as a great shock to Mr. Cattani. Although volume was slightly greater than in the first half of 1967, profit was down to 8.8 percent of sales, an all-time low. The comparison, with all figures expressed as percentages of net sales, was as follows:

	Six Months 1968	Six Months 1967
Net sales	100.0%	100.0%
Production costs	77.6%	72.3%
Selling and administrative costs	13.6	13.9
Profit	8.8	13.8

Mr. Pareto knew that the company's problem must be either low prices or excessive costs. Unfortunately, the cost data already available told him little about the cost-price relationship for individual jobs. Tipografia Stanca's operating costs were classified routinely into twenty categories, such as salaries, pressroom wages, production materials, depreciation, and so forth. Individual job cost sheets were not used, and the cost of goods in process was estimated only once a year, at the end of the fiscal year.

Detailed data were available on only two kinds of items: paper stock issued and labor time. When stock was issued, a requisition form was filled out, showing the kind of stock issued, the quantity, the unit cost, and the production order number. Similar details were reported when unused stock was returned to the stockroom.

As for labor, each employee directly engaged in working on production orders filled in a time sheet each day, on which he recorded the time he started on a given task, the time he finished it or moved on to other work, and (in the case of time spent directly on a specific production order) the order number. His department number and pay grade were recorded on the time sheet by the payroll clerk.

Mr. Pareto's first step was to establish some overall cost relationships. Employees, for example, fell into three different pay grades, with the following regular hourly wage rates:

Pay Grade	Regular Hourly Wage Rate
1	L. 1,200
2	800
3	600

These rates applied to a regular work week of forty-four hours a week. For work in excess of this number of hours, employees were paid an overtime premium of 50 percent of their regular hourly wage. Overtime premiums were negligible when the work load was light, but in a normal year they averaged about 5 percent of the total amount of hourly wages computed at the regular hourly wage rate. In a normal year this was approximately L.40 per direct labor hour.

In addition to their wages, the employees also received various kinds of benefits, including vacation pay, health insurance, and old-age pensions. The cost of these benefits to Tipografia Stanca amounted to about 70 per-

Exhibit 1   Partial List of Materials Requisitions
For the Week of October 5–9

Req. No.	Job No.	Amount[a]
4058	A-467	30,000
R162	A-469	(2,000)
4059	A-467	6,000
4060	A-442	600
R163	A-455	(900)
R164	A-472	(800)
4061	A-467	3,600
R165	A-465	(1,200)
4062	A-467	9,600
4063	A-471	32,000
4064	A-473	26,400
4065	A-458	2,200
R166	A-467	(3,300)
4066	A-481	17,600

[a] Amounts in parentheses are returned materials.

cent of the total payroll. Mr. Pareto estimated that all other shop overhead costs—that is, all copy department, composing room and pressroom costs other than direct materials, direct labor, overtime premiums, and employee benefits on direct labor payrolls—would average L.400 per direct labor hour in a normal year.

Armed with these estimates of general relationships, Mr. Pareto then proceeded to determine the costs of several recent production orders. One of these was order A-467. This was received for copyediting on Monday, October 5, and delivered to the customer on Friday, October 9. Mr. Cattani had quoted a price of L.180,000 on this job in advance, on the basis of an estimate of L.48,000 for paper stock and forty-five direct labor hours. All requisitions and time records relating to order A-467 are included in the lists in Exhibits 1 and 2. (To save space, some of the details shown on the requisitions and time tickets have been omitted from these exhibits.)

Exhibit 2   **Partial Summary of Labor Time Sheets**
For the Week of October 5–9

Employee No.	Pay Grade	Dept.	Job No.	Hours
14	2	Copy	A-463	6.6
14	2	Copy	A-467	1.4
15	1	Copy	A-467	3.3
15	1	Copy	a	2.7
15	1	Copy	A-467	8.8
18	3	Press	A-467	4.0
18	3	Press	A-472	4.6
22	1	Composing	A-455	3.8
22	1	Composing	A-467	8.4[b]
22	1	Composing	a	1.5
23	2	Press	A-458	3.4
23	2	Press	A-467	4.7
23	2	Press	a	1.1
23	2	Press	A-459	2.5[b]
24	2	Copy	A-470	7.4
28	1	Press	A-467	7.0
28	1	Press	A-458	1.0
31	3	Press	a	8.0
33	1	Composing	A-471	7.6
33	1	Composing	A-472	4.2
40	2	Press	A-469	3.6
40	2	Press	A-467	4.9
40	2	Press	a	0.2
43	1	Press	A-467	3.5
43	1	Press	A-481	5.8

a Indicates time spent on general work in the department and not on any one job.

b Employee No. 22 worked 6 hours of overtime during the week, none of them on job A-467, while employee No. 23 worked 8 hours of overtime, including 4.0 hours spent on job A-467.

A/S DANSK MINOX, COPENHAGEN

A/S Dansk Minox in Copenhagen, specializing in branded vacuum-packed meat and other food products, has for many years sold vacuum-packed sliced pork in gravy, a very popular dish in Denmark. In 1965 the product represented about 15 percent of the firm's total sales in the country in a product range that comprises thirty products. The Danish housewife very often serves this dish together with a red cabbage salad. This salad is rather time-consuming to prepare at home and certain competitors of A/S Dansk Minox had recently introduced red cabbage salad in either vacuum-packed, canned, or frozen form. However, A/S Dansk Minox estimated that the major part of the red cabbage sold was still prepared at home, and although sales of ready-made red cabbage salad expanded rapidly, it was felt—and consumer research confirmed this—that there was still a great untapped potential for such a product.

At the end of 1965, A/S Dansk Minox had not marketed vacuum-packed red cabbage salad, but in view of existing market potential, and since it was so often eaten together with sliced pork, the company management considered producing red cabbage salad also. A/S Dansk Minox had during the last year considered introducing a speciality line of complete meals, which were to be sold in an attractive carton containing vacuum-sealed bags with the different ingredients for the meal. The management decided that the first product in this speciality line was to be "sliced pork in gravy with red cabbage," and the product was to be packed in a carton containing the standard vacuum-sealed bag with sliced pork plus another bag with the red cabbage. Cost allocation problems arose in this connection, leading to long discussions between the marketing and finance departments of the Danish company.

The standard product "sliced pork in gravy" was sold in a 450-gram bag at a consumer price of D.Cr. 4.85. This was the "ideal" quantity for an average family, giving between three and four servings. Therefore, when considering the "complete meal" product, the marketing department did not wish to change the quantity of sliced pork in gravy. Extensive testing showed that the average family consumed between 500 and 600 grams of red cabbage salad with 450 grams of sliced pork in gravy. It was therefore decided to sell the "complete meal" product in a 1-kilogram pack, containing the standard 450-gram bag with sliced pork in gravy plus another vacuum-sealed bag with 550 grams of red cabbage salad.

The marketing department received the following preliminary selling price calculation from the Finance Department, based on the assumption that the new product should produce approximately the same profit per kilogram as the standard sliced pork in gravy. For comparison, the selling price calculation for standard sliced pork in gravy is also given, both for 1 kilogram and for 450 grams, to show that the raw material costs and labor costs for sliced pork in gravy are exactly the same in both the existing standard pack of this product and in the new 1-kilogram "complete meal" pack.

	"Complete Meal" 1 kg.	*Sliced Pork in Gravy* 1 kg.	*Sliced Pork in Gravy* 450 g.
		(All amounts are in D.Cr.)	
Consumer price....................	8.20	10.78	4.85
Less turnover tax (12.5% of consumer price before tax)	.91	1.20	.54
Consumer price before tax	7.29	9.58	4.31
Retailer's margin (27.5% of price to retailer)	1.57	2.07	.93
Price to retailer.....................	5.72	7.51	3.38
Raw material, sliced pork	1.67	3.71	1.67
Raw material, red cabbage.............	.50	—	—
Labor, sliced pork	.25	.56	.25
Labor, red cabbage	.25	—	—
Packaging material	.26	.24	.11
Transport and storage................	.20	.20	.09
Margins and discounts to wholesalers (8% of price to retailer)	.46	.60	.27
Sundry variable costs	.10	.10	.04
Total variable costs	3.69	5.41	2.43
Marginal contribution	2.03	2.10	.95
Production fixed expenses	1.20	1.20	.54
Other product-related fixed expenses	.30	.30	.14
General selling and administrative expense and overhead (4% of price to retailer)..	.23	.30	.14
Total fixed expenses...............	1.73	1.80	.82
Net operating profit	0.30	0.30	.13

The difference in consumer price between the two packs as proposed by the Finance Department meant that the consumer would have to pay D.Cr. 3.35 (8.20 − 4.85) for the red cabbage salad, since the sliced pork in gravy content of the two packs was the same. The Marketing Department protested that this price difference was prohibitive, since the ingredients for making the red cabbage salad at home could be bought for approximately D.Cr. 1.10 and the labor costs at home (if counted at all) would not amount to more than approximately 0.70. The Marketing Department argued that A/S Dansk Minox could not expect the consumer to pay more than D.Cr. 2.00 at the most for the red cabbage salad and added convenience, thus leaving a consumer price for the new pack of 4.85 + 2.00 or 6.85. The Marketing Department contended, furthermore, that the selling price calculation showed that the raw material and labor costs amounted to only 0.75 for the red cabbage salad and that it was unreasonable that the other cost elements should result in a consumer price difference of 3.35.

Since the only difference between the standard pack and the "complete meal" pack was the red cabbage and a more elaborate package, the Marketing and Finance Departments listed those cost elements that varied between the 1,000 g. "complete meal" pack and the 450 g. standard pack with sliced pork in gravy. These elements were the following:

	"Complete Meal" 1 kg.	*Sliced Pork in Gravy* 450 g.	*Difference*
Raw material, red cabbage salad	.50	—	.50
Labor, red cabbage salad	.25	—	.25
Packaging material	.26	.11	.15
Transport and storage	.20	.09	.11
Margins and discounts.................	.46	.27	.19
Sundry variable costs	.10	.04	.06
Production fixed expense...............	1.20	.54	.66
Other product-related fixed expenses......	.30	.14	.16
General overhead	.23	.14	.09
Totals	3.50	1.33	2.17

The retail margin and the turnover tax were added to the cost difference of D.Cr. 2.17 plus the difference in operating profit of D.Cr. 0.17 to arrive at the previously mentioned selling price difference of D.Cr. 3.35. As an approximation, the consumer price is computed by multiplying the retail price by 1.45. This means that if the Marketing Department wished a new price of D.Cr. 6.85 for the "complete meal" pack (D.Cr. 2.00 more than the standard pack with sliced pork in gravy), the difference in the price to the retailer could not exceed approximately D.Cr. 1.38 (D.Cr. 2.00 divided by 1.45). Thus, with a consumer price of D.Cr. 6.85 and an unchanged net operating profit per pack, the difference in the cost elements in the selling price calculation would have to be reduced from D.Cr. 2.17 to 1.38 (a reduction of 0.79).

There was no disagreement between the Marketing and Finance Departments with regard to the raw material, labor, packaging material, transport and storage, and sundry variable costs. The item "Other product-related fixed expenses" covered mainly advertising; consequently, the Marketing Department could not argue with the Finance Department about this item, either, since it was under the control of the Marketing Department. The two items "Margins and discounts" and "General overheads" are, as a standard rule in the company, calculated as fixed percentages of the price to the retailer (8 percent and 4 percent, respectively). Although this procedure might be open to question, the Marketing Department was satisfied that the costs would decrease automatically if a lower selling price could be agreed upon.

The main discussion, therefore, centered upon the item "Production fixed expenses." After internal agreement on the sales budget every year, the total production fixed expenses were divided by the total sales quantity, expressed in kilograms. This computation resulted in a rate of D.Cr. 1.20 per kilogram for the year under consideration. This rate was then applied to all products from the company's factory. There was no need to buy any new equipment for making the red cabbage salad, and there was spare capacity available for the estimated production of the new "complete meal" product. The estimated sales of the new product were included in the budgeted sales quantity.

The Finance Department claimed that any departure downwards from the rate of D.Cr. 1.20 per kilogram for production fixed expenses would result in an undercoverage of fixed expenses. The Marketing Department replied that a strict application of this rule would lead to unreasonable consequences in this case, where a relatively cheap component (red cabbage) is added to an expensive component (sliced pork in gravy), and where the cheap component more than doubles the weight of the new pack and thus also doubles the fixed burden charged to the product. The Finance Department stated that it would be impractical to use different burden rates per kilogram for different products. It was supported in this view by the managing director, who said that the product should not be introduced if a normal selling price calculation did not show an operating profit.

The Marketing Department responded that selling the new product at D.Cr. 8.20 per pack was out of the question; therefore, only two alternatives remained:

1. Abandon the whole project.
2. Establish a consumer price of D.Cr. 6.85 and a price to the retailer of D.Cr. 4.78. The 8 percent margins and discounts to wholesalers and the 4 percent general overhead would then amount to 0.38 + 0.19 instead of 0.46 + 0.23, a reduction of 0.12. If the production fixed expense were then reduced from 1.20 to 0.54, the same amount as for one

standard pack of sliced pork in gravy, expenses in the selling price calculation would then be reduced by a total of 0.78. This is almost exactly the necessary reduction of 0.79 mentioned earlier.

The managing director decided in spite of the Marketing Department's arguments that the new product should not be introduced without full coverage of fixed expenses. It was introduced at a consumer price of D.Cr. 8.20, and the sales budget was set at eighty-five metric tons. (A metric ton is equal to 1,000 kilograms.) This was about 45 percent of the budgeted sales of the standard pack of sliced pork in gravy, which reflected the assumption that the upward sales trend of recent years would continue. In other words, the company did not expect that the new "complete meal" product would steal sales from the standard pack. Some customers would certainly switch over from the old product to the new, but these losses would be offset by the added sales resulting from greater consumer awareness of Minox products due to the planned advertising campaigns for the "complete meal" item.

In the months that followed, a number of complaints about the high price of the new product were received from retailers and consumers, and sales for the first year amounted to only thirty tons in contrast to the budgeted eighty-five tons. Sales of the standard pack, on the other hand, exceeded the budgeted amount by a small percentage.

3

Marketing Management

In this course, the fundamental question that serves as an integrating element is:

> What does the manager need to know to plan, execute, and control effectively the activities associated with the sale and distribution of the firm's products and/or services?

The primary objective of the course is to develop skills in solving complex problems dealing with marketing variables, particularly in areas such as:

Identification and Quantification of Market
Opportunities
Planning Marketing Strategy and Tactics
Evaluation of Effectiveness

Distinguishing characteristics of the course:

1. Proceeds from the general to the specific, e.g., start with role of marketing in the firm—the general framework for marketing planning—market analysis and tools to aid in decision-making and ends up with detailed strategy and tactics cases. Frequently marketing is examined in the reverse order.

139

2. Integration of new technology of planning, evaluation, and research throughout the course, e.g., use of models of buyer behavior, computer simulation models for planning and evaluation of strategy. A more typical approach leaves much of this material out or else covers it in special sessions that have been set aside for the purpose.

The advantage of this approach is greater credibility of value of analytical tools and research as aids to decision-making—realization that the manager needs to know about potentials and limitations in order to use them effectively and work with specialists who develop them.

The major areas to be covered in this course are:

I. *Introduction to Marketing Management*
   Introduction
   Implementation of the Marketing Concept
   Planning in Marketing
   Marketing Management and Management Science Techniques
   Analysis of Market Opportunity
   Quantification of Market Potentials
   Marketing Information and Sales Forecasting Systems
   Marketing Research
   Marketing Organization
II. *Strategies and Tactics*
   Product Life Cycles and Product Strategies
   Pricing Strategies
   Distribution Strategies
   Personal Selling
   Advertising and Promotion
   Development of the Total Marketing Plan
   Social and Economic Considerations

LAUNDROWASH S.p.A. (A)

In February 1961, Mr. Mario Paino, owner of Laundrowash S.p.A., was wondering what price schedules he should set for his new Turin automatic laundry. Laundrowash S.p.A., which was scheduled to open May 9, 1961, was to be the first American-style automatic coin-operated laundry in Italy.

Mr. Paino, a successful Italian investor living in Rome, had recently acquired the Speed Wash coin-operated laundry equipment franchise for Italy. After acquiring the franchise, he had made many attempts to interest Italian investors in coin-operated laundries, but each time these attempts were greeted with skepticism. Many investors were interested but felt the market risks of this radical new service were too great to justify their making the first move. After a number of unsuccessful attempts to interest investors, Mr. Paino decided to form a corporation called Laundrowash S.p.A. and open his own Speed Wash coin-operated laundry. Although his main objective remained to distribute coin-operated equipment, he felt that a successfully operating laundry would provide the evidence he needed to convince investors that coin-ops could be profitable in Italy.

Definition and Development of Coin-ops in the U.S.

The term "coin-op" developed in the United States. It was used there to describe unattended (or attended by one clerk) laundries where customers operated automatic washers, dryers, and soap and bleach dispensers themselves by dropping coins in the appropriate slots. In a coin-operated laundry, each machine was equipped with a coin meter that automatically operated the machine when the correct amount of change was inserted.

In the United States, the forerunners of coin-ops were "laundrettes." The laundrette was a laundry where the customers' clothes were washed by laundry attendants. This type of laundry offered a same-day, rough-dry service where the clothes were simply washed by machine and dried in an automatic dryer. Usually, they also offered a more expensive "semi-finished" service where clothes were hand folded after drying. Although most laundrettes used automatic equipment, their labor cost for attendants limited their ability to compete on a price basis with coin-ops. It also limited the hours per day that they could remain open, so that their costs were not spread over a twenty-four-hour day. Because of their higher cost structure, the cost per pound to the housewife was greater than that of the coin-ops.

Coin-ops were first introduced in the U.S. at the close of World War II. Their installation was on a small scale, however, and made little market impression. Initial attempts to establish them on a large scale failed, partly because then existing machines and metering devices were unreliable.

With rising labor costs and development of effective coin-metering equipment and more reliable machines, the way was open for the installation of self-service laundries in America. The business got its start in California, where people were more accustomed to self-service facilities. By 1958, an estimated 4,000 to 5,000 coin-ops were spread over the country, and new ones were being established at the rate of one per day.

In early 1960, *Coin-Op Magazine* estimated that there were 25,000 automatic laundries in the U.S., and that during the year another 3,000 would open their doors. Using an average figure of 20 machines per laundry, this meant that there were 500,000 coin-operated machines in the U.S. in January of 1960, and expectations were that an additional 60,000 would be installed during the year. Throughout the rise of the coin-ops, annual sales of four million automatic machines for home use remained steady.

One of the reasons for this rapid growth, according to *Barrons,*[1] was the lower cost to the housewife.

> A housewife can wash a load of clothes in one (coin-operated machine) for 10 or 20 cents, and she can use a dryer that will take up to four loads of washing for 1 cent per minute. Indeed, all her laundering for a week can be done in an hour for no more than $1.25, or far less than the payments on a washing machine of her own.

In 1960, the average prices in the U.S. were less than 25 cents per wash, and 10 cents per five-minute drying cycle.

In America, small investors were attracted to coin-ops by the low initial cash outlay, the small claim on their time, and the prospect of a high return on investment. ALD Inc., the largest equipment supplier to the trade, estimated that a laundry containing twenty regular 9 lb. (4-kilo) automatic

---

[1] November 10, 1958. *Barron's* is a well-known U.S. financial publication.

machines and one large 25 lb. (11-kilo) machine for rugs, eight dryers, and all necessary auxiliary equipment such as changemakers, water softeners, boilers, heaters, and sinks would cost, completely installed, $23,000. Another estimate of laundry costs was made by an appraisal bulletin published in January, 1959, which suggested that on the average the total cost of all equipment and installation charges averaged about $700 per washer. Using this guide, the total investment for the average twenty machine laundry in the U.S. was around $14,000. It further reported:

> Income and operating information is rather sketchy, but we have obtained figures in St. Louis from what we consider reliable sources. A good average sized coin-up in the St. Louis area will gross about $15,000 during this year. In order to do this volume of business, the laundry would have to be in a good location and should operate 24 hours a day, 365 days a year. We found a few coin-ops gross as high as $30,000 per year.
>
> Insofar as the expenses are concerned, on a coin-op doing an annual gross of $15,000, the breakdown will be about like this:

	Monthly	*Yearly*
Rent	$100	$1,200
Utilities	200	2,400
Maintenance	50	600
Insurance (including vandalism coverage)	30	360
Taxes	10	120
Miscellaneous	150	1,800
	$540	$6,480

The Italian Market

After forming Laundrowash S.p.A. in 1960 to operate the first coin-op laundry in Italy, Mr. Paino's first step was to investigate potential cities as sites for his automatic laundry. In checking market statistics, he quickly found that considerable variations existed in different regions. For example, average per capita Gross National Product for 1959 in Italy was listed as $545. In the same year a survey in the industrial north[2] revealed a much different figure: a sample of 97,000 workers in metallurgical and mechanical firms showed that payments to them averaged $2,200 per year including

---

[2] Turin Industrial Association, May 1959. Results published in *Setting up a Business in Italy*. Investment Information Office, Rome, 1960.

direct payments, indirect payments, and charges for social welfare. Statistics for the province of Turin, in the north, showed on car owner for every 22 persons while this figure for Nuovo, in comparatively backward Sardinia, was 272. The average figure for Italy of 77 (1956) was anything but indicative of the real picture. A close look at the figures confirmed Mr. Paino's conclusion that Italy was economically two countries: the highly developed north and the relatively underdeveloped south.

Because of the much higher living standards there, Mr. Paino decided to concentrate his search in northern Italy. In the north, Turin seemed the best choice for a number of reasons. Since 1946, the city had grown from 700,000 to over one million in population. With less than $\frac{1}{25}$ of the country's population, it paid almost 20 percent of the national tax bill. It was the fourth largest city in Italy, located in the heart of the industrial Po Valley where workers enjoyed a standard of living rivaling that of the most advanced European countries. After several visits to Turin, Mr. Paino concluded that it was a dynamic modern city. whose population was receptive to new ideas. Therefore, when he was offered a chance to sign a two-year lease for a 5 × 13 metre shop on Via Rosselli, he accepted with the thought of setting up his first coin-op laundry there.

The Site

Via Rosselli was a wide, tree-lined street at the southwest edge of Turin. A street plan of Turin showing the location of the automatic laundry and the other shops in the block is given in Exhibit 1. The area was predominantly residential with most families living in apartment buildings ranging from four to seven stories in height. All buildings within approximately 2,000 metres of the laundry appeared to be of postwar construction. The apartments in the immediate area were of excellent quality and had been constructed within the last five years. The average four-room apartment was renting for around $65 per month. There were no single unit dwellings in the area.

The inhabitants were mainly middle-class families, with a few professionals and managers. Occupationally, they were about evenly divided between office workers and skilled factory workers, with most families having more than one wage earner. Mr. Paino estimated that average family income was around $200 per month and that there was about one car for every twenty people in the area.

Turin was divided into twenty zones for statistical reporting. The automatic laundry site was located at the southern end of zone seventeen. Exhibit 2 shows population statistics for zone seventeen and total figures for all twenty zones.

Exhibit 1

Laundrowash S.p.A. (A)

Street Plan Showing the Site of the Automatic Laundry

Wine Shop	China Shop	Dress Shop	Baby Clothing Shop	Watch Shop	Furniture Shop	Automatic Laundry Shop	Health Center	Women's Purse Shop	Hard-Ware Shop	Cloth Shop	Sports Shop	Cloth. Shop

Via Rosselli

Coffee Bar & Billiard Hall	Butcher Shop	Shoe Shop	Fruit Shop	Milk Shop	Grocery Store	Vegetable Shop	Household Goods and Furniture Shop

←———— One city block ————→

Exhibit 2

Laundrowash S.p.A. (A)

Population Statistics for the proposed Laundrowash Zone[a]
(30 January, 1959)

	Blue Collar Workers		Office Workers		Managers		Self-employed		Self-employed Professionals		Part-time Workers		Non-Working Population		Total
	Number	%	Number	%	Number	%	Number	%	Number	%	Number	%	Number	%	
LAUNDROWASH Zone (17)	26,232	24.0	17,682	16.0	790	0.7	6,033	5.0	391	0.3	2,162	2.0	57,395	52.0	110,685
City Total (percentages only)		21.0		14.0		1.0		7.0		1.0		2.0		54.0	

[a] Note: For statistical reporting purposes, Turin was divided into twenty zones.
Source: Citta di Torino

146

Available Laundry Facilities

For the Turin housewife, there were three ways of getting her wash done. She could have it done by a "charwoman," do it herself at home, or send it to a commerical laundry. A great deal of washing was done by "charwomen" who charged from 200 (20.32) to 250 lire ($0.40) per hour plus soap. These women would come into homes and wash or would do the laundry in their own homes.

The housewife did her laundry at home by machine if she owned one, but since this was rare, the more usual method was by hand. Exhibit 3 shows washing machine sales and market saturation figures for Italy. Mr. Paino estimated that the saturation index for Turin was double the national average.

Exhibit 3   **Laundrowash S.p.A. (A)**

Washing Machine Sales and Saturation in Italy

	Sales			Saturation Index		
Year	Number (000)	Average price in lire	Total value in lire (000)	Household Units (000)	Number with machines (000)	Percentage with machines
1950	10	80,000	800,000	5,910	11	.18
1951	20	80,000	1,600,000	6,260	30	.49
1952	23	85,000	1,955,000	6,560	50	.76
1953	30	85,000	2,550,000	6,810	80	1.17
1954	40	90,000	3,600,000	7,300	115	1.57
1955	52	90,000	4,680,000	7,600	160	2.10
1956	74	100,000	7,400,000	8,000	225	2.80
1957	90	100,000	9,020,000	8,350	300	3.60
1958	120	110,000	13,200,000	8,700	400	4.60
1959	190	110,000	20,900,000	9,100	570	6.25

Source: Apparecchi Elettrodomestici, anno 111, No. 8, Agosto 1960, page 64.

There were approximately two-hundred commercial laundries in Turin. Their per-kilo rates for unfinished dry laundry ranged from 110 to 160 lire while finished rates per kilo were from 170 to 235 lire. Average finished piece rates ranged from 160–200 lire per shirt and from 130–150 lire per sheet.

Although confident that his laundry would succeed, Mr. Paino recognized that the success in the United States of coin-op laundries did not necessarily mean that they would be successful in Italy. The standard of living, for example, was different and there were definite customs and cultural patterns in Italy that might retard the early acceptance of the automatic laundry idea. Several people had pointed to the disappointing sales of supermarkets, which had recently opened in Turin, as an example of what was in store for other American ideas that were transplanted to Italy. Mr. Paino, however, felt that lessons learned from the supermarket experience supported his belief in the future of automatic laundries. He noted that especially among middle- and upper middle-class housewives it was a "status symbol" to be seen in a supermarket. By going to a supermarket, the housewife proved that she was "modern" and "up to date."

Housewives did not continue to trade in supermarkets, according to Mr. Paino, because the great majority were without cars and found supermarkets too inconvenient. He reasoned that the need to feel "modern" that motivated many women to try supermarkets would also motivate them to try an automatic laundry. Once they had tried them, he was convinced women would continue to use the laundries.

Investment Costs

Exhibit 4 was Mr. Paino's estimate of the cost of equipping and installing a laundry with sixteen 9 lb. (4-kilo) machines, one 25 lb. (11-kilo) rug washer, six dryers, and all necessary auxiliary equipment, leasehold improvements, and furniture. The estimated total investment cost of $30,900 shown in Exhibit 4 was almost double that of the average cost of an equivalent sized U.S. laundry.

Exhibit 4   **Laundrowash S.p.A. (A)**

Investment Required for Turin Automatic Laundry

Equipment	No. of Units	Cost per Unit	Total Cost
4-kilo Speed Wash washers with meter	16	$ 524	$8,384
11-kilo washer with meter	1	1,179	1,179
Speed Wash dryers with meter	6	758	4,548
Water extractor, with meter	1	758	758
Hot water storage tank	1	1,400	1,400
Water softener	1	2,213	2,213
Water heater	1	2,710	2,710
Soap and bleach dispenser	1	758	758
Outdoor electric sign	1	454	454
Indoor instructions signs		252	252
Furniture		179	179
Equipment total			22,835
Installation costs and leasehold improvements			8,065
Total investment required			$30,900

Mr. Paino observed that "clearly the reason for the high investment cost is the expensive imported auxiliary equipment." A typical example of the cost of importing was the hot water storage tank shown below:

All equipment in Exhibit 4 was imported. For the type of equipment

Cost of Imported Hot Water Storage Tank

U.S. Factory Cost	$ 592
Freight: Factory to New York	62
Freight: New York to Genoa	300
Duty and Misc. Import Taxes	406
Total Landed Cost in Italy	$1,360

necessary, no Italian source existed. Although Mr. Paino was concerned about the high costs, he was not completely discouraged. He did observe that "it is quite evident that if I am ever going to make a success of my Speed Wash franchise, I must find a cheaper Italian source of auxiliary equipment." He reasoned that investors would be concerned with the total cost of opening a laundry, and that lowering this figure by bringing down auxiliary equipment costs would lower the cost of entering the business and, therefore, make it more attractive as an investment.

The cost of importing washers was not so high as the cost of the auxiliary equipment. The landed cost in Genoa of a $215 (factory price) Speed Wash automatic washer was $325. Mr. Paino planned to sell these machines to coin-op investors at the landed price plus a 38 percent markup.

Mr. Paino's estimate of monthly operating expenses is shown below:

Estimated Monthly Operating Expenses

Fixed Expenses

Rent	$175
Maintenance	80
Salaries (attendants and janitor)	140
Insurance	30
Depreciation	500
	$925

Variable Expenses

Utilities (gas, fuel oil and electricity)
15% of gross wash and dry income

The depreciation figure was based on five-year straight-line (20 percent) rates applied against the estimated total investment of $30,900. The variable expense for utilities of 15 percent of gross wash and dry income was taken from an estimated income statement that ALD Inc. (the largest U.S. coin-op distributor) mailed to prospective investors. Italian electricity costs were about the same as those in America, but gas costs were higher. However, for estimating purposes, the 15 percent figure was considered satisfactory although Mr. Paino felt it might be on the low side.

Equipment Capacity

The 4-kilo washers had a twenty-minute cycle while the 11-kilo washer had a thirty-minute cycle. The dryers had five-minute cycles and were capable of drying the average 4-kilo load in two cycles. With a twenty-four-hour operation, therefore, the theoretical capacity of each washer was 72 loads per day, while each dryer had a theoretical capacity of 144 4-kilo loads per day. Loading time was the limiting factor on theoretical capacity. One estimate of actual washer capacity was published by ECON-O-WASH, a U.S. installer of coin-ops, who advised investors that a twenty-minute cycle would produce over 60 loads per day.

The supply vending machine was designed to sell packets of soap and bleach. An American laundry detergent could be imported and put up in individual wash packets at a total cost of 18 lire per packet. There was a possibility that an Italian manufacturer might be able to deliver an equivalent soap for 15 lire per package. Bleach was available at a price of 18 lire per packet.

Coin meters were available capable of accepting any combination of Italian coins, except five 100 lire coins or a single 500 lire coin.

Pricing

A critical problem for Mr. Paino was to decide what prices to charge for washing, drying, and supplies. Table I below shows Italian coins and their exchange value in U.S. dollars.

Table I

Italian Coins	U.S. $ Value (620 lire = $1)
5 lire	$0.008
10 "	0.016
20 "	0.032
50 "	0.08
100 "	0.16
500 "	0.80

In his attempt to select prices that would maximize long-run profitability, Mr. Paino was having considerable difficulty appraising elasticity of demand for his new service. He was aware of U.S. prices, but felt they were only a very rough guide in Italy, especially because of much higher Italian investment costs.

LAUNDROWASH S.p.A. (B)

In August 1961, Mr. Mario Paino reviewed his first few months of opera-tion and was concerned about what he could do to increase sales in his new laundry.[1] Mr. Paino had, three months earlier, opened in Turin what he believed to be the first American-style coin-operated automatic laundry in Italy. Initial results were extremely disappointing.

Mr. Paino had equipped the Turin laundry with sixteen Speed Wash 4-kilo washers, one 11-kilo washer, six dryers, one water extractor, and a soap and bleach dispenser. The laundry opened on May 9, 1961. Prices were L.200 for the 4-kilo washers, L.400 for the 11-kilo washer, L.50 for each five-minute dryer cycle, and L.50 per packet for the soap and bleach. The water extractor, which was equipped with a L.50 coin meter, was not used due to mechanical difficulties.[2] Hours of operation were from 8:00 to 12:00, and from 15:00 to 19:00, Monday through Saturday. Local regulations made it illegal to operate on Sunday.

Advertising and Promotion

Preopening advertising and promotion consisted of movie slides announc-ing Laundrowash, two pamphlets describing the new laundry, and free wash coupons, which were inserted with the two pamphlets into 1,000 mail boxes in the Via Rosselli area. Several days after the laundry opened, the slides were discontinued, and no more free wash coupons were distributed.

One of the pamphlets opened to three pages printed on both sides. An English translation of this pamphlet is reproduced in Appendix A. The second pamphlet was larger and opened to two pages printed on both sides. In addition to a large two-color picture of the interior of the laundry, it repeated most of the text of the three-page pamphlet.

---

1 See Laundrowash S.p.A. (A), p. 141.
2 As of mid-August, Mr. Paino had not been able to locate a mechanic who could repair the machine.

Exhibit 1

Laundrowash S.p.A. (B)
Laundrowash Sales

1961, week ending	Washing Operations			Income			Total	
	Paid	Free	Total	Washers Lire	Dryers Lire	Soap Lire	Lire	U.S.$ equivalent[a]
May 14	51	86	137	10,200	3,700	3,400	17,300	28.00
May 21	124	20	144	24,800	5,650	10,000	40,450	65.00
May 28	133		133	26,600	6,450	12,350	45,400	73.00
June 4	159	10	169	31,800	6,450	13,800	52,050	84.00
June 11	171	6	177	34,200	7,200	15,200	56,600	91.00
June 18	217	1	218	43,400	6,200	19,200	68,800	110.00
June 25	217		217	43,400	7,350	17,600	68,350	109.00
July 2	216	1	217	43,200	6,850	19,100	69,150	111.00
July 9	232		232	46,400	4,150	19,800	70,350	113.00
July 16	176		176	35,600	4,400	14,250	54,250	88.00
July 23	162		162	32,400	5,000	13,300	50,700	82.00
July 30	226		226	45,200	6,700	14,300	66,200	107.00
August 6	225		255	45,000	7,300	14,750	67,050	108.00

[a] One U.S.$ = L.620.
Source: Company Records.

There were 86 redemptions of free wash coupons during the first week of business. In the second week this number fell to 20, and in successive weeks it dropped to ten, 6, and 1. The last coupon was redeemed in July, bringing the total redemption to 124.

Operating Results

Laundrowash sales, including free washes, for the first thirteen weeks are shown in Exhibit 1. Although complete expense reports were not available, preliminary data indicated that fixed expenses were as expected ($925 per month, including $500 for depreciation), while variable expenses were around 13 to 14 percent of gross wash and dry income.

Mr. Paino was extremely discouraged by the laundry's performance. He estimated that for the month ending August 6, 1961, his "out-of-pocket" expenses exceeded income by almost $100, and that including depreciation, operating losses were at least $600.

As a rough estimate, Mr. Paino calculated that sales would have to increase to L.666,000 per month in order for the store to break even.[3] His break-even calculation, which is reproduced in Exhibit 2, was figured on the basis of washer and dryer operation only.

Exhibit 2　　　　**Laundrowash S.p.A. (B)**
Break-Even Calculation for Laundrowash S.p.A.[a]

Break-even: the point at which fixed plus variable expenses = total revenue.
Assumption: Each wash load L.200 ($0.32) is matched with 10 minutes drying time L.100 ($0.16) producing a total revenue of $0.48 per "load."
Let X = the number of break-even "loads" per month.
(Revenue per load × No. of loads = Fixed Costs + variable costs)

$$\$0.48(X) = \$\ 925 + (14\%)(0.48X)$$
$$0.48(X) = \$\ 925 + 0.0672X$$
$$0.4128X = \$\ 925$$
$$X = 2,240\ (\text{"loads"})$$

No. of break-even "loads" per month = 2,240
Break-even revenue per month　= $1,075 (L.666,500)
Break-even revenue per week　= $ 268 (L.166.622)

[a] Excluding soap, bleach, water extractor, and 11-kilo washer sales.
Source: Mr. Paino's records.

Mr. Paino was puzzled by the laundry's failure to achieve a profitable sales level. Although he was unhappy about the continuing losses, he remained firm in his belief that coin-ops could be profitable in Italy. He

---

[3] Break-even: the point at which fixed plus variable cost equals total revenue.

felt that a major problem was educating people to accept coin-ops. For example, women were observed entering Laundrowash with their laundry concealed in suitcases because they were afraid of being seen on the street with dirty laundry.

Mr. Paino wondered if an advertising and promotion campaign was needed to overcome the public's resistance to coin-ops. One promotion possibility was a formal opening ceremony with the dignitaries from the U.S. Consulate and Italian Foreign Trade Department as guests of honor.

APPENDIX A

LAUNDROWASH S.P.A. (B)

Text of Laundrowash Pamphlet

(Translation from the Italian by Miss G. Schori).

Page 1: Announcing a shop for Automatic Laundry equipped with commercial laundry machines.
Welcome neighbors !! to your Speed Wash automatic laundry, open every day of the week.

Page 2: Welcome neighbors!
To your Speed Wash self-service laundry, designed and furnished only for you, yes, it is your shop, and you should feel right at home. Now you can do your own laundry just as you do at home, with the assurance that there are plenty of machines, big dryers, and unlimited hot and soft water. You can save 50% doing your laundry this way.

Finished are the days when you have to do laundry in small loads. Now you can use as many washing machines as you need, and you will be through with your laundry in less than an hour.
The cost is so little that it would be more expensive to do it at home even if you had a free washing and drying machine. We can save you money, because we do not need to pay personnel. We offer you this saving and reduce the cost of your laundry.

Page 3: The four ingredients of a good wash:
A really good wash requires:
—a good plant
—a good detergent
—plenty of hot water
—soft water

Our laundry is furnished with the best equipment available, constructed with the utmost care by Speed Wash. The Speed Wash washer does not have an agitator that damages your laundry, and dirty water is removed so that it does not go through your laundry as it does in conventional machines. You need 77 litres of water at 80° C to wash 4 kilograms dry weight. The heaters you have in your house have a capacity ranging from 80–120 litres of which only 45 to 50 litres are warm enough to provide a good wash. You would need at least 6 hours to wash a weekly laundry of 20 kilos because you would have to wait for your boiler to heat the water. The Speed Wash laundry has enough water to provide continuous washing for each machine in the laundry.

Page 4: To dry your laundry at home you need many hours. Instead your Speed Wash laundry has big commercial dryers which circulate your laundry in a big cylinder drying it quickly and giving a soft dry wash.

The water used on the Speed Wash automatic laundry is as filtered and soft as rain water. We use soft water because hard water minerals make the soap less efficient and leave deposits. The Speed Wash machine NEEDS LESS THAN ONE CUP OF DETERGENT.

The reason this is so is that with soft water you get a better wash with less soap. This is another saving for you.

DO NOT USE TOO MUCH DETERGENT: you will only get too many bubbles.

Your Speed Wash automatic laundry was created to lighten your work and lessen your fatigue, from the boring days you spent doing laundry. Remember that this is your neighborhood washing place. Cooperate with your neighbors to make it and keep it a nice and gay place where you can do your weekly laundry.

Page 5: You will obtain a whiter and cleaner wash using the Speed Wash commercial laundry. This laundry uses purified soft water that is as soft as rain.

Page 6: The woman who wants the best of everything uses the Speed Wash Laundrowash.
—You will get a better wash than you get at home.
—You can do your entire weekly wash in an hour by using several machines.
—You will get scientifically clean, deodorized clothes with machines that are frequently sterilized.

—You can dry your clothes cheaply and quickly.

—You can do the laundry yourself with all the advantages and none of the disadvantages of home.

—You will reduce the cost of your wash by 50% and do your wash in a pleasant atmosphere with your friends and neighbors.

LAUNDROWASH S.p.A. (C)

In December 1961, Mr. Mario Paino reported the following sales for his Turin coin-operated laundry:

Week Ending		Gross Sales Lire
August	4	67,050
"	11	60,250
"	18	51,800
"	25	80,350
September	1	83,200
"	8	87,500
"	15	119,850
"	22	154,500
"	29	162,000
October	6	154,950
"	13	146,250
"	20	186,700
"	27	178,500
November	3	228,050
"	10	190,750
"	17	205,550
"	24	191,750
December	1	208,250
"	8	209,000
"	15	243,650

Two changes had been introduced at the laundry. Early in September, a point system was inaugurated whereby a woman received a small card valued at one point each time she used a washer; twenty points entitled the customer to a free wash, while one hundred points could be redeemed for a small three-wheeled cart.[1]

In December over eight thousand points had been distributed, and twenty-two free washes had been claimed. Mr. Paino felt that the point system had a tremendous incentive effect on housewives.

---

[1] The cost of the carts to Mr. Paino was 1200 Lire.

157

The second change involved hours of operation, which were extended on October 1. Instead of operating Monday through Saturday from 8:00 to 12:00 and 15:00 to 19:00, Mr. Paino kept the laundry open continuously from 8:00 to 22:00 Monday through Saturday, and from 9:00 to 12:00 on Sunday. Although local regulations forbade Sunday business, he planned to continue Sunday operations until he was ordered to stop.

TINTA N.V.[1]

In the Autumn of 1957, Mr. W. M. Jansen, Account Executive for the Holland branch of the American advertising agency Woodhouse-Pearsen, Inc., was assigned the task of creating a successful brand image for "Tinta," a do-it-yourself hair dye produced by a major Dutch cosmetics manufacturer. Extensive brand image promotion was to be the main effort in the Tinta sales campaign, starting at the beginning of 1958.

The Woodhouse-Pearsen office in Amsterdam, Holland had been established in 1952 to represent the parent company with headquarters in Chicago, Illinois, U.S.A. The Amsterdam office employed approximately eighty people; smaller Woodhouse-Pearsen branches were maintained in The Hague and Rotterdam with staffs of fifteen to twenty employees each.

In addition to some major Dutch clients, the agency worked with Dutch branches of American concerns such as licensed manufacturers, exclusive agents, and service organizations. This manner of operation had greatly stimulated Woodhouse-Pearsen's growth in Holland since these American subsidiaries and representatives liked working with a progressive advertising agency that provided an American approach to publicity, together with a capable Dutch staff of copywriters and researchers. This efficient American-European approach had attracted major Dutch clients.

Mr. Jansen, Account Executive, (see Appendix C for organization chart) handled the accounts of:

1. Snel N.V., the licensed Dutch manufacturer of the American pharmaceutical company Whitney and Luke, Inc.
2. Visser N.V., makers of "Ramex," a portable dictating machine.
3. Bettinger Rubber Company N.V., who manufactured the "Diana" Tires for cars and trucks.
4. Richter N.V., a well-known company in Dutch heavy industry.
5. Tinta N.V., a large cosmetics manufacturer, known for its "Tinta" hair dye.

---

[1] N.V. (Naamloze Venootschap), a limited liability company or corporation.

The Tinta account had come to Woodhouse-Pearsen in early 1956. Since that date the agency had successfully handled all advertising and sales promotion work for Tinta do-it-yourself toning, dyeing, and blonding hair creams.[2] These products combined a shampoo and hair dye into one operation that could easily be applied by the user at home in thirty minutes. According to the manufacturer's description, Tinta treatments would remain effective from two to three weeks. The cream, which was packed in 80-gram tubes, was available in "natural" colors such as blond, black, and brown and in a wide range of "fashion" colors including titian, ashblond, copper, mauve, and red.

In September 1957, Tinta's president, Mr. W. H. Otten, and Mr. Jansen had had several meetings to appraise Tinta's market position and to prepare plans for an aggressive 1958 advertising campaign. In a report to the Amsterdam office manager, Mr. Jansen summarized his meetings with Mr. Otten and concluded that several marketing and promotion problems were handicapping his assignment of creating a successful Tinta brand image for 1958.

Tinta had almost 100 percent of the do-it-yourself hair dye market in Holland. As of September 1957, Tinta products were still only available in such retail outlets as druggists and perfumeries, since Mr. Otten did not believe the institutional outlets, (hairdressers, beauty shops), would be interested in selling Tinta products. Also, he thought that even if the institutional outlets carried the Tinta line, they would not generate a significant sales volume. Mr. Otten also felt that by using these outlets, he might antagonize his major hair dye competitor, Tobi N.V., who sold exclusively to the institutional market. He feared that by "encroaching" upon Tobi's territory, he might provoke Tobi introducing a competing line of do-it-yourself hair dyes. Since Tobi's net sales were estimated by Mr. Otten to be ten times those of Tinta, he was anxious to avoid direct competition with Tobi. Thus for marketing and competitive reasons, Tinta N.V. distributed its products to wholesalers and retailers only, dividing sales equally between them.

Distribution of Tinta Hair Dyes in Holland[a]

Outlets	Total Clients	Prospective Clients	% Distribution
Drugstores	11,300	11,500	98%
Perfumeries, department stores	2,830	3,000	94%

a Source: Woodhouse-Pearsen Company files 100 Dutch Florin = Swiss Francs 120

2 The toning cream slightly reinforced or deemphasized hair color (i.e., "touched up"), the dyeing cream completely changed hair color, and the blonding cream maintained or emphasized natural or dyed blond hair. Collectively, these creams were referred to as hair dyes.

Tinta's president was primarily looking for stability in sales, a peaceful relationship with the Tobi company, and a brand image readily acceptable by Dutch middle-class customers. Mr. Jansen pointed out, however, that this policy was unrealistic in view of Tinta's market position and conflicted directly with Mr. Otten's expressed desire "to put new life into Tinta, and to bring our product into the hands of every Dutch woman. . . ." Mr. Jansen therefore suggested that beginning with 1958, Tinta should sell to institutional outlets too. He pointed out that a customer often sought a hairdresser's expert advice in selecting a hair dye. As a result of Tobi's dominant position in the institutional market, however, hairdressers were often known to remark disparagingly about Tinta's products and to claim that "Tinta makes your hair brittle" or "affects your scalp" or "a Tinta hair treatment does not last longer than a week." The attitude of these hair dressers towards Tinta was not improved by the company's failure to attempt distribution through these institutional outlets.

Mr. Jansen warned Tinta's president that Tobi N.V. might very well decide to introduce do-it-yourself hair dyes; in that case Tobi would certainly aim for distribution through drugstores and perfumeries and present massive competition in Tinta's traditional type of outlets.

The Tobi company, with an advertising budget of Fl. 9–10.5 million had always followed an aggressive advertising and merchandising policy when introducing new products or announcing a new hair dye color. Tinta, on the other hand, never formally publicized a new product; it merely appeared among a salesman's samples during a customer call. The company customarily spent approximately 10 percent of net sales on advertising and promotion. Mr. Otten feared that any sudden change in Tinta's publicity might indicate to competitors that his company aimed to increase sales. In spite of this conservative policy, Tinta's outstanding quality and attractive prices had accounted for the company's steadily-increasing sales. A Tinta tube of hair cream for home application retailed at Fl. 1.50 while the charge for a comparable Tobi hair dye treatment at a beauty shop ranged from Fl. 17 to Fl. 26.

Mr. Jansen thought that in the future Tinta might even consider increasing its price to Fl. 2.50 per tube. A higher retail price would permit the company to enlarge its advertising budget, while a more expensive Tinta product would carry a definite prestige appeal on the market. Mr. Jansen felt that a higher price might also help induce hairdressers and beauty shop operators to carry Tinta products. He stressed the fact that Tinta should adopt a more aggressive pricing policy.

Mr. Otten and Mr. Jansen discussed whether Tinta's "coupon for free sample" plan should be continued in 1958. As a stimulant to sales, the Tinta company had been using coupons in its magazine advertisements since 1956. Each coupon could be exchanged for a free regular-sized sample tube of Tinta hair dye. Mr. Jansen did not favor a continuation of this promotional method since the expenses of the plan were deducted from Tinta's annual advertising budget. From a merchandising point of view, Mr. Jansen considered the plan cumbersome and expensive, as well as relatively unproductive of results. He estimated that total free samples accounted for 5–10 percent of annual Tinta sales and presented the following figures on company experience with free samples through coupons:

1955—Of a total $3\frac{1}{2}$ million units produced, 270,000 were given away.

1956—Of a total 4.4 million units produced, 350,000 free samples were exchanged for coupons.

1957—(1/1–9/1) Total production amounted to 5.6 million units, of which 450,000 units were given away.

Mr. Jansen pointed out that Tinta's free sample campaign represented an annual charge of Fl. 178,500 to the company, including postage and wages for full-time coupon plan personnel. Although the company had not set a limit on free samples per customer, an audit showed that fewer than 1 percent of the coupons were returned by the same people. Mr. Jansen felt, however, that the company was actually losing sales through its coupon plan, rather than stimulating buying. He recommended that the plans be terminated at the end of 1957.

Since Tinta N.V. had been selling to drugstores and perfumeries only, possible future introduction of Tobi do-it-yourself hair dyes in these outlets could present serious competition to the Tinta company. At the end of 1957, it had thus become very important to create a distinct Tinta brand image that would firmly fix into customers' minds the advantages and qualities of a Tinta product. In this matter of brand image, Mr. Jansen's ideas conflicted with Mr. Otten's. Tinta's president was mainly interested in mass marketing and mass production and believed that his company's publicity should stress a conservative brand image, appealing to Holland's middle-income classes. This policy was reflected in Tinta's $\frac{1}{4}$ and $\frac{1}{2}$ page black-and-white advertisements and occasional full color ads, which had appeared regularly in women's fashion magazines and weekly newspapers. These advertisements featured much descriptive copy explaining the quality and use of the product; they commonly included the drawing of a female profile displaying an attractive hairdo. Mr. Jansen felt, however, that Tinta in looking for a striking brand image for 1958, should not continue the conservative repetition of black-and-white advertisements. He suggested that the company radically alter its policy and introduce full-page, four-color advertisements exclusively. These advertisements, with a minimum of descriptive copy, would feature large-size, actual photographs showing Tinta users in desirable luxurious settings.

A summer 1957 opinion study by the Woodhouse-Pearsen agency had indicated that, in spite of female readers' stated preference for "normal" and "everyday" situations in advertising, their greatest amount of attention was drawn to the "idealized," "dream-like" type of advertisements in magazines. The research department felt that the latter type of publicity was most likely to stimulate attention, interest, and buying, because it could sell a *promise* (beauty) or an *illusion*; such advertisements would appeal to women *emotionally,* not rationally. Mr. Otten disagreed, saying "Women want a hair dye that is foolproof, easy and uncomplicated to apply, and offers a wide variety of colors. Therefore these selling points should be the basic advertising ideas, not—as the agency suggests—'a promise of beauty.' This is too vague an argument and one that could be used by any cosmetics manufacturer."

Mr. Jansen suggested the creation of a high-class brand image for Tinta's 1958 sales campaign. He believed that once the impression had been conveyed that women in the upper-income classes accepted hair dyeing as a common practice, this example would be more readily accepted by middle-income customers. Mr. Jansen observed that "in order to sell color, one must show color" and as examples of Tinta's new style proposed the following samples of advertisements:

—a dignified looking woman wearing a white mink stole displaying a mauve-tinted hairdo in an "opera" setting;

—an attractive red-haired girl behind the wheel of an expensive convertible;

—a beautiful young woman with gold blond hair lounging on the deck of a sailboat.

This type of advertisement, Mr. Jansen felt, should supplement in two-week intervals the black-and-white advertisements in women's magazines during the remaining months of 1957. Early in 1958 they would replace black-and-white advertisements entirely and feature Tinta products exclusively in women's home and fashion magazines.

As part of its 1958 Tinta publicity presentation, the Woodhouse-Pearsen marketing and research departments had prepared two extensive research reports. Mr. Jansen felt that these studies, summaries of which are presented in Appendices A and B, factually substantiated his recommendations for the new Tinta campaign. A survey of Dutch advertising media costs is reproduced in Appendix A.

APPENDIX A

Tinta Market Study I[1]

This study mainly concerned an analysis of the 1957 Tinta advertisements in Dutch publications. It investigated the feasibility of four-color advertisements during the second half of 1957, and for 1958.

---

1 Woodhouse-Pearsen Company files.

In 1957 our selected publications reached 87 percent of all female readers, i.e., 60 percent of the total female adult population (i.e., over the age of 16). We concentrated our advertisements in those media read in the more densely populated areas and aimed at a "key" group of customers, i.e., women of all ages and from all social classes. This means that a total of 2,300,000 women were approached by Tinta advertisements from a total of 2,650,000 female readers.

Our advertisements appeared in women's home and fashion magazines, and were repeated every three to four weeks.

During the second half year in 1957, we had a budget for Tinta of Fl. 57,406 at our disposal. We intend to make the following monthly advertisement allotments:

July	Fl. 10,033
August	12,449
September	13,616
October	13,854
November	7,454
	Fl. 57,406

We propose to distribute our funds among eleven publications as follows:

Newspapers		
Het Vrije Volk-Landelijk	Fl.	4,922
De Telegraef		5,853
Nieuwe Rotterdamse Courant		3,111
De Volkskrant		3,272
Neerlandia Pers		1,855
Ladies' Fashion and Home Journals		
Margriet		16,334
Libelle/Beatrijs		10,512
Eva		7,571
Rosita		2,431
Moeder		1,449
Plattelandsvrouw		90

We believe the advantages of this policy to be:

1. A substantial amount in discounts dependent upon the volume of advertising.
2. A cautious reminder through the repetition of our advertisements each three to four weeks in these magazines (each two weeks in women's magazines). Tinta advertisements will thus not easily be forgotten.

As a disadvantage we note the fact that small size black-and-white advertisements command less attention than actual photo, four-color advertisements.

We therefore suggest the use of color advertisements for which we list the following advantages and disadvantages:

Pro

—Large-size color advertisements create a lasting impression; in addition we intend to continue our small-size black-and-white advertisements until the end of 1957.

—The introduction of color advertisements now would be a preparation for our 1958 sales campaign, which would exclusively feature four-color advertisements.

—We would reduce the number of publications used to five, total issue of two million; this is still more than 50 percent of the eleven papers we intend to use during the second half of 1957.

Con

—We are selling a "continuous" thought, which would be repeated each three to ten weeks, thus reminding readers irregularly.

—We will have to limit the number of publications we use and must concentrate on a "general" type of magazine, not so much on women's papers.

—Our total bookings will be reduced, and we stand to lose approximately Fl. 6,615.

—During the second half of 1957, the publishers will increase their rates; this may cause us a loss of approximately Fl. 4,410 to Fl. 5,512.

—There will be a reduction in the number of publications to which we subscribe.

—We will achieve a concentrated color impact in a small number of publications, rather than a more widespread black-and-white impact in a large number of newspapers.

—By concentrating on color advertisements only in a smaller number of publications, we stand to lose approximately Fl. 12,127 in rebates; this would account for about 21 percent of our total 1957 rebates at Fl. 57,330 and would represent more than two full-page, (i.e., two page spread), color advertisements.

—We therefore recommend till the end of 1957 a combination of color and black-and-white advertising; we would favor a combination of four-color advertisements in papers one to three.

The report concluded with statistical information regarding:

1. Consumer preference for color over black-and-white advertisements in leading U.S. magazines.
2. Tinta's advertising budget 1955–1957.
3. A comparison of Tinta's and Tobi's monthly advertising expenses in 1957.

4. The total market for beauty aids in Holland.
5. A breakdown of expenses by type of beauty aids used.

Table 1   **A Comparison of Consumer Preference
for Color over Black-and-White
Advertisements in Leading U.S. Magazines**

	Black-and-White 1 page spread	Four colors, full-spread	Advantage of color
Collier's	100	114.3	14.3
Saturday Evening Post	100	135.2	35.2
Life	100	109.9	9.9
Color favorite by an average of 19.8			

Table 2   **Tinta's Advertising Budget 1955–1957**
A Breakdown by Media
(in Fl.)

	1955	1956	1957
Insertions	121,391	151,924	149,071
Printed matter	4,410	6,726	8,820
Point of sale	20,947	20,727	35,170
Movie slides	22,050	22,711	27,783
Reserve	7,601	9,922	10,950
Market research	—	2,646	2,977
Market consultation	9,922	11,025	11,025
Miscellaneous	—	6,394	3,087
	186,321	232,075	248,883

**Table 3   A Comparison of Tinta and Tobi
Monthly Magazine Advertising Expenses in 1957**

Months	Tinta Fl.	Tobi (Est.) Fl.
January	9,877	2,317
February	3,785	50,049
March	14,131	174,602
April	21,701	139,600
May	17,864	171,774
June	16,883	175,069
July	17,856	169,126
August	18,129	131,867
September	27,644	173,693
October	9,497	233,375
November	15,214	186,297
December	3,532	26,544
Total	176,113	1,634,313

Table 4   Total Market for Beauty Aids in Holland
1952–1957
(in millions of Fl.)

1952	55
1953	65
1954	74
1955	83
1956	103
1957	120

Table 5   1956 Expenses[a] on Beauty Aids in Holland
Breakdown by Type
(in millions of Fl.)

Head and hair	35.00
Skin	20.00
Perfume, etc.	18.00
Teeth	13.00
Powder	6.00
Beauty, miscellaneous	3.00

[a] Does not include a number of beauty aids such as expensive beauty soaps, eye makeups, weight controls, etc.

APPENDIX B

Tinta Market Study II[1]

The purpose of this study was to gather up-to-date information about Tinta users in terms of: motivations for using a hair dye, personality of user, hairdresser-vs.-home application and user experiences with Tinta products; 1,553 women were interviewed.

Size city by number of inhabitants	*Percentage interviewed*
under 2,000	10%
2,000–5,000	7%
5,000–20,000	14%
20,000–100,000	17%
100,000–500,000	19%
over 500,000	33%
	100%

[1] Woodhouse-Pearsen Company files.

Sample questions asked during Market Study II:

1. "Which of the following beauty aids have you used?"

Total answers: 100%
No beauty aids used: 25%
Beauty aids used: 75%
   (Total answers will exceed 75% since more than one
   answer to each question was possible.)

Lipstick	65%
Face Powder	51%
Tinta toning cream for hair	13%
Tinty dyeing cream for hair	4%
Tinta blonding cream for hair	3%
Other hair treatments	11%
Nail polish	45%
Mascara	14%
Eyebrow pencil	38%

2. "Do you believe that a 'modern' woman can, by herself, satisfactorily tone, dye, blond or perma-wave her hair?"

	Tone	Dye	Blond	Perma-Wave
Yes	46%	18%	19%	34%
No	23%	46%	41%	40%
No Opinion	31%	36%	40%	26%
	100%	100%	100%	100%

3. "Do you think that the price for a Tinta tube (toning dyeing, blonding), is expensive, about right, or inexpensive?"

Answers	
Expensive	19%
Inexpensive	11%
About right	64%
No Opinion	6%
	100%

Conclusions of the Tinta Market Study II

1. *Motivations for the home use of Tinta Products* The expectations of a woman treating her hair with color culminate in the desire to have natural beauty for her hair. She wants beauty without striking changes and prefers "natural" changes to "fashionable" ones. The home treatment is stimulated by the product's low price; continual hair-dyeing at home is considerably cheaper than professional treatment at the hairdresser's.

2. *Tinta users belong to the middle-and lower-income classes* Most of them are self-employed and live in greater numbers in middle-sized cities than in large cities. The Tinta toning cream is particularly well-

liked by the 18–25 year and 36–50 year age groups. The dyeing and blonding cream is mainly used by the 36–50 year age group; the younger and older groups use these products less often. The Tinta Products' user can be described as a modern, life-loving, and sportive kind of woman, interested in outside life, next to her household work.

3. *Reaction toward using a Tinta dyeing, toning, or blonding product* The greatest amount of interest seems to exist for Tinta's toning cream. This was indicated by 61 percent of the women interviewed, 46 percent of whom stated that home application is possible. The least positive reaction concerns Tinta's blonding cream; opinions about this product differ according to social groups and age levels. Approximately 7 percent of the women questioned use a home toning product, 3 percent dye their hair and 2 percent blond it. The creams used in the present market situation, for home treatments, are almost exclusively Tinta products. For those women using Tinta products only sporadically, the results are: 13 percent use hair toning cream, 4 percent use Tinta cream for dyeing, and 3 percent demand a Tinta product for hair blonding.

4. *The "advice" from hairdresser and/or druggist* It seems that the hairdresser, for questions concerning hair treatment, enjoys more consumer confidence than the druggist. While the druggist is also considered as an expert, a visit to the hairdresser stems from a natural female wish to be served and cared for.

5. *Beauty shop versus home treatment* Dyeing, toning, and blonding all take place at the beauty shop; 2 percent of the women interviewed exclusively dye their hair themselves, 1 percent do this sporadically, and 15 percent visit the hairdresser for dyeing exclusively. A more favorable relation exists for home toning: 7 percent of the women use Tinta's toning cream and 18 percent go to the beauty shop. Visits to the hairdressers are frequent: 44 percent go regularly, while 21 percent make only occasional visits.

6. *Comments about the use of Tinta products* After some experimentation, women do not find it difficult to use Tinta products. With certain exceptions, the instructions enclosed with each tube are customarily followed by the user. Favorable results with Tinta products exceed unfavorable experiences. Exceptions are those users whose skin and/or hair type stand up less favorably under a Tinta treatment. The end result and the method of employment of Tinta products meet most women's desires regarding the home treatment of their hair.

The market study concluded that favorite colors were: gold blond, light blond, medium brown, and dark brown. Chestnut and medium blond were considered second choice. Liked and disliked in about equal proportions were silver white, mahogany, and hazelnut brown. Disliked were titian red, copper, black, and ash blond. Considered as uninteresting were dark blond, light brown, medium ash blond, and silver blue.

APPENDIX C

Organization Chart of Woodhouse-Pearsen, Inc.

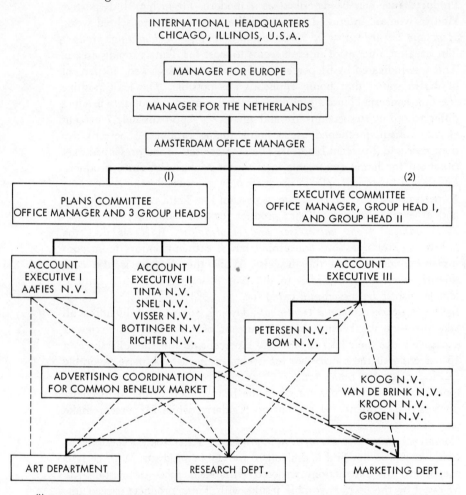

(1) Functions of the Plans Committee: "approve all creative plans which are presented to clients."

(2) Functions of the Executive Committee: (a) all law business; (b) company policy; (c) hiring and firing of executive personnel, including copy-writers; (d) all questions regarding billing, i.e., setting price for contracts with clients.

CHAMBREY CÉRAMIQUES S.A. (A)

Chambrey Céramiques S.A. of Paris, France was a large manufacturer of ceramic products, including domestic ware, sanitary ware, and various industrial ceramic products. Late in 1960 executives of Chambrey were approached by representatives of Allied Ceramics Inc., of Philadelphia, Pennsylvania, and offered exclusive continental European rights to manufacture a type of electronic resistor[1] developed and patented by Allied. On an initial appraisal, Chambrey management thought the proposition attractive; the resistors could well be a profitable addition to the company's line, and their manufacture was dependent on ceramics technology, a field in which Chambrey had considerable experience. They were hesitant to make a final decision, however, before they had specific detailed information on the potential market for such resistors in continental Europe. They were therefore considering initiating a research project to provide the necessary marketing information.

The Company

Chambrey was founded early in the nineteenth century as a family firm specializing in the manufacture of pottery. Over the years the company had grown and diversified to include the manufacture of other ceramic lines. By 1959, sales volume was about NF. 80,000,000, and the company employed about 2,500 people. The company was controlled by descendants of the founders, although a substantial portion of the common stock had been issued to the public at various times to finance expansion. All of Chambrey's manufacturing facilities were located in France, but sales were made to many European countries, particularly those that were members of the EEC.

---

[1] A brief description of this term and other basic electrical concepts is given in Appendix A.

Products

Domestic ware, including many kinds of household items ranging from fine bone china to cheaper earthenware were the dominant products in the company's line, accounting for about 50 percent of 1959 sales. These products were distributed to the retail trade in several European countries by various china, glass, and hardware wholesalers. A small Chambrey salesforce serviced the wholesaling organization.

Sanitary ware, primarily bathroom fittings, were another important line of products, accounting for about 25 percent of 1959 sales. A direct salesforce sold this line to plumbing supply houses and some large contractors.

The final major line of products included the insulating and corrosion-resistant porcelains sold primarily to the chemical and electrical industries. This product line ranged from porcelain apparatus and piping for the chemical industry to insulating porcelains for the use of the electrical industry in the manufacture of such products as plugs, switches, and electronic sets and components. Some of these products, such as the chemical apparatus, were fairly well standardized, but others were manufactured to suit the particular needs of a user. A combination of direct sales and sales through specialized dealers handling electrical or laboratory supplies was used to distribute this line. These products accounted for about 20 percent of Chambrey's 1959 sales and were the fastest growing and most profitable of the company's lines.

Resistors

The manufacture and sale of resistors seemed to Chambrey executives to be a reasonable extension of their present line of industrial ceramic products. An intimate knowledge of ceramics and ceramics technology was necessary to make the resistors developed by the Allied Company. The manufacturing process, as explained by the Allied representatives, consisted of several steps. First, a special ceramic composition was made and extruded into long, thin rods. These rods formed the base of the resistor. Second, a film of metal oxide was fused to the ceramic base; this film was the conducting medium of the resistor. Third, the film was spiraled, i.e., portions of the coating were removed so the electric current would have to travel a predetermined distance in passing through the resistor; the spiraling, the type of material of the film, and the thickness of film determined the ohmic resistance of the resistor. Fourth, the long rod was cut in proper length to produce a number of resistors. Finally, wire leads were attached to the ends of the resistors and an insulating coat was applied to protect the film.

The Allied Proposal

For initial manufacturing and selling in the European market, it was proposed that Chambrey execute only the third, fourth, and fifth production steps. The ceramic rod with fused film would be imported from Allied in the United States. In this way, the very high investment necessary to manufacture the ceramic rod and to fuse the film would be avoided, or at least postponed until the market possibilities had been fully explored. Chambrey executives estimated that the investment in plant and equipment necessary to carry out the latter three stages of manufacture would be about NF. 750,000. The equipment necessary for the first two stages would require an additional investment of about NF. 3,000,000. Production and royalty costs, which would be almost wholly variable for the last three stages, were roughly estimated by Chambrey management at about 70 percent of the probable selling price of the various ratings of resistors.

The resistors produced by the Allied process reportedly had characteristics superior to many resistors currently on the market. For example, their precision and stability were reported to be far better than almost all the graphite or carbon composition resistors on the market. However, in general, they were more expensive to make than other types of resistors and had to be sold at considerably higher prices (see Appendix A).

Chambrey executives speculated that users of resistors would seek to achieve some sort of balance between the desired technical characteristics (in which they thought there was generally a reasonable amount of freedom) and cost. Because of this, they thought it would be necessary to have a fairly precise knowledge of the needs of the users of resistors before estimates of potential sales could be made and before production or marketing strategy could be planned. For example, they thought they would need to know what particular types and quantities of resistors were chosen for specific tasks, why these resistors were favored, and how the Allied line of resistors matched the needs of the market.

Available Information

Other than a general knowledge of the electronics industry (such as is presented in Appendix B), Chambrey executives had little specific information on resistor users or makers in their hands. They were aware that the Allied Company had achieved excellent sales and profits with the resistors in question in the United States, but they were not sure that such experience would be duplicated in Europe. The Allied representatives, who were familiar only with the American market, were unable to provide specific information on the European market.

A factor that accentuated management's desire for information was their belief that manufacturing and selling resistors would be a departure from the traditional role of the company in supplying ceramic products to the electrical equipment industry. Historically, Chambrey was a manufacturer of subassemblies for use in the industry; the adoption of resistors was viewed as a change in Chambrey's role from that of an outside supplier to one of active participation in the industry.

Chambrey management had no internal marketing research organization on which they could call to provide the needed information. They were considering initiating a research project to be done by a professional research organization to provide the necessary information.

APPENDIX A

CHAMBREY CÉRAMIQUES S.A. (A)

Some Basic Electrical Concepts

An understanding of the function of resistors in electrical circuits rests on a knowledge of some basic electrical concepts. A brief description of these concepts follows, with a description of the major characteristics and types of resistors.

1. *Electromotive force (e.m.f.)* This is the electrical force that causes a flow of electrons (current) in an electric circuit. This force can be developed in many ways, e.g., by chemical action in dry cell batteries or mechanical action in a generator. The unit e.m.f. is the volt—thus a six-volt battery provides a source of e.m.f. equal to six volts.
2. *Circuit* Before useful work can be performed by the e.m.f., a circuit must be available through which the electric current can travel. An electric circuit must always be complete, that is, it must start at the source of the e.m.f., go through the load or loads it is energizing (e.g., toasters, light bulbs, vacuum cleaners) and then return to its starting point. The material through which the current actually flows in a circuit is called a conductor.
3. *Current* The term current used in the preceding descriptions refers to the flow of electrons through an electrical circuit. The unit for current is called the ampere—thus we say that the current in a circuit is five amperes.
4. *Resistance* All electrical circuits and loads are composed of conductors in one form or another. Every conductor possesses some degree of resistance to the flow of current. Such resistance is found in all electrical

circuits in varying degree, depending on such factors as the length of the circuit, cross-sectional area, the materials used and the particular characteristics of the loads. The unit of resistance is called the ohm.

5. *Relationship of e.m.f., current, and resistance* These three factors are related in an electrical circuit by Ohm's law, the equation:

$$E = IR \qquad \text{where } E = \text{e.m.f. in volts}$$
$$I = \text{current in amperes}$$
$$R = \text{resistance in ohms}$$

6. *Voltage drop* Voltage drop occurs when a current flows through a resistance. For example, in the circuit drawn below the voltage across the terminals of the source of e.m.f. (measured by a voltmeter attached across *AB*) is six volts. If we assume that

$$R_2 = 2 \text{ ohms}$$

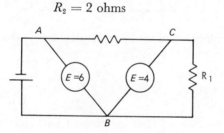

there is no resistance other than R_1, and R_2 in the circuit, that the resistance of R_2 is two ohms and that a current of one ampere is flowing, we can calculate the voltage drop across the resistance R_2 by:

$$E = IR \qquad \text{where } R_2 = 2 \text{ ohms}$$
$$I = 1 \text{ ampere}$$
$$E = 2 \text{ volts}$$

Therefore the voltage drop is two volts, and the remaining voltage across *CB* is four volts.

7. *Resistors* It is often necessary to introduce resistance into a circuit to produce a voltage drop. This is generally the case where the e.m.f. is higher than that required for the load. For example, in the following circuit, assuming no resistance in the transmission lines, we may wish to have an e.m.f. of four volts to obtain the desirable current of, say, one ampere through R_1, which we might assume to be an electric light. Any greater e.m.f. would drive too large a current through the light bulb R_1, and burn it out. Our source of e.m.f. is six volts,

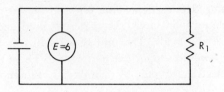

however, and must be reduced. We can reduce the voltage across the light bulb by introducing an additional resistance into the circuit (R_2) as below:

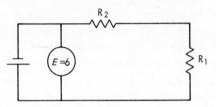

We can calculate the value of this resistance R_2 by considering:

1. the voltage drop required;
2. the current in the circuit.

In this case we desire a voltage drop of two volts and we have a current of one ampere in the circuit. Therefore, as previously demonstrated, the value of the resistance to be inserted in the circuit can be determined by:

$$E = IR \qquad \text{with } I = 1 \text{ ampere}$$
$$E = 2 \text{ volts}$$

and $R_2 = 2$ ohms

When we wish to introduce a resistance into a circuit, such as above, we use a device called a resistor.

Physically, most resistors generally look like small cylindrical units with wire leads on each end. Other shapes and a great variation of sizes are quite common, however. Resistors are generally made from such materials as wire, carbon, graphite, and certain molded compositions, depending on the use for which they are intended.

8. *Electrical power* When a source of e.m.f. forces a current through a circuit, energy is expended. Energy is the capacity to do work, and the rate at which it is done is power. For measuring electrical power the unit used is the watt. One watt is the power used when an e.m.f. of one volt forces one ampere of current to flow. Or:

$$W = EI \qquad \text{where } W = \text{power in watts}$$
$$E = \text{e.m.f. in volts}$$
$$I = \text{current in amperes}$$

When a current passes through a resistance (or resistor) electrical energy is dissipated. The amount of power so dissipated can be found by using the equation:[1]

$$W = I^2R \qquad \text{where } W = \text{watts dissipated}$$
$$I = \text{current in amperes}$$
$$R = \text{resistance in ohms}$$

The energy is dissipated in the form of heat. Therefore it is necessary to rate resistors in watts as well as their ohmic value. For example, a two ohm resistor rated at two watts would burn out quickly if required to dissipate ten watts.

9. *Characteristics of resistors*   For a given circuit where the current and the required voltage drop are known, the ohmic value (the amount of resistance) and thence the power dissipation required of a resistor can be calculated. The ohmic value called for must be accurately calculated or too large or too small a voltage drop may occur. And the resistor used must accurately supply the resistance called for, or again too large or too small a voltage drop might occur. Power dissipation does not enter into the function of a resistor so long as it is not overloaded. Therefore this factor need not be so precisely calculated and controlled. Generally a healthy "safety margin" is used by specifying a resistor with a power dissipation capacity substantially higher than that required theoretically.

Some additional concepts are particularly important in selecting resistors.

a. *Precision*   Precision denotes the percentage variation of the ohmic value of a resistor from its nominal value. A resistor nominally rated at four ohms, for example, may have been manufactured with a precision of ± 20 percent. Thus the actual resistance, in fact, could be from 3.2 to 4.8 ohms.

b. *Stability*   Stability denotes the variation in the resistance or ohmic value over a period of time. For example, as a resistor heats up as current passes through it, the resistance offered to the current changes. The degree of such change is one aspect of stability.

c. *Reliability*   Reliability is a concept very close to stability, but deals with the variation in resistance over a period of time, including such factors as temperature, mechanical, and moisture conditions.

---

[1] This equation is obtained by combining the equations $E = IR$ and $W = EI$.

d. *Physical dimensions*   The physical dimensions of the resistor are quite important in many applications where space is limited or weight is very important, e.g., circuits in rockets.

e. *Properties in high frequency*   In some alternating-current circuits, some types of resistors tend to exhibit inductive reactance (which opposes the flow of current much like resistance). This phenomena is related to the frequency of the current in cycles and, particularly in high-frequency circuits, is undesirable.

f. *Noise*   When an electrical current passes through a conductor, a rearrangement of the atomic structure of the matter takes place. This sets up in the matter a phenomena known as "noise." In sound reproduction particularly, this background noise must be kept to a minimum so that it doesn't interfere with the transmission. Noise is expressed in terms of volts/volt. The higher the volts/volt the worse the noise interference.

10. *Kinds of resistors*   There are many different kinds of resistors, each offering different combinations of resistance, power dissipation, precision, stability, cost, and so on. Generally, they can be classified into the following categories:

a. Carbon composition resistors, which are generally the least expensive, have the lowest precision and stability, etc. In 1960, these resistors were commonly sold by French manufacturers for from 5 to 15 centimes each.

b. Carbon deposited resistors, which consist of a carbon or carbon composition film deposited on a glass or ceramic base. These resistors were sold in France in 1960 for about 15 to 25 centimes each. They have precision and stability characteristics somewhat better than the ordinary graphite or carbon resistors.

c. Wire-wound resistors are used where high power dissipation is necessary, Prices are quite varied depending on application. This type of resistor is generally quite bulky and exhibits high reactance in high frequency circuits.

d. Metal oxide resistors, which consist of a metal oxide coat on a base of nonconductive material such as ceramic or glass, have good precision and stability characteristics. These characteristics are generally better than carbon, graphite, or carbon composition varieties. They were sold in 1960 for 35 to 50 centimes each. Chambrey was considering the manufacture of resistors in this category.

Another type of metal film resistor is the pure metal film resistor. Such resistors are similar to the metal oxide film resistors except that the film is pure metal fused to the glass or ceramic base under vacuum. The precision, stability, and reliability of these resistors is significantly better than any other type. Selling prices in 1960 were very high, ranging upwards from NF. 1 each.

APPENDIX B

Note on the French Electronics Industry[1]

The "electronics industry" in France was considered to consist of those firms whose products were based significantly on the use of electronic[2] principles. As such, it included a very large number of component-part and finished-goods manufacturers who made products varying from electronic tubes, transistors, and other components to television sets, hearing aids, and computers. These many firms were classified into four basic divisions.

1. Finished equipment manufacturers who produced for the consumer market. Products included such items as radios, television sets, and hearing aids.
2. Finished equipment manufacturers who produced for the industrial and governmental markets. Products included such items as computers, other data-processing equipment, radar, and radio and television broadcasting equipment.
3. The manufacturers of component parts such as resistors, capacitors, and transistors.
4. The manufacturers of electronic tubes.

The Finished Equipment Manufacturers

These manufacturers were primarily assemblers, bringing together the necessary components to produce sets—the final products ready for use by consumers or industry. These manufacturers usually produced some of the components used in their sets, but all relied to some degree on the purchase of components produced by independent firms.

There were distinct differences between the firms that produced for the industrial market and those that produced for the consumer market. The

[1] The major source of this information was "L'Industrie Electronique par la Federation Nationale Des Industries Electroniques," Société Nouvelle Mercure, Paris.
[2] Electronics was a broad term describing that area between electrical engineering and physics where basic circuit elements such as tubes, transistors, and magnetic amplifiers were used to control electrons and many of the other fundamental particles and radiations of matter.

manufacture of industrial products was generally more complicated and afforded few opportunities for mass production. Often, in fact, industrial products were "tailor made" to the technical needs of the buyers. Consumer products, on the other hand, were relatively less complex in design and manufacture and could often be mass-produced. Generally, therefore, the two sectors were considered almost as two separate industries, each with its own problems and opportunities. The two sectors met on common ground only in the use of similar or identical component parts.

The following tables present some basic statistics on the French finished equipment manufacturers in 1958:

Table 1   **Radio and Television Receiver Manufacturers[a]**

Number of Employees	Number of Firms	Total Personnel Employed	Total Sales in NF. × 1,000
Over 500	6	8,381	349,500
201–500	6	1,772	63,300
101–200	7	1,057	66,080
51–100	16	742	60,370
21–50	24	416	19,510
11–20	26	378	26,650
6–10	52		
Total	137	12,746	585,410
Amateur production	587	772	23,400
Grand Total	724	13,518	608,810

[a] No statistics were available on other consumer goods manufacturers. Amateur producers were generally unincorporated and produced primarily for their own needs.

Table 2   **Industrial Goods Manufacturers**

Number of Employees	Number of Firms	Total Personnel Employed	Total Sales in NF. × 1,000
Over 1,000	7	15,527	447,320
301–1,000	6	2,104	63,210
101–300	14	2,203	42,290
51–100	9	622	16,140
21–50	17	575	22,630
11–20	8	117	2,840
6–10	5	38	980
Total	66	21,186	595,410
Amateur production	49	38	690
Grand Total	115	21,224	596,100

As can be noted in the preceding tables, there was a tendency for a few large firms to dominate the finished equipment manufacturing sectors of the industry. Moreover, industry sources estimated that this concentration would increase in the future because of increasing product complexity, which necessitated high expenditures on research and large capital investments.

The unit production of radios and television sets in France for three years is given below:

Table 3   **Unit Production of Radio and Television Sets**

	1956	1957	1958
Radios	1,450,000	1,586,000	1,522,000
Television sets	260,000	343,000	372,000

The Component Part Manufacturers

The third and fourth branches of the industry[3] were suppliers of component parts to the finished equipment manufacturers.

The production of the various component parts required specialized technology and manufacturing processes. The manufacturers of transistors, for example, required highly specialized knowledge and machinery, both of which were quite different than the requirements for the manufacture of, say, capacitors. Primarily for these reasons the manufacturers of components tended to be specialized, producing only one or more related components and sometimes only certain specifications of one component.

The following tables present basic information on the French component part manufacturers in 1958:

Table 4   **Component Parts Manufacturers**

Number of Employees	Number of Firms	Total Personnel Employed	Total Sales in NF. × 1,000
Over 500	2	1,442	24,330
201–500	13	4,374	117,940
101–200	17	2,368	55,360
51–100	25	1,724	52,570
21–50	45	1,599	45,780
11–20	34	531	14,280
6–10	29	224	6,810
Total	165	12,262	317,070
Amateur production	181	153	3,540
Grand Total	346	12,415	320,610

---

[3] The reasons for separating the manufacturers of electronic tubes from the manufacturers of other components are not stated in the publication supplying the information.

Table 5   Electronic Tube Manufacturers

Number of Employees	Number of Firms	Total Personnel Employed	Total Sales in NF. × 1,000
Over 1,000	4	6,916	141,470
201–1,000	3	929	6,230
51–200	4	474	53,240
6–50	5	133	2,400
Total	16	8,452	203,340
Amateur production	11	11	320
Grand Total	27	8,463	203,660

For the manufacture of certain components only a relatively small capital investment was required. If an individual or group had the requisite technical knowledge they would probably have little difficulty raising sufficient capital to go into production. This factor, plus the previously mentioned tendency to specialization, probably accounts for the relatively large number of small firms in component part manufacturing.

A detailed breakdown of the production of various component parts in units is given in the following table. No more detailed statistics were available in published sources.

Table 6   Component Part Production in Units

	1956	1957	1958
Receiving tubes	21,500,000	28,000,000	27,000,000
Cathode tubes	215,000	360,000	460,000
Variable capacitors	1,370,000	2,101,000	1,792,500
Speakers for radios	1,910,000	2,360,000	3,033,000
Carbon resistors	110,000,000	106,000,000	104,000,000
Other types of resistors	(N.A.)	(N.A.)	30,000 to 50,000,000
Potentiometers	6,170,000	5,650,000	8,526,000
Transformers	1,270,000	1,700,000	1,300,000

It was estimated that the radio and television manufacturers were the major users of resistors, consuming about 100,000,000 units in 1958. The majority of the resistors used by these manufacturers were the cheaper, low precision, carbon composition types.

The Growth of the Electronics Industry as a Whole

The following table clearly presents the remarkable growth of the French electronic industry in the years prior to 1959:

Table 7   **The French Electronics Industry**
Index of Total Sales (1952 = 100)

Year	Products	Industrial Products	Component Parts	Electronic Tubes	Total
1952	100	100	100	100	100
1953	115	127	109	125	120
1954	137	185	154	121	156
1955	185	215	209	147	194
1956	270	221	286	180	241
1957	341	258	384	259	304
1958	403	276	431	316	349
Percent of total industry sales in 1958	36%	31%	21%	12%	100%

Industry sources were confident that the past growth of the French electronics industry would continue well into the future. They pointed to the worldwide trend of greater utilization of electronics both in the industrial and consumer fields and to the seemingly continuous discovery of new applications for electronic-based products. In addition they cited the relatively low saturation of electronic equipment in France as compared to countries like the United States; for example, television broadcasts were available to only 60 percent of the French population in 1958, while the corresponding figure in the United States was almost 100 percent.

Import and Export Trade

The following tables present import and export statistics regarding electronic products:

Table 8   **French Imports of Electronic Equipment**
NF. × 1,000

	1955	1956	1957	1958
Consumer goods	12,400	13,400	13,250	5,020
Industrial goods	12,200	23,000	32,880	32,370
Component parts	11,000	18,700	22,650	16,650
Electronic tubes	21,900	24,700	27,200	38,040

Industry sources estimated that foreign trade would increase in the future, particularly within the Common Market, but that a rough balance would be maintained between imports and exports.

Table 9   French Exports of Electronic Equipment
NF. × 1,000

	1955	*1956*	*1957*	*1958*
Consumer goods	21,600	25,150	4,600	4,510
Industrial goods	53,800	52,000	68,000	77,210
Component parts	13,500	16,900	15,100	13,370
Electronic tubes	12,900	19,400	18,300	24,670

The Free World Electronics Industry

The following table presents statistics on the electronics industry of the Free World. Since different definitions of the industry are used in the various countries, the figures are not perfectly comparable. Some compensations have been made in the French figures to make them more comparable. Despite these limitations the figures are useful for a gross comparison of the various countries.

Table 10   The Electronics Industry of the Free World, 1957

Country	*Total Number of People Employed*	*Total Sales*	*Exports*
		Converted to French Francs NF. × 1,000,000	
West Germany	115,000	2,170	630
France	60,000	1,500	140
Italy	30,000	350	18
Holland	22,000	420	280
Belgium	19,000	315	70
Luxembourg	5,000	35	—
Total Common Mkt.	250,000	4,790	1,138
Great Britain	190,000	2,550	332
United States	700,000	26,250	385

CHAMBREY CÉRAMIQUES S.A. (B)

In November 1960, management of Chambrey Céramiques S.A. authorized a research program to provide needed information on the market for resistors in Europe.[1] Subsequently, proposals that broadly outlined the scope and objectives of the study were sent to four Paris-based marketing research organizations. Of these four, three submitted bids to Chambrey for the execution of the study. Management faced the task of either selecting one of these firms to do the study or searching for alternative methods or organizations.

Following the decision to research the resistor market, the task of coordinating and supervising the actual research had been assumed by Mr. Bernard Guyot, Sales Director for Industrial Ceramic Products. Mr. Guyot's first step was to prepare a brief statement of the problem facing Chambrey and mail it to four research houses who had done good research in the past. Excerpts from this letter follow:

> ...the overall objective of the research would be to provide Chambrey with basic market information to guide our decision on adopting this product line and to give direction to our initial marketing, if the product is adopted. Specifically, such questions as the following should be answered:
> —Who are the major users of resistors?
> —Who are the major producers of resistors?
> —In what quantities and types are resistors employed?
> —Why are particular types of resistors chosen for specific tasks?
> —Are there any particular marketing opportunities for the line of resistors Chambrey anticipates marketing?
> ...we would anticipate selling the resistors to all European countries with the exception of England. Therefore, although our major market would probably be in France, the research should not necessarily be confined to France alone.
> ...we would appreciate a statement of the time required to

---

1 See Chambrey Céramiques S.A. (A), p. 171.

execute any study proposed. While we are under no great time pressure, we feel that our decision whether to enter this market should be made as soon as reasonably possible.

...no budget limitations have been placed on this study other than the fact that the research expenditure should be reasonable in relation to our anticipated initial investment of some NF. 750,000.

...if you require further information, we are available to meet with you to discuss the problem.

The following are summaries of the subsequent negotiations of the four companies with Mr. Guyot. In Appendix A the detailed bids of the three firms interested in doing the research are presented.

1. VERNAY AND BONVIN S.A.   This company was Chambrey's advertising agency and had done research for Chambrey in the past on domestic ware. A few days after he had mailed the proposals, Mr. Guyot phoned the marketing research director at Vernay and Bonvin, Mr. Capelle, and asked him for his reactions to the problem. Mr. Capelle said that although the study looked interesting he was afraid that Vernay and Bonvin could not undertake it, because they had no experience in research for industrial products, and, moreover, they had a large backlog of consumer product studies to complete. In further conversation with Mr. Guyot, Mr. Capelle offered the opinion that most good research houses in Paris were very busy and had substantial backlogs of projects.

2. ANDRÉ FELLER S.A   In Mr. Guyot's opinion this firm was probably the best marketing research house in France. Shortly after the proposals had been sent out, a representative from this firm called on Mr. Guyot and explained that André Feller was interested in executing the study, but, since it was presently fully occupied with other studies, it could not start the Chambrey study until November, 1961. In reply to a question from Mr. Guyot, the André Feller representative estimated that the probable costs for executing the study in France would be from NF. 15,000 to NF. 20,000. He would not make a firm commitment on the price, however. The representative left a submission from André Feller with Mr. Guyot for his consideration.

André Feller S.A.'s submission claimed that it was the largest French marketing research agency, with a permanent staff of sixty and a part-time staff of three hundred specialized field investigators. The company claimed ability to execute general marketing research projects, motivation studies, industrial research studies, advertising research, and product, price, and brand name research. In addition, André Feller was associated with ten research houses in various European countries and through this association was equipped to conduct international studies.

The Feller submission made no specific references to the Chambrey study.

3. DOUGLAS JOHNSTONE AND ASSOCIATES. This firm specialized primarily in management consulting but made a definite bid for the Chambrey research study after personally discussing the work with Mr. Guyot. During these meetings Mr. Guyot was impressed by the apparent capabilities of the Douglas Johnstone personnel, two of whom were electronic engineers. He was, however, disturbed by what he called "high-pressure" approach of this firm and wondered whether they had ulterior motives in bidding for the study. For example, at one point, a director of Douglas Johnstone visited Chambrey, and bypassing Mr. Guyot, talked directly with Chambrey's president about the study.

The submission of Douglas Johnstone and Associates dwelt specifically with the Chambrey problem. The company proposed to execute about eighty interviews with key customers and competitors in France, Italy, Germany, Switzerland, and Holland. It was claimed that these interviews would provide the statistical and technical data needed by Chambrey. The total cost of the project, which was to be completed in four months, was estimated at NF. 80.000, including traveling expenses.

4. NADEN ADVERTISING S.A. This company, which was primarily an advertising agency, also made a definite bid for the research job. Mr. Guyot was personally acquainted with the director of marketing research at Naden, Mr. G. Favez. Mr. Guyot explained that Mr. Favez had done a small but excellent study on sanitary ware for Chambrey when he was with another company. In conversation with Mr. Guyot about the study, Mr. Favez admitted that neither he nor his Naden research staff had much experience in research on industrial products. However, he stated that Naden was anxious to do the study and would give it an all-out effort. Naden was prepared to start on the study within a few weeks. In addition, Mr. Favez mentioned that Naden would be willing to hire an electrical engineer for a period of time to handle the interviewing and any other technical aspects of the job.

In its submission, Naden proposed that the research be conducted in two distinct steps: (1) establishing a complete list of companies using resistors; and (2) interviewing all or a sample of these companies to obtain information regarding the quantities, kinds, specifications, etc., of the resistors used.

Naden limited the scope of the research in their proposal to the French market but explained (during one of the interviews with Mr. Guyot) that it could extend the study to other European countries if Chambrey so desired. Naden estimated that the research in France would be completed in four or five months, and maximum cost would be NF. 4,700 plus traveling expenses, if any.

After the written submissions had been received, Mr. Guyot felt he should propose a recommendation regarding the research bids for the consideration of Chambrey management.

APPENDIX A

CHAMBREY CÉRAMIQUES S.A. (B)

Submissions of the Market Research Firms

1. *André Feller S.A.* André Feller S.A. was founded in 1953 by Mr. André Feller. Presently, it is the largest French marketing research agency. It has a permanent staff of sixty people and more than three hundred specialized part-time field investigators.

André Feller S.A. and ten foreign marketing research agencies are members of a European society of marketing research, which constitutes the most important group of marketing research agencies in Europe.

André Feller S.A. offers to its clients a complete scope of abilities and methods in economic and commercial studies.

    a. *Market research.* The study of the marketing of a product has as its object the accumulation in a numerical manner of the greatest possible amount of information concerning the production, sale, and consumption of the product.

The principal information furnished by a marketing research are:
—The total volume of the market (in quantity or in trade figures);
—The place held by different makes on the market;
—The characteristics of the clientèle of the different makes;
—The channels of distribution by which the production passes and the prices used;
—The buying habits of the clientèle;
—The consumption habits (who consumes, where, when, how).

Marketing research can be executed in two ways:
    (1) The collection and analysis of the economical and statistical documentation existing (documentation emanating from public or private organisms). André Feller S.A. practices this method with the aid of a specialized documentation service.
    (2) Field research, which consists of interviewing a representative sample of the producers, or consumers of the product and to extrapolate the results obtained by this sample. In doing field research, André Feller S.A. uses a specialized staff of investigators and statisticians. André Feller S.A. has made nearly two hundred studies of this nature since 1953.

    b. *Motivation studies* The objective of motivation studies is an understanding of the psychological factors that make the consumers, retailers, industrialists, etc. react as they do. Motivation studies are thus clearly distinguished from the standard or classic marketing studies that tend to study the exterior aspect of consumer behavior and not the profound reasons behind the behavior. André Feller S.A. was the first institute in Europe to conduct motivation studies. It employs ten psychosociologists for this type of research. André Feller S.A. has made important motivation studies since 1954.

c. *Research in industrial marketing* Marketing research of industrial products (motors, plant, transformers, raw materials, factory equipment, etc.) demands a certain adaptation of the methods in marketing research and the employment of a specialized personnel having basic technical abilities. André Feller S.A. employs a team of engineers and industrial investigators and has made industrial research in very varied fields (electricity, chemical products, glass industry, plant, motors, building materials, etc.).

d. *Advertising research* With a view to guiding the advertising strategy endeavors of its clients and of then measuring the results, André Feller S.A. uses the classic methods of pretest and posttest. André Feller S.A. also has methods of testing that resolve problems that, up till now, have been reputed to be insoluble (for example: to measure *the real interest* held by the readers for an advertisement).

e. *Tests of products, of condition, of price and names* The object of these tests is to determine in advance the reception that the public will give to a new product, a new packing, a new make, a new selling price, etc. The techniques of these tests are drawn from those used in field research and motivational studies.

f. *Marketing studies at the European and international scale* As a result of the formation of the Common Market, André Feller and ten other important institutes of Marketing Research have formed an agreement to cooperate on international studies. Member companies are located in: Germany, Austria, Belgium, Denmark, France, Great Britain, Italy, Norway, Holland, Sweden, and Switzerland. The entire group is composed of three hundred marketing research specialists and three thousand field investigators. Every year the institute as a whole makes five hundred thousand interviews with the European public.

Due to its economic documentation service and to its centralized structure, this group of companies is capable of making very complete, very rapid, and also very economical marketing studies according to the European scale for its clients.

2. *Douglas Johnstone and Associates* Following our meetings, we are happy to offer our services in attaining two precise goals:

1. To execute technical market research in the field of metal film resistors.

2. To provide for you, in the course of this research, the whole of our technique so that Chambrey will be able to perform future research in such areas, if necessary.

We trust that you will personally follow our research activity during the time at your disposal; but, it is understood, you may, in addition, delegate any other member of your personnel, be it the future salesman of the resistors or any other person, to collaborate with us to the extent you choose.

The different stages of our research will be developed as follows:

The basic research work will be a series of interviews with the manufacturing chiefs, the engineers, the heads of the research office, and the directors of factories or companies. It is possible for this field to be enlarged should other sources of information from which the research may benefit present themselves.

Recognizing your desire to export resistors, we foresee covering the market in the following countries: France, Italy, Germany, Switzerland, and Holland with the help of about eighty visits. Among these visits, a certain number will probably turn out to provide more information than others; these cases will be studied very thoroughly.

These visits will be carried out with the principal prospective customers and with rival manufacturers.

After the campaign of visits has been established, we shall carry out the interviews in such a manner that they will furnish not only statistical information but technical data that will allow you to undertake the delicate operation of starting up your prospective production process.

The reports on each company will be as complete as possible including the tabulated answers to the questionnaire and a general statement regarding the position of the company in the industry.

We shall submit two reports during the contract, in order that you can carefully study our progress.

And we shall establish a general report, which will include a general analysis of the results and an attempt will be made to enumerate the most important alternatives for future action.

We propose forming a research team to discuss the questionnaire and execution of the research. It would include two qualified engineers from our office, in addition to yourself and one of your associates. Our engineers would conduct all the field work and tabulation.

In order to allow for careful preparation for the interviews with qualified people of each of the firms to be visited, we believe that it would be useful to carry out the research over a period of four months. Our fees, traveling expenses included, are NF. 20,000 per month payable net monthly to our account with Credit Lyonnais in Paris, this making a total sum of NF. 80,000.

We sincerely hope that we shall have the opportunity to work in collaboration with your company.

3. *Naden Advertising S.A.*

   a. *General datum on the research*   The market for resistors is extremely widespread since they are used in products as different as electric motors and radar.

   It is not a question of studying the entire market for resistors but of studying the market for resistors possessing characteristics such as those you will possibly be producing.

   The resistors that you contemplate manufacturing are assumed to be products of excellent quality.

   This consideration alone should limit the sale of the rival products.

   The enquiry would be made anonymously. If it were necessary to name our client we could furnish the name of the American company of whom you would be the licensee. In any case, the name of your company would not be declared.

   While we do not have an investigator on our permanent staff that has the technical background that seems to be necessary, we have made arrangements to hire an electrical engineer on a temporary basis for the execution of the interviews and for technical interpretations and feel confident that this man has the experience and qualifications to do the necessary work, and, additionally, the first interviews by this investigator will be closely followed so that his investigating qualities may be judged.

   b. *Aim*   The aim of the research is to determine the actual market for resistors.

   More precisely it is a question of studying a limited number of industries to determine:
   —The quantities of resistors employed;
   —The qualities and technical characteristics of the resistors used in various applications;
   —The reason why certain types of resistors are used.

   This research will be limited to the categories of industries we decide to consult.

   In addition, it is conceivable that we might abstain from asking for information regarding resistors having characteristics that are not competitive with the models you contemplate manufacturing.

   c. *Methods*

      (1) The first stage of the research would consist of establishing a list of industries.

We would establish a list of industries likely to use the kinds of resistances under study.

(2)   You would then supply us with any information in your possession regarding the importance of companies engaged in all or part of these industries.

We would undertake, in cases where you cannot supply this information, to investigate the companies or important groups that are missing.

(3)   We would then submit the complete list of companies or groups with whom the research should be made for your approval.

(4)   Finally, as a second stage, all the enterprises on the list would be questioned by a person possessing the qualities of an investigator and technician.

d.   *Realization*

(1)   The questionnaire will be designed to include the following information:

—what is the number of resistors bought each year by the company for use in industrial manufactured products?

—at what point in the manufacturing process is each kind of resistor integrated into the product?

—what are the electrical characteristics of the circuit before and after the resistor?

—what are the characteristics of each type of resistor: physical characteristics (dimension, material), electrical characteristics?

—what are the reasons that determine the choice of such material, of such design, of such a make, of such characteristics (particularly the assessment of endurance)?

—what are the actual tendencies in the use of different types of resistors?

(2)   People to be questioned   Experience alone will allow us to determine the best people to interview. Nevertheless we think that the following should be interrogated:

—a representative of the purchasing office who would be furnishing quantitative information; and

—a representative of the engineering and technical service, who would be able to furnish information on the conditions of the use of the resistors and the justifications for the choice of a certain type.

(3)   *Time*   From the moment you give us authorization to execute the research, we would estimate the following timing:

—First stage, resulting in the establishment of the list of firms to be questioned: fifteen days to three weeks.

—Second stage, interviews of the firms. If we count on five categories of industries and on eight firms for each category, we arrive at a total of forty interviews.

At this moment we should make two hypotheses:

—either one interview is sufficient to obtain the necessary information on one firm;

—or else, other interviews should be made, either with several people in one company or with several establishments.[1]

Assuming one interview, the first part of the inquiry will last one-and-a-half months on the condition that the time devoted to traveling be limited. That is to say, if all these interviews take place in a 50-kilometer radius of Paris.

Assuming two or more interviews the time delay would be of a two-and-a-half-month order, under the same reservations as those made previously regarding the time devoted to traveling.

Under the conditions, the report, which will require considerable work to compile, could be presented four or five months after the start of the enquiry.

(4)　*Fees*　The cost of the first stage obviously depends on the amount of information that would have to be obtained from sources other than Chambrey. The cost may nevertheless be estimated between NF. 500 and NF. 1,000. The cost of the inquiry, the interviews and the editing of the report depends on the number of interviews contemplated.

—in the case of an interview per company: NF. 2,100.

—in the case of two or perhaps more interviews per company: NF. 4,200.

In conclusion, the total cost of the research would be:

—first hypothesis　　　　:　　　NF. 2,600

—second hypothesis　　　:　　　NF. 4,700

It is understood that traveling expenses and the time spent away in the provinces would be in addition, if such journeys prove necessary.

(5)　*Remarks*.　We think we should now draw your attention to certain points.

(a)　Qualification of person being interviewed　The experience acquired in industrial inquiries has shown us that it is sometimes very difficult to know the person who had the responsibility of the choice of the product in his hands. Often several

---

[1] In the same company, for example, two factories geographically distinct.

functions intervene: technical service, manufacturing service, purchasing service, etc. . . .

It is with this in mind that we foresee the possible necessity of conducting several interviews.

(b) Nonunity of the firm   It is possible that a firm has several branches, for example, a head office and two manufacturing factories.

In a certain number of cases, the orders may all pass through the head office, or, on the contrary, be made by each factory for its own requirements.

It is thus possible that to obtain the necessary information it would not be necessary to visit the factories.

On the other hand, perhaps the factories alone indicate the reasons for the use of a certain kind of resistor and the head office only verifies the order. In this case it would be necessary to visit the factory.

(c) Quantitative information   We hope to be able to obtain quantitative information classified by the type of resistor used.

This is possible on two conditions: the first is that these statistics exist (as we think) and in sufficient detail; the second is that the firm being interviewed agrees to furnish them.

Perhaps we are going to throw ourselves into difficulty on this subject: for a technician should be able to deduce, from the characteristics and the quantities of resistors employed, the firms production, an element that the enterprise obviously wants to keep secret.

On first thoughts, this consideration seems particularly valid with respect to radio and television manufacturers.

(d) Concentration of the industries   We have assumed a concentration of the industries to be interviewed; that is to say, we expect to see more than 70 percent of the trade figures realized by a number of firms less than ten.

But if this hypothesis proves inexact and, for example, 50 percent of the trade figures are made by sixty or eighty small firms, the research should be given up, or in any case, the proposed method of research should be altered.

For, if such were the case it would no longer be forty firms that should be interviewed but perhaps two hundred or three hundred, which would constitute a difficult sampling problem.

CHAMBREY CÉRAMIQUES S.A. (C)

Mr. Guyot's recommendation that Naden Advertising S.A. be selected for the research on the market for resistors was accepted by Chambrey management.[1] Thus, in January 1961, Mr. Guyot met with Mr. G. Favez, Mme. M. Grysel, and Mr. E. Renouf of Naden Advertising to discuss detailed procedure for the research. Mr. Favez was the Research Director and Mme. Grysel was a senior member of the advertising agency's Research Department. Mr. Renouf was the electrical engineer hired by Naden for the Chambrey project. He had no previous experience in research.

At their meeting, the following procedures were developed for the research:

1. The research was to be executed in two stages, as outlined in the Naden proposal. Only after the results of the first stage were available would Chambrey give final authorization to the second stage.
2. The cost for the first stage of the study was to be a maximum of NF. 1,300 not including traveling expenses. Payment was to be made on delivery of the report. It was understood that the majority of the information required to complete the first stage would be available at the "Exhibition for Component Parts" to be held soon in Paris. Interviews at the exhibition or at any other place were to be carried out by Mr. Renouf in the company of Mr. Favez.
3. The agreed cost of the second stage, should it be authorized, was to be based on the number of interviews conducted.

40 interviews	NF. 2,600
80 "	NF. 4,700
200 "	NF. 11,750

These quotes were maximum charges for interviewing and did not include traveling and hotel expenses. Payment was to be made as follows:

---

[1] See Chambrey Céramiques S.A. (A), p. 171, and (B), p. 177.

1/3 on the authorization of the second stage,
1/3 after the questionnaire was finalized,
1/3 on the delivery of the final report.

4. No specific cost estimates were considered for research in foreign countries, although the Naden representatives estimated that costs in each foreign country would be approximately the same as those incurred in France.
5. Mr. Favez would be responsible for the research on the part of Naden Advertising S.A.

On March 1, 1961, the report on the first stage of the research was submitted by Mr. Favez to Mr. Guyot. It was now necessary for Mr. Guyot to decide on the execution of the second stage of the research. Excerpts of the first stage report follow:

Excerpts from Naden Report

The objectives of this first stage of the research program were to:

1. Establish a list of the manufacturers of resistors.
2. Attempt to enumerate the characteristics of resistors manufactured.
3. Establish a list of users of resistors.

The greatest part of the information contained in this report was obtained at the Exhibition of Component Parts. Exhibitors were questioned, and the published material they provided was studied.

1. GENERALITIES ON RESISTORS   It appears that the choice of a specific resistor depends on: dimensions, precision, stability, noise, power dissipation, and properties in high frequency.

a. *Dimensions*   The aggregate, carbon deposited, metal oxide, and pure metal film resistors are generally less cumbersome than wire wound resistors. This is particularly true when the resistance is high but the maximum power dissipation is low. Subminiature resistors of the carbon deposited and metal oxide and pure metal film types have been developed for use in transistor circuits and miniaturized equipment such as electronic calculating machines, hearing aids, and subminiature military equipment.
b. *Precision*   Precision of the resistor type can be controlled by the manufacturing process. Carbon composition resistors are usually produced with a precision in the order of ± 10 percent and sometimes ± 5 percent. Wired resistors can be made with precision lower than ± 1

percent. Carbon deposited, metal oxide and pure metal film resistors can be manufactured with precisions less than ± 1 percent.

c. *Stability*   Stability is mostly a function of the material of which the resistor is constructed. Carbon composition resistors and some of those with fine metal and carbon coatings often show variations in resistance when temperature mounts. And after this their resistance does not return to its initial value. Wire wound resistors do not show these characteristics. Neither do pure metal film resistors, which demonstrate very high stability.

d. *Noise*   Carbon composition, carbon deposited, and wire wound resistors have high noise voltage relative to metal oxide and pure metal film resistors. Several manufacturers have perfected processes to produce low noise metal oxide and pure metal film resistors.

e. *Power dissipation*   The carbon composition resistors, and probably the carbon deposited, metal oxide, and pure metal film resistors are not widely used for power dissipations greater than two watts and certainly not for dissipation in excess of four watts. Wired resistors are available for power dissipation up to one hundred and two hundred watts; besides, covered by enamel, they can support operating temperatures of several hundred degrees centigrade.

f. *Properties in high frequency*   Carbon composition, carbon deposited, and the metal film resistors behave practically as pure resistors up to extremely high frequencies. Wired resistors, however, show reactances frequently to the same extent as the resistance itself at high frequencies.

Exhibit 1, following, is a list of the present manufacturers and sources of resistors in France and the general types of resistors they supply. The list is classified into domestic and foreign sources and in each of these categories the sources are ranked according to their importance.

Exhibit 2, 3, and 4 are summary comparisons of principal characteristics of competitive metal oxide resistors. Included in these exhibits are the resistors Chambrey contemplates manufacturing.

Exhibit 5 is a list of all the significant users of resistors classified into industry groups and within each classification ranked according to importance. It would appear that, in view of price considerations, the market for Chambrey resistors lies mostly with the manufacturers of electronic equipment in the industrial and military fields. Hence, we have carefully sub-divided these users.

Exhibit 1 Chambrey Céramiques S.A. (C)

List of Manufacturers of Resistors

A. Domestic Manufacturers

Name		*Types of Resistors Produced*
1. Reyrenn S.A.	a.	Metal oxide and pure metal film resistors
	b.	Carbon deposited resistors
	c.	Wire wound resistors
2. Conzett & Faye S.A.	a.	Carbon deposited resistors
	b.	Subminiature carbon deposited resistors
3. Luzet Electroniques S.A.	a.	Metal oxide and pure metal film resistors
	b.	Wire wound resistors
4. Multiwatt	a.	Metal oxide and metal film resistors on glass bases
5. Meylan Recherches S.A.	a.	Metal oxide and metal film resistors on glass bases
	b.	Carbon deposited resistors
6. Prelaz Resistances S.A.	a.	Carbon deposited
	b.	Carbon deposited with high resistance
	c.	Carbon composition resistors
7. Appac S.A.	a.	Carbon deposited
	b.	Wire wound resistors
8. Celpos S.A.	a.	Carbon deposited
	b.	Subminiature
9. Venage S.A.	a.	High stability carbon deposited
10. Darnol	a.	Carbon deposited
11. Veuve	a.	Miniature wire wound resistors
12. Allaz	a.	Carbon composition resistors
	b.	Wire wound resistors
13 Délitroz and Rosset S.A.	a.	Carbon composition resistors
	b.	Wire wound resistors
14. Christinet S.A.	a.	Wire wound resistors of high precision
15. Resistances Bobinées S.A.	a.	Ceramic coated wire wound resistors
16. Société Duriez	a.	Wire wound resistors
17. Fráncey S.A.	a.	Wire wound resistors
18. A.G.O.P.	a.	Wire wound resistors
19. Penseyres & Cie. S.A.	a.	Variable resistors
20. Metzener Georges	a.	Wire wound resistors
21. Sté. Anonyme Kussner	a.	?

B. Foreign Sources of Resistors

Name		*Types of Resistors Produced*
1. Adolf Kleinert	a.	Carbon deposited
(West Germany)	b.	Metal oxide and pure metal film resistors
	c.	Wire wound resistors
2. Electro-Components	a.	Metal oxide and pure metal film resistors
(U.S.A.)	b.	Miniature resistors
	c.	Wire wound resistors
3. Johnback Instruments	a.	High resistance resistors
(U.S.A.)		
4. Smithson Electronics	a.	Carbon composition resistors
(U.S.A.)	b.	Metal oxide and pure metal film resistors

Exhibit 1 (cont.)

Name	Types of Resistors Produced
5. Shultz (West Germany)	a. Carbon deposited resistors b. Wire wound resistors
6. Doenzer (West Germany)	a. Carbon deposited resistors
7. Chicago Resistors (U.S.A.)	a. Carbon composition resistors b. High stability carbon deposited resistors
8. Geibelhaus (West Germany)	a. Carbon deposited resistors b. Wire wound resistors
9. Electroequipment (U.S.A.)	a. Carbon deposited resistors b. Metal oxide and pure metal film resistors c. Wire wound resistors
10. Kostelecky, V. (Hungary)	a. Carbon deposited resistors b. Wire wound resistors
11. Chernowski (Poland)	a. Carbon deposited resistors
12. J. M. Hansen (Denmark)	a. Carbon composition resistors b. Wire wound resistors

Exhibit 2

Chambrey Céramiques S.A. (C)

For Metal Oxide Film Resistors

Precision

Precision Characteristics	Category of Resistor						
	Coated with Epoxy Resin	*High Power Dissipation*	*Hermetically Sealed in Ceramic Coat*	*Noninductive*	*Subminiature*	*High Stability*	*High Resistance*
±15%				A		A	E
±10%	B	B	B	A, B	C	A	E
±5%	B	A, B	B	B	C	A	
±3%	B				C		
±2%	B	B	B	B	C	A	E
±1%	B	B	B	B	C	A, D, S	
±0.5%	B		B	B	C	A, D, S	
±0.2% and under			B		C		

Key: A—Chambrey
B—Reyrenn
C—Luzet Electroniques
D—Meylan Rescherchers
E—Multiwatt
S—Electroequipment (U.S.A.)

Exhibit 3

Chambrey Céramiques S.A. (C)

For Metal Oxide Film Resistors

Noise

Noise Characteristics (volts/volts)	Category of Resistor						
	Coated with Epoxy Resin	High Power Dissipation	Hermetically Sealed in Ceramic Coat	Noninductive	Subminiature	High Stability	High Resistance
0.8 µV/V							E
0.5 µV/V							
0.4 µV/V							
0.3 µV/V							
0.2 µV/V	B	A, B		A, B	C	A	
0.1 µV/V	D					D	
0.05 µV/V							E
0.01 µV/V							E

1 µV = 1/1,000,000 Volt
Key: same as Exhibit 2

Exhibit 4

Chambrey Céramiques S.A. (C)

For Metal Oxide Film Resistors

Temperature Coefficient
in %/C°

Temperature Coefficient / Category of Resistor	Coated with Epoxy Resin	High Power Dissipation	Hermetically Sealed in Ceramic Coat	Noninductive	Subminiature	High Stability	High Resistance
±0.0050%/C°	B		B	B	C, S	D, S	
±0.0075%/C°	B, D		B	B	C	D	
±0.01%/C°	D		B	B		D	
±0.015%/C°		B				A	
±0.025%/C°		A		A	A	A	E
±0.05%/C°					A	A	E
±0.075%/C°							E
±0.1%/C°							E

Key: same as Exhibit 2

Exhibit 5   Chambrey Céramiques S.A. (C)

Users of Resistors

Category 1—Radio and TV set manufacturers—Sound Reproduction Equipment Makers
  1.   La Radio Technique
  2.   Pathé Marconi
  3.   Teppaz—Lyon
  4.   Cie. Radio France
  5.   Ribet Desjardins
  6.   Oceanic
  7.   Polydict

Category 2—Manufacturers of Instruments and Measuring Equipment
  8.   Philips Industrie
  9.   C.R.C.—St. Etienne
 10.   Ferisol
 11.   A.O.I.P.
 12.   Intertechnique
 13.   Ribet Desjardins
 14.   METRIX—Annecy
 15.   LIE BELIE

Category 3—Manufacturers of Computers
 16.   Cie des MACHINES BULL
 17.   IBM FRANCE
 18.   BURROUGHS
 19.   SAMAS

Category 4—Manufacturers of Military Electronic Equipment
 20.   S.N.C.A.N.—Chatillon (Seine) (ex DERVEAUX)
 21.   Sté EUROPEENNE DE TELEGUIDAGE S E T E L
 22.   MATRA
 23.   S.A.R.A.M.
 24.   C.S.F.

Category 5—Manufacturers of Radio and TV Transmitting Equipment and Telephone Equip-
          ment
 25.   THOMSON HOUSTON
 26.   C.S.F.
 27.   T.R.T.
 28.   N.O.R.
 29.   LABORATOIRE GENERAL DES TELECOMMUNICATIONS
 30.   MERLIN GERIN
 31.   L.M.T.

Category 6—Other Industrial Electronics Equipment Manufacturers
 32.   S.M.E.

Category 7—Research Centres
 33.   C.N.R.S.
 34.   C.N.E.T.
 35.   S.T.T.A.
 36.   C.E.A.
 37.   Service des Études de la RADIODIFFUSION-TELEVISION FRANCAISE
 38.   THOMSON

Exhibit 5 (cont.)

39.	C.S.F.
40.	L.E.P.
41.	LABORATOIRE NATIONAL D'ESSAIS DU CONSERVATOIRE DES ARTS ET METIERS

Category 8—Miscellaneous

42.	Ets F.R.B.
43.	L.I.R.E.
44.	S.E.F.
45.	MASSIOT
46.	MECI
47.	LCC

CHAMBREY CÉRAMIQUES S.A. (D)

After discussions of the results of the first stage of the research with several Chambrey executives, on March 25, 1961, Mr. Guyot authorized the execution of the second stage by Naden Advertising S.A.[1]

Subsequently, Mr. Guyot arranged meetings with Mr. Favez and Mr. Renouf of Naden Advertising to discuss the sample of users to be interviewed and to draw up a questionnaire.

With regard to sampling, it was decided to approach all the firms listed as users of resistors in Naden Advertising's first report. It was admitted that some of these firms might not answer the questions posed with the result that the 100 percent sample might not be realized. The approach to a company and the selection of the person or persons to interview were left to the discretion of the interviewer.

A tentative questionnaire was prepared (Exhibit 1) with the thought that this questionnaire would be tested on a few users and then modified, if necessary. These initial test interviews were to be conducted by both Mr. Favez and Mr. Renouf; in this way Mr. Favez could check Mr. Renouf's qualifications as an interviewer. The recommendations arising from these initial interviews are contained in Exhibit 2.

Exhibit 1 **Chambrey Céramiques S.A. (D)**
Questionnaire on Resistors

1. Do you use resistors in the manufacture of your products?

   Yes   No

2. If yes, what type of resistor(s) do you use?
   —carbon composition resistors
   —wire wound resistors
   —metal film resistors
   —carbon deposited resistors

---

[1] See Chambrey Céramiques S.A. (A), p. 171, (B), p. 177, (C), p. 195.

3. In exactly what products are the different kinds of resistors used? (Reply to each type of resistor cited in question 2.)

4. *Carbon Composition Resistors*
    a. Exactly what type of carbon composition resistors do you use?
        —ordinary carbon composition resistors
        —miniature carbon composition resistors
    b. (1) At what power do you use the carbon composition resistors?
        (2) What is the normal power?
        (3) What is the maximum power?
    c. What is the maximum tension (volts) at which you use carbon composition resistors?
    d. (1) What are the preferred ohmic values of these resistors at the ambient temperatures?
        (2) What is the precision you demand for these resistors ($\pm$ %)?
    e. What is the coefficient of temperature required of these resistors?
    f. What are the dimensions commonly used for these resistors?
        —length.....right exterior section....
    g. At what frequency do these resistors function?
    h. What is the kind of lining of your resistors?
    i. (1) Are your carbon composition resistors coated?
        (2) If so, how?

Questions 5, 6, and 7 are exactly the same as above but on wire wound resistors, metal coated resistors, and carbon deposited resistors.

Quantitative Questions

8. Can you tell me how your annual consumption of resistors is divided by absolute quantities or by percentage, according to the following criteria?

		Absolute Quantity	%
a.	*Dimension*		
	—normal resistors	....	....
	—miniature resistors	....	....
	—subminiature resistors	....	....
b.	*Power* (Watts)		
	— between $\frac{1}{50}$ and $\frac{1}{16}$	....	....
	— $\frac{1}{16}$	....	....
	— $\frac{1}{8}$	....	....
	— $\frac{1}{4}$	....	....
	— $\frac{1}{2}$	....	....
	— 1	....	....
	— 2	....	....
	— 3	....	....
	+ 3	....	....

c. *Precision*
Less than ±1%   . . . .
±1%   . . . .
±2%   . . . .
±5%   . . . .
Greater than ± > 5%   . . . .
d. What is your total purchase of resistors per year?

Commercial Questions

9. a. What makes of resistors do you buy? (for each category)
—carbon composition resistors   . . . .
—wire wound resistors   . . . .
—metal film resistors   . . . .
—carbon deposited resistors   . . . .
b. Do you have many supplying distributors for each category?
If yes —carbon composition resistors   . . . .
—wire wound resistors   . . . .
—metal film resistors   . . . .
—carbon deposited resistors   . . . .
c. What is the packing unit in which your resistors are delivered?
d. In what quantities do you buy your resistors? (For each of the
four categories)
e. How many purchases do you make for each category of resistors?
(For each of the four categories)
f. What is the waiting period between the time the order is placed
and the time of delivery?
g. (1) Can you tell me, for each category of resistor, what price
you pay for miniature and subminiature resistors. (For each
of the four categories)
(2) Are prices quoted with or without the inclusion of taxes?
(3) Do you obtain discounts?
If yes —by quantity?
—on basis of annual purchases?
(4) What are the technical characteristics, for each category of
resistors, for which you have previously indicated the price?
(5) At what price do you purchase each of the categories and
type of resistor that you use?

Reception

10. a. What norms or specifications do you use to check resistors?
—general norms
—special norms of the company

b. In your enterprise how do you control the specifications of the resistors you purchase?
—by utilizing specifications of the manufacturer
—by checking in your laboratory
If yes, answer c.

c. On what characteristics do you base your control?

d. What kind of controls do you have on the method of delivery of your resistors?

e. How is the choice of resistors to be checked made?
—all the resistors
—a random sample
—others ways

f. Who carries out the technical investigations that make it possible for you to obtain resistors corresponding exactly to your demand?

g. Can you determine, sometimes, in the material you sell, technical weaknesses due to the resistors?
If yes, what problems?

General Questions

11. a. Are you still using the same category of resistors as you used two years ago? If yes, what developments in characteristics have been made in that time?

b. What will the technical characteristics of the resistors of the future be?

c. What, in your opinion, are the best makes of resistors?

d. What do you think of the foreign brands in comparison with the French?

e. Does this apply to all foreign makes? If "yes" or "no," which?

Exhibit 2   **Chambrey Céramiques S.A. (D)**

Mr. Favez's Report on the Initial Interviews
Research on Resistors—Part 2

Accompanied by Mr. Renouf, I contacted four companies to check the questionnaire. We can make the following remarks regarding the questionnaire:

1. The length of time required to complete the questionnaire is from one to one and one-half hours.
2. Certain questions should be changed.
3. The required information is of both a technical and a commercial nature, and therefore two or more interviews will be required at each

company, in most cases. It was sometimes difficult to obtain interviews with responsible people.

With regard to point 2 we suggest the following changes in the questionnaire:

a. Question 9.a. should be omitted and the information on the make should be asked at the beginning of group questions 4, 5, 6, 7, the questions becoming 4.b. to 5.b. etc.

   In fact, very frequently, the make of resistor is given fairly quickly and the references, in particular dimensional, are made there, for example: "these are the standard dimensions of the make"—

   The question would become:
   "What make do you buy   (usually)?
                             (exceptionally)?

b. Regarding the questions 4.b. to 5.b. etc. These comprise not more than one question with three headings: essential power, maximum power, coefficient security.

   In fact, most of the time the users employ the resistors at half or quarter of their theoretical power.
   Questions 4.b. to 5.b. etc.
   The intervals that are given us of the micro-volt to the kilo-volt range make the interest of this question very limited and we suggest its omission.

c. *Questions 4.d.(1) to 5.d.(1) etc.*
   The word "preferential" should not be included. The question would be replaced by the following: "What are, in ohms, the values of the resistors that you use most frequently?
   Question 8
   The question would be changed in the following way: "Can you tell us how your consumption of resistors divides itself out, in percentages according to the following criteria?" And the words "dimension," "power," etc., would be preceded by the word criterion.

   The column "absolute numbers" would be omitted and a question 8.a.(6) would appear (if absolute quantity not furnished): "What is your approximate annual consumption of all types of resistors?"

d. *Question 9.a.* is omitted (see a)

e. *Question 9.b.*
   In the observed cases purveyors do not exist, the resistor users applying directly to the manufacturers.

   The information on the different makes was supplied to us each time.

   The supplying distributor is only of interest when it regards imported resistors.

Because of this we suggest that the question be omitted.

The question 9.g.(4) should actually be placed immediately after 9.g.(1), the price being defined with regard to the precise characteristics.

f. *Question 9.g.(3)*

Unfavorable reaction. This question would be omitted and replaced by the following, which would supply us with the same information: "Does this price include discounts?" Yes or No.

g. *Questions 10.c. to 10.d.*

These questions are badly interpreted and the same reply is given to question 10.c. and question 10.d.

We suggest the omission of question 10.c.

h. *Question 10.f.*

This question is actually badly drawn up: badly interpreted.

The replies that we have obtained with other formulas show that the actual manufacturers believe they can find resistors corresponding to their requirements on the market.

We suggest the omission of this question.

We would be very obliged if you would kindly give us your opinion on the proposed changes, as soon as you can, if necessary by telephone, in such a way that we may modify the actual questionnaire.

We think that Mr. Renouf is quite capable of conducting these interviews.

AU BON MARCHÉ A.G.

Au Bon Marché A.G. (ABM) was a small, fast-growing chain of medium-sized department stores located in Switzerland. Mr. Hans Mahler, Jr., General Manager of ABM, said the chain was operated on a policy of "passing the advantages of mass production and loss distribution costs to the consumer by selling on a low-price, high-volume basis." He cited, for example, the fact that ABM operated on an average gross margin about 28 percent as compared to the margins of 33 to 35 percent common in full-line department stores in Switzerland.

Since most Swiss manufacturers refused to sell their branded products to any retailer who did not agree to sell at manufacturer-set prices,[1] ABM's management felt that the only way to make their policy of low prices fully effective was to introduce private brands (i.e., ABM's own brands of merchandise). Thus, in the two years since ABM had opened its first store, it had introduced twenty private brands on merchandise as diverse as detergents and Eau de Cologne. In the spring of 1958, Mr. Mahler and his executives were considering the introduction of several new private brands.

The Company

Early in the 1950s, the management of Globus A.G.; an important chain of Swiss department stores (Zürich, Basel, St. Gall, Chur, and Aargau), was studying the possibility of expanding by opening additional branch stores. Because of the increasing costs and difficulty in obtaining sufficiently large sites in Switzerland for additional outlets similar to its existing full-line department stores, Globus was particularly interested in the ways and means

---

[1] Swiss legislation permitted combines and agreements to fix and maintain prices. Exceptions were rents and some agricultural products such as milk and eggs, which were sold at government controlled prices. The majority of Swiss products sold under a manufacturer's brand were price-fixed. Policing of the fixed prices was carried out by both producer and distributor organizations.

211

Exhibit 1

Au Bon Marché A.G.
Organization

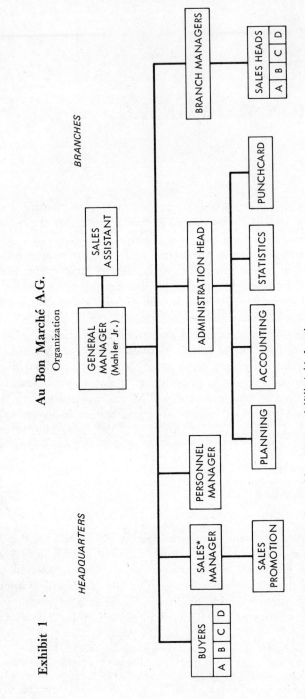

HEADQUARTERS

BRANCHES

* Mr. Mahler Jr., with the special aid of his assistant, fulfilled this function.

by which stores of smaller selling area could be established. At least tentatively, 1,000 m^2 to 1,200 m^2 was believed to be a feasible size.[2]

A special study group, headed by Mr. Mahler, the son of Globus's president and a recent graduate of the Harvard Business School, was assigned to study the expansion problem. After detailed research studies the group recommended the adoption of "a bold new merchandising concept" whereby 1,000 m^2 to 1,200 m^2 stores would be used to sell a limited assortment of merchandies on a low-price, high-volume basis, with a minimum of supporting services and promotion.

The recommendations were accepted by Globus's management, and late in 1954 the formation of a new and separate organization to operate the new stores was authorized. The new organization, as yet unnamed, was to have independent management and staff, but Globus would provide financial support, technical services, and give organizational advice. Mr. Mahler was appointed general manager, and, in turn, he appointed most of his research team to responsible positions in the new organization. An organization chart for the new group is given in Exhibit 1. (Relationships among the various positions will be presented later in the case.)

In the meantime, Globus had purchased property in the city of Biel in 1953 and in 1954 had acquired majority holdings in "Au Bon Marché," an unprofitable textile store in Berne. Both properties were turned over to the new organization which, after some consideration, took the name "Au Bon Marché."

Mr. Mahler and his group took over operation of the Berne store in May 1955. The new ABM management operated this store on an experimental basis for almost a year as they liquidated old inventory, developed sources of supply, trained personnel, and made renovations in the building. Then, in March 1956, the newly remodeled store, consisting of two floors with a total selling area of 890 m^2, was officially opened. Sales from this store were Sfr. 6,800,000[3] in the remainder of 1956 and Sfr. 9,900,000 in 1957.

In Biel a new three-story building with 1,200 m^2 of selling area was erected on the property Globus had purchased and was opened in November 1956. Sales from this store were Sfr. 6,000,000 in 1957, its first full year of operation.

ABM management was encouraged by the sales of these two stores and scheduled an aggressive program of future expansion. Additional openings were planned at the end of 1958 in Basel and less than a year later in Winterthur. Further expansion in other cities was scheduled at later dates.

---

2 One m^2 is approximately equal to 10.8 sq. feet.

3 All monetary figures will be stated in Swiss francs. One American dollar was approximately equal to 4.3 Swiss francs.

Merchandise Policy

During the research study and the following period of experimentation, ABM management concluded that with a selling area of only 1,000 m^2 to 1,200 m^2 in each store, a policy of restricted assortment would have to be adopted and that many of the merchandise groups usually offered in full-line department stores would have to be excluded. In addition, the range of items within the accepted groups of merchandise would have to be carefully controlled. Consequently, ABM stores offered only about 3,500 articles as compared to the approximate 70,000 articles offered by full-line department stores such as Globus.

A great deal of time and effort had been devoted to selecting ABM's merchandise line from the customary assortment list of a full-line store. Only standardized consumer goods for daily use and with a fast turnover potential were included. The composition of the merchandise line is given in Exhibit 2.

Exhibit 2   **Au Bon Marché**

Sales Volume Shares

Group of Goods	Percentage of No. of Articles	Percentage of Sales Volume ABM-Berne	Percentage of Sales Volume ABM-Biel
Foodstuffs and stimulants	11.7	4.9	9.7
Beauty aids and toilet articles	7.1	2.9	3.6
Ready-made clothing	22.8	50.0	39.0
Ready-made clothing accessories	6.5	18.6	17.4
Material for clothes making	3.9	2.8	3.6
Furniture and accessories	9.3	7.1	8.0
Domestic furnishings and fittings	17.2	5.7	8.6
Education, entertainment, travel, sport, games	21.5	8.0	10.1
	100.0	100.0	100.0

Total sales volume

	ABM-Berne	ABM-Biel
1956	Sfr. 6.8 million	—
1957	Sfr. 9.9 million	Sfr. 6.0 million

Buying and Selling Organizations

A major ABM policy was that buying was to govern sales and, further, that there was to be a clear separation of the buying and selling functions. Thus, a strongly centralized organization had been established (Exhibit 1) with great emphasis given to the buyers and the planning section (assortment control).

There were four buyers in the ABM organization, each handling a certain assortment of articles that could be roughly grouped as follows:

1. Babies', girls', and ladies' clothing; household linens; handkerchiefs; haberdashery.
2. Hygiene items; men's and boys' clothing; stockings and socks; gloves; umbrellas; stationery; leather goods; jewelry.
3. Bedclothes; tablecloths; household decorations; electrical equipment; dishes and cutlery; cleaning equipment; workshop tools; garden tools; sporting goods; toys; souvenirs.
4. Foods and related items.

The task of the buyers in cooperation with the planning group was to determine the nature and selling price of each article to be sold and determine its relative importance in the total merchandise assortment. After the buyers had made the qualitative choice of the merchandise and found suppliers, it became the responsibility of the store personnel to place the quantitative orders and to ensure that sufficient stock was maintained.

Each ABM store had a branch manager and four sales heads who corresponded to the four buyers. In turn, each sales head had one or more salesgirl supervisors, each of whom supervised several sales clerks. The branch managers and their staffs were responsible for quantitative orders for merchandise, control of stock levels, and efficient operation of the stores.

Every season meetings of the general manager, buyer, planning executives, branch store managers, and sales heads were held to review the existing assortment of merchandise in the light of actual sales experience. Items that had proved their sales potential were continued on the assortment list and poor selling items were eliminated. In addition, in the course of these conferences, suggestions were made regarding future composition, structure, and pricing of the assortment.

Sales and stock budgets were established for each month six months ahead by the branch managers and head office management. Two formal revisions of these budgets were made. Management of ABM regarded these budgets as devices for directing sales effort and keeping stocks under control.

On the whole, management was satisfied with the way the organization was operating. However, some problems regarding prerogatives and procedures had arisen between the buyers on the one hand and the store managers and department heads on the other. Some buyers, for example, tended to interfere with the branch selling functions by ordering specific quantities of merchandise without consulting branch personnel. Management thought such problems would decrease with time, as the personnel became better acquainted with the procedures and when written descriptions of procedures and responsibilities could be distributed.

Sales had developed quite satisfactorily in ABM management's opinion, being about 17 percent above budget. An unexpected occurrence had been the important volume contributed by textile sales, which were accounting for over 50 percent of total sales and were running 30–40 percent over budget. A breakdown of sales by various merchandise groups is given in Exhibit 2.

While pleased with the sales progress, ABM management was concerned about the trend in inventory levels; inventory turnover had been decreasing recently and actual stocks were considerably higher than budgeted (Exhibit 3). Inventory turnover figures were already considerably below the objective of 5.5 established by the planning department to meet profitability goals and

Exhibit 3   **Au Bon Marché**

Selected Figures on Sales Volume;
Stock/Sales Ratio
Stock Turnover and Budgeted Stock

| | ABM-Berne | | ABM-Total | | | |
	Stock/ Sales	Stock Turnover	Stock/ Sales	Turn- over	Stocks (Sfr. × 1000)	Budgeted Stock
1956						
March	2.04	—	2.04	—	866	865
April	2.66	—	2.66	—	1098	1098
May	2.83	—	2.94	—	1374	1323
June	3.23	—	3.35	—	1588	1533
July	3.15	—	3.30	—	1843	1761
August	3.76	—	3.97	—	1768	1676
September	3.56	—	3.76	—	1651	1563
October	2.49	—	2.62	—	1601	1522
November	2.76	—	2.44	—	2884	2668
December	1.32	—	1.62	—	3371	2738
1957						
January	3.00	—	3.42	—	3054	2675
February	3.28	4.49	3.84	4.12	3049	2605
March	2.84	4.41	3.51	3.95	3584	2871
April	2.40	4.46	3.16	3.91	3957	3005
May	2.76	4.44	3.76	3.81	4262	3129
June	2.66	4.52	3.59	3.78	4540	3365
July	2.44	4.63	3.35	3.78	4590	3343
August	2.91	4.68	4.29	3.69	4632	3145
September	3.14	4.65	4.54	3.58	4960	3434
October	2.82	4.55	4.03	3.47	5472	3834
November	2.78	4.48	3.79	3.36	6031	4431
December	1.70	4.59	2.34	3.39	6272	4560
1958						
January	2.99	4.63	4.66	3.35	5141	3305
February	3.23	4.60	5.00	3.27	4680	3028
March	2.63	4.64	4.25	3.23	5081	3149

to insure that sufficient internally generated funds would be available for future expansion.

Services, Advertising, and Sales Promotion

The ABM stores were designed for semiself-service shopping; the store layout and merchandise presentation were arranged in such a way that the customer could find a desired item quickly and could make his choice without strong personal selling effort. Customer services such as delivery, credit facilities, elaborate wrappings, etc., were dispensed with entirely. The stores, however, were pleasantly decorated, had piped music, and every effort was made to create an atmosphere that would invite the customer to shop around.

ABM did no advertising. Sales promotion was limited to in-store merchandising media such as window displays, point-of-sale displays, and special layout arrangements. All such in-store sales promotions were planned at ABM headquarters by the sales promotion department. The branch managers and their subordinates were not consulted.

Pricing

ABM's pricing objective was to offer favorable prices on good quality merchandise appealing not only to the middle- and low-income groups but to all price-conscious consumers. Mr. Mahler remarked that, "we work with the elasticity of demand" and also pointed out that "with a small assortment and a desire for large volume, low prices are necessary."

One principle of ABM's pricing policy was not to be undersold, and to this end it carefully watched the prices of all competitive stores in its trading areas. For example, ABM closely watched the prices of Migros—a large chain renowned for its aggressive pricing methods primarily in goods but also in soft goods. While it matched low prices quoted by competitors, ABM did not sell any merchandise on a "loss-leader" basis.

Competition

Because of the range of merchandise offered and their downtown location, the ABM stores found themselves in competition with many retailers, including full-line department stores, variety stores, food stores, and, of course, Migros outlets.

The Berne ABM store, for example, was located on the main shopping street about midway between the two largest department stores. Also on this street, in the three blocks between the department stores, were a large Migros store, a variety chain store, and many large and small specialized stores. It was the case writer's impression that, in terms of location and physical appearance and facilities, the ABM store was competitive with the other outlets. It was also the case writer's impression that prices at the ABM Berne store were, for the most part, the same as or slightly lower than prices for similar merchandise in competitive stores. However, the ABM store carried a limited assortment of merchandise, a limited variety of brands of the products it did carry and, as a consequence, offered a limited price range to the consumer.

Competitive stores, particularly the department stores and with the exception of Migros,[4] generally carried a greater assortment of merchandise, several brands of each product, and offered a fairly wide choice of prices to the consumer.

All the competitive stores carried at least some private brands, and invariably it was these private brands that were in direct price competition with ABM's merchandise. For example, ABM carried only private-branded nylon hosiery primarily at two prices, 2.95 francs and 3.95 francs. All the competitive stores visited by the case writer also carried private brands of nylon hose at these prices and, in addition, many carried a number of national brands at higher prices.

Private Brands

ABM management's goals in introducing private brands were: (1) to maintain and enhance ABM's reputation for competitive, aggressive pricing; (2) to create a broad image of selling quality goods at low prices; and (3) to cut down inventory and space requirements by eliminating manufacturer brands where possible.

By 1958, ABM had introduced twenty private brands and had eliminated approximately fifty previously carried brands in the process. Some examples of ABM private brands with related sales volume, prices, and margin statistics are given in Exhibit 4.

The private brands carried by AMB were defined in two broad categories. The first included all articles that carried the "ABM" name alone or in conjunction with a private trade name. Examples of items in this category were detergent and Eau de Cologne. The second category included those articles that, because of their "fashion" nature and the fact that they might be used for gifts, did not carry the ABM name but had special wrappings and names. Articles in this category were the "Soldanella" brand nylon hose and "New Pioneer" nail polish.

ABM management had adopted no formal written policy on the selec-

---

[4] See Appendix A for a short description of this important force in Swiss retailing.

Exhibit 4   **Au Bon Marché**

Selected Examples of Private Brands
and Relevant Statistics

Merchandise	*Brands*	*Sales Price*	*Approximate Sales—1957*	*Approximate Markup*
1. Detergent	Lux	1.40	2,400 francs	17%
	ABM[a]	0.95	3,300 francs	16%
2. Eau de Cologne	ABM[a]	—	6,400 francs	28%
	Others[b] (Manufacturer Brands)	—	13,600 francs	35%
3. Nail Polish	New Pioneer[a] No other brands	0.90	1,260 francs	27%
4. Hosiery	Soldanella[a]	—	175,200 francs	28%
	ABM[a] No other brands		64,800 francs	27%

a Private brands
b ABM's alcohol was only 60 percent whereas the others were 90 percent

tion of private brands nor, for that matter, on the extent to which private branding was desirable. Up to the present most decisions had been made on an individual basis. Mr. Mahler explained, however, that the following conditions were usually considered in decisions to adopt private brands:

The article must be of first-class quality.

The article should be suitable to, and promote, self-service. (The customer's confidence eliminates necessity of any sales talk).

By its packaging, the private brand article must have an effective appearance that would increase its sales potential.

Price and demand should be constant over the seasons of the year.

Management recognized that margins on private brands were often lower than on national brands but were willing to accept this if the private brand seemed to have the potential of higher turnover at lower prices.

The Private Brand Proposals

It was against this background that Mr. Mahler, the buyers, the store managers, and store sales heads met in early 1958 to consider the following private brand proposals:

1. *Toilet Soap* ABM was carrying four manufacturer brands of toilet
   soap: Lux, Cadum, Palmolive, and Maya. The sales prices, sales
   volumes, and margins (on selling price) on these products were:

Lux	Selling price:	Sfr. 0.85/bar
	Sales volume:	approx. 41,000 bars/year
	Margin:	33%
Cadum	Selling price:	Sfr. 0.85/bar
	Sales volume:	approx. 18,000 bars/year
	Margin:	36%
Palmolive	Selling price:	Sfr. 0.75/bar
	Sales volume:	approx. 18,500 bars/year
	Margin:	35%
Maya	Selling price:	Sfr. 1.00/bar
	Sales volume:	approx. 14,000 bars/year
	Margin:	37%

All these soaps were price-fixed, and the manufacturers did extensive
consumer advertising.

The group "D" buyer proposed that ABM adopt a private brand soap
to sell at Sfr. 0.50. It would be the same size bar as the manufacturer brands
ABM carried and could be purchased from a reputable soap manufacturer
for Sfr. 0.33 per bar. The manufacturer agreed to absorb packaging, package
design, and delivery costs if ABM would guarantee an annual volume of
at least 25,000 bars. Otherwise, these costs would have to be further negotiated. The buyer also recommended that the present manufacturer brands
be kept if the private brand were adopted.

2. *Household Starch* ABM presently carried one national brand of household starch. Statistics were:

Selling price:	Sfr. 1.85 packeage
Sales volume:	approx. 1,600 packages/year
Margin:	23.5%

This starch was price-fixed. It was not a heavily advertised brand.

The group "D" buyer recommended the adoption of a private brand of
starch to be sold for Sfr. 1.95 for a package containing four times more
starch than the national brand package. Arrangements had been made,
again with a reputable manufacturer, to purchase such starch, packaged and
labeled, for 1.25 francs per package in lots of 1,000 packages. Delivery
expenses were not considered to be material. ABM would have to bear the
costs of package design and registration, which were estimated at about

350 francs. In this case the buyer recommended the elimination of the national brand.

3. *Men's and Boys' Underwear*   ABM was selling a manufacturer brand of men's and boys' underwear. The composite statistics were:

Average sales price: Sfr. 3.75 piece
Total sales volume: approx. 45,000 pieces/year
Average margin: approx. 24%

The prices on this brand were not fixed. The manufacturer did a small amount of consumer advertising.

The group "B" buyer had located a manufacturer willing to supply identical quality merchandise at prices that would yield ABM a margin of 28 percent if present retail prices were maintained. One condition was the elimination of the present manufacturer brand. The buyer recommended accepting this offer and the branding of the underwear with an "ABM" label.

4. *Women's Sweaters*   ABM was presently importing branded woolen sweaters from Italy. Sales volume was well over 100,000 francs at a margin of 33 percent and average sales price of about 20 francs. There were no attempts to fix retail prices on this brand.

Another Italian supplier had offered to supply sweaters of the same quality to ABM at lower prices provided they carry an ABM private label. If such sweaters were sold at present prices, the group "A" buyer estimated the margin would be about 40 percent. The buyer thus recommended accepting this supplier's offer. He also recommended that the present manufacturer brand be retained and that a special private brand name, not specifically mentioning ABM, be given to the new sweaters.

APPENDIX A

AU BON MARCHÉ A.G.

Selected Notes on the Migros Organization[1]

The (Migros) organization...manufactures, wholesales, and retails food and related nonfood items; distributes and will soon refine, gasoline; has its own bank; publishes its own newspapers; has its own political party with representation in the Conseil National; runs an extensive tourist travel plan

---

[1] These notes were taken from "The Changing Pattern of Europe's Grocery Trade" by R. Davis, Stanford University, 1959.

throughout Europe; has a book club and supports a number of cultural and social activities.

A few statistics summarize the major elements of the (Migros store) policy;

Migros Stores by Number and Type					
Type	*1951*	*1952*	*1953*	*1954*	*1957*
Service	159	145	134	109	52
Self-service	82	121	145	179	291
Van	70	68	70	71	100
	311	334	349	359	443

Not only has Migros increased its retail outlets 40 percent in seven years but it has been fast converting its service stores. Thus, while van outlets kept pace with the overall expansion, service stores declined 70 percent and self-service operations more than doubled. In fact, in 1958, it was Migros policy, when building, to put up only self-service outlets. The significance of self-service is magnified when we realize that such stores outsell in total the service operations nine to one.

The annual sales growth of the Migros food stores averaged 20 percent in 1956 and 1957, so that by 1957 total sales were about 600,000,000 Swiss francs at retail, $4\frac{1}{2}$ percent of all Swiss retail sales and 9 percent to 10 percent of food sales, not counting alcohol or cigarettes. Certainly, the growth has been dramatic when we compare today's volume with the 303,000,000 franc volume in 1952 and the 85,000,000 franc volume at the end of World War II.

The Migros price policy is one of the major points for which the organization is attacked by Swiss manufacturers and distributive trades. Migros carries no items with fixed prices, which means that it stocks few national brands. There are some exceptions, to be sure, but they include items distributed by official or semiofficial organizations and, of course, imports. If a Swiss manufacturer were to sell his national brands to Migros, all other Swiss distributive outlets would be closed to him. The supplying of private labels, however, is possible and a number of brand producers do just that. But, for a national brand, Migros is an either/or proposition. Either you supply Migros and no one else or you supply the rest of the trade and not Migros.

The price appeal is naturally one of Migros's major selling points, completing its three-sided marketing formula of quality, self-service, and price.

Other than its policy of carrying no price-maintained merchandise, Migros's outstanding product policy is that of limited items. The firm stocks no duplicating items or brands. . . . As a consequence the company is able to operate efficiently with limited stocks.

Limited stocks explain, in part, Migros's ability to sell more per square foot ($7 each week) than many comparable stores in the United States.

A final characteristic of Migros, certainly in contrast with most European competition, is the heavy emphasis on self-service.

Self service was the result of three factors in Migros:

1. The desire for more volume in the same space.
2. The desire to service the rapidly growing number of customers.
3. The desire to expand sales.

The conversion to self-service, as we have seen, has been rapid. . . . Self-service is by no means complete, however, even in the supermarkets. Vegetables, fruits, delicatessen items, charcuterie, and flowers are service items, while meat is typically offered on both a service and self-service basis. A few stores in Zürich do offer self-service meat only. Customer resistance generally precludes the latter approach, particularly in the larger markets.

On the average, 40 percent of the space (in Migros supermarkets) is devoted to nonfoods, which account for 30 percent of the sales. But the company, in contrast to American supermarkets, discounts its nonfood items as a fundamental principle, resulting in a situation of little or no profit on such merchandise.

4

Production
and Operations Management

Emphasis in this area is placed on the development and utilization of the "Systems Concept" to provide economical and effective solutions for problems arising in production and operations management. The course objectives are specifically:

A. To develop an understanding of the technological, economic, and human aspects of the creation of goods and services and of how these factors interrelate as an operating system.

B. To develop skill in identifying and analyzing important managerial decisions that affect the efficient operation of an enterprise:
   —Design of operating systems
   —Planning and scheduling of operations
   —Control of inventories, schedules, quality, and cost
   —Modernization and technological change
   —Use of computers

C. To develop insight into the dynamic behavior of complex interactive systems.

D. To develop an understanding of applications of modern techniques of analysis to management decisions. Emphasis will be placed upon the manager's role when relating to technical specialists who apply these concepts.

224

E. To provide an appreciation of relationships between production and operations managers and other activities in an organization.

The course will be divided into four parts, each of which has a central focus:

Part 1   *The scope of operations management and operations as systems of interrelated parts*   This section is designed to (a) give an introduction, (b) present a systems viewpoint, and (c) establish the usefulness of breaking down an operating system into its parts in order to understand each and to study the related concepts and tools.

Part 2   *Design of operating systems*   This section covers relationships among men and machines, flows of materials, and information. Systems design determines how these components affect each other and how they influence cost, quality, and availability of products and services. Topics covered by the cases and readings include system design, work planning, manpower standards and productivity, line balancing, and improvement curve theory.

Part 3   *Planning and control of operations*   In this section planning and control of flows through an operating system will be considered. Central to this is the role of a control system that reflects the basic system design. Scheduling and inventories are major areas of emphasis and are seen as complementary one to another. In addition, other concepts will be covered: network analysis with PERT/ CPM, industrial dynamics, quality and reliability, simulation.

Part 4   *Automation and technology*   This section will consider the impact on management of technology and automation. Some attention will be given to the management of research and development.

These four parts are not mutually exclusive, and there is considerable overlap among them. Although each part will be concerned with particular problem areas, running throughout the course will be questions of interrelationships between the operations part of an enterprise and other functions.

BAYERISCHE MASCHINEN
WERKE GmbH

The first few observer seats and control stands had just been shipped by
the Bayerische Maschinen Werke GmbH[1] (BMW) from Anderbach, Germany, to the Kellering Aircraft Company (KAC) on the West Coast of the
U.S. Mr. Hans von Halle, Sales Manager of the Aircraft Division of BMW,
planned to review the condition of the DM 3,000,000[2] contract and evaluate
the difficulties and problems experienced to date on this program for 150
seats, one hundred control stands, and related tooling. He faced the necessity
of recommending a future policy for his company regarding the expansion
or the elimination of sales effort directed toward prime contractors in the
U.S. aerospace industry.

Company Background

Bayerische Maschinen Werke GmbH was the surviving entity of a 1955
merger between BMW and Allgemeine Flugzeug Werke (AFW). BMW
itself, before the merger, had a history dating back to the early 1920s when
it had been founded as a machine shop in Anderbach, a small town not
far from Nuremberg. Throughout the pre-World War II years the machine
shop had grown in size until it was converted, during the war, into an am-
munition factory that suffered complete destruction as a result of military
action. After the war the plant was reconstructed as a repair yard for
railroad cars and later eventually expanded as a railroad car, hydraulic
press, and truck trailer manufacturing facility.

The AFW half of the present company had been founded in Potsdam
and was one of the pioneers in aircraft manufacturing. The company
had been a major contributor of military aircraft during the First World
War and had gone on, between the two wars, to create an excellent reputa-

---

1 GmbH is the abbreviation for *Gesellschaft mit beschränkter Haftung*. This is a "close
corporation" form of business organization having limited liability and whose stock is
privately held.
2 German Marks: DM 4.00 = $1.00

tion for itself in civilian aircraft by establishing several world speed, altitude, and endurance records. Immediately prior to World War II, the company again began producing military aircraft and continued to do so, despite severe destruction, during the war. The partition of Germany at the war's end resulted in their manufacturing facilities being located in the Eastern Zone, and these were dismantled and taken to the Soviet Union. All land, buildings, and equipment was expropriated by the Soviet Occupation Government. Most of the company's management and engineering personnel, however, managed to escape to the West, and the company was reestablished in Nuremburg. Here the AFW staff, forbidden by the Allied Powers from building airplanes, were only able to do limited design work on modern airframes and related projects.

In 1955, airspace sovereignty was returned to the Federal Republic of Germany (FRG), and AFW found itself with technical knowledge about aircraft but with no manufacturing facilities. It was under these circumstances that the BMW-AFW merger was arranged; with BMW supplying capital, facilities, and manufacturing know-how, and AFW supplying aircraft technology and a small organization that believed it could undertake new product design and development work. At the completion of the merger the old AFW offices were moved from Nuremburg to the BMW plant at Anderbach, and the company was reorganized into a Railroad Division (that included truck trailers and hydraulic presses) and an Aircraft Division.

Recent History

By the early 1960s the Aircraft Division of the company had established itself as a reliable supplier on several NATO subcontracts, on parts contracts awarded by the newly reconstituted Luftwaffe, and on subcontracts from several German commercial airplane companies. The designs were supplied by the buyers, and BMW's work consisted of the manufacture and assembly of such items as wings, wing sections, tail assemblies, fuel tanks, compartment bulkheads, airducts, doors, helicopter rotor blades, cockpit canopies, and radomes. Many of these items required extensive development effort in such fields as plastics, metal bonding, and other new techniques. As a result of this effort, BMW gained a reputation for a high level of competency.

In addition to its subcontract work, the company produced and marketed several small civilian aircrafts, including both piston and jet designs. One sports plane was of a prewar design, and another was built under a license from the foreign designer. Concurrently the Railroad Division had rapidly expanded its own domestic and foreign sales volume as a designer and manufacturer of original equipment. Between 1957 and 1964, the combined company operations tripled in turnover (sales) from DM 23 million to DM 70 million.

Manufacturing Location and Employees

BMW's entire facilities were located in the small town of Anderbach. The town was located on South Germany's rail and highway network, with direct connections to the major rail and air centers of Nuremburg and Munich. Thus, it had excellent transportation arrangements to the whole of Western Europe.

Although Anderbach was too far from Nuremburg for daily commutation, BMW had relatively little trouble—by German standards—in encouraging employees to come to work for the company. The town could be classified as a typically quaint Bavarian town and was well-liked by Germans as a place to live and work. The surroundings were pleasant, and housing was adequate.

Most of the BMW workers lived in the adjacent countryside, and many drove to work by auto. As a result, the company faced the necessity of expanding its four hundred-car parking lot. This was in contrast to the prewar situation when only the managing director and a few other executives came to work in private autos.

BMW, with 2500 workers, was the largest employer in the town that had a total population of 11,000. Located on an adjoining property was a major farm implement manufacturer that employed 800 people. The other businesses were the typical supporting service activities for such a community.

Despite its generally favorable location, however, BMW did have some problems in finding enough skilled employees to fulfill all its operating requirements. In the mid 1960s unemployment was virtually nonexistent throughout FRG. For any skilled worker who might temporarily be out of a job there were usually several job openings in his home location. This made it difficult to get workers to move to Anderbach.

As a result BMW found it necessary to recruit and transport to Anderbach approximately one hundred Turkish workers who were employed on a two-year contract basis. These foreign employees were hired by the production manager who periodically visited Turkey and made the necessary arrangements through a Turkish Government Agency. The Turkish workers spoke little or no German, but one of their group had a good command of the German language and did the necessary translating so that there were few communication problems. Although some of the workers developed skills such as welding, most of them were assigned unskilled manual tasks. After saving up a "nest egg" during their two-year contract most of the Turkish workers returned to their native land. Some, however, preferred to stay as long as possible.

Initial Contacts

When Kellering Airplane Company invited BMW to submit a bid, the top management was delighted since they had long desired to do sub-contract work for a U.S. firm. They felt that such work would give them entry to the U.S. aerospace industry and access to its technology. They saw in the U.S. some of the world's largest airplane makers and the most scientifically advanced aerospace organizations. If BMW were able to establish a direct link with U.S. firms, it could open for them a large and profitable market and permit them to participate in a rich technical information pool.

Kellering was also interested in establishing relationships with overseas suppliers. The firm's own facilities were operating at full capacity, and the company had a growing order backlog. Although it was expanding its facilities rapidly at a rate that would double its size in five years, the company still found it imperative to maintain and even enlarge its broadly based network of suppliers in the U.S. and Canada. Kellering felt foreign suppliers had the advantage of low labor costs, created relationships that could provide a potential base for stronger sales entry by Kellering into foreign markets, and offered Kellering the opportunity for making technical contacts with other foreign aerospace companies. In any case, Kellering felt they needed some direct experience with a major overseas supplier before they could determine their own long-range policy regarding foreign procurement.

Kellering had previously been involved in an engineering agreement on a consulting basis with a South German aircraft company for the joint design and development of military hardware for NATO. It was through this activity that Kellering first heard of BMW. On a trip to Germany regarding the NATO project, several of the Kellering executives visited BMW to inspect the plant. During this visit they informally questioned the management as to their willingness to bid on a U.S. subcontract. BMW management indicated that they would like to submit a bid on anything they could handle. They also carefully pointed out their long experience in the airframe business, their previous subcontract performance (some of which involved U.S. designs), and their competence and familiarity with such methods used in the aircraft industry as PERT and improvement curves.

Shortly after this visit, BMW was invited to bid on a contract for observer seats and control stands to be used on a large commercial jet airplane that Kellering was building. The observer seats were installed on such aircraft immediately behind the pilot and copilot for use by government inspectors, instructors, trainees, and visitors. The seat was a mechanical device con-structed of welded steel tubing with upholstered cushions and with a lever system to adjust its position. The control stand was located between the pilot and copilot and was a mechanical-electrical/electronic device with levers, switches, and cable connections to actuate devices for moving the aerodynamic control surfaces of the airplane. By moving these surfaces the pilot could trim the vertical and horizontal position of the airplane and control the flaps and airbrakes in the wings for landing. Because of its importance to the flight characteristics and to the safety of the airplane, the specifications for the control stands were comprehensive and had precise requirements for performance and tolerances.

Preparing the Bid

With the invitation to bid in hand, BMW set about to prepare their bid price. They knew that several U.S. companies along with BMW were invited to bid, and they realized that despite Kellering's interest to place an overseas subcontract, they would have to submit the lowest bid to win the award. Their competitive advantage was a labor rate that averaged DM 3.60 per hour, which they knew was substantially lower than those in the U.S. Their handicaps were in their limited familiarity with U.S. procedures, especially those of Kellering; and their geographic remoteness from Kellering, which would add to shipping costs and the costs of communication. Communication costs could be high, not only from the standpoint of transmission but also from the standpoint of translation and interpretation. Transmission costs could be controlled by the careful use of inexpensive communication channels, but the cost of translation and comprehension of the many documents involved, however, remained an imponderable.

A set of drawings and specifications for bidding purposes were provided BMW by Kellering. These were studied by the engineers and estimators who developed a tentative manufacturing plan and determined the bid price in the normal BMW manner, as shown in Exhibit 1.

Cost Estimates

The direct labor component of Exhibit 1 was derived by estimating the required man-hours and multiplying by the standard labor rate. This was primarily a task of estimating productivity since 80 percent of the jobs at BMW were on a piece rate basis using a 100 percent incentive plan—either by group or by individual. The remaining 20 percent of the jobs were on a time wage basis for such operations as chemical processing. Piece rates were established by time studies using a stop watch method in accordance with the REFA system—a standard time study procedure used throughout Germany. This system provided standards for such things as personal allowances, cycles to be timed, and leveling procedures. The motion and time study engineers applying the REFA system were required to have a

Exhibit 1　　　　　　　　　　　**Estimating Sheet**

Observers Seat—150 Shipsets

Direct Expense:	Hours	Rate	Total
Direct labor hours	126		
Sustaining labor hours	13		
Total labor hours	139		
Direct labor rate		DM 3.25	DM 451
Engineering and sustaining tooling			45
Total labor cost			496
Overhead expense:			
Production		47%	212
Engineering and tooling		300%	135
Material		25%	24
Material			96
Factory Cost			963
General and administrative expense,			
contingencies, taxes, and profit		20%	193
Total			1,156
Packaging			48
Sales price per shipset			1,204
Total contract price—150 shipsets			1,660,000
Total tooling costs			18,000
Total program costs			DM 1,678,000

Control Stand—100 Shipsets

Direct Expense:			
Direct labor hours	660		
Sustaining labor hours	132		
Total labor hours	792		
Direct labor rate		DM 4.85	DM 3,850
Engineering & sustaining tooling			575
Total labor cost			4,425
Overhead Expense:			
Production		47%	1,815
Engineering and tooling		300%	1,725
Material		25%	510
Material			2,025
Factory Cost			10,500
General and administrative expense,			
contingencies, taxes, and profit		20%	2,100
Total			12,600
Customer variation			385
			12,985
Packaging			350
Sales price per shipset			13,335
Total contract price—100 shipsets			1,333,500
Total tooling costs			128,000
Total program costs			DM 1,461,500

The Kellering buyer had also requested firm fixed costs for transportation and insurance and had requested that the BMW bid include allowances for the following clauses, which were to be part of the contract:

Observer Seat Engineering Change Allowance

The prices include the total cost effect of all future engineering, planning, and schedule, production, rework, tooling, termination, and obsolescence costs created by engineering changes, which may exceed the statement of work hereunder, the total price of which is less than $75.00 per change per shipset or less than $4,000 per change for the entire contract, whichever is first exceeded.

Control Stand Engineering Change Allowance

The price shall include all engineering, planning and schedule, production, rework, tooling, termination, and obsolescence costs created by engineering changes, which may exceed the statement of work, hereunder, the total price which is less then $150 per change per shipset or less than $10,000 per change for the entire contract, whichever is first exceeded.

The above dollar figures are applicable to price increases only. Changes exceeding the above limitation will be negotiated separately by the parties.

certificate indicating that they had completed a special course of study in the technique and had passed a standardized examination. Labor unions generally accepted without questions the piece rates established by persons who had the REFA certificate. The normalized time was set at 100 percent. The piece rates were established by applying a base labor rate to the time required on an 80 percent speed basis. If an actual operation resulted in workers operating at 30 percent above the normal speed, then the planning department rechecked the study.

Production overhead was derived from direct labor costs broken down by cost centers. Each cost center had its own overhead rate, which ranged from 150 percent (carpenters, upholsterers, etc.) to as high as 2,000 percent (for the chemical processing department). An overall average labor overhead rate normally amounted to about 250 percent of direct labor cost.

To the estimated total material requirements per unit was applied an associated overhead rate covering such items as transportation, receiving, purchasing, inventory control, and material handling. The largest costs were for purchasing and inventory control.

The "technical cost" included engineering and development work, their associated overhead, and some supervision. The technical overhead was normally allocated at fixed rates based on direct labor man-hours.

The categories for general and administrative expenses included allowances for sales expense, taxes, contingencies, and profit. The long-term cost trend for general and administrative expenditure (excluding contingencies, taxes, and profits) had averaged about 10 percent of total manufacturing costs.

Turnover taxes required special attention. There was a turnover tax of 4 percent on items manufactured for domestic consumption (except no tax was applied in West Berlin for items shipped out of Berlin). But there was no turnover tax on items manufactured for export, and in addition, manufacturers of export items received a 3.2 percent ad valorem tax rebate under the export compensation tax in order to encourage export shipment.

Dealers (wholesalers) paid a domestic turnover tax of 10 percent but no tax on exports. The dealers received a 7.2 percent tax rebate for export—4 percent to compensate for the manufacturers' turnover tax paid by the dealer and the 3.2 percent export compensation tax.

Normally BMW included in their contracts an escalation clause for changes in the cost of materials and wages. During recent years the cost increases subject to the escalation clause had averaged about 4.25 percent per year. Kellering would not accept such an escalation clause; hence the BMW made an estimate of future cost increases and included this in their estimate for contingencies. Thus, they carried the full risk for such cost changes.

Tooling costs were estimated in a similar manner but were treated in a separate formal contract. BMW had investigated prices and costs in the U.S. When BMW management reviewed their final bid, they felt confident that they were not only competitive but probably the low bidder.

The Contract Award

As it turned out BMW had, in fact, submitted the low bid. After sending a small team of Kellering engineers, from the NATO project, to briefly inspect their facilities, Kellering accepted the bid and awarded BMW the observer seat and control stand contract. Usually the Kellering buyer went to great lengths to help new suppliers become acquainted with Kellering methods and procedures. But after receiving the favorable report of the visit by the senior executives, Mr. Tim Lester, the Kellering buyer, felt BMW could be treated in the same fashion as any experienced U.S. supplier and that special assistance to BMW was not necessary. He was also aware of the distance and language barriers.

Shortly after the contract was awarded, Mr. Hans von Halle, Sales Manager of BMW, came to the U.S. to review the details of the contract at the home office of Kellering. Mr. von Halle had an engineering degree from a university in Germany and had a variety of experiences in commercial activities, including one year in the U.S. when he worked as a sales engineer for a major pump company. He was about thirty-five years old, an enthusiastic salesman, and the son of the managing director of BMW.

Contract Provisions

The final contract agreed to by both companies was typical of the form used by Kellering but had several features that were new to BMW. One such new aspect was the provision for value engineering. This provided for a 50–50 percent sharing between Kellering and BMW of all savings accruing from the application of value engineering principles to the work under the contract.

The delivery requirements were clearly and explicitly established by the contract. Delivery of the seats was to begin in nine months at a limited rate. The first stands were due in thirteen months. The delivery rate was to accelerate to a maximum of twelve seats and eight control stands per month, and then taper off until the contract was completed.

The contract also contained procedures for progress reporting. This was to be done monthly with Gantt-type charts identifying "milestones," such as the receipt of drawings, procurement of material, completion of manufacture, and shipments. These charts showed both the actual and planned performances—side by side—and were forwarded to both the Kellering U.S. Headquarters and to the Kellering NATO project team in Germany who might be able to provide assistance if difficulties were encountered by BMW.

A vital section of the contract covered the quality control policies that were to be implemented by detailed procedures. These were to be developed by BMW into a Q.C. manual, subject to approval by Kellering. The Q.C. procedures used by BMW on previous work had been reviewed by the Kellering inspection team, and their apparent similarity to the requirements of the contract had convinced them that BMW could perform satisfactorily. The contract did not provide for source inspection (final inspection at the supplier's plant, subject to guarantees) but the final inspection and acceptance were to be conducted at the home plant of Kellering.

Related to quality control and inspection was the requirement for approval by the U.S. Federal Aviation Agency. The FAA had to pass on all equipment that went into U.S. made planes. This approval consisted of two distinct aspects: (1) approval of the design and (2) approval of the manufacture. Although the FAA had an office in Brussels and could perform its inspections and grant its approval without too much difficulty, BMW would have preferred to deal with PFL, the German counterpart of the FAA. They had heard that this had been done in other situations, and they felt PFL could at least have been asked to certify the manufacture of the seats and stands because the FAA had already certified the design that had been made by Kellering.

In submitting their bid, BMW had been required to submit a breakdown of their price as shown in Exhibit 1. The contract included a clause regarding the cost control and accounting procedures. These procedures at BMW had also been checked by the Kellering review team before the contract was awarded, and it appeared that they followed the generally accepted U.S. concepts about accounting methods, although there were certain differences reflecting European practice. To ensure that Kellering could obtain experience in German accounting methods, Kellering had included a clause in the contract giving them the right to audit BMW's books where they pertained to the contract. Commenting on the bid requirements for a cost breakdown and for the audit, Mr. von Halle said, "We would not have accepted such clauses from anyone but Kellering. We have great respect for them and we were anxious to do business with them." Although BMW had been audited frequently in the past by FRG, such audits were always associated with "cost plus" contracts. Mr. von Halle did not think such an audit was either necessary or justified on a fixed-price contract.

A final provision of the contract gave Kellering an option, effective for eighteen months, for additional quantities. One hundred and fifty seats could be ordered at a unit price reduction of 10 percent, and one hundred stands could be ordered at a unit price reduction of 30 percent. These prices were established on the basis of the expected improvement curve performance.

Drawings and Specifications

As soon as the contract went into effect, BMW began to receive the necessary drawings, specifications, manuals, and documentation from Kellering. Although BMW had had previous experience on its NATO contracts in dealing with U.S. firms, the adaptation phase still had its difficulties. Mr. von Halle said, "Any changeover, even from one U.S. manufacturer to another, is difficult. This is especially true if the changeover involves differences in language and measuring system."

The translation aspects were particularly difficult for BMW. Since only about twenty persons in the company spoke English (some very limited), it was desirable that all documents be translated into German. In Anderbach, BMW did not have ready access to outside translation facilities that were available in larger cities. Furthemore, the type of translation involved did not appear to justify permanent "expert" translators who could command up to DM 1,600 per month more in salary than a technician with merely a knowledge of English. There were some 1,500 pages of text to be translated at a rate of about two to four pages per hour. This work was greatly reduced, however, by published translations that were available, such as those covering many U.S. Military Specifications (Mil Specs). In addition the Kellering engineers in Germany were available to assist with the translating of special technical terms. More important than the *cost* of translation was the *time lag* involved. If a particular piece of information was immediately needed and if that information had never been translated, it might take several hours to make the translation and get the information to the production personnel. This lost time, however, could delay the schedule by as much as a full day.

Drawings were received from Kellering in the form of a transparency for each plan. BMW entered the German translation directly onto the transparency, side by side with the original English wording, including the metric equivalents for the English units of measure. Thus, below a dimension shown in inches would be the equivalent dimension in centimeters. The transparency was then used to reproduce the necessary blueprints or black and white prints for shop use.

The problem of translating dimensions from the English system to metric system and vice versa was generally a minor one. BMW had, from its previous work, a large supply of gauges and tools based on the decimal inch, and the company's workmen were largely familiar with this system. Although all dimensions on the drawings were given in both centimeters and decimal inches, BMW did most of its work in decimal inches.

Another problem was the cross-referencing of the various parts on a drawing. In many cases BMW engineers found the Kellering system of cross-referencing complex and confusing. Furthermore, after tracing a particular part number back through the system to its original drawing, BMW engineers on several occasions found that Kellering had not sent them the required detailed drawings. Communicating this lack to the U.S. and getting the required drawings could consume several weeks. The engineering staff of BMW felt that all cross-referenced detail drawings pertaining to the contract should have been assembled in the U.S. and sent, as a complete set, to Germany. They felt the delay in receiving some drawings had a serious effect on the production schedule.

Besides having to identify cross-references, BMW also had to deal with changes and modifications. Internal procedures for dealing with changes had been established for the various NATO contracts that they had previously worked on. There were new problems, however, with *modifications*. Unlike changes, these did not alter the basic drawing but introduced a minor modification for only a few units to suit one particular customer of Kellering. BMW was still receiving modifications eight weeks beyond the promised cutoff-date for units that were to be delivered in four months, and this created serious production problems.

Parts Procurement

Another problem area involved approved sources of supply for purchased parts and materials. During the final negotiations it was clear to BMW that all purchasing would have to be done in strict conformity to the specifications required by Kellering. BMF understood, however, that they could use any supplier who could certify that their material was in accordance with the required specifications. On the basis of this understanding, BMW purchased some special control cable from a well-known French company that supplied the European Aircraft Industry. This order suggested new sales possibilities to the French company. They had their U.S. representative contact the buyer at Kellering headquarters on the basis that if they could provide parts for Kellering through BMW, they should also be able to sell directly to Kellering for other purposes. The Kellering buyer who discussed the matter with the French representative immediately checked the Kellering approved list of suppliers and was surprised to find that the French company was not on the list. The buyer then sent a telegram to BMW advising them that the French cable could not be used on the Kellering contract. From this incident BMW learned that they could only purchase from suppliers who were previously approved by Kellering. The only suppliers that were approved were located in the U.S.

The French company requested Kellering to add them to their approved list of suppliers. The Kellering buyers responded that they already had two suppliers in the U.S. that they felt were sufficient because the special cable was purchased in small quantities. To send an inspection team to France to certify the French company could not be economically justified.

BMW felt that some of their purchasing problems could be avoided if Kellering would remove their restriction requiring the use of specified U.S. sources and would permit the use of European suppliers and the corresponding European specifications. Many equivalent parts were available in almost identical form from competent European sources. BMW felt that they did not yet have enough business in the U.S. to establish a permanent U.S. representative for their U.S. purchases. Most U.S. suppliers were not export oriented and increased their prices to overseas customers. The customers also had to bear the extra cost of shipment, duties, and insurance. Even at the higher prices many U.S. firms were still not interested in overseas customers because of the unfamiliar procedures that were entailed, especially during a prosperous period in the U.S. when it was relatively easy to sell to domestic customers. Thus BMW was forced in many cases to depend on their freight forwarding companies to handle many administrative details that suppliers might refuse to do. Mr. von Halle, underlining the importance of the freight forwarder, asserted that a skillful and cooperative freight forwarder was a necessity to purchase from and ship to U.S. firms.

An example of a purchasing problem that arose was that of obtaining special tubing of an odd shape, which was required by the FAA specification. This tubing was only available in the U.S. from a single supplier. BMW had a great amount of difficulty locating and contacting the supplier, which it did without help from Kellering. Even then, the tubing did not exactly meet the precise specifications, but further investigation revealed, however, that it was acceptable to Kellering. Later BMW learned that the Kellering buyer would have been glad to assist if he had been notified of BMW's problem. Mr. von Halle's response was "Kellering didn't clearly advise us at the beginning that they would help us, and anyway we had to show them that we were capable of independently doing our own job."

BMW management was very concerned about the problems of drawing interpretation and sources of supply because of the effect on delivery. If additional Kellering subcontracts were to be obtained they believed that they had to perform well on the present one. If necessary, BMW was prepared to reduce the six to eight weeks delivery required by ocean and rail transport and to ship the finished units to the U.S. by air at their expense.

Communications

BMW management felt that their relationship with Kellering was generally satisfactory, but they would have preferred a greater degree of mutuality. Mr. von Halle recognized the reasons for using English exclusively in BMW's dealings with Kellering, but he would have appreciated some use of German in informal discussions. With most other foreign customers correspondence was carried on in the language of the customer, but usually some German was used in personal negotiations. With French customers it was normal practice for all correspondence to be sent and received in both German and French. Although it was obvious to the Kellering people that the contract was being performed by a German firm, there was almost no one at Kellering who could or would use German.

This was reflected in Kellering's communications with BMW. Almost all communications were written in English, that required about four days transit time by air mail and three weeks by surface mail. Kellering had a sales office in Paris with a direct telex connection to its U.S. headquarters. On a few occasions BMW sent telex messages through the Paris office for important matters that necessitated immediate response. It usually required only fifteen minutes to complete the transmission, but because of the nine-hour time difference between the two locations, one company office was closed when the other was open. Thus, it was difficult to get immediate response. Except for one or two occasions the telephone was not used, even for pressing problems when the expense could have been justified.

Immediately after Mr. von Halle's trip to the U.S. after the contract was awarded, there was little face to face contact between the two firms except for occasional visits from the Kellering engineers in Germany. As the contract progressed Mr. von Halle was concerned that his views and his problems were not completely understood by the Kellering management. Finally, three months after the contract award, BMW sent one of their engineers to the Kellering headquarters to review technical problems on the drawings and to clarify some matters that were very difficult to translate. Six months after the contract award, Mr. Tim Lester, the Kellering buyer responsible for the BMW contract, visited Anderbach for a general review of the situation. One month later he was followed by Carl Gothel who came as the resident inspector. In the following month, two executives from BMW stopped off at the Kellering headquarters while on other business to the U.S. and were able to clarify some technical questions and special problems.

Quality Control

The quality control department at Kellering was completely independent of other functional departments and, through its own line organization, reported directly to the president. It was the policy of this department to provide a resident inspector at the plant of those suppliers who had large and complicated contracts that required inspection during the manufacturing process. In this way the department was able to catch many errors during manufacture and thus to save the cost and time of shipping parts back to the supplier if they were not satisfactory. In addition to handling quality control matters, the resident inspector was to assist the subcontractors with other activities such as materials, engineering, production planning, manufacturing processes, etc. He was not, however, involved in contract negotiations as such, although he was aware of the general terms of the contract.

The department had always planned to send a representative to BMW at the proper time. Mr. Gothel arrived at BMW as the resident inspector six weeks prior to the scheduled first shipment. Mr. Gothel's arrival, however, was unexpected by most of the BMW executives, and for several weeks he was merely greeted courteously but largely ignored by the plant personnel. But after he made it known that he planned to reject the first units because of defects, and the local BMW quality control supervisor was instructed to accept Mr. Gothel's authority, his comments, advice, and suggestions began to receive more careful attention. Nevertheless, there was open hostility between Mr. Gothel, and the BMW quality control department members who complained and resisted for the following overt reasons:

1. Mr. Gothel's interpretation of the specifications was only one point of view, and there was no need for BMW to comply with his interpretation when they could read the same specification and arrive at a different interpretation.
2. His recommendations were contrary to BMW's previous procedures.
3. He required records to be kept that were unnecessary.
4. His recommendations and requests involved additional costs that were not provided for in the original estimate.

Exhibit 2   **Excerpts from Quality Control Requirements
for Kellering Suppliers**

Section 1   General

1.1   Policy

The contractual obligations of the Kellering Company, and the highly competitive and technical nature of the industry, cause quality control requirements
to assume a most vital role. The proportion of the Kellering product fabricated
by suppliers, the greater complexity of many of such components, and the
essentially high level of reliability make it impractical or impossible to adequately assure product quality by inspections and controls at Kellering plants
alone.

In order to assure product quality, appropriate inspections must be made,
controls initiated, and/or data gathered for each phase of the life cycle of the
product, from the refining and compounding of raw materials to customer
service.

Therefore, since Kellering is obligated to assure the overall quality of the
end product, including its service reliability, Kellering must verify that each
supplier of material going into the end product is aware of, is enforcing, and
is recording accomplishment of adequate quality controls.

This requires that all work performed pursuant to a Kellering purchase
order shall be subject to inspection, surveillance, test, and quality control audit
by Kellering at all reasonable times, including the period of performance, and
at all places, including the plant or plants of the supplier or any of its suppliers
engaged in the performance of work to fulfill the Kellering purchase order.

.   .   .

Section 2   Publication of requirements

2.1   Procedures

The supplier shall establish and maintain written procedures defining his
Quality Control system. These procedures shall be subject to the right of
disapproval by Kellering

A. Management responsibility for the Quality Control function will be set
   forth on the supplier's organization chart. The responsibility for the Quality
   Control function will be so placed that schedules and cost will not compromise quality.

Section 3   Records and Stamps

3.1.   Records

Adequate records of inspections and tests performed under the responsibility
of the supplier shall be maintained.

.   .   .

Section 4   Facilities

4.1   Measurement and Test Equipment

All test and measurement equipment used to check product components and systems, to check materials that are used in a product, or to check control of the processing of a product, shall be checked against a standard that has greater accuracy. The required accuracy of shop test and measurement equipment is the accuracy required to evaluate the most precise tolerances of any item required to be checked by the equipment. The standards against which test and measurement equipment is periodically checked shall have their accuracy verified directly by or through a precise comparison with legal standards traceable to the National Bureau of Standards.

Section 5   Procurement Control

5.1   Procurement by the Supplier

The supplier shall assume the responsibility for the quality of all purchased materials, articles, and services. This responsibility includes:

A. Selection of qualified procurement sources.

Section 6   Process control

Section 7   Product Control

Section 8   Functional Tests

Section 9   Special Procedures

9.1   Discrepancy controls

The quality control procedures will assure that non-conforming materials, tools, or test equipment will be identified as discrepant, segregated and reviewed for disposition.

9.1.2   Reliability
9.2   Single Standard Quality Control
9.3   Statistical Quality Control
9.4.   Training
9.5   Quality Control Audit Program

The supplier shall audit the adequacy of quality program procedures, inspections, tests, process controls, and certifications performed in each area on a timely basis. The audit shall be performed by an impartial team familiar with written procedures and standards applicable to the areas being audited but not having specific line responsibilities in those areas.

The audit shall include examination of all quality operations and documentation, comparison with established requirements, notification of required corrective action, and follow up to assess results of corrective action. An example of an examination of an inspection operation would include, but not be limited to:

A. A reinspection of work accepted by the inspectors in the area.
B. An investigation of the availability of all required documents.
C. A determination of the familiarity of personnel concerned with required documents.
D. A review of failure analysis and corrective action taken.
E. An evaluation of the adequacy of acceptance and rejection documents.

5. The additional record keeping and inspections procedures that were requested required more manpower, and the quality control department did not have sufficient people with the ability needed to comply with Gothel's recommendations.
6. None of the other customers of BMW required such quality control procedures and Gothel's request involved unnecessary special favors for only Kellering's benefit.

Mr. Gothel based his activities on a document entitled "Quality Control Requirements for Kellering Suppliers," which established basic policies and was incorporated as a part of the contract with BMW. Exhibit 2 contains excerpts from this document. He also had a supplementary document: "Operating Instructions Manual for Resident QC Inspectors" of which twenty-seven pages was largely concerned with the manner of making a survey of the subcontractors QC procedures to properly qualify the supplier in compliance with the contract.

Resident Inspector's Opinions

Mr. Gothel was asked by the case writer to comment on his observations and problems at BMW.

I have had a hard time trying to find direct answers to who does what. They have an organization chart, all right, (see Exhibit 3) but several people seem to be doing the same job; on the other hand, for some problems I can find no one who accepts responsibility. Many times my questions merely get a shrug of the shoulder answer.

Exhibit 3   **Organization Chart**
Bayerische Maschinen Werke GmbH

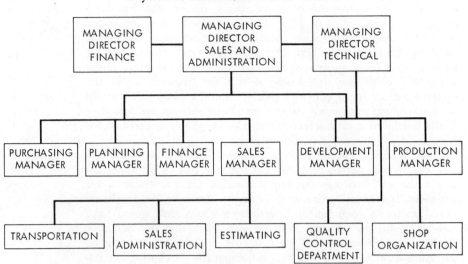

The production manager is a very capable man, but he has five major programs under his jurisdiction, only one of which is the Kellering project, and he cannot give it sufficient attention. I feel there is a serious "management gap" at the middle level. Part of the trouble is that too many decisions must be made at the top level. Lower-level people have a great deal of trouble getting prompt decisions about their problems—many of which could have been delegated to a lower level. There is not enough information filtering down from the top management regarding basic policy, terms of the contract, relationships with customers, and other types of information that would help coordinate the job. At the same time, they don't give the shop much information on how to do a job—they just throw the blueprints into the shop and let the workmen figure out what to do. If some materials or parts are missing the workmen are just hung-up because no special group is assigned to expedite deliveries.

It's also very difficult for lower-level people to get their problems passed up the line. For example, the most trivial kind of capital expenditure has to be approved at top levels, and usually it is not accepted if it was not entered in the capital budget that may have been made a long time ago. As a result, new problems turn up that require minor tools or equipment, but these cannot be quickly purchased. This causes serious production delays, or the shop finds a way to get around the problem by an expensive method that does not require the tools or equipment.

We had a mix-up because of this and because of language misunderstanding. The throttle handles and reversing levers on the control stand have to be tested for the torque required to move them. The test specifications call for the use of a precision scale. At home this means the use of a measuring device that has been certified as to its accuracy. Here they understood "precision scale" to mean a simple spring scale, and I found them using a scale for weighing fish to run the test. Obviously this was unsatisfactory. I insisted they get a proper device. Then the question was raised when they could buy it because it was not allowed for in the budget, and getting approval for this "capital expenditure" would involve a substantial delay. After a lot of pressure on my part they finally borrowed a satisfactory precision scale that was certified for accuracy from another aircraft company.

I have to keep pushing them to use some imagination when they run into an unexpected problem. Let me give you an example. On one of the seat drawings the length specified for a few screws was too short. It was an engineering oversight. At home the mechanic would go to an open bin and get longer screws that would have enough threads to properly hold the nuts. Here they did not have the extra length screws and work on the job stopped because no one knew what to do. Finally they requested the purchasing department to buy longer screws. Because of the specifications these screws had to be purchased in the U.S., and it would take at least six weeks to get delivery. That's the way they left it. When I heard about it I blew my top because this meant that the first deliveries would be delayed another six weeks beyond the current schedule, which was already late. I insisted that they get the screws right now, somehow! Finally, at my suggestion, they contacted Lufthansa and found that they could get the few screws that were needed immediately from the airline's maintenance stores.

One of my biggest problems is to get them to put things down in writing. For example, when a part is rejected by their inspector it is usually done on a verbal basis and the part is thrown in the junk pile. Once in a while it even gets pulled out of the junk pile and slipped back into production. Our quality control policy manual requires them to tag every rejection with a full explanation so that we can retrace problems and get the correction made at the proper place. This sometimes means changing shop procedure or even going all the way back to get a change in the drawing. In order to control these rejected parts they are supposed to have a locked rejection cage to provide secure segregation of bad parts. This cage requirement is in the policy manual and everyone here says they are going to set it up, but so far there is no cage.

The inspectors here seem to have great faith in what other people say is okay. They have to learn to check everything. For example, on a special control knob for the stand the inspectors assumed that the dimensions were okay because the vendor stated the part was made in accordance with the specifications. They didn't even make a first part inspection, let alone check all of the shipment. Later on I found that the part did not fit properly and had to reject it.

Although the shop people here have had a great deal of experience in working on prejet aircraft parts, they have not quite grasped the jet age situation. For example, a minor gouge on a forging is okay for plane flying at 200 miles an hour. But in a 600 miles per hour plane minor scratches and gouges can cause concentrated stresses that may result in failure. This concept has not yet been fully recognized here. They also leave too much to the workman to decide on how to make the part. They need a great many more detailed process specifications to explain to the worker exactly how each operation should be done. These fellows complain badly when I insist on this because they say they are expert mechanics. I agree, but they don't understand the new situation.

Let me explain what I want to avoid. On my previous job I checked a landing gear part that was a forging and failed in service, causing a great deal of havoc. After much investigation, we traced the error to a workman who had drilled a hole in the forging. He used a dull drill and exceeded the feed speed stated in the process specifications. Because of the dull drill the inside of the hole had minor scratches, and the fast speed caused the part to overheat around the hole during drilling. In use, under great stress, vibration and severe weather conditions, the scratches in the hole allowed some corrosion to begin, and the extra heat from the drilling had changed the crystalline structure so that the corrosion cracks rapidly developed through the part, like a hot knife going through butter. This minor mistake on the part of the mechanic could have jeopardized a five million dollar airplane and the lives of more than one hundred people.

The buyer at Kellering has to start at the negotiating table to stress the need for quality and precise adherence to process specifications. Most buyers don't fully understand this and do an inadequate job of conditioning the vendor. The buyer tells the vendor he has to provide good quality in accordance with the specifications. The vendor says yes, but nobody really understands what this means. It is bad enough in the States, but over here the problem is really fierce.

They have very good people here. Most of their mechanics have been through a long apprentice program. They are better trained and can do a larger variety of jobs than most of the mechanics back at home. As a result they do not place so much importance on inspection because they depend on the mechanic to do the job right in the first place. The inspectors and quality control people are paid less than the mechanics; hence they get less effective people to do this work than they should have. Also, because the inspectors are paid less than the mechanics, they hesitate to reject parts or complain about workmanship. With these old habit patterns in quality control, the inspectors cannot understand why I insist on so many details, and this forms a mental handicap that prevents improvement. I have many fights here with the people, but now they are beginning to understand what I want and why, and they are starting to comply with the requirements in the policy manual.

This problem of poor communications up the line of command is partially due to too much respect for authority and social position. For example, one of the top executives here was going back to the Kellering headquarters for a meeting. BMW needed a small part very badly that was readily available at Kellering spares-pool stores. The local shop people here refused to ask him to get the item and bring it back in his pocket because they felt he was too high an executive to help them.

I suppose the problems here are the same as with any new subcontractor in U.S. who is not completely familiar with our requirements and system. Here, of course, we have the additional problem of language translation. Why didn't buyers at Kellering expect and prepare for these problems?

Background of Resident Inspector

Mr. Gothel was about thirty-five years of age. He was selected for the BMW job because of his experience, personality, and German background. As a child he had learned German from his parents, although he had not used it during his adult life to any extent. Upon graduating from high school he joined the U.S. Air Force. After receiving his basic training, he advanced to flight engineer and had extensive experience as a flight crew member. Later he became an instructor to teach maintenance and emergency procedures. After five years in the Air Force, he joined the Kellering Company and was assigned to the Preflight Quality Control Department. Here he was involved with final inspection procedures of completed airplanes prior to their first test flight. After one year in this assignment, he was moved to the Material Review Department where he investigated material failures and the processing of material that did not conform to specifications. As a result of the care he displayed in this job, after two years he was advanced to work in the Customer Service Department where he remained for the next seven years prior to his assignment at BMW. In the Customer Service Department he processed complaints from customers under contract warranties, and became very much aware of how minor and trivial errors in the manufacture and maintenance of airplanes could create serious problems. For example, he was involved in a situation in which scratches on highly stressed parts had caused serious failures. He was also aware of an occasion where a service mechanic had merely connected the control surface cables backwards and caused a plane to crash with a serious loss of life.

After accepting his new assignment to BMW, Gothel received what was considered to be an adequate amount of indoctrination regarding his new job, was given an airplane ticket and a letter of introduction, and sent off to Anderbach.

Upon his arrival at the Nuremburg airport, he discovered that his language facility was more limited than he had realized. Because of an unfortunate mix-up he was not met at the airport by the local representative of Kellering who had been assigned to meet him. After some trouble with the local telephone and with making himself understood by a taxi driver, he managed to get to the railroad station and took a train to Anderbach where he arranged to stay at a hotel.

Family Problems

Two weeks later his wife and eight-year-old daughter arrived from the U.S. They did not speak German. Since there was no English-speaking school in Anderbach for his daughter, the family decided to move to Endigen where such a school was available because of several large U.S. military bases located in the vicinity. This required Gothel to commute each day by railroad between Endigen and Anderbach; a trip of approximately forty-five minutes each way. Endigen was an old community with a population of about 125,000 but had modern facilities and many shops for English-speaking customers.

Mrs. Gothel had a great deal of trouble learning German and, for a time, stopped taking lessons. At first she only traded at those shops and stores where the sales people spoke English. Mr. Gothel commented that "as a result, we always paid the highest prices." Their language limitation also restricted social contracts with local people but caused the family to be closely drawn together. They did find a comfortable apartment from a "For Rent" listing at the local U.S. army base. They paid, however, a substantially higher rental than would have been charged to a native German. This appeared to be the only reason that local landlords rented apartments to U.S. people. Fortunately, their landlord spoke English, and they developed very pleasant relationships with him and his wife. After several months in their new location, Mrs. Gothel's ability to speak German improved, and she became more comfortable with shopkeepers and neighbors.

Parker's Opinions

The quality control problem at BMW was repeatedly called to the attention of the Kellering management by means of weekly reports that Mr. Gothel sent back. Exhibits 4 and 6 are excerpts from some of these

Exhibit 4   **Activity Report**[a]

Observations and thoughts that occur
during the Q.C. survey.

During discussions with the managing director, the
impression is conveyed that there is a great interest in
obtaining and holding Kellering Company business, This
establishes the fact that the intent to attempt to comply
with our policy manual exists, however, at this point the
intent to comply seems to end in the form of the resistance or nondevelopment of the Quality Control department.
The thought seems to be "lets operate on a shoestring,"
which connotes to me that the Quality Control department
in Europe does not have the stature that it has in the
USA.

The Quality Control inspectors are not paid as high as
the work force so there is a continual problem in obtaining
good Q.C. people. It would appear at this point desirable
to strengthen the Q.C. department by an increase in wages,
which would attract more people, and then a selection of
the best candidates could be made. This kind of an action
is apparently not in the picture because the one Q.C. man
who is the real spark plug for the stand production has
not been advanced in wages. Whether this situation is a
company policy or Q.C. department policy I have not determined.

Another disturbing thought is the fact that aircraft
production is under a railroad man and not under an aircraft man. The thought of an aircraft Q.C. man reporting
to a railroad man suggests the possibility of diluted
standards and of course the lack of aircraft guidance at
that level.

Another disturbing line of reasoning put forth by some
people in the Q.C. organization is that "Kellering must
consider that BMW has other contracts also and that Kellering cannot expect special attention," which is quite
a distorted line of reasoning. It has to be recalled that
we expect only what is required by the basic purchase
agreement, part of which of course is an adequate Q.C.
organization. An adequate Q.C. organization cannot be
construed as "special attention" in any form.

a Written by Gothel three months after his arrival at BMW.

It is my personal opinion that the Q.C. organization can be termed as being of the "old school" that is not readily receptive to the jet age requirements. To date there has been very little Q.C. response to organizing along the lines of our policies.

The argument that BMW did not receive the Kellering Q.C. policy manual until two months ago, rather than during the initial contract negotiation, has in all probability some merit, however, it appears to be an excuse of convenience. Aircraft production in general, regardless of who it is for, has certain basic guides to work to. These guides of course, are the drawings and all the related specifications that are called for by the drawings. Additional requirements for a Q.C. department are adequate records of the work accomplished through the medium of inspection operating procedures and rejection and rework systems, all of which can be termed as "standard Q.C. tools." These standard Q.C. tools have not existed.

The proposed solution to the entire problem is for high level management to direct the BMW Q.C. organization to begin compliance with our policy manual.

Gothel

Exhibit 5

William Morrissey
International Office
Kellering Headquarters

Subject: Your TWX Re: Gothel Problem

Bill:
  At your request, I drove up to Anderbach yesterday to
a. Familiarize myself with the facility as a potentially
   continuing Kellering subcontractor and
b. to investigate the "Gothel" problem.

  I had considerable discussion with Gothel and a German
who is part of the Q.C. organization and is assigned to
work with Gothel, sort of as his opposite number. I also
toured the plant with them and finally, had about a half-
hour discussion with von Halle.
  I came away with the following findings and conclusions:

1. Findings
a. BMW had to start production of the seats and flight
   control stands in question before it had access to any
   translations of Kellering manufacturing and inspection
   process standards.
b. The job of translating these standards is now being
   accomplished at a rapid pace.
c. BMW had to start work on the flight control stands
   working from Kellering detailed final assembly and part
   drawings, which are so different from comparable German
   blueprints, that the average German production worker
   has to have quite a lot of exposure before he can really
   "read" them.
d. The Germans do not traditionally keep Q.C. records that
   are remotely comparable, quality and quantitywise, to
   ours.
e. Inspection processes employed routinely at BMW for
   production of aeroplane seat category hardware are
   generally not yet comparable to what we would require
   of a vendor in the U.S.
f. The inspection processes identified above are improving quickly as Gothel continues to identify when necessary requirements for improvement.

g. The first seat category hardware presented to Gothel for "buy-off" was definitely characterized by deficiencies that would have caused rejection at Kellering shops.

Examples:

1. Nuts on bolts without washers
2. Faulty rivets
3. Faulty machining, etc.

h. BMW is doing repair work on FRG Luftwaffe airframe structures that would compare favorably with similar work done in the U.S.

i. Gothel has, per copies of memos to the BMW workforce managers, demonstrated considerable understanding of their problems and has stretched application of our standards as far as any Q.C. supervisor in Kellering would ever back him up.

j. BMW people felt at first that Gothel was nitpicking and overdoing the Q.C. bit.

k. Gothel felt at first that BMW was so far behind us, Q.C. wise, that they would just never be able to "hack it."

l. BMW no longer feels that Gothel is exaggerating the Q.C. bit.

m. Gothel is convinced now that BMW is making good progress and will soon be capable of passing the "Source Certification Inspection" that they have not yet been subjected to but will ultimately have to pass to be able to continue on as a supplier to Kellering.

II. Conclusions

a. The Gothel problem stemmed essentially from:

(1) Inadequate time for proper BMW preparation and indoctrination before initiation of production.
(2) Basic initial differences between Kellering and BMW approach to Q.C.
(3) BMW standards for production of something like "seat" hardware being initially admittedly lower than minimum Kellering quality requirements.
(4) Naturally, the language problem.

b. The "Gothel problem" has essentially gone away because:

(1) Gothel has been able to get across to BMW that there are certain minimum standards that he has to enforce without hopelessly alienating them.

(2) BMW wants more Kellering business and has realized now that part of getting it is learning to live with a "Gothel."

(3) The overall situation is improving very rapidly.

(4) To have to go through a "Gothel problem" cycle in breaking in a new foreign vendor source is to be expected.

(5) BMW was probably "lucky" in drawing a Q.C. inspector who has been as "understanding" as Gothel has apparently been.

III. Actions

a. I think I was able to help ease the situation further by:

(1) Commending Gothel for demonstrating the "understanding" that he has to date and encouraging him to continue in that vein. He now feels like he is not quite so isolated and on his own.

(2) Explaining better to the BMW people that Gothel is only the first stage in a screening operation that goes on until Kellering has, in fact, delivered the assembled aeroplane to a customer, ... that Gothel could do them more harm in the long run by backing off from standards to a degree that he knows would not be "bought" than by insisting that they meet his interpretation of Kellering standards.

Finally I received a call from Gothel a few minutes ago to tell me that the managing director for production came to his office yesterday afternoon after I left and made a very impressive speech to him to the effect that BMW is in complete sympathy with Kellering Q.C. standards and intends to do anything and everything Gothel requires to be able to routinely meet those standards.

Sincerely,
Jan Parker

(Note: This memorandum was written six months after Gothel arrived at BMW.)

Exhibit 6   **Activity Report**[a]

Control Stands

The first control stand has been completed, and things were really humming this week. Every member of the BMW organization, from the Director on down, felt that they had to be on the scene, and I am not sure whether they became part of the problem or part of the solution.

At the last minute, the BMW Q.C. department decided that they could not come up with a satisfactory inspection package, so I had to make up one. Now that a sample one exists, it can serve as a pattern for future ones.

The first stand appeared to be a pretty good item, considering everything. The proof of the thing, of course, will be the acceptance by Kellering Receiving Inspection and the actual installation into the airplane. I'd appreciate any and all comments on the thing in order to initiate any correction that would be required. I sit with baited breath wondering what I have overlooked. There are times when a person cannot see the forest for the trees when you are very close to a thing.

Planning

The response to my request for a more complete planning package has been most gratifying. The planning package that is emerging is quite complete and in detail. The planning portion of the survey will receive a "satisfactory" classification.

The department is absorbing the Kellering way very readily.

Quality Control

I am of the opinion that as the result of meetings between the Q.C. people and myself, I am on the verge of a breakthrough. It appears that I have finally gotten their attention, and there are indications that compliance with our policies is forthcoming. I realize that 100 percent compliance with it is not a reality, however, I'm going to shoot for the moon. The possibility of some new Q.C.

---

[a] Written by Gothel eight months after his arrival at BMW.

people who will be more effective than the present ones appears to be in the formation process.

Lufthansa three-seat combination

I have learned Lufthansa has contacted an Engineering organization to produce a three-seat combination for use in their new airplanes. The seat will weigh about ten to twelve pounds less than the seat that Kellering uses, and its reclining feature is based on a sliding sitting platform rather than the conventional tilting back type. The prototype seat has a fairly clean look about it. I have no idea as to who will manufacture it, to what specifications, and where it will be installed.

F-104 Failures

The F-104 failures that have plagued the airplanes produced in Europe, appear to have ended. I believe the last one fell and that, according to the newspaper, is the predicted end of the thing. Many top German Generals have resigned and implications are flying back and forth between the military and politicians. One of the accusations by the military is that they were forced to buy the airplane under political pressure and some of the material purchased was defective. It is not possible to ferret out just what was defective, although steel strengths are being discussed. There existed an interchangeability problem also. The military selected a number of airplanes at random and proceeded to remove and attempt to interchange the more major components. The test revealed that interchangeability between components manufactured in different countries was not controlled very well.

The above situation alerts me to watch for anything and everything in European production.

                                                        Gothel

reports. As a result, the Kellering management decided to make an independent check and sent Mr. Jan Parker from the Kellering NATO Team to check on the "Gothel" problem. The report of his short visit is included as Exhibit 5. He also commented to the case writer that he could understand why BMW had troubles with the drawings. For example, Kellering's drawings had a large number of "flag" notes that are uncommon with many other companies. In addition, the drawings for electrical cables have a special complex system for designating wires and this was completely new to BMW. Most of the important drawings got to BMW on time but a few dribbled in late. These late drawings, however, caused a great deal of trouble because they were difficult to identify and to determine if they were really needed.

Mr. Parker stated that "I feel one of the real problems here is that they have an organization that is mixed up in too many different kinds of work. I don't like aircraft work being done with railroad work and truck trailer work, even if they are in physically separated facilities. Each type of work requires the mechanics to have a certain mental approach to the production methods, and I think it is easy for the workers to get confused when they are switched back and forth between rough railroad car work and precise aircraft work."

"It is also possible that the Q.C. requirements were overstressed. Rather than pursue a practical and responsible approach, it is easy to reject a part in case of doubt."

Dobrin's Opinions

Mr. Hans Dobrin, the financial officer for BMW, commented on the problem. "I'm not a technical man myself, but I think I know a little bit about the problem. The top management here is very anxious to follow all of the Kellering requirements, but the problem is with the lower-level people. You must appreciate that our mechanics all have a long apprentice background, and they feel they know how to do things without detailed process specifications. In fact, they are insulted when you tell them how to do their job.

"The Kellering drawings had many errors, even though they were minor ones. The layout is relatively poor compared to the beautiful draftsmanship on most German drawings, and many drawings were late. As a result, some of the plant people lost confidence in the precise requirements and felt that it was not absolutely necessary to follow what, to them, seemed to be unnecessary detail in the specifications.

"Also many of the people don't fully understand what Gothel is driving at. They feel he is going in opposite directions at the same time. On one hand he claims that the shop people don't show enough initiative and imagination in solving their problems, as illustrated by the difficulty with the short screws and the fish scale. On the other hand, he claims they are too independent because they won't precisely follow detailed specifications that they believe are unnecessarily restrictive. You Americans have to make up your mind what you are really complaining about and what you want us to do. Why doesn't Kellering just tell us what they want and leave us alone to do the job?"

Review of Progress

The first shipment of observer seats was ready to ship eight weeks late, and the first control stand was ready six weeks late. The responsibility for late delivery clearly belonged to BMW, according to Tim Lester, the buyer at Kellering; nevertheless, the items were urgently needed, and BMW was authorized to make these first shipments by air to save time that surface transportation would require. Kellering agreed to pay for the extra air freight charges. The observer seats were accepted by the Kellering Quality Control Department.

Just after the shipment of the first control stand was made, but before the unit had passed final inspection at the Kellering plant, Mr. von Halle received an inquiry from Kellering inviting him to negotiate for a follow-on order for additional controls stands and observer seats. He now faced the necessity to make an effective assessment of past costs and future expectations.

Cost accounting details were generally available about forty-five days after the end of a month. When available, the data was reasonably accurate regarding direct labor costs for the assembly of each unit that was completed and the lot cost of parts that were fabricated awaiting assembly. The total accumulated project man-hours at the end of the monthly accounting periods was also known, but there was no formal method of determining the percent of completion of work in progress.

Since Mr. von Halle was familiar with improvement curve theory, he expected the cost per unit to be quite high at the beginning of the contract but to rapidly decrease as work progressed. The problem was how to interpret the high cost of the first few units that were delivered and how to project future costs using the improvement curve.

Mr. von Halle's latest cost data included most of the information regarding the first shipment of seats, but it only contained partial information about the stands. After carefully reviewing the limited accounting figures that he had available, and discussing the project with various foremen and other executives, Mr. von Halle came to the tentative conclusion that the observer seat project was progressing satisfactorily from a cost point of view, but the control stand project costs appeared to be running very substantially above expectations. He now felt, that at the time they prepared their bids, they did not have enough drawings and specifications to fully understand the project. In addition, some of the documents that were on hand had not been translated and thus were not considered at the time of bidding. They also underestimated the cost of obtaining parts from the U.S. and the air-freight charges for expediting delivery to BMW.

From the limited data he had available, Mr. von Halle had to decide what to do about his present contract and how to react to the invitation to negotiate for additional quantities of seats and stands.

THE CRESTA
AUTOMOBILE COMPANY

Early in 1963 the Executive Committee was considering a proposal of Mr. White, the Technical Director, to spend approximately 1,250,000 Sfrs. to construct a piece of automation equipment for the body assembly division. The Executive Committee was composed of the president, the commercial director, and the technical director.

The proposal concerned the company's most popular model of car, designated model "A," which was sold throughout Europe and was also exported to other continents. It competed with comparable models of automobiles produced by Fiat, Volkswagen, and Renault. Exhibit 1 shows the average daily production of this Cresta model for each of the last four years.

Exhibit 1   Cresta Automobile Company
Average Daily Production of Model "A"
1958–1962

1958	1,721
1960	1,943
1961	2,196
1962	2,263

Description of the Project

The proposal that Mr. White had put forward was one developed by the Planning Department, which was under his direction. The proposal concerned the assembly of three major pieces: the right front fender, a center section, and the left front fender. Each of these three pieces was itself an assembly of many individual parts; the center section, for instance, included the grill, hood, windscreen frame, and part of the roof.

At present, these pieces were being assembled by six teams of eight men each. Each of the teams had a work station at which were located a set of fixtures and several pieces of welding equipment. The parts arrived from previous assembly operations on conveyors and were loaded into the fixtures by work loaders. These fixtures held the three assemblies in the proper relationships to one another. After the pieces had been placed in the fixtures, the welders welded at a total of thirty-seven different locations to effect the assembly. When the welding was completed, the work handlers removed the assembled unit, loaded it on a conveyor for transportation to the next work station, and then repeated the cycle of loading three new pieces. Some of the welding operations were spot welding, but several were seam welds, the longest of which was 15 cm. Most of the seam welds joined curved rather than straight joints. Each piece was thoroughly inspected immediately after its completion, and those with defects were shunted off to one side of the main conveyor, where a repair welder corrected the faults, if possible.

The Assembly Department management was of the opinion that the output of this section was not as high as it might be, based on studies by the Work Study section. Some attempts had been made to increase the output on the existing lines, but these efforts had been strongly resisted by the workers. The work study analysis indicated that five, rather than six, teams should have been able to produce the current hourly output, which was 125 cars per hour, or about 21 cars per team. According to the Work Study Department, an output of 25 cars per hour per team could be achieved using the present methods. Historically, Cresta labor relations had been marked by an absence of labor strife, however, and the management was reluctant to risk a rupture over the issue of these six work stations.

The Cresta plant operated two eight-hour shifts, five days a week; occasionally the plant had worked overtime. The company employed more than twenty thousand workers, all of whom were paid on a nonincentive basis.

Investment Required and Forecasted Savings

The Planning Department estimated that to design, build, and break in automated equipment to perform these particular assembly operations would cost 1,150,000 Sfrs.; to this figure had been added a provision for contingencies of 100,000 Sfrs., making the total proposed expenditures 1,250,000 Sfrs. Accompanying the proposal were detailed estimates and a sketch showing the general way in which the equipment would function. Further development of the general approach and detailed design work would not begin until and unless the project was approved by the Executive Committee. It was estimated that ten months would be required to complete the project, once it had been approved. After ten months it was expected that the equipment would be producing acceptable output at about 50 percent of its design capacity; another six to twelve months would be required to bring the equipment up to its designed capacity of 125 cars per hour. In the past it had been very difficult to estimate accurately the time required to complete the project. Additional time of 20 to 30 percent of the original estimate had been required on nearly half of similar projects undertaken.

It was estimated by the Planning Department that the proposed equipment would save forty-three men per shift. In addition to the direct labor operators (six teams of eight men each) there were additional maintenance, service, and inspection personnel totaling eleven persons, or a total assigned manpower of fifty-nine persons each shift. The planned automatic equipment would require a crew of eleven operators and five maintenance and service personnel each shift. In computing direct labor savings, the Planning Department used the plant-wide average hourly wage of 4.1 Sfrs.

The company's factory overhead rate for the body division as a whole was 150 percent of its direct labor cost. Each section, however, had its own rate, and in certain highly mechanized sections of this division (comparable in a general way to the one being proposed) rates of about 400 percent were used.

The floor space required by the current hand method of assembly totaled 6,000 square metres, while the preliminary layout for the automatic equipment required only 2,200 square metres. While the replacement cost for a similar building would currently amount to about 450 Sfrs. per square metre, the Planning Department did not attempt to impute any savings as a result of the reduced requirement for floor space. The report pointed out, however, that it was a factor to be considered, especially since the floor space involved was among the most expensive owned by the company, having high ceilings and wide bays because of the huge hydraulic presses installed in the vicinity.

In the past it had been company policy to require all capital investments in special (as distinguished from general purpose equipment) to show a payback of the original outlay in two years or less. In practice, most of the projects had bettered that standard by a considerable margin.

Other Considerations

Cresta's Planning Group had executed two earlier projects of this general type, but the parts to be dealt with in the project proposed were considerably larger than any heretofore assembled with automatic assembly equipment. Several of the seams to be welded were longer and more complex in shape than any heretofore encountered. There were several automatic feeding devices for supplying small parts in the proposed design; projects involving automatic feeding had been completed in the past but not projects involving the particular parts used in the proposed project. One of the major sources of problems in earlier projects had been minor variations in the quality of parts and subassemblies supplied from preceding operations. A high degree of precision was required to obtain good fits of the parts, so that they could be properly positioned in their fixtures for the automatic equipment and so automatic welding heads would function properly. It had been the company's experience in earlier projects that once these kinds of problems had been solved, the quality of output from automatic assembly equipment had been markedly superior to the quality achieved under previous methods of hand assembly.

One of the major risks involved in the proposed equipment would be the possibility of design changes of sufficient magnitude making the assembly equipment obsolete. The automobile industry had become quite competitive during the preceding twelve months. One indication for Cresta was the disappearance of an order backlog, the first time this had happened since the company began production after the conclusion of World War II. There were indications that in the immediate future, overcapacity might well exist in the automobile industry in the European Common Market countries. The Cresta management believed that increased competition would probably increase the necessity for making design changes much more rapidly in the future than had been the case in the past. They believed that this was especially true of body styling changes.

All the foregoing factors, plus indications that economic expansion was tending to slow down in many of Cresta's markets, also created some uncertainty with respect to the future volume of production that would be required. The company's current forecast called for an annual volume of 500,000 cars of the model "A" type; in the past, the volume estimates used had, in the event, turned out to be conservative, with actual sales running 10 to 20 percent greater than forecast.

The design for the special automatic equipment contemplated the possibility of certain changes being required as a result of changes in body part designs. The leeway provided, however, was relatively restricted, and it was the management's opinion that it was an impossible task to try to predict the nature and extent of design changes of this sort.

The Planning Group indicated that no problems were expected in connection with the displacement of workers by the proposed equipment. In view of the existing labor shortage, all of the people displaced could be transferred to other positions within the plant at equivalent levels of wages. Two years before, the management had had extensive discussions with the company's Works Council on the displacement problem. The full implications of a major project for the workers affected had been examined in detail and had apparently satisfied all those concerned. Therefore, in the opinion of the management the members of the Works Council and the workers in general were now convinced that continued automation was not a real threat and also made the work easier for the operators of automatic equipment, in comparison with hand assembly procedures.

According to the Planning Group, another important benefit, flowing from the ability to transfer surplus workers to other jobs would be to avoid substantial expenditures for the workers' social improvement. It was company policy to pay substantial fringe benefits to its workers and to subsidize housing facilities for them by building apartment houses for Cresta employees. If additional workers had to be hired, instead of using the forty-three to be transferred, then these social charges could not be avoided. When all these social charges and indirect employment costs were taken into account, the Planning Group estimated that their cost to Cresta was about equal to 100 percent of the wages paid to a typical employee in the course of a year.

Finally, the Planning Group suggested that some of the risk of obsolescence of the equipment might be overcome if the company would establish a policy that there would be no redesign of the pieces involved in these assembly operations unless the changes were approved by the Planning Department in advance. Such a policy could be expected to reduce the number of changes actually made and, hopefully, permit necessary changes to be made in a way that would avoid making the proposed equipment obsolete.

KÖNIG MACHINE WORKS, GmbH (A)

As the result of a prolonged period of prosperity, the König Machine Works, a European manufacturer of heavy industrial machinery, had built up a large backlog. The plant had been operating at peak capacity for several years, but the top management of the company had become concerned about the long delays the company was forced to quote in bidding on new orders. Historically, such long delays were typical of boom periods in the industry. For this very reason, however, ability to quote earlier deliveries than competitors was an important aspect of competition, and it was believed that the company's current competitive position would be considerably strengthened if something could be done to reduce delivery delays.

Engineer Escher, who was assigned to the Planning Department, had recently read several articles in professional journals concerning the PERT technique, and he decided to conduct an experiment to find out whether it might be a useful tool to help accomplish a reduction in delivery delays. The experiment started with choosing a recently completed order and charting the tasks involved on a network diagram. Next, Engineer Escher gathered the time actually consumed for each task from the dossier on the order. Then Engineer Escher examined the network chart to discover ways in which the manufacturing cycle time required to process this particular kind of product could have been reduced.

The object of this experiment was a radial compressor (vacuum blower) recently built for a paper mill. A typical radial compressor is pictured in Exhibit 1. König constructed this type of equipment to order (as it did for the large majority of all lines of equipment it manufactured). In every case, however, a radial compressor was a variation of one of five standard basic designs. The choice among the basic designs depended upon the capacity required. Each customer's order also required a variety of custom modifications and attachments, depending on the application involved and the specifications desired by the customer. König had sold nineteen radial compressors during the past twelve months.

The PERT network compiled by Engineer Escher (Exhibit 2) included only the major parts and assemblies. His chart showed the activities related

Exhibit 1   König Machine Works, GmbH (A)
                              Typical Radial Compressor

to the purchasing of major parts all in one location, to the left of Event 4. Activities related to manufactured parts, and to the assembly of both manufactured and purchased parts, were drawn to the right of Event 4. Purchased parts were required to be available at the time Event 76 occurred, the beginning of the assembly process.

Elapsed time on Engineer Escher's chart was expressed in "TE's" a unit of time equal to three working days. König was currently working one shift per day, six days per week.

The major purchased parts were a pump, a squirrel-cage electric motor, a gear box, and a safety coupling. The major manufactured parts included on the chart were: the casing; the diffusor; the rotor; the shaft; the spacers; the turbine wheels, each with its set of blades; the lubrication piping system; the oil tank; an oil cooling unit; and a clutch.

Two of the major purchased parts were inventoried items, the pump and the squirrel-cage motor, while the other two major purchased items could vary considerably from one order to the next, and were bought as required for each customer's order. Stocks were also maintained of most of the work

Exhibit 2   König Machine Works, GmbH (A)

Network Chart for Actual Manufacturing Cycle

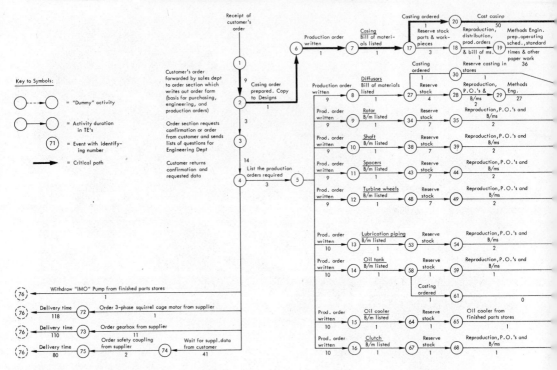

pieces (such as castings, or forgings) from which the major manufactured parts were fabricated. The casing, however, was an exception; no stocks were maintained, and each casing was cast in the company's foundry for a specific customer's order. The casings were large and heavy, they ranged from two to four metric tons in weight, depending upon which of the five basic designs was involved. The raw casing casting was valued at 3,200 DM for the order chosen by Engineer Escher (which can be compared with 185,000 DM for the sales price of this item).

Turbine blades for the turbine wheels were also manufactured to order, although they were of a standard design. Blades varied in diameter and in width. The diameter varied with the customer's performance requirements and with the number of stages, which could range from one to four. Within each stage, however, all blades had the same diameter and from stage to stage varied in width. While stocks of other turbine wheel work pieces were maintained, the blade "blanks" were cast by a special precision casting process especially for each customer's order.

The characteristics of the motive power that the customer would supply to turn the compressor affected the selection of the safety coupling. Before

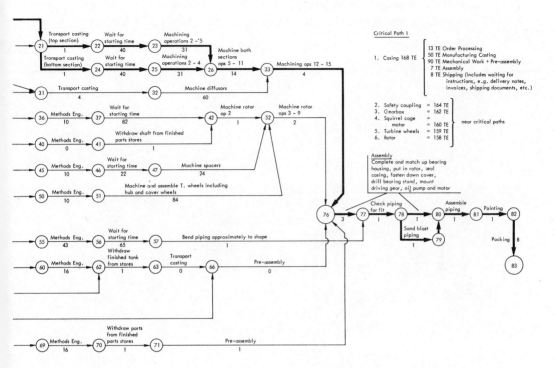

the appropriate safety coupling could be ordered from the subcontractor, the size of connecting shaft, the amount of torque involved, and the safety margin desired by the customers had to be determined by correspondence with the customer. In the case of this customer's order, it took the Purchasing Department 41 TE's to acquire this data (activity 4–74).

Even though squirrel-cage electric motor was a stock item, the store room was out of stock when this particular customer's order was received, and it took 118 TE's to replenish their supply.

Mid-way in the assembly process the oil ductwork was fitted for size. After this was done, the ductwork was removed and taken to the sand-blasting section. There it was sand-blasted to prepare it for painting, after which it was returned to the assembly section for assembly to the equipment.

The various activities described as "Wait for Starting Time" (such as activity 22–23, with a duration of 40 TE's) represented the time elapsed on this order between delivery of the work piece to the Fabricating Departments and the time the departments actually began fabricating operations. The reason for this kind of delay was other shop orders in the departments that had arrived earlier and that were also waiting their turn.

Engineer Escher's network chart (Exhibit 2) showed that the critical path for this particular order was the one for the casing. Exhibit 2 shows a summary of the time consumed by each of the major classes of activities in the casing's path. It also shows the total time consumed by the paths for four other parts.

KÖNIG MACHINE WORKS, GmbH (B)

After Engineer Escher had compiled a network chart for the customer's order, which he had selected, he set about finding ways to reduce the total manufacturing cycle time required to produce this kind of product. Exhibit 1 shows the network for the revised procedures, which reduced the total manufacturing cycle time required from 168 TE's to 75 TE's. Exhibit 2 compares the original time utilized for each activity with the revised time and shows the reductions that Engineer Escher accomplished (in a few cases, there was a small increase in the time allowed). Exhibit 2 also gives a brief explanation for each of the changed times.

When the results of these studies were presented to the Sales Departments at a group meeting for all the company's sales engineers, the audience appeared to be very favorably impressed with the usefulness of PERT as a technique to reduce delivery times for a large proportion of the company's products.

Exhibit 1

König Machine Works, GmbH (B)
Revised Network Chart

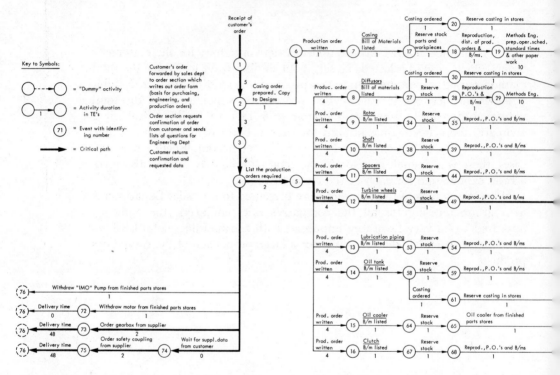

Key to Symbols:

○---→○ = "Dummy" activity

○—1—→○ = Activity duration in TE's

(71) = Event with identifying number

—→ = Critical path

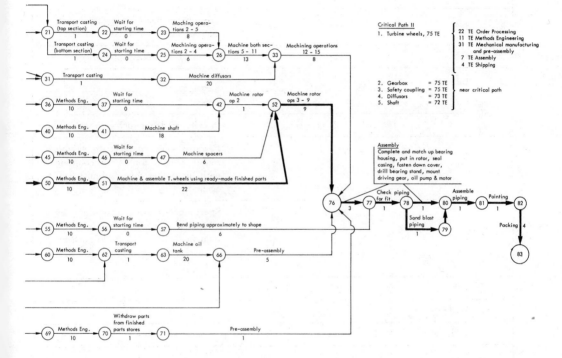

Exhibit 2   **König Machine Works, GmbH (B)**

Comparison of Actual and Revised Activity Times

Activity From Event	To Event	Original time	Revised time	Difference (original minus revised)	Explanation for Changes in Time
1–2		9	5	−4	Rationalization and speeding up of office procedure
2–3		3	3		—
2–6		1	1		—
3–4		14	6	−8	Pressure on customer, e.g., delay on his part may lead to late delivery
4–5		3	2	−1	Speeding up office procedure
4–76		1	1		—
4–72		1	1		—
4–73		11	2	−9	Priority grade for such orders
4–74		41	0	−41	Require sales engineer to submit required data for safety coupling with his or her form (submitted at event 1)
5–8		9	4	−5	Speeding up office procedure by means of office schedule (planned sequence of writing prod. orders) + increasing capacity more order clerks
5–9		9	4	−5	″
5–10		9	4	−5	″
5–11		9	4	−5	″
5–12		9	4	−5	″
5–13		9	4	−5	″
5–14		9	4	−5	″
5–15		9	4	−5	″
5–16		9	4	−5	″
6–7		1	1		—
7–17		1	1		
8–27		1	1		

Exhibit 2 (cont.)

Activity From Event	To Event	Original time	Revised time	Difference (original minus revised)	Explanation for Changes in Time
9–34		1	1		
10–38		1	1		
11–43		1	1		
12–48		1	1		
13–53		1	1		
14–58		1	1		
15–64		1	1		
16–67		1	1		
17–18		3	1	−2	Speeding up office procedure
18–19		1	1		
19–21		36	10	−26	Elimination of waiting time in Methods Engineering Department used standard operation schedules
20–21		50	1	−49	Cast casings held in stock—series production. Sales program justifies this more
21–22		1	1		
21–24		1	1		
22–23		40	0	−40	Improved machine loading, reduce backlog in this department
23–26		31	8	−23	Reduced waiting time, reduce backlog, improved machine loading
24–25		40	0	−40	as (22–23)
25–26		31	6	−25	as (23–26)
26–33		14	13	−1	Reduced waiting time
27–28		4	1	−3	Speeding up office procedure, planned sequence of work
27–30		1	1		
28–29		2	1	−1	Speeding up office procedure

Exhibit 2 (cont.)

Activity From Event	To Event	Original time	Revised time	Difference (original minus revised)	Explanation for Changes in Time
29–31		27	10	−17	Elimination of waiting time in Methods Engineering, use of standard operation schedules
30–31		1	1		
31–32		4	1	−3	Reservation of transport
32–33		60	20	−40	Elimination of waiting time, improved machine loading, reduced backlog
33–76		4	8	+4	Removal of need for "crashing" through improved machine loading e.g. (25–26) (32–33)
34–35		7	1	−6	as (27–28)
35–36		2	1	−1	as (28–29)
36–37		10	10		
37–42		82	0	−82	Improved machine loading, reduce backlog
38–39		7	1	−6	as (27–28)
39–40		2	1	−1	as (28–29)
40–41		0	10	+10	Due to policy change finished shafts will no longer be held in stock. Reduction of invested capital
41–42		1	18	+17	as (40–41)
42–52		1	1		
43–44		7	1	−6	as (27–28)
44–45		2	1	−1	as (28–29)
45–46		10	10		
46–47		22	0	−22	Improved machine loading, reduced backlog
47–52		24	6	−18	Improved machine loading, reduced backlog
48–49		7	1	−6	as (27–28)
49–50		2	1	−1	as (28–29)

Exhibit 2 (cont.)

Activity From Event	To Event	Original time	Revised time	Difference (original minus revised)	Explanation for Changes in Time
50–51		10	10		
51–52		84	22	−62	Use of ready-made finished parts. Series production of standard parts (for inventory)
52–76		2	9	+7	Removal of need for "crashing" through use of finished parts (51–52)
53–54		5	1	−4	as (27–28)
54–55		2	1	−1	as (28–29)
55–56		43	10	−33	as (29–31)
56–57		65	0	−65	Improved machine loading, reduced backlog
57–77		1	6	+5	No need for "crash" program because: (a) (55–56) improvement in time; (b) "float" is available
58–59		1	1		
58–61		1	1		
59–60		1	1		
60–62		16	10	−6	as (29–31)
61–62		0	1	+1	Fully maintained costing, no longer held in stores—only raw casting
62–63		1	1		
63–66		0	20	+20	Required to machine tank casting
64–65		1	1		
65–66		1	1		
66–76		0	5	+5	Required after machining under new policy
67–68		1	1		
68–69		1	1		
69–70		16	10	−6	Elimination of waiting time in Methods Engineering, use of standard operation schedules

Exhibit 2 (cont.)

Activity From Event To Event	Original time	Revised time	Difference (original minus revised)	Explanation for Changes in Time
70–71	1	1		
71–76	1	1		
72–76	118	0	−118	Improved inventory control. New project begun to raise level of warehouse performance
73–76	110	48	−62	Other supplier found
74–75	2	2		
75–76	80	48	−32	Other supplier found
76–77	3	3		
77–78	1	1		
78–79	1	1		
78–80	1	1		
79–80	0	0		
80–81	1	1		
81–82	1	1		
82–83	8	4	−4	Earlier orientation of administrative departments leading to on-time availability of documents

UNITED FOOD
PRODUCTS COMPANY

In March 1964, Mr. H. van Roehm, Managing Director of United Food Products (Benelux) S.A., said to the case writer:

> If members of your Institute can tell us how to improve our distribution system this would be more than recompense for the cooperation we're giving you in describing our situation. Distribution problems are among our most difficult ones to solve. With about 56,000 retail grocery outlets to serve about eight million people in Belgium and Luxembourg, we can't realize the efficiencies of mass distribution like they can in the U.S. where there are only one and a half retail grocery outlets per one thousand persons. I'm reasonably satisfied with our performance in buying, production, sales, and advertising, but I think we've got to improve our effectiveness in distribution.

Company Background

ORGANIZATION   United Food Products, U.S.A., produced and sold a growing variety of consumer food products: breakfast cereals, dehydrated soups, instant coffee, and various flours and cake mixes. Unlike some of its large U.S. competitors that had competed in European markets for over fifty years, United had not marketed its products in continental Europe until 1953. However, since 1931 when it purchased the Henry Morehead Company, Ltd., which operated a factory at Hull in England, the parent company was actively developing markets for its breakfast cereals, dry soups, and instant coffee in the United Kingdom. In 1953, United Food Products Company (Geneva) S.A. was established as a continental headquarters for directing the development of new markets. The Geneva company did not operate factories; its function was confined to market development. As one of its first actions the Geneva organization moved into the marketing region of the European Economic Community (EEC). In 1953 it contracted with Mr. van Roehm of Brussels, Belgium, to act as General Sales Agent in the Belgium and Luxembourg markets and with Mr. P. van der Woeld as General Sales Agent for Holland. Products were imported from the factory in England. By 1955, sales of the "Potage-Minute" dry soups had increased so that an arrangement was made for the Moulins Généraux S.A., a diversified Belgian food processor, to produce "Potage-Minute" for the Benelux markets. Sales continued to more than double each year. In 1955, the general agency arrangement for Benelux was terminated, and a new company, United Food Products Co. (Benelux) S.A., was established with Mr. van Roehm as General Manager. Main offices were shifted from Brussels to Antwerp, and a construction of a new $4,000,000 factory was started in Louvain. Mr. van der Woeld was continued as General Sales Agent for Holland, but his contract was administered by the new Benelux Company, instead of by the Geneva company. Imports from England were discontinued shortly after the new factory went on stream in the fall of 1956. Exhibit 1 is an abbreviated organization chart of United Food Products Co. (Benelux) S.A.

PRODUCTION   Most breakfast cereals were made by either rolling out, as in the case of flake cereals, or steam-exploding, as in the case of "puffed" or "popped" cereals, the individual cereal grains. The flakes or pops were then mixed with various flavoring ingredients such as salt, malt, sugar, barley, and corn syrup and sent to ovens where they were carefully baked to the desired crispness. Some breakfast cereals—those of the formed type— were made by grinding the cereal grains, together with the flavoring ingredients to form a paste. The paste was then extruded into the desired shape and sent to the baking operation. The cereal was then packaged in branded cartons and sent to the factory warehouse for shipment to customers. Shelf-life for breakfast cereals was limited, because after eight months the flakes might become stale or spotty. Except for rolling and exploding, the same processing and packaging equipment was used for all flake and exploded products. Alteration of the final recipe and package size to suit the particular needs of a market presented no major manufacturing problem. In 1963, the Louvain factory produced two hundred different combinations or recipe and package sizes of eight different brands for the Benelux-Holland market.

Intensive market research into housewives' menu planning and taste peculiarities in different regions led to the necessity for specific recipes and package-sizes sold in each region. This was in accord with a long-established United Foods policy on marketing and product quality.

The packaging equipment installed at Louvain was of European design; it operated at lower speeds than the equipment used in the U.S., but it could be changed for different package-sizes in eight hours. Comparable changeovers required as much as twenty-four hours in the U.S.

From 1953 to 1963 shipments to the Benelux-Holland markets had doubled every two years, and management believed this rate of growth would continue through 1968.

United Food Products Company

Benelux Company Organization

Exhibit 1

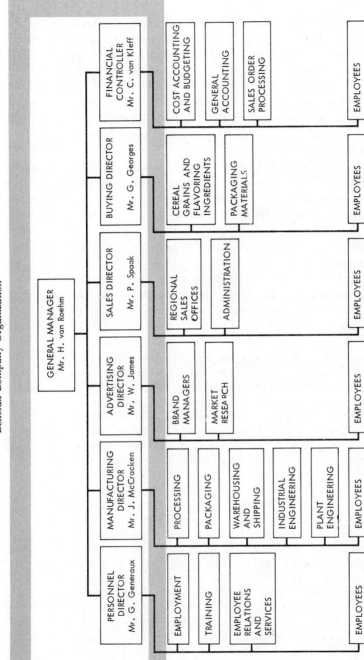

Source: Mr. H. van Roehm, General Manager

DISTRIBUTION   From 1953 to 1956, while he was the General Sales Agent exclusively for United Foods, Mr. van Roehm engaged a contract trucking firm, Coerts S.A., that owned and operated a warehouse in Brussels to store all the shipments from England and to deliver most of the shipments made to Belgian wholesalers. Some of the wholesaler-customers picked up their own orders from the Brussels warehouse, under an arrangement known as *laissez-suivre,* to be described in detail later. Deliveries to the Holland market were also made from the "outside warehouse" in Brussels via a Dutch trucking firm.

Since 1956 two additional Belgian trucking firms, de Steeg and Knokkaert, made deliveries to Belgium and Luxembourg customers respectively from the factory warehouse in Louvain, while the Brussels and Dutch truckers made deliveries from the outside warehouse in Brussels. Railroad rates and delivery times were so unfavorable within the Benelux area that United Foods management felt rail transport to be out of the question for at least the next five years.

In 1960, the factory warehouse in Louvain was expanded to twice its original size; still the Brussels warehouse had to be rented. Commenting on the continued necessity for outside warehouse space, Mr. J. McCracken, Director of Manufacturing, said,

> We've had such an increase in the number of brands and package sizes while we've boosted our overall volume of shipments that, in order to store factory output and load shipments forty-eight hours after receiving orders from our customers, we've had to utilize the Brussels warehouse. This outside space was needed even though sometimes it meant trucking cases of breakfast cereal from Louvain to Brussels and back again before shipping them to customers in Belgium and Luxembourg. In addition to being a depot for loading shipments to customers, the Brussels warehouse is used to store our safety stocks while the Louvain warehouse is used to store what we call "planning" stocks. Actually, we carry two distinct kinds of planning stocks. One kind provides us with standby inventory so that we can use the same equipment for processing different brand-sizes. This type of planning stock allows us to schedule production runs in Economic Lot Sizes. The other type of planning stocks allow us to build inventory in anticipation of scheduled promotional efforts. Our safety stocks don't move as fast as our planning stocks; safety stock is an amount we maintain to cushion the effects of surges in the difference between production and shipping rates for each brand-size of product. These safety stocks have to be physically turned over once every thirteen weeks, so we are certain to send good quality products to our customers.

In mid-1963, after several months of study by industrial engineers, Mr. van Roehm endorsed a proposal to again double the size of the factory warehouse. The study showed that significant savings could be realized, mainly by eliminating the need for the outside warehouse space in Brussels. The proposal was finally approved by executives at continental headquarters in Geneva, and a construction project was planned for completion by August 1, 1964.

In February 1964, the company completed negotiations to purchase Mr. van der Woeld's business in Holland. This meant a transfer of the administration of Mr. van der Woeld's marketing and accounting functions to the United Foods Benelux organization in Antwerp. The transfer was to be completed by May 15, 1964.

It was against this background that Mr. van Roehm expressed his concern for strengthening the organization and procedures for distributing products to customers in Belgium, Holland, and Luxembourg. As he put it,

> How much more profit we actually realize by eliminating the outside warehouse and by taking over marketing management in Holland will depend as much upon controlling the costs of giving our customers an efficient delivery service as it will upon more efficient marketing that we expect to be able to do in Holland.

Detailed Description of the Present Distribution System

The load and performance of any distribution system are affected by marketing and production activities, as well as the organization and facilities chosen to deliver products from the factory to customers. Hence, this discussion will highlight relevant details of advertising, sales, and factory warehousing activities as well as the methods and procedures for distribution.

MARKETING CONSIDERATIONS   The company marketed eight different brands of breakfast cereal, each in three standard package sizes. To promote the sales of each brand-size each of four brand managers, working in conjunction with Mr. James, the Advertising Director, would plan a variety of special sales promotions during a year. All divisions of United Foods operated on a basis of a year comprised of thirteen four-week periods, called sales canvass periods. Sales promotions were planned for twelve canvass periods in a coming year; these plans were updated four times a year. Sales promotions usually consisted of "special packs" containing offers of lower prices, premium coupons, or premiums inserted in the package. Mr. James said,

> We budget promotions expenses according to several key factors: (1) the goals we set for the market share for each brand, (2) the availability of new, attractive promotion schemes, (3) the marginal income we have to work with for each brand-size. We usually

plan to promote each brand four times a year. But during the year we actually stage some promotions during canvass periods and at frequencies different from our plans. We have to do this mainly for two reasons: (1) to counteract promotional efforts of our competitors, and (2) to take advantage of "hot" promotional schemes that may become available during the year. As you know, United Foods has a reputation for its emphasis on advertising and sales promotion activities. Of course, before we stage a promotion, we consult with the Sales, Buying, and Manufacturing Departments to be sure they can support each scheme, because each scheme means a fast filling and emptying of pipelines with special packages that have to be on the shelves of all our retailers at the same time. To be effective, a special promotion stock should be exhausted by the end of a four-week canvass period. I know these special promotion schemes create problems for the boys in Sales, Manufacturing, and Buying, but they boost our volume and market share. As Advertising Director, I have to concentrate mainly on boosting sales volume, even though I realize my promotional budget for each scheme doesn't precisely account for all the expenses incurred by the Buying, Manufacturing, and Distribution departments that have to shift from standard packs to special packs for each promotion. It's their problem to live within their budget.

Mr. Spaak, Director of Sales, highlighted procedures of his organization:

We have analyzed and classified our wholesale and retail customers and our selling efforts (see Exhibit 2). The first three to five days of each canvass period are spent concentrating on our wholesaler-customers; the next eight to ten days on retailer-customers. The remaining five to ten days are for repeat-calls at our top wholesaler-customers. In this way our salesmen are able to give our customers the best service. In fact our emphasis is on helping our customers to plan to boost their sales. Each salesman makes an analysis of a customer's future needs for restocking each brand and size and submits his analysis to the wholesaler or retailer. He also advises the customer about plans and schedules for special advertising product-displays and special pack-promotions during the canvass period. The customer then adjusts the proposed order quantities up or down, signs the order, and the salesman mails it back to our Sales Office in Antwerp at the end of the day. From a variety of market research sources we've found that on the average, wholesalers carry approximately a one-month stock and retailers between a two- and three-month stock. Nevertheless we have good reason to believe that at any one point in time an average of 6 percent of our Belgian retailers are out of stock in Flakes-O-Corn. For FLOCODAV and Oat Pops the figures are 7 percent and 8 percent respectively, and for Sparkies and Rice Puffies 1 percent and 11 percent.

Exhibit 2 — **United Food Products Company**

Analysis and Classification of Customer Sales Efforts

Market Served	No. of Wholesalers	No. of Retailers	Population
Belgium and Luxembourg	860	58,400	9,300,000
Holland	635	23,500	11,000,000

Sales-Manpower Allocation (Belgium and Luxembourg only)

Wholesaler	Average Call Frequency	No. in Class
Class 1	14 days	563
Class 2	35 days	257
Retailer		
Class 1	35 days	18,600
Class 2	70 days	13,100
Class 3		26,500

Each salesman is expected to make a weighted average of sixteen calls per working day; a call at a wholesaler-customer is weighted 1.5 times a call at a retailer-customer.

Customer classifications are established by such criteria as customer's estimated annual turnover, his purchases of United Foods brands and package-sizes, and his affiliation (or independence from) a retail buying group (or volunteer retail chain stores).

Source: Mr. P. Spaak, Director of Sales

OFFICE AND CLERICAL CONSIDERATIONS   The "Sales Office" received customers' orders, checked the status of customers' credit, and prepared five copies of the invoice (one copy being the waybill or shipping instructions) for each order. These tasks were completed by the end of the day after a salesman mailed the customer's order. The Sales Office was managed by Mr. van Kleff, Financial Controller, who said,

> It may seem unusual that these activities are part of my organization instead of Mr. Spaak's, but we've found that they function best this way, because they are closely related to our accounting activities. As you would expect, our Sales Office activities are much heavier during the first half than during the last half of a sales canvass period. During the first half we've processed as many as 425 orders per day, and during the last half we've processed as few as 15 orders per day. Orders received on peak days may not be processed until the day after receipt.

Waybills were then transmitted by messenger to the office of the trucking company designated to deliver the order.

Deliveries to customers were performed either by trucking companies under contract with United Food Products Co. (Benelux) S.A. or by the customers themselves, under terms known as *laissez-suivre*. This means that a customer received a price allowance because he used his own trucks to pick up his orders. The amount of the allowance was determined more by negotiations with the customer than by a rationalized formula. About 17 percent of the total shipments to Belgium and Luxembourg markets were under the *laissez-suivre* arrangement. The customer could pick up his order any time at his convenience up to seven days after he placed his order with the United salesman. Commenting on this arrangement, Mr. McCracken said,

> The seven-day limit for the customer to pick up his order has proved to be meaningless. Frequently customers will pick up only part of their order because there's no space on their truck. Most of the time, our *laissez-suivre* customers have several orders at our warehouse, waiting to be picked up. It is very difficult for us to schedule the work of preparing shipments (stock picking, assembling cases in the order on the shipping platform, counting and verifying cases with quantities ordered, etc.). This is because *laissez-suivre* customers don't give us advance notice of when their truck will pick up their orders. And of course, when they do arrive, we have to give a customer's truck priority over our contractors' trucks that may have to be loaded at the same time. You can see the disruptions that occur when our planned work has to be stopped while our warehouse and shipping crews work to load a customer's truck.

SHIPMENTS TO BENELUX MARKETS   As mentioned earlier, by 16:30 each day, the Sales Office transmitted waybills to each of three contract trucking firms responsible for delivering 83 percent of total shipments to customers in Belgium and Luxembourg. The largest of the three trucking firms, Coerts, operated the outside warehouse in Brussels and handled deliveries between his warehouse in Brussels and the factory warehouse in Louvain (23 kilometers), as well as deliveries from his warehouse to customers.

Each contract-hauler had a dispatcher who decided (1) which of his available trucks would be used to haul customers' orders, (2) the route of travel to be taken by each truck (hence, the sequence in which customers' orders were to be loaded and unloaded).

Frequently, in making these decisions, the dispatcher was not able to load all cases ordered by all customers located along a route to be traveled during the day by one truck. This meant that he would either have to send another partially loaded truck if available, or plan to deliver portions of customers' orders the next day his truck would travel this route. This meant that the warehouse had to keep an accounting record of quantities ordered and quantities actually shipped to customers. A map showing the geographical districts served by each trucker is given in Exhibit 3. The distribution of shipments to the various districts is given in Exhibit 4.

WAREHOUSING AND SHIPPING   In the early afternoon of each day, at about 2:00 P.M., the truckers sent a summary of the delivery plans to the Shipping Department in Louvain. These delivery plans enabled the foreman of the Shipping Department to schedule the activities of warehouse and shipping personnel who prepared the shipments to be loaded each day. This schedule was completed by 4:00 P.M. each day and usually planned the activities through the morning and early afternoon of the following day.

The factory warehouse was operated daily between the hours of 06:00 and 23:00, five days a week. For each order, the required number of cases of each brand-size was picked from designated factory stocks. If a truck was at the shipping platform waiting to be loaded, the cases were moved directly to the truck; otherwise they were assembled by truckloads in the shipping area and then loaded on a highway truck.

Stock picking and loading were done by means of an industrial clamp-truck. The clamps enabled the truck to grasp the cases quickly, without using pallets or skids. If a highway truck were to be loaded with cases of only one brand-size, then a single clamp truck could pick the stock and load at the rate of 1,500 cases per hour; this rate was reduced to 500 cases per hour for truckloads of mixed brand-sizes. Since single brand-size was usually stored in several warehouse locations in order to maximize the utilization of total factory warehouse space, the shipping foreman had to designate to the clamp truck operator the particular stock-location of cases to be picked for each customer's order. The foreman also tried to move out the oldest stocks first. He could, however, if stocks were not near the maximum point, ship more recent stocks in an effort to cut handling costs.

Industrial engineers had developed a rationalized routine to help the warehouse and shipping foremen in their work of storing cases coming in via the packaging line conveyors and loading delivery trucks at the shipping dock. This routine required the maintenance of a master stock location and warehouse space availability file and a detailed checklist of steps in planning for efficient utilization of warehouse space, manpower, and materials handling equipment as well as for efficient materials handling methods.

SHIPMENTS TO HOLLAND   Shipments to Holland customers were presently being dispatched from the Brussels (outside) warehouse via the Dutch trucking company. This company operated three intermediate storage and dispatch depots. Daily, Mr. van der Woeld's office in Rotterdam sent via telex to the trucking company a list of customers' orders to be delivered. The trucking dispatcher then prepared the daily schedule of pickups and

Exhibit 3   **United Food Products Benelux S.A.**
District Map of Belgium and Luxembourg

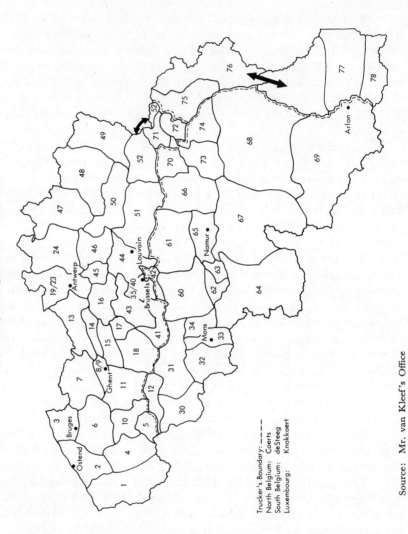

Trucker's Boundary: — — —
North Belgium: Coerts
South Belgium: deSteeg
Luxembourg: Knokkaert

Source: Mr. van Kleef's Office

Exhibit 4   **United Food Products Company**

Area	Number of Customers	% of Total Shipments
1	23	1.114
2	25	1.451
3	25	1.335
4	19	1.841
5	32	.520
6	25	.738
7	23	1.342
8/9	45	2.328
10	21	.702
11	40	.891
12	24	2.054
13	25	.563
14	32	2.089
15	21	.709
16	19	1.336
17	22	1.198
18	19	.523
19/23	115	14.320
24	27	1.659
30	25	2.202
31	24	.689
32	18	.638
33	23	1.295
34	24	1.406
35/40	137	14.026
41	12	.811
42	15	.366
43	18	1.583
44	25	1.864
45	28	.981
46	23	1.231
47	23	1.024
48	10	.940
49	10	.324
50	9	1.584
51	15	1.254
52	9	1.135
60	19	1.688
61	11	.765
62	27	2.992
63	23	1.597
64	11	.639
65	17	1.726
66	20	1.218
67	10	.854
68	19	1.702
69	18	1.314

Exhibit 4 (cont.)

Area	Number of Customers	% of Total Shipments
70	18	1.205
71	25	.449
72	27	1.150
73	11	.449
74	22	.781
75	28	1.333
Liege	4	2.702
Grand-Duche de Luxembourg 76/78		7.020
Rounding		.350
		100.000

routings to customers. Shipments destined for northern Holland were delivered directly from Brussels to retailers. Shipments to the remaining sections of Holland were routed to customers (wholesalers and retailers) via one of the three intermediate depots, otherwise called "shuttle points," where they were reloaded and routed further to final destinations.

Mr. McCracken said,

> We are not satisfied with this Dutch shuttle-point system. We've had too many damaged cases returned by our Holland customers. When we checked into the cause of this we found that storage facilities were not adequate and handling was careless. Once we learned that cases were stored temporarily on the deck of a ship in Rotterdam, under a tarpaulin. Another time we saw depot crews using a greased wooden ramp to slide our cases down to the truck dock.

United Foods managers all agreed that distribution procedures for the Holland market would have to be changed, but they were not certain about what changes should be made.

VARIATIONS IN SHIPPING ACTIVITIES   Pursuant to plans for expanding and improving the Louvain warehousing activities, the industrial engineers made some studies to measure the variations in shipments. They determined that 4 percent of shipments in Belgium were in lots of ten to twenty-four cases, 17 percent of shipments were in lots of twenty-five to ninety-nine cases, and the remaining 79 percent was in lots of over one hundred cases each. They also derived a graph showing the number of cases shipped each day for three different sales canvass periods given in Exhibit 5 and a table summarizing numbers of truck arrivals and truck departures per hour from the Louvain warehouse each day for three consecutive operating days given by Exhibit 6.

Exhibit 5   **United Food Products Company**

Sales Canvass Period 30/9-25/10

Graph Showing Number of Cases Shipped Each Day of Sales Canvass Period
30 Sept.-25 Oct. 1963

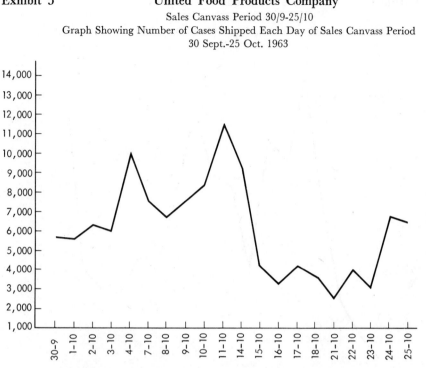

Notes: A "case" at United Food Products Company was actually a weighted average
of all case sizes for all products and brands. Each case weighs approximately 12 kg.
Source: Industrial Engineering Department

Mr. McCracken made the following comments about these variations:

Our analysis of these variations shows that about 70 percent
of our total shipments are made during the first half of a canvass
period. The number of cases shipped on the peak shipping days
is about five times the number shipped on the low shipping days.
If we're going to stick rigidly to our policy of shipping forty-eight
hours after a customer gives us his order, then we're going to have
to tolerate overtime and idle time of our warehouse personnel and
equipment.

Warehousing and shipping expenses are part of our manufacturing departmental budget, not of the Sales Department. Yet it is
the deliberate concentration of sales and advertising efforts early in
each canvass period that causes our performance to look poor as
far as budget measures are concerned. I agree that sales promotions have boosted our market share and sales volume, but they
also make it more expensive for us to give prompt delivery service
to customers.

Exhibit 5 (cont.)   **United Food Products Company**

Sales Canvass Period 28/10-22/11

Graph Showing Number of Cases Shipped Each Day of Sales Canvass Period
28 Oct.-22 Nov. 1963

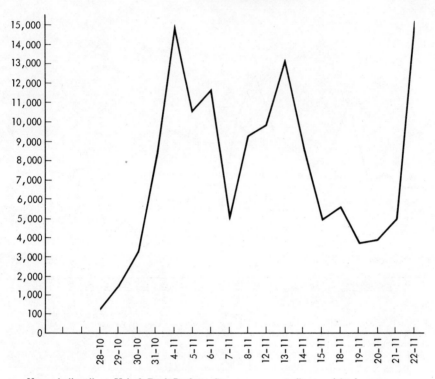

Note: A "case" at United Food Products Company was actually a weighted average
of all case sizes for all products and brands. Each case weighs approximately 12 kg.
Source: Industrial Engineering Department

Arrangements with the three contract trucking firms delivering to the Belgium and Luxembourg markets have been negotiated by the Sales Department. Reimbursements to these contractors were based on Belgian Francs per ton and amounted to 460 francs per ton for Coerts S.A., 580 francs per ton for de Steeg, and an average of 700 francs per ton for Knokkaert.[1] In addition, Coerts also received 85 francs per ton for performing the loading operation at their Brussels warehouse. Mr. McCracken thought that these reimbursements might preferably be based on the number of cases delivered instead of tonnage and that the number of pickups and deliveries

---

[1] One Belgian Franc is approximately equal to two U.S. cents.

Exhibit 5 (cont.)   United Food Products Company

Sales Canvass Period 25/11-20/12
Graph Showing Number of Cases Shipped Each Day of Sales Canvass Period
25 Nov.-20 Dec. 1963

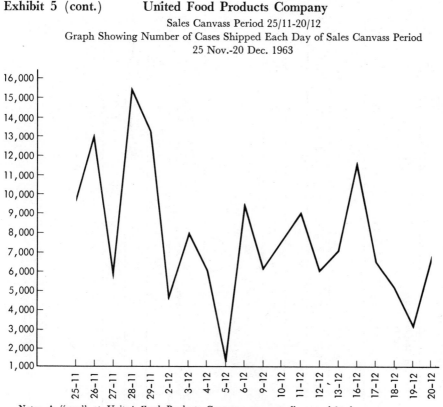

Note: A "case" at United Food Products Company was actually a weighted average
of all case sizes for all products and brands. Each case weighs approximately 12 kg.
Source: Industrial Engineering Department

should also be accounted for in reimbursing the trucking firms. The Dutch trucking firm operated under similar arrangements and negotiated with Mr. van der Woeld in Rotterdam.

Mr. Van Roehm said,

I realize that our contract trucking firms make their own truck-routing and dispatching decisions daily and that these decisions have significant effects on our distribution costs and services to customers. If our organization were to make these decisions would they become the responsibility of the Sales Department or the Manufacturing Department? Even if we did manage the traffic problems of distribution, how could I be certain that we should solve them any more economically than they're being solved now by the contract trucking firm?

Exhibit 6

United Food Products Company

Summary of Truck Arrival and Service Times for Canvass Period

January 3—February 14, 1964

(31 working days)

Truck Arrival per Hour

Hour of Day

	6	7	8	9	10	11	12	13	14	15	16	17	18	19	20
Total—31 days	35	40	60	44	24	27	24	42	44	39	21	28	6	6	1
Average	1,13	1,29	1,94	1,42	0,77	0,87	0,77	1,35	1,42	1,26	0,68	0,90	0,19	0,19	0,03
Maximum	4	6	4	7	3	3	4	5	4	3	3	4	2	2	1
Minimum	0	0	0	0	0	0	0	0	0	0	0	0	0	0	0

Truck Departure per Hour

Hour of Day

	6	7	8	9	10	11	12	13	14	15	16	17	18	19	20
Total—31 days	1	11	34	33	45	34	18	47	42	47	50	27	20	20	12
Average	0,03	0,35	1,10	1,06	1,45	1,10	0,58	1,52	1,35	1,52	1,61	0,87	0,65	0,65	0,39
Maximum	1	2	3	5	6	6	4	4	5	4	3	4	2	3	2
Minimum	0	0	0	0	0	0	0	0	0	0	0	0	0	0	0

No arrivals or departures after 20:00
Source: Industrial Engineering Files

Exhibit 6 (cont.)

Summary of Truck Arrival and Service Times for
Canvass Period January 3–February 14, 1964
(31 working days)

| Date | Truck Arrival per Hour | | | | Truck Departure per Hour | | | |
	Total Each Day	Average	Max.	Min.	Total Each Day	Average	Max.	Min.
Jan. 3	10	0,59	3	0	10	0,59	3	0
″ 6	22	1,29	7	0	22	1,29	3	0
″ 7	18	1,06	4	0	18	1,06	6	0
″ 8	17	1	4	0	17	1	3	0
″ 9	13	0,76	3	0	13	0,76	3	0
″ 10	11	0,65	3	0	11	0,65	2	0
″ 13	16	0,94	4	0	16	0,94	3	0
″ 14	20	1,18	5	0	20	1,18	4	0
″ 15	21	1,24	4	0	21	1,24	4	0
″ 16	20	1,18	4	0	20	1,18	4	0
″ 17	5	0,29	2	0	5	0,29	2	0
″ 20	10	0,59	2	0	10	0,59	3	0
″ 21	11	0,65	2	0	11	0,65	2	0
″ 22	7	0,41	2	0	7	0,41	2	0
″ 23	10	0,59	2	0	10	0,59	2	0
″ 24	11	0,65	3	0	11	0,65	2	0
″ 27	21	1,24	6	0	21	1,24	5	0
″ 28	26	1,53	4	0	26	1,53	5	0
″ 29	8	0,47	2	0	8	0,47	3	0
″ 30	7	0,41	2	0	7	0,41	1	0
″ 31	11	0,65	4	0	11	0,65	2	0
Feb. 3	15	0,88	4	0	15	0,88	4	0
″ 4	13	0,76	4	0	13	0,76	3	0
″ 5	17	1	4	0	17	1	6	0
″ 6	19	1,12	4	0	19	1,12	4	0
″ 7	21	1,24	4	0	21	1,24	4	0
″ 10	18	1,06	4	0	18	1,06	3	0
″ 11	10	0,59	3	0	10	0,59	2	0
″ 12	6	0,35	2	0	6	0,35	2	0
″ 13	12	0,71	4	0	12	0,71	3	0
″ 14	15	0,88	3	0	15	0,88	3	0

Source: Industrial Engineering Files

5

Organizational Behavior

In this course an opportunity is provided to acquire understanding of the behavior of people individually and in groups. The demands that the human factors in an organization place upon the administrator are considerable. But, under the pressure of day-to-day activities with their inevitable crises, executives often handle in a piecemeal fashion or neglect entirely their responsibilities involving people. It is easier to work with inanimate things—facts, figures, or machines—than with human beings; and administrators tend to concentrate on these kinds of activities while letting the people take care of themselves—often to the detriment of total effectiveness.

Administrators would like some simple, concise set of rules that will tell them how to deal more effectively with people. They would like a proven way to achieve cooperation and teamwork. Unfortunately, such a set of rules does not exist. The "Ten Successful Steps in Dealing with People" or a list of "Guidelines for Effective Administration" do not stand up under either critical scrutiny or the test of practical application. Observing quite quickly that such lists of rules are of little practical value, administrators often assume that an effective approach to the human elements of administration cannot be developed; and they conduct their activities concerning people on an opportunistic, unsystematic basis.

Such an approach is not necessary. Effective approaches to the problems involved in the administration of people can be developed although to do so requires a great deal of thought and effort. Some materials that are presented in this course will assist in the development of such approaches. The major purposes include helping the administrator to increase his effectiveness in dealing with people; developing his awareness of the existence of both individual and organizational goals in an administrative situation; and assisting him in developing methods of encouraging cooperation toward the achievement of both types of goals. An additional purpose is to assist the administrator in increasing his knowledge and awareness of himself as an individual.

Human Skills of an Administrator

To this point, we have spoken of human skills only in a very general sense. More precisely, however, the human skill of an administrator has three distinct elements. First, the administrator must have proficiency and skill in understanding the basic human forces active in his organization. He must understand the fundamental concepts of motivation and behavior that affect the activities of the people with whom he works, the true nature of authority and influence, and the ramifications of his pattern of leadership upon the actions of individuals and groups of individuals. He must be aware of the factors that prevent or promote effective communication within the organization and recognize that in many instances people perceive the same situation in greatly differing ways. He must know, and know intimately, the subtleties of relationships with both superiors and subordinates, and he must fully appreciate the impact of his assumptions, attitudes, and actions upon such relationships. Further, he must realize that these relationships are not constant but are continually changing. He must understand the problems involved in the initiation and administration of change in organizations and the ramifications of the organizational structure and control techniques upon total effectiveness. In brief, he must possess substantial knowledge about human behavior characteristics.

Second, the administrator must have a high degree of skill in analyzing complex human situations. He must be able to use his knowledge of organizational behavior as a framework within which to analyze specific human problems, determine what factors and forces present, and then, based on this analysis, select from those alternative courses available to him what seems most likely to alleviate or resolve the problem. Of critical importance at this stage is an administrator's ability to recognize and deal effectively not only with facts but also with attitudes, opinions, and sentiments—including those that he himself brings to the situation.

Finally, the human skill of an administrator involves ability in implementing a plan of action. For example, having decided that the best approach in gaining greater cooperation from a group of individuals is to influence the informal leaders of the group, he must be able actually to influence these individuals. He must have skills in "doing"; he must be able to carry out his intentions successfully.

We will deal with each of these kinds of skills in this course. The specific topic areas we will cover include:

Individual Motivation and Behavior
Group Dynamics in Organizations
Leadership Styles
Communication in Organizations
Organization and Control
Administrative Relationships
The Administration of Change
The Management of Conflict
Values and Value Systems

CONSTRUCTION EQUIPMENT INTERNATIONAL AG (A)

Construction Equipment International, AG, with headquarters in Zürich, is a wholly owned subsidiary of Road Machinery of America Inc., the headquarters of which are in Detroit, Michigan, U.S.A. For many years, the parent company has been one of the leading manufacturers in the U.S. of material handling equipment, lifts, and hoists, concrete mixing machinery, and heavy asphalt processing machines used in highway construction.

In the past ten years, there was a rapid increase in the foreign operations of RMA, first in terms of sales to independent distributors in Europe, South America, Australia, and the Far East and later in terms of manufacturing plants abroad. At first, all the selling was managed from the parent company's Detroit headquarters—that is, sales representatives were trained and stationed throughout the world, the market potential by country was estimated, customer orders were received from dealers, and shipments were made from the U.S.

The Establishment of Overseas Companies

Concurrent with the rapid growth of foreign sales, RMA top management took two important organizational steps. They set up manufacturing plants in certain countries under subsidiary companies (i.e., RMA Belgium with two thousand employees today, twenty of whom are U.S. nationals, and RMA U.K., with four thousand employees today, twelve of whom are U.S. nationals). These companies report to the manufacturing department in Detroit. Second, they set up a company in Zürich to sell company products all over the world, except in the U.S., Canada, and South America.

Somewhat over 40 percent of all RMA sales volume worldwide, including domestic sales in the U.S., results from sales made outside the United States. RMA, therefore, might be categorized as multinational company, and CEIAG has become a principal selling arm, for all countries except the U.S., Canada, and South America.

CEIAG has changed markedly in the last six years. Six years ago there were about fifty employees in the Zürich headquarters: twenty-seven U.S. nationals acting as managers and sales representatives, and twenty-three non-U.S. nationals, serving in clerical capacities such as order handling, bookkeeping and secretarial work. In addition, there were about forty sales representatives, serving territories from Bombay and Johannesburg to Salzburg. All these representatives were U.S. nationals, hired and trained in the U.S.

One year later—five years ago—there were 220 people in the Zürich headquarters, and the number of direct representatives throughout the world was increasing rapidly. Today the Zürich headquarters employs 330 people. There are seven major departments and department heads. With the exception of the manager of employee relations, all these managers are U.S. nationals, hired and trained in the U.S. In addition, there are forty-four members of middle management—division managers and assistant division managers within the seven major departments. Of these, thirty-six are U.S. citizens hired in the U.S., and eight are "local hires." The term "local hire" is used to denote employees hired by CEIAG, under the policies of the latter, rather than those hired by RMA under its policies. All these eight are heads of inside work divisions, office management, or accounting.

In addition, as of the time of writing of this case, the field force worldwide has increased to sixty-three sales representatives throughout the world, fifty-three of whom are U.S. foreign service employees, and ten of whom are "local hires."

In summary, in the short time since Michel Mottier, a young French clerical worker in Zürich, was sent to Detroit for training five years ago, the number of non-U.S. sales representatives worldwide has increased from zero to ten out of sixty-three; and the number of division middle managers of non-U.S. origin has increased to eight out of forty-four. However, all top management (the managing director and seven major department managers) are U.S. citizens except one.

Michel Mottier

Michel Mottier was employed by CEIAG on August 13, five years ago. At that time he had been employed by a Swiss firm. He speaks four languages— French, English, German, and Italian. At the time of employment, Mr. Hans Giorgetti, Personnel Director, explained to him the employment rules that were then explained to all "local hires." Among other things, Mr. Giorgetti told him "frankly, Mr. Mottier, there is not much chance that men who have not been trained in the United States will be transferred to the position of sales representative. This is a United States Company, manufacturing and selling products primarily made in the U.S. We have no sales representatives who are not from the United States. However, we can offer you exceptional work, we think, in the Zürich office." At that time, it was the opinion of many executives in Detroit, and in Zürich, that selling methods and managerial methods in the United States required that both sales representative and managerial positions could best be filled by men who had been brought up in the United States, trained in the American educational system, and trained in the sales and managerial organization of RMA in the U.S. For example, there was one instance in Zürich in which a young man came to the personnel director and said that unless he could be assured of promotions beyond his present job, he would have to leave. The man's department manager, in this case, felt that the man in question was competent in his present job but that he should be allowed to leave, "since I can replace him with an engineer trained in the U.S.—it is much easier to work with men who, through training and experience, think like I do."

But in the case of Mottier, the head of the Parts Sales Department, William Brown, to whom he reported, responded differently when Mottier inquired of his own chances for advancement. Brown assessed that Mottier was as qualified as anyone he knew (including Americans) to advance as an outside parts sales representative. He wrote to the head of the RMA Parts Sales Department in Detroit, saying, "there is no point in this man sitting here doing internal administrative work when he has all of the potential qualities of a line sales representative—language, intelligence, energy, and personal skills." Brown requested that Mottier be sent to Detroit for a two-year training program operated for college graduates about his own age and training.

Mottier was soon sent to Detroit and spent eight months in the college training program of RMA. During his stay there, he attracted the attention of some of the executives in line sales management. They judged that he would be a valuable sales representative selling in the United States and informed the Zürich company of this fact, asking if he could be released. At this point, the Zürich personnel director, together with the manager of Parts Sales of CEIAG, reasoned "if he is good enough for selling the U.S., we would like to have him selling back here." Mottier became the first non-U.S. national to become a parts sales representative for CEIAG.

Training Placement and Compensation of Graduates

According to Mr. Giorgetti, Personnel Director, CEIAG, with its growing sales of technical equipment to large dealers in many countries, has an acute problem in finding enough qualified sales engineers to handle the business in its many and diverse sales territories. In the first place, all companies in the industrialized world have need for this type of person. This is as true in West Germany and the U.K. as it is in the United States. But for an international company like CEIAG, the supply of talent is even tighter. Applicants must not only know mechanical engineering, but they must know both the culture and the language of the territory to which they are assigned. Mr. Giorgetti gives the example of a recently placed sales representative in Lagos. This man was called upon to help the leader solve a technical problem with his employee-mechanics, who were attempting to respond to an important customer requirement for repairing and adjusting equipment. In this case, the representative was able to spend time with the mechanics, on the shop floor, conversing with them in French, and gaining their acceptance of his ideas. As a third important qualification, which adds to recruiting difficulty in a tight labor market, the men chosen should have a knowledge of English for integrating well into the parent company environment, and of still a third language. This last qualification is necessary in a multinational company for two reasons—to enable transfer and promotion earlier in the career and to provide for higher management talent later in the career.

Finally, there is a qualification that the man have the personal and human characteristics necessary for dealing with many customers. This, as is well-known in all countries, is a difficult combination to find, especially if the man must also have a good engineering education.

All these reasons, according to Mr. Giorgetti, contribute to a shortage of qualified people on the demand side. But management is faced with other necessities on the supply side. One of these is to maintain good relations with the professors of engineering at better technical schools, in order that they will call CEIAG to the attention of their graduates and, at the same time, inform the company of prospective trainees. For example, the company has at times been pressed to raise starting salaries for trainees as a means of attracting qualified people. In Switzerland, there are a few such schools and professors that are important, among which are the Polytechnic Federal High School in Zürich and the Ecole Polytechnique of the University of Lausanne. Currently, the company is offering trainees Swiss francs 1,600 to 2,000 per month ($368–$460). This range is slightly higher than the average for Swiss firms. Mr. Giorgetti states that if U.S. companies went substantially higher than this, professors and department heads, many of whom maintain excellent relationships with Swiss companies, which also are in need for talent, would react unfavorably.

It is therefore the company policy on compensation to pay people who are employed locally approximately the range paid by local employers.

> Not only does this keep our company in better relationship with people in the various countries, including other industrialists and governments—we cannot afford to disrupt the local economies— but it also makes sense competitively and economically. For example, if we are hiring a sales engineer in Scotland, the going rate for graduates of the best universities might be payment in Pounds in

the equivalent of U.S. $1,600, whereas the same average rate in universities in the U.S. is perhaps $8,000. If Detroit were to try to establish a single rate for hiring mechanical engineers all over the world, it would not work for the company or for other industrial companies in the countries concerned.

We are very careful, however, to pay people who are hired in one country certain added benefits if they are assigned to a foreign post. These added benefits take the form of post allowances, quarters allowances, education allowances, and foreign service allowances, including periodic returns home for extended vacations.

Mr. Giorgetti further stated that "the formulation and administration of personnel policies in a multinational company is sometimes a difficult thing. We are sometimes faced with particular problems that require a great deal of thought." As an example, Mr. Giorgetti cited one such problem that arose this year.

Hans Buhler and Richard Steadman

Hans Buhler and Richard Steadman are two men who have been working in Zürich for a little over one year. Both of them were hired directly out of college. Buhler from the Eidgenossische Technische Hochschule in Zürich and Steadman from Purdue University in the U.S. Both were hired to go through a college training program lasting about two years, which was set up by RMA management in Detroit. In this program, men are given about five months' orientation and formal classroom type work in Detroit, and this is followed by two on-the-job assignments lasting about twelve to eighteen months. Buhler and Steadman are now residing in Zürich and have been assigned on-the-job training positions in the area of dealer training operations. Both men have substantially the same training in mechanical engineering at their respective colleges. Both men are married but have not yet had children, Buhler is twenty-six and Steadman is twenty-seven. Buhler was hired by CEIAG and Steadman by RMA.

One of the projects to which the men have been assigned is the development of a one-week course designed to train the salesmen of one of CEIAG's largest dealers, Société pour Machines Industrielles S.A.. This latter company, located in Paris, has six hundred employees engaged in large machine shops, maintenance shops, and service shops, as well as twenty salesmen who sell RMA products all over France. The director of Sales Training in Zürich decided on the need for this program, and SMI management in Paris has received it enthusiastically. It was also decided that this course should be held in Geneva and conducted in French so that the salesmen of SMI could easily understand and so that there would be a smoother working relationship between instructors and CEIAG personnel on the one hand and SMI salesmen and sales manager on the other.

Buhler and Steadman worked very hard on their assignments. First, they studied the new equipment to be covered in the program, sought out engineering specifications from many sources, and prepared and presented lecture-discussions, which were received with high compliment by the SMI salesman. They also planned the mechanics of the conference, hotel arrangements, transportation arrangements, and such matters as coffee socials and the final dinner.

At a social hour preceding the final dinner, two of the salesmen from France, together with a member of management in the Paris customer-firm, paid a high compliment to Buhler. Several members of CEIAG top management were present at this dinner. Mr. Giorgetti was almost always invited to such meetings because of his facility in speaking with customers in French, English, and German. At this particular time, Buhler and Giorgetti were standing by the fireplace in the restaurant when the three men from Paris came over. One of them said to Giorgetti: Hans, this has been an excellent conference. Not only have we improved our own knowledge of sales engineering, but we have respected Steadman and Buhler for their ability to arrange a conference without flaw. Buhler, here, speaks French as well as we do and is quick on his feet with answers to our questions. Steadman is a fine engineer and will make a good sales engineer."

After the three men parted, Giorgetti said to Buhler, in German, "they really think a lot of you and Dick Steadman. And I might say that our company management is happy that you two do such good work."

Hans Buhler answered, laughing in a good natured way, "Well, we surely worked hard, and I'm happy that you and the men from Paris think of us this way. I enjoy working with CEIAG people, especially with Dick Steadman. Everything would really be fine if some day you would pay us the same as our friends."

Mr. Giorgetti states that he and Buhler continued to have a pleasant conversation and pleasant visits with men from the French company. However, the remark of Buhler stuck in his mind.

Management faces some difficult problems in formulating policies for compensation, worldwide. Let me explain to you what I think Hans Buhler meant.

Buhler was hired here at Sfr. 2,000 per month, equivalent to U.S. $464. We raised him to the equivalent of $500 a month after six months, when he went to Detroit for training. In the U.S. he is entitled to the standard 20 percent foreign service allowance (equivalent to $100) and to a housing allowance that is worth an equivalent of about $150. This brings him to a total "take home" payment of about $750 while he was living in Detroit. This was definitely in line with the going rates being paid to his fellow trainees (about $750 in salary) who were hired in the U.S. universities, including his fellow worker here, Dick Steadman.

At the completion of training in the U.S., Hans was brought back to Zürich with a raise, and then given a second raise, to the point where he is making Sfr. 2,800, the equivalent of $644 per month. However, he no longer receives foreign service or housing allowances. He is treated under CEIAG policy as a person hired in his native country and permanently working here. This policy, as I have already explained, is necessary to keep from jeopardizing the local economy and the company economics.

Now let us look at Dick Steadman's salary history. He was hired at approximately the same time by Detroit as Buhler was by Zürich. According to the competitive market for graduate engineers in the U.S., he was started at $750 per month. At the conclusion of his U.S. training, he was assigned to Zürich as a U.S. foreign service employee, at a salary of $850 a month (he had one raise on the U.S. to $800). In Zürich, he is entitled to the standard 20 percent foreign service allowance ($170) and to the post allowance, which amounts to about $176—this is designed to cover the difference in cost of living (excluding housing) between Zürich and Washington, D.C.

Thus, Steadman's base pay plus allowances comes to about $1,196 a month while he lives in Zürich.

Our management in both Detroit and Zürich is constantly on the alert to compensation problems such as this, and particularly when we are dealing with talented young men who are productive like these. At the same time, you can see that salary administration in a big international company like RMA, and a large international subsidiary like CEIAG, is not an easy job. I would be interested in what you think about this example.[1]

---

[1] This case was written, edited, and submitted to Mr. Giorgetti and Mr. Kermit Hansen, Managing Director (President) of CEIAG for their approval. After making some minor corrections of fact, Mr. Hansen said:

"I agree completely with the statement made by Hans Giorgetti in the last paragraph. It seems to me that the obvious solution is to equalize pay between the two. However, opposed to this is the absolute necessity for maintaining salary levels in line with local practices. This is what makes the problem such a tough one."

CONSTRUCTION EQUIPMENT INTERNATIONAL, AG (B)

Construction Equipment International, AG, with headquarters in Zürich, is a wholly owned subsidiary of Road Machinery of America, Inc., the headquarters of which are in Detroit, Michigan, U.S.A. For many years, the latter company has been a leading manufacturer of material handling equipment, lifts and hoists, concrete mixing machinery, and allied products. Information on company operations, and on personnel policies, is to be found in Construction Equipment International (A), p. 295.

This case has to do with the thoughts and reactions of Willi Studer, thirty years old, toward his career, his employment by CEIAG, his training in Detroit, U.S.A., and his work in the Zürich headquarters of CEIAG. At the time of writing of this case—(the same as CEIAG A)—Willi Studer has been in Zürich for sixteen months in a sales engineering assignment in which he does certain sales planning work, helps to plan and conduct (lecturing) presentations to train dealer salesmen on technical qualities of the company's lift and hoist machinery, and sometimes travels with dealer salesmen in countries such as France, Germany, or Switzerland. This latter function involves direct help to final customers and training of dealer salesmen at the same time. For example, in traveling with a salesman, Studer faces such customer questions as "what kind of a machine do I need to charge a brick stone oven with a narrow and low clearance?" Drawing on his knowledge of company products, plus his training as a mechanical engineer, Willi is an important link in the company's relations to its large dealers (the one in Paris has six hundred employees), their salesmen, and the final customer.

At the opening of the interview, the case writer stated that all that is needed for a good case is to describe facts and opinions about career and employment and suggested that "we start by simply asking what your career was before joining CEIAG, and how you happened to come to work for this company."

Incidently, the interview was conducted in good English, with a slight accent. Most of the words below are those used by Willi Studer.

> I joined CEIAG after I saw an advertisement for employment in
> a newspaper while I was waiting in the railroad station at Chur.

I guess there are a lot of reasons why I chose this. I was born in a small town in the Bernese Oberland and later moved to Luzern with my family. My first connection with Americans was when I was about eight years old. This was after World War II, and the American soldiers came here on vacation, in uniform. I knew how to ask for chewing gum, and it was a thrill to ask for it. I somehow got the impression that the Americans are nice, and even then I thought something like "they have a high standard of living, and they don't seem narrow minded, and someday you will make better money working for an American business."

Anyway, I went to primary school until I was thirteen, then middle school until sixteen. Having decided to be a mechanical engineer, I took an apprenticeship for four years, until twenty. You see, there are two ways to be an engineer in Switzerland. One way is apprenticeship, and then three years of engineering school. The other way is to go to the Eidgenossische Technische Hochschule (ETH, Zürich) for eight semesters or four years. After the apprenticeship, I was in the Swiss Army for almost a year, and then went to the Central Swiss Technical School (ZTL) for three years. I was then twenty-four.

After that, I got a job with a big American oil company, took a training program in their research center in England, and was assigned as a sales engineer on technical problems—giving schools and presentations to salesmen about company products, their uses and applications. Sometimes the job involved going to factories and helping solve complaints. I started there at Sfr. 1,100 per month when I was hired, and was making Sfr. 1,800[1] when I resigned three years later. Actually, I enjoyed the work, but the longer term prospects weren't too good for advancement. Switzerland is a smaller country, and it is impossible to have a company with all chiefs and no indians, also, there were too many young people ahead of me. Maybe in twenty years I could have been a product manager or technical manager. They wanted to send me to a six-months training program in their research laboratories in the U.S. My wife and I both wanted to know and learn about the U.S. first hand, but under company policy my wife couldn't go (I couldn't afford to pay for her stay myself).

So I resigned after I saw that advertisement in Chur and after being interviewed at CEIAG by several people, even though the new job paid slightly less money. In the interviews, the main thing they looked at was how well I speak English and other languages. You know, it is not too easy to find good engineers who also have good knowledge of languages. All the way through school, some people are good at things like languages and others are good at things like arithmetic or physics. CEIAG told me what I will do for three years, including training for two years, which is spent in the com-

---

[1] One Swiss franc equals twenty-three U.S. cents. One U.S. dollar equals 4.30 Swiss francs.

pany headquarters in the U.S. They also told me what I'd earn and that the trend in the company is to give over more and more of the management of overseas business to people who are native to the countries where the factories and markets are. Maybe even some day the whole overseas company will be managed by Europeans. My starting salary was Sfr. 1,600 as compared with my previous salary of Sfr. 1,800 plus a car. Maybe today I'd be getting Sfr. 2,500 if I were to stay with the old job. The really big thing was the long training stay in the U.S. and an opportunity to learn how people live over there and how they think, as well as how to speak the language really well.

At this point, Willi Studer gave an example of what he meant by an opportunity "to know how people live," and why this is important. He said that it is just as important for him to know how people in the U.S. live, as it is for U.S. nationals to know how people in other countries live.

Take for instance one time when my boss here at CEIAG asked me to conduct a study of how French agency companies (our potential customers) finance their purchase of machinery for their own sales operations. Our management needs this kind of information to plan our own capital requirements. We needed to know, among other things, whether the French businessman pays cash for his equipment, how much credit he gets, what kinds of interest rates he pays, where he gets his money (from manufacturers such as RMA?) and so on. Well, I could understand how our management needs to know this, but I knew we could not put these kinds of questions on a questionnaire or ask them in an interview. You can't go to a French businessman and say "do you pay cash for your machinery"—he would consider this a serious invasion of his privacy, even more than in the U.S. And yet, that was one of the proposed questions on the form.

The conversation then turned to the type of work experiences Willi Studer has had with CEIAG and, in a training capacity, with RMA in the U.S. Shortly after being hired in Zürich, Willi went with his wife to Detroit for a formal classroom type training program combined with rotation to various jobs for direct on-the-job training. The length of this training in the United States was about two years.

The first five months were spent in study of teaching materials, in lectures, and in discussions on a wide range of information about RMA—its products, its engineering, its finance, etc. This gave us a real grounding in both the technical aspects of the company and its management. I think we got very much out of this, and at times we (the trainees) were assigned as group coordinators for conducting discussions. That was good training, too, and it gave us satisfaction.

This was followed by six months of sales engineering on-the-job training. I'll give you one example of what we did. Dealers all over the United States would contact us, either by letter or telephone, asking such questions as: "I have this certain metal plate that was used on the old model machine, number 58, and I wonder if it can be used successfully on the new machine, number 62. If I do use it, what modifications in the machine, and the plate, must be made?" or "I have a complaint from customers that such-and-such machine makes too much noise. What can be done to reduce the noise?"

From there, I went on to the construction department. After that, I spent four months in the used equipment section, and six months in dealer training. In the first, we acted as consultants to dealers at their places of business. In the second, we conducted training programs for dealer salesmen all over the nation who would come to Detroit. There, we explained the technical characteristics of products, the various uses and applications of products, and any other questions that these salesmen wanted to raise.

At this point, the case writer stated that there were two other subjects he wanted to explore: how Willi feels about working in a U.S. company, and how he feels about his own status and position in comparison to the status and position of U.S. citizens working for CEIAG in Zürich. Particularly, the case writer was interested in working conditions and pay.

Well, I like working for this company. In comparison to European companies, I think I can speak up and have somebody listen, and I think I can get more interesting work and get moved up faster. For the past sixteen months I've been doing sales planning work, dealer training work in Zürich, and some traveling with dealer salesmen. The salesmen learn from me, and I learn about company product applications from them.

There are at least eight Americans here in Zürich who got out of the Detroit training program about the same time (within two months) as I did. I know for certain that they are making more money than I am, partly because the pay rates for mechanical engineers hired in the U.S. is more than here, and partly because they are being paid foreign service allowances. Of course, I am now in my home country, and not getting such allowances.

My wife and I do notice the difference in the way an American here lives with his wife and the way we live. They spend a lot more money. For them, it is somewhat like being on vacation. They travel to Paris and Rome, and they go all over. If they see an antique or something, and its price is reasonable, they buy it. We all give parties and have people to dinner, but I know we have to be more careful about how much we spend on this.

I know they (the company) cannot pay the same salaries. Its just a question of demand and supply. If they can hire mechanical engineers at a given price, why should they pay more? When I got back from Detroit, and had been in Zürich a while, I did think I was getting too little. I went in and raised the question, and found out that a raise from 2,000 to Sfr. 2,400 was already in the mill. Since then, I've gotten two raises, up to Sfr. 3,240, and this represents a hell of an improvement. I know this isn't as much as the Americans, but its probably more than I would be getting from a Swiss company.

From an employee standpoint it's simple. You can look at it in two ways. If you look at it as a Swiss, working in a Swiss Company, you're happy. If you look at it as a mechanical engineer working in an international company and see that, because of language, you are sometimes doing a little more for the company than people without this qualification, you're unhappy.

The case writer then said that the interview was almost over and commented that, on the whole, Willi Studer seemed to be competent in his job and to have good prospects ahead. He wondered out loud if, in this employment situation, there were any other matters that ever made Willi feel unhappy.

Well, two or three years ago, people came into Zürich after the training in Detroit, stayed maybe a month, and then got a field assignment. That's the thing I have looked forward to all along. You get a territory, you have a lot of room to produce on your own, you are looked upon by the company as a full professional employee, and you begin to feel responsible for what happens. Now we are staying here (the others and I) for fifteen or sixteen months already, and I don't see the possibility of getting assigned in the immediate future. The percentage of details in our job means that there just simply isn't enough responsibility to justify our training!

Understand this, though, this is not a real gripe. I know I am going to make it and be successful, the question is only when.

CONSTRUCTION EQUIPMENT INTERNATIONAL, AG (C)

Construction Equipment International AG, (CEIAG), with head-quarters in Zürich, is a wholly owned subsidiary of Road Machinery of America, Inc., (RMA), the headquarters of which are in Detroit, Michigan, U.S.A. For many years, the parent company has been one of the leading manufacturers in the U.S. of material handling equipment, lifts and hoists, concrete mixing machinery, and heavy asphalt processing machines used in highway construction. Measured by sales volume, the company would be in the top five corporations in the U.S. engaged in the production of these products.

This case concerns information about the employment and subsequent career, in both CEIAG and RMA, of Jonathan Cook, a British engineer. This information is related by Mr. Hans Giorgetti, manager of personnel and employee relations at CEIAG headquarters in Zürich. Particularly, this case reports on the compensation, placement, and transfer of Cook from the company viewpoint and the career moves and location moves of Cook from his own standpoint.

Jonathan Cook is a graduate of St. Andrews University, Scotland, which is regarded in academic circles as one of the top universities in science in the U.K. Eleven years ago, Cook was employed as a sales engineer, at the age of thirty-two, by Construction Equipment Ltd., a wholly owned subsidiary of RMA. This subsidiary has both manufacturing plants in the U.K. and a selling organization. Cook was employed at a salary of £2,000 per year, equivalent approximately to Swiss francs 2,000 per month or U.S. $460 per month. Stationed at Edinburgh, Scotland, company appraisal forms reveal that he was judged by his superiors to be a very competent sales engineer, interested in company products, and successful in his work with dealers throughout England and Scotland. He remained in this position for five years, until he was thirty-eight, receiving four salary raises during this period. Each time the sales manager in the U.K. reported to him that he had earned increases through hard work and competence.

About six years ago, Construction Equipment International, AG, which is the selling arm of RMA throughout most of the world, except for Canada,

U.S., and South America, badly needed a highly competent sales engineer in Delhi, India. This position seemed to the CEIAG Sales Manager for Asia and the Middle East (The Central Division) to be especially important and difficult to fill. First, there was at the time a shortage of trained engineers who also had the personalities to become good sales representatives. This was difficult enough. But the Indian representative would have unusual demands made on him. There is one very important equipment dealer in Delhi who has a large organization, selling machines all over India. This organization would be helped greatly by a good engineer to train its salesmen in technical applications of the company's products. In the words of Hans Giorgetti, "this is a helluva complicated job—import regulations, relations with the Indian Government, financing of machinery, Agency for Economic Development projects, and the works. Whoever has the job is the official link between sales, engineering, and management of both CEIAG and the customer-dealer. During the three years Jonathan Cook was there he did an excellent job. In the annual reviews of performance with the Sales Manager of the Central (Asian) division, he was given high ratings."

Mr. Giorgetti also recalled how Jonathan Cook happened to get the job in India.

At a company meeting in Zürich, the sales manager for Asia, Jack King, met the sales manager for the U.K., Brian Quinn. As is customary at these meetings, managers frequently informally exchange information on personnel. In the course of conversation, King asks Quinn who are his best salesmen in the United Kingdom. Quinn describes a few people in great detail and seems enthusiastic about what a good group he has working in England and Scotland. He is particularly vivid in describing Cook. A few months later, when King had the difficult job of finding a man for New Delhi, he searched at several places in the CEIAG organization but had not found a man he thought qualified. Then he remembered the name Jonathan Cook and some of the description Quinn had given him. Because Construction Equipment Ltd. is a separate subsidiary within RMA, King had to check with the proper officials in England and then ask Mr. Georgetti to handle the official employment transfer for CEIAG in Zürich. This was duly accomplished, and Cook was moved to New Delhi at a salary of Sfr. 3,100 ($713) a month.

Since he was doing a good job, he got good raises while there. At the time he left, his base salary was good—Sfr. 4,000 per month, or the equivalent of $920. But his total compensation was even better. Under CEIAG compensation policy, he was getting 20 percent foreign service allowance (Sfr. 800), a 10 percent hardship location allowance (Sfr. 400) and a housing allowance equivalent to Sfr. 1,120 a month. All of this gave him a total of Sfr. 6,320 or U.S. $1,450 a month.

It is the company policy not to keep a man in India for more than three years. And so, the Asian Sales Manager contacted various people here in Zürich after Cook had spent two and one-half years there. He said that Cook had done a fine job. In addition to me, he contacted the head of the Product Development Division and the head of the Sales Training Department, here in Zürich. He probably also contacted other people, as well as sales managers he knows in other parts of the world. These contacts were for the purpose of locating a good transfer for Cook—a position where he could have responsibilities commensurate with his experience and level and a salary fitting for a man making what his salary was at that time.

None of these inquiries produced a spot, and so we discussed the situation here in Zürich among our management. It was decided that, no such position being immediately available in CEIAG, the best thing might be to consider the possibilities in the U.S., in the parent company RMA. After all, their organization is bigger than ours, and the salaries there are higher for sales positions. It was further decided that the General Sales Manager of CEIAG would recommend him to the head of the sales organization of RMA in Detroit. This was done, completed with the qualifications and past performance of Jonathan Cook.

RMA management responded with a position of Sales Representative in Toronto, Canada. This was three years ago, when Cook was forty-one, and he seemed very enthusiastic to get the job. In deciding what to pay him, RMA personnel people in Detroit, with information supplied by me, took note of the fact that he was making a total of Sfr. 6,320, including foreign service, hardship, and housing allowances. They were also aware that if Cook were hired by RMA, rather than CEIAG, he would be considered as a "local hire"—a man hired by the domestic company to work domestic territory. Since he would no longer be an employee of the Zürich company, he would not therefore be considered as doing "foreign service." Rather, he would be just like any other domestic employee (the domestic area is considered to cover the U.S. and Canada). Therefore, to be equitable, it was decided that he should have at least the equivalent of what he was making in Delhi but without the housing allowance. So they took the Sfr. 6,320 total remuneration in Delhi, subtracted out the Sfr. 1,120 he was getting for housing, and reasoned that he was getting Sfr. 5,200 compensation for services. This is equal to about $1,200 a month. Therefore, RMA offered him the equivalent of U.S. $1,200 a month in Toronto, all payable as salary. This seemed acceptable to Cook. I am guessing that, while the amount in Toronto was exactly the same he had been getting in Delhi for his services, it appealed to him that his base salary increase was from $920 to $1,200. In other words, this is something permanent—and it raises a man's status in the company—whereas the difference, $280, which had been paid in the form of foreign service and hardship, operating out of the Zürich company, might someday be taken away and does not classify a man in such a high salary scale.

Well, Jonathan Cook stayed in Toronto three years, from ages forty-one to forty-four. Like his other positions, he did well in the job, produced a good amount of business and goodwill for the company, and got high recommendations from the manager above him. In fact, he did well enough that some of the top sales managers in Detroit judged him highly. He was brought to Detroit in a sales management position, at a salary of $1,600 per month. I was glad that he was a foreign national who had been promoted through ranks of CEIAG to a managerial position in the parent company.

After two months in Detroit, Cook asked for an appointment to see the executive in whose department he worked, his line manager. He said that he and his wife had been discussing the difficulties of living in the U.S. and particularly the cost of living and the cost of trips back to their native Scotland, where both of them had strong ties. Cook said that he felt rather deeply the need for some additional compensation. As one means of granting such compensation, he wondered if the company might give him an educational allowance for his children—similar to the allowances available to certain RMA foreign service personnel under RMA policies, and to certain CEIAG foreign service personnel, under CEIAG policies.

In the judgment of RMA management, even though they regarded Cook highly, this simply was not possible. Some stable policies on compensation are absolutely necessary to maintain equity between people, and the policy was clear. RMA has its own policies for people it hires, and, under these, those people who are hired by RMA for a domestic position accept the practices of all domestic RMA personnel. To grant Cook any foreign service allowances would look discriminatory to other managers in the Detroit headquarters. Cook also pointed out that he felt he should be given an extended home leave every two years, to his native country, like other foreign nationals. But company policy clearly classified him as an employee hired by RMA for employment in RMA's domestic territory of operations. This he knew when he took the job.

In due time, Cook apparently became more and more dissatisfied with the situation. His immediate superior and the personnel management people in Detroit knew it. Knowing that Jonathan Cook was a very capable employee and that he had very valuable experience in both the Detroit company and the Zürich company, they talked with him several times about his career with the company. Together, they reached a solution. RMA management contacted the management of Construction Equipment Ltd. in England, and they were glad to have such a man return to the company from where he started. Everyone seemed satisfied. Cook was transferred back to England (employed by Construction International Ltd.) at a salary of £3,500 a year, or about $812 a month. The management in both Detroit and London recognized that this was less than the $1,600 he had been getting in Detroit, but they also judged his job in the U.K. to be one of similar interest and prestige, and the salary to be one that is fully in line with this kind of job in the U.K. Jonathan Cook was in on these discussions, and he too, said that the salary was acceptable.

About a month after Cook reported into work in London and just about his forty-third birthday, he resigned from Construction Equipment Ltd. and took a job with a large company in England.

Mr. Giorgetti completed the information on Jonathan Cook's career in RMA—CEILtd.—CEIAG by stating that Cook's case, though a unique one in many ways, represents the kind of tough problems faced by a complex of companies operating over national borders and in a variety of cultures.

The case writer concluded the interview by observing that RMA seemed to him to have some characteristics of a multinational company. He recalled that somewhere near 45 percent of all RMA sales are made outside of the United States and Canada. He said that, while RMA does not seem to be as international in its operations as some of the multinational companies such as Unilever in London, or Nestlé in Switzerland, it certainly has some of the same characteristics.

FRASSATI COMPANY (A)

On May 1, 1959, Dr. Mazzini, Personnel Director of the Frassati Company was considering the position that he should take at a meeting with the Internal Commission of the company. This meeting, scheduled for May 5, was a fortnightly meeting at which the chairman of the Internal Commission had asked to discuss the unsatisfactory state of affairs in the special tool section of the Cedano plant. In September 1958 management had extended its system of job evaluation and incentive payment into the Cedano plant where it had met with an unenthusiastic reception. Despite increased productivity in the department, there had been continual grumbling by the workers concerned, and this grumbling had finally been brought to management's attention through the representations of the Internal Commission.

The Frassati Company

The Frassati Company had been founded by P. R. Frassati at the end of the nineteenth century. Originally, the company had been exclusively a fabricator of light iron and steel products for use in general engineering. Under aggressive leadership of its founder and his son, the company had expanded rapidly and successfully and now operated eight plants throughout Italy with a total work force of about sixteen thousand men. In 1959 the company produced a wide variety of iron and steel products ranging from heavy structural steel girders to small nuts and bolts. A substantial percentage of total output was exported and, in common with most Italian industry, the company had enjoyed a period of rising sales and profits through 1958 and 1959.

The largest of the company's plants, employing about eight thousand workers, was situated at Valate, just outside Milan. This plant produced the full range of the company's products and was the largest and most important plant in the company. The remaining plants in the company were smaller and were widely dispersed throughout the country. Each of these smaller plants tended to be more specialized in its production. One of these smaller plants at Cedano was essentially a satellite of Valate and was situated just a few kilometers away from it.

In 1946, the company had organized a Central Personnel Department under Dr. Mazzini. Before the war he had been personnel manager for another well-known Italian firm and during the war had been active in the Resistance. Under Dr. Mazzini's leadership the personnel office had grown into a department employing over three hundred people with responsibility for labor relations, personnel policies, and welfare services. Frassati Company was highly regarded by the rest of Italian industry as being a leader in the development and practice of enlightened personnel management.

Due to the importance of the Valate plant in the company's overall organization and the fact that developments at this plant tended to act as precedents for the other plants, the personnel policies at this plant were directly controlled by the Central Personnel Department. In particular, the Central Personnel Department carried full responsibility for relations with the Internal Commission representing the Valate and Cedano plants.

This Internal Commission consisted of fifteen members elected by the workers, four representing salaried employees and eleven representing hourly paid workers. Management believed that eight of these members were affiliated with the CGIL union, five with the CISL union and two with the UIL union. Management's relationships with the Internal Commission were kept on a strictly formal basis. Discussion was restricted to the provisions of the collective contract and to the detailed requirements of the labor laws in Italy. Meetings were held every other week to discuss complaints or questions about workload changes, production benefits or incentive earnings, etc. Dr. Mazzini normally delegated responsibility for these meetings to a senior assistant but would attend himself on important questions. In addition, various operating managers from the plant at Valate would be invited to take part in the discussions if their specialized knowledge could contribute to the effectiveness of the meeting.

About 2,300 (30 percent) of the company's workers in the Valate and Cedano plants were thought to be active dues-paying union members. Of these it was estimated that 1,100 men were members of the CGIL union; 600 were members of the CISL union and 600 were members of the UIL union. As is characteristic of the Italian labor structure, there was no *union* organization inside the factory, and the majority of management-union discussions or negotiations were held with the appropriate union officers in the provincial Chambers of Labor in Milan.

Labor Policies

The company had clearly defined personnel policies particularly in two areas—incentive wages and strikes. For many years the company had followed the practice of paying workers incentive wages whenever possible. Each worker was guaranteed a base wage in accordance with the current collective agreement signed by the unions. However, for production above a certain stated minimum, increased payments were made to the worker based on his additional production. Maximum increments to pay were 30 percent of the base rates.

In the Valate plant base rates and incentive rates had been set for many years on the basis of scientific job evaluation except in the Maintenance Department where the difficulties of establishing a sound basis for work measurement had been the greatest. It had also not been possible to devise a satisfactory system for use at the Cedano plant.

Consequently, in the Maintenance Department and at the Cedano plant, while incentive pay was used, the rates were for many years based on standards that had come to be set by practice and custom. In 1952, management had started to introduce standards set by time study measurement for the Maintenance Department and by 1958 over six hundred highly skilled craftsmen employed on maintenance were being paid on the basis of scientific job measurement.

Management had found that on each occasion of introducing the new system one important factor that had constantly to be kept in mind was the overall internal structure of wages. Inside the company there was a well-established monetary grading of jobs, which was known by the workers. Any serious alteration in the relative pay for jobs that carried a historical position in this grading system would have serious repercussions on the entire wage structure and spread discontent over a wide area.

As far as strikes were concerned, management had also adopted a clear policy. This policy had been established in 1952 in defense against the wave of political strikes that had swept the country. Participants in a political strike would be punished; participants in a strike for economic reasons would not be punished. In this connection management distinguished clearly between a strike in which workers failed to report for work and a protest movement with some element of "go-slow" involved. A strike according to Italian practice is a refusal of workers to report for work. This is legally permitted. On the other hand, a "go-slow" or "sit-down" protest movement is not legally regarded as a strike but rather as an act of noncollaboration. Hence management regarded participation in such activity as a punishable offense. For example, in 1953 the workers in a particular plant had made a "declaration of noncollaboration with management," and management had reacted by cutting all wages by 15 percent.[1]

---

[1] The assumption is made in Italian law that, if a worker reports for work, he will do a full day's work under the direction of management. Failure to do this by some concerted protest action is not a strike but an act of noncollaboration.

The Cedano Plant

The Cedano plant was a satellite of the main Valate plant; it was sited only a few kilometers away and was solely concerned with the production of light structural steel parts. While some of the parts manufactured were standard items such as steel brackets and small steel fittings for general use in construction, this plant also carried out a significant proportion of special order work. The plant was supervised by Mr. Rita, a mechanical engineer, who was generally regarded as an efficient manager and a good leader. Under Mr. Rita were four separate sections, assembly, adjustments, materials, and special tools. Each section had a section supervisor with four or more foremen who reported to him.

In 1956, a study had been carried out at Cedano to see whether productivity could be increased by the application of more efficient methods and the use of time standards. The study itself was kept secret trom the workers and the lower line management. The results of this study clearly indicated that substantial savings could be made. For example, it was estimated that for an expenditure of about five million lira, savings of over twenty million lira per year could be obtained.

The study had included three separate steps:

1. Methods and work simplification, standardization of particular steps in the job, analysis and standardization of the tools to be used, and the introduction of new procedures for ordering work.
2. The application of time standards.
3. The introduction of incentive payments related to these standards.

As a result of the study made, the company decided that a piecework system based on a well-known American type formula would be most suitable. One characteristic of this system was that it allowed some elasticity in setting standards, thus reducing the effort involved in estimating costs for a particular job. The whole system was fully discussed with the Central Personnel Department to check whether introduction of the system would contravene the collective agreements with the unions or the plant rules negotiated with the Internal Commission. The Personnel Department offered no objections, but one result of these discussions was that it was decided to introduce the same incentive curve[2] at Cedano as had already been applied elsewhere in the company.

The new system was first introduced into the adjustments section of the

---

[2] The incentive curve is the curve relating production above the minimum with the additional wage paid as an incentive.

Cedano plant. The company ran a special index of productivity that showed that productivity jumped from a figure of 93 to 133 within a year. Normal productivity was represented by a figure of 100.

In the special tooling section special jigs and tools for use throughout the company as well as for extra-company sales were manufactured. In this section there was a fairly stable workforce of 350 men, including 140 lathe operators and skilled fitters (finissagio). These 140 men received higher pay than the remainder of the workers in this section. They were long service workers, and they were generally acknowledged as the key men in the section, both by management and fellow workers.

In accordance with company policy, a system of incentive pay had been operating in this section for many years. No job measurement or time study work had been carried out in setting standards. The levels of production for minimum rates of pay had been established on the basis of what management knew of past practices and performance. For the two years 1956 and 1957, the workers generally earned the maximum incentive pay that was permissible under the system.

Early in 1958, Mr. Rita was reviewing the operations in this special tool section and felt that the time had come to introduce the new methods and incentive system. Accordingly, he approached Dr. Mazzini to discuss such a step. Following this discussion, Mr. Rita went ahead with his plans, and methods and time study men from the Central Time and Motion Study Department of the company came down to the plant to set the standards in this section.

In September 1958, Mr. Rita reviewed the results of the work done by the methods and time study men. As a result of this review he decided to introduce the system forthwith and gave the appropriate instructions to the special tool section supervisor. New types of work sheets were issued out to the foremen with instructions that they were to be used for future computation of wages. By the end of the month, the system was in full operation.

The nature of the new system of work sheets was fairly simple in concept. Each job was preplanned to the extent that a detailed routing of the job with instructions about the work to be done at each stage were specified. Each operation was given a standard time based on the results of the time studies. Completion of the job within this time limit automatically qualified a man for his base rate, and if the job was completed in a shorter time he qualified for different amounts of incentive pay in accordance with a predetermined scale called the incentive curve.

During the subsequent months, productivity rose and labor and wage costs in the section were lowered, although no workers had to be laid off. Under the new arrangements of better organized and more systematic work, many workers were in fact working harder since delays in the flow of work were largely eliminated. Most workers took time to adjust to the new required rate of working, and they found that their wages were falling below their previous levels. The average drop in actual earnings throughout the section was 4–5 percent, while productivity, according to the index, increased by 50 percent.

The section supervisor and foremen noticed that there was a certain amount of grumbling by a number of workers. Typical complaints were based on such things as machine interference preventing the worker from achieving maximum productivity or differences in quality of raw materials that affected the volume of output. Some workers complained that they had old machines with a slower rate of operation than other workers with new machines and that this fact prevented the workers on the old machines from earning full incentive pay. Individual cases of this type were referred by the foremen or supervisor to the methods and time study men for reassessment. No *formal* complaints or grievances were registered until February 1959.

At this time the whole question was discussed at a meeting of Dr. Mazzini with the Internal Commission. The Commission protested against the system on grounds of principle, saying that management had no right to introduce the system, the system was inequitable, and it must be eliminated. Management took the following position:

1. Management refused to discuss its right to introduce a new system.

2. Management was perfectly prepared to discuss the equity of the new arrangements at those positions where there were particular complaints. These positions could be discussed on a case-by-case basis between management or the time study men and the operator, any worker's committee, and the Internal Commission.

Dr. Mazzini stated subsequently that he made it plain at the meeting that he was prepared to discuss the complete method and timing of any particular job but that he was not prepared to discuss the system. The Internal Commission rejected this approach by management stating that the whole new system was unacceptable. No further discussion of the matter took place with the Internal Commission although a few individual cases of difficulty were solved within the section with the assistance of the methods and time study men.

On April 30, 1959, the Chairman of the Internal Commission informed Dr. Mazzini in writing that at the next meeting of the management with the Internal Commission on May 5, the Internal Commission wished to discuss the situation in the special tool section at Cedano. He stated that as a result of complaints that had been forwarded to him and his own investigation of the situation, the Internal Commission must insist on the following points:

1. The new system of job measurement and incentive pay in the special tooling section was unfair to the workers in that section and was totally unacceptable as a system.
2. If elimination of the system was not possible, a substantial increase in incentive pay was required as compensation for such an inequitable system.[3]

3 This case was prepared by Basil W. Denning under the direction of Professor Stephen H. Fuller as a basis for class discussion.

FRASSATI COMPANY (B)

At the meeting on May 5, 1959, in reply to the demands of the Internal Commission, Dr. Mazzini restated the position that had been taken in February. This position was that he would not discuss management's right to introduce the system but that he was prepared to discuss individual situations on a case-by-case basis. No additional offer was made. The members of the Internal Commission rejected management's offer to discuss the application of the system, and no agreement on any future procedure was reached.

Work continued in the special tool section where management noticed that the increased level of productivity was sustained and costs remained lower. Management recognized that the workers were in fact working harder and that the general level of pay was still averaging 5 percent below previous levels. Management noticed also that the grumbling of the workers had not significantly decreased, but there were no more official complaints or representations by the Internal Commission until July 1960.

During the summer of 1960, among others, the Communist and Socialist political parties had been growing increasingly dissatisfied with the national government of Signor Tambroni, the Prime Minister. This dissatisfaction arose from the fact that Signor Tambroni relied on the votes of the M.S.I. pro-Fascist parliamentary representatives to maintain his majority, with a somewhat more right wing government policy as a result. When the M.S.I. party announced that it would hold a national convention in Genoa in June 1960, protest riots took place in a number of Italian cities. As a further demonstration, the CGIL planned a one-day national strike in protest against M.S.I. participation in the government. This strike was called for July 9, and the large majority of Frassati workers throughout the country obeyed the strike.

All the workers in the special tool section of the Cedano plant, however, stopped work on July 8 and stayed out for three days, resuming work July 11.

FRASSATI COMPANY (C)

The CGIL representatives in the Provincial Chamber of Labor noted that the workers in the special tool section of the Cedano plant had struck for three days, and they interpreted this action as a significant measure of the dissatisfaction with the new incentive payment scheme. Accordingly, they contacted the provincial CISL and UIL representatives and made a joint request to the employers' representatives at Confindustria to arrange a meeting with the management of the Frassati Company on July 21. Dr. Mazzini, reluctant to have a meeting so soon after the strike and desiring to separate company problems from political ones, agreed to meet with the union representatives on July 29.

At this meeting held between the provincial organization of Confindustria and the three Provincial Chambers of Labor, the unions were represented by noted regional and national labor leaders in the metal-working industry. Indeed, the presidents of the CISL and UIL federations of metal-working unions headed their respective delegations because of the importance that any agreements reached with the Frassati Company might have as precedents in other companies in the industry.

At the meeting Dr. Mazzini restated management's positions as outlined in February 1959. Although he continued to refuse to discuss management's right to introduce the new system, he did say that management would conduct an intensive survey of all the work that had been carried out to see if any errors could be found or any corrective measures could be taken by management to improve the system. For example, he suggested that management would thoroughly investigate the extent to which foremen were attempting to iron out difficulties as they arose. He also mentioned the possibility of calling in an outside consultant.

As a result of these various suggestions, Dr. Mazzini said that he felt that the unions were beginning to signal a shift in their position by arguing about the technical merits of the system rather than about the right of management to introduce it at all. While no formal agreement on future procedure was reached, it was agreed to hold a further meeting in two months' time at

320

which management would offer the results of its survey. All outstanding issues could be discussed in the light of this survey at that time.

The following day the union leaders called a meeting of the workers of the special tool section outside the plant at which they announced the results of the discussions of the previous day. They recommended that the workers cooperate with management in the survey being made and then bring up any issues that remained unresolved in time for the September meeting. The workers refused to accept this recommendation and stated that they were not satisfied that the union had adequately represented their interests. It was apparent that they were still thinking in terms of militant action to force abolishment of the system in their section.

FRASSATI COMPANY (D)

Although no final agreement was reached at the meeting on July 29, management proceeded on the basis of the tentative understanding that they felt had been reached with the unions. Accordingly, the survey of the whole new system, as it had been applied in the special tool section, was carried out.

The most significant findings arose in the general area of communications between the supervisor, foremen, methods and time study men, and workers. Since the supervisor and the foremen had not been adequately instructed in the details and operation of the new system, when faced with a complaint, they had been forced to call in the methods and time study men to iron out the difficulty. This had resulted in an apparent diminution of their authority and appeared as a reflection on their ability to supervise production. As a result of their feelings about this situation they resented the methods and time study men almost as much as the workers did, and thus were not giving their full cooperation either to the time study men or to the workers. Various actions were taken by management to improve this situation including a redefinition of the supervisor's and foremen's responsibilities, which laid particular stress on the fact that they were ultimately responsible for the productivity of their men. The methods and time study men retained the responsibility for the times, and individual discussions were held with each methods and time study man to understand his difficulties. One important result of these various discussions was that the methods and time study men who had been working at Cedano were permanently transferred to the Cedano plant to work under Mr. Rita. In addition, management arranged for a careful recheck of all jobs carried out during the previous year. This reexamination revealed that about 2 percent of all jobs were actually in dispute. In these cases management initiated adjustments as necessary and, in management's opinion, these measures significantly improved the climate in the section.

However, on August 22 and 23, all men in the special tooling section at Cedano went on strike. They also declared and carried out a second strike

322

on August 26. Neither of these strikes were sponsored by the union. Management did not punish any of the strikers.

At the meeting between management and union leaders on September 9, the unions agreed that the situation had much improved as a result of management action. Hence, the union leaders stated that they would accept the situation and adopt the proposed consultation procedure outlined by management at every meeting since February 1959. However, they also demanded that each worker should be given a cash grant of 10,000 lira as an indemnity. They justified this demand by drawing attention to the hardships imposed on the workers during the period of difficulty and argued that these hardships could have been avoided if management had introduced the system in a more effective manner. Management felt that the objections of the unions would be heard no more if they granted the 10,000 lira.

FRASSATI COMPANY (E)

At the meeting on September 9, management firmly rejected the union demand for 10,000 lira per man.

At a further meeting between the union representatives and management on November 3, the union leaders withdrew their demand for the 10,000 lira cash indemnity. At this meeting the unions accepted the new incentive pay system. In addition, agreement was reached on a consultation procedure to be used in case of disagreement about any particular job. This agreement was spelled out in two documents. The significant portions of the two agreements are attached as Appendix A.

APPENDIX A

FRASSATI COMPANY (E)

Minutes of Agreement

1. In accordance with the general conditions governing incentive and piece work rates and agreements previously reached it is agreed between management and the Internal Commission that:

   a. When it becomes necessary to issue or revise any rates, the appropriate company officials will inform both the workers concerned and the Internal Commission in advance. The giving of this information in no way changes the normal procedure for making time studies or setting rates.

   b. When the rates for new or revised standards are established, the rates will be exhibited on the notice board and, at the worker's request, explained in detail to him.

   No new or revised standard will be brought into force until fifteen days have elapsed from the time of exhibiting this notice on the board.

   c. At the end of the fifteen days, the new rates will automatically be introduced. For the first twenty days, payment of at least 53 percent of the maximum incentive pay will be guaranteed. After twenty days have elapsed, the rates will be enforced without the guarantee. Nevertheless, disagreement about the new rates may still be registered via the grievance procedure separately agreed.

d. Where there is no disagreement about the new rates, the fifteen days' notice period may be reduced at the request of the Internal Commission. When this occurs, the new rates will be introduced immediately, and there will be no guarantee of 53 percent of maximum incentive pay.

e. Unresolved disagreements between workers and management at the shop floor level will be referred to the Internal Commission.

2. It is further agreed that:

a. Should a noticeable drop occur in the earnings of any worker on piece work or incentive pay, the worker concerned or the Internal Commission may submit the case within fifteen days to management in order to determine the cause of the reduction in pay.

b. Whenever, as a result of the examination of grievances submitted by the worker or by the Internal Commission within the fifteen days' time limit, an incentive or piece work rate is altered, final payment for the work that provoked the grievance shall be made on the basis of the finally agreed rate.

HELVETICUS COMPANY (A)

In August 1957, a problem arose at the Helveticus Company that indicated to members of the personnel staff that cooperation between their department and executives of the production division was less that satisfactory. At the end of the series of events leading up to this problem, which are described below, the members of the personnel staff were considering how they should deal with the immediate difficulty facing them. At the same time, they were considering what steps they should take to improve relationships with production executives in the future.

The Helveticus Company, founded in 1872, was a major European producer of textile machinery. It was located in St. Gall, Switzerland and employed approximately 3,300 wage-paid workers and 1,500 salaried employees.

The Production Division, which employed roughly 2,700 of the wage-paid workers and 200 of the salaried employees, was the largest division in the firm. (See Exhibit 1 for a partial organization chart of the company.) This division comprised five production departments and a number of supporting staff departments. Each production department was headed by a departmental superintendent, who reported to the Production Manager, Mr. Hans Wohl. A total of seventy-four salaried production foremen reported to the five departmental superintendents.

The Personnel Department was made up of fourteen staff members and was divided into two sections. The larger of these two was the nine-man worker section, which had been established in the early 1930s. This section had jurisdiction over the 3,300 wage-paid personnel of the company.

The other section was the five-man employee section, which had been established in 1944. This section had jurisdiction over the 1,500 salaried employees of the company, of whom 900 were technical personnel (chiefly engineers and draftsmen) and 600 office workers.

Exhibit 1   **Partial Organization Chart**

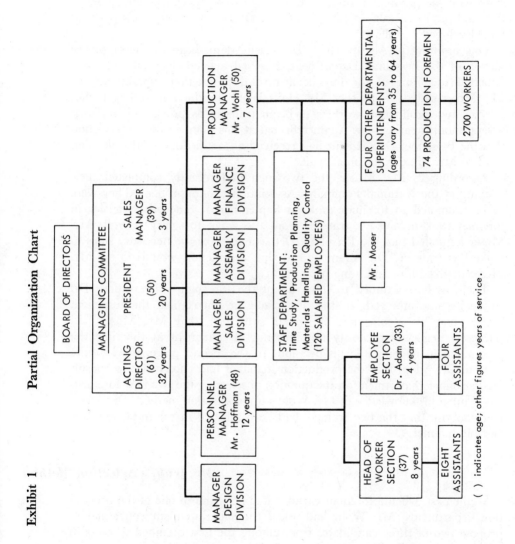

( ) indicates age; other figures years of service.

327

Events Leading up to the Current Difficulty

The latest problem, which indicated to the personnel staff that relationships with the production division were unsatisfactory, concerned the selection and setting of salaries for two new production foremen. This problem had developed as follows.

One morning in August 1957, Dr. Karl Adam, head of the employee section of the Personnel Department, received a telephone call from Mr. Albert Moser, one of the five departmental production superintendents. Mr. Moser stated briefly that Mr. Hans Wohl, Production Manager, had selected two production workers to begin training as production foremen several months earlier. Dr. Adam reflected at this point in the conversation that the Personnel Department had received no notification of this decision prior to Mr. Moser's telephone call.

According to Mr. Moser, the two men had recently completed their training at the National Foreman's Association training school. They were to be promoted to foreman rank on September 1. Since the transfer to foreman rank involved a transfer from the wage to salary payroll, Mr. Moser requested that the Personnel Department take the necessary steps to make this transfer. Dr. Adam agreed that the section would do so. Mr. Moser thanked him and hung up.

Then, as he continued to think about the foregoing conversation, Dr. Adam became annoyed. In the first place, he entertained the suspicion, based upon his recollection of similar situations, that Mr. Moser had purposely neglected to notify the Personnel Department at the time the production manager made his decision. In the second place, it was quite clear to Dr. Adam that the production manager had chosen not to consult the Personnel Department on the question of selecting the two new foremen. Based upon his knowledge of Mr. Wohl's usual selection method, Dr. Adam was doubtful that the two trainees had been selected in the most objective possible manner.

Mr. Wohl's Selection Method

In the past, when a foreman vacancy had occurred in one of the production departments, Mr. Wohl had asked the superintendent concerned to propose two or three candidates from among the best qualified workers in his department. In Dr. Adam's opinion, the candidates proposed were usually those personally best known to the superintendent. He doubted that these men were always those with the greatest foreman potential.

Nevertheless, Mr. Wohl chose the man he believed to be most qualified from among these candidates, on the basis of his personal evaluation of each man. Occasionally he requested the Personnel Department to obtain a handwriting analysis from an outside expert, but he had never asked for further advice or recommendations. (See Exhibit 2 for a typical hand-writing analyst's report prepared for the company.)

Exhibit 2   **Excerpts from Handwriting Analyst's Report[a]**

Rudolf S.

This man lacks many qualities required to be a foreman. Within his natural limitations, however, there are some positive factors. He might do well in a job that requires more exactitude in production and other technical matters than ability to supervise men. On balance, he might be an adequate foreman, although I think that mentally he should be classified as inflexible, and probably limited in ability.

Mr. S. has worked hard to acquire the education he has and is willing to improve it further. This is somewhat remarkable, since he has difficulty in grasping complicated matters. He is, however, tenacious and persevering and does not give up before he has reached his goal. Thus, if the necessary patience is invested in him, his training should not turn out badly.

He has one important capability : he is a very good calculator (this talent clearly stands above the general level of his abilities).... He will always choose the procedure that gives the greatest precision.... As a foreman he will expect his subordinates to accept his own view of what is to be considered good performance without discussing the matter with them.... He will be rather skeptical of new ideas since he often does not understand the consequences of them.... He lacks understanding of other people to a large extent.

---

[a] Handwriting analyses were made for the Helveticus Company by an outside expert. He required a page of handwritten script and certain additional information such as the age of the writer and the position for which he was being considered.

Dr. Adam and the other members of the personnel staff felt that this selection method left much to be desired. They were of the opinion that they could be of substantial assistance to Mr. Wohl in selecting new foremen if given an opportunity to do so. They pointed out, for example, that they had access to the personnel records of each worker, which showed his educational background, previous experience, and wage history. In addition, they had available to them the merit rating reports described in Exhibit 3.

The members of the personnel staff believed that when a vacancy occurred they should be asked to review these records for all potential supervisors in the Production Division. Following that, they would interview the most likely candidates. Finally, on the basis of the interviews and their analyses of the men's records, they would present a list of the most promis-

Exhibit 3   Merit Rating Procedure for Worker Personnel

The merit rating procedure for worker personnel was established in 1955, in accordance with a plan proposed by the head of the worker section. It was developed in meetings with line executives and worker representatives and approved by the Managing Committee.

Each worker was rated twice yearly by a committee of up to six persons: the production superintendent for his department, his section foreman, the lead hand for his group, a representative of the workers' committee, a member of the worker section of the personnel department, and occasionally by a member of the quality control department.

Rating was based on ten factors grouped into three main categories: Quality of Work (weight of 4) Reliability and General Behavior (weight of 2), and Versatility and Transferability (weight of 1). Points were awarded for each of the ten factors, weighted according to category, and totaled.

Records of all ratings, with the point totals, were kept in the worker section of the personnel department. There they were available to the personnel staff and to the line executives concerned upon request. A set of records such as these was kept, for example, for both Schmidt and his fellow trainee.

The principal use of the merit rating records was to help determine, in conjunction with job evaluation results and other considerations, individual hourly wage rates. The records were also available for reference on other matters, such as promotions, although their frequent use for such purposes had not yet become the custom in 1957.

ing men in the division for Mr. Wohl to choose from. They believed that such a procedure would not only be helpful to Mr. Wohl but would also enable them to carry out more fully their responsibilities to top management. (See Exhibit 4 for responsibilities of the employee section as specified by the Managing Committee of the company.)

Transfer Procedure

In spite of his dissatisfaction with the way the selection procedure had been handled, Dr. Adam requested one of his assistants to take the steps necessary to transfer the two trainees to the salary payroll, in accordance with Mr. Moser's telephone request.

The assistant's first step was to prepare a salary recommendation for each of the two trainees. To do this he consulted the production foreman salary chart (see Exhibit 5 for a copy of the chart and description of how it was prepared). Then, taking into consideration the trainees' ages and various

Exhibit 4

Responsibilities of Employee
Section as Specified by the Managing Committee[a]

1. Periodic study of employee personnel needs, within the framework of departmental salary budgets, emphasizing necessary qualifications for each position.
2. Development and use of effective recruiting and selection procedures.
3. Correspondence with job applicants and maintenance of all subsequent personnel records.
4. Reception and introduction of all new employees.
5. Treatment of all retirement questions.
6. Maintenance of statistical data on personnel turnover.
7. Personnel exchange with firms abroad.
8. Promotion of work simplification and specialization of office work.
9. Recommendations for changes in salary and bonus policies to the Managing Committee.
10. Development and use of effective employee rating methods.
11. Determination of individual salaries and bonuses in cooperation with department supervisors.
12. Determination of working conditions (hours of work, plant hygiene, etc.)
13. Treatment of training questions.
14. Personnel counseling.

a The responsibilities of the worker section were similar to these but included several additional duties, such as apprentice training.

Exhibit 5   **Foreman Salary Chart**

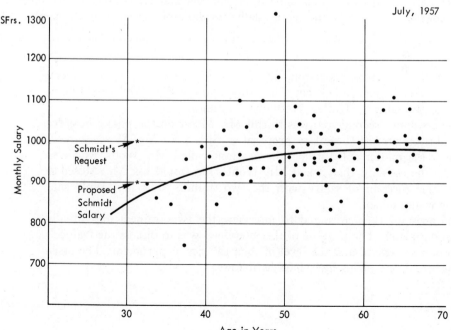

Exhibit 5 (cont.)

The series of salary charts used in the Helveticus Company were prepared in 1955 by the personnel staff on the basis of the individual salary records in their files. Individual salaries were plotted as a function of age, and then a curve was drawn freehand through the plotted points, as shown in this exhibit.

Prior to 1955, individual salaries were set by line supervisors, in principle after consultation with the personnel staff. Since 1955, the salary charts had served as starting points for salary discussions. Using the charts, the personnel staff assistants suggested individual salaries to the line supervisors of the employees (such as foremen) under consideration. An attempt was made to have individual salaries fall on or near the curve. Deviations were permissible, however, provided that they could be justified on the basis of years of service, training, experience, merit rating reports, or other considerations.

Responsibility for final approval of individual salaries rested with the immediate line supervisor, although in many cases the personnel staff assistant also referred his salary recommendation to the division manager concerned for review and approval.

The shape and level of the salary curves, which reflected the company's overall salary policy with respect to particular groups of employees, were the responsibility of the employee section. Once yearly, the salary charts were reviewed by the Managing Committee, at which time Dr. Adam made recommendations for changing the salary curves. At the same time, he was often called upon to justify "out of line" (unusually high or low) salaries. In September 1957, Dr. Adam was planning to recommend that the salaries of the older production foremen be increased relative to those of the younger foremen.

---

other factors, such as education, years of service, experience, and merit rating reports, he concluded that a monthly salary of Sfrs. 900[1] would be in line with the salaries of other production foremen.

The assistant's second step was to call Mr. Moser on the phone in order to ask his opinion of the salary proposal of Sfrs. 900. Mr. Moser agreed. To clear the matter still further, the assistant called Mr. Wohl, who also agreed. The assistant then asked Mr. Wohl if he would ask Mr. Moser to discuss the question of salary with the two trainees, and Mr. Wohl said that he would do so.

The assistant then arranged to interview the two trainees individually several days later. The purpose of the interviews was to discuss the trainee's promotion in general and the level of their salaries in particular. The assistant reported one of his interviews as follows:

---

[1] About $210.

Memorandum

September 1, 1957.

Mr. Schmidt, age 31

On August 31, Schmidt finished foreman training. According to his departmental superintendent, Mr. Moser, Schmidt is to be transferred from worker to employee status on September 1. His salary will be Sfrs. 900 per month.

I told Mr. Schmidt that his transfer to the salaried employee payroll had been approved for September 1, and that his salary had been fixed at 900 francs, as I believed he had already been informed by Mr. Moser according to Mr. Wohl's instructions. Mr. Schmidt replied that it was quite true that Mr. Moser had told him that he would become a salaried employee when he finished training. When he asked about his salary however, Mr. Moser told him only that he would certainly be agreeably surprised. Mr. Moser did not state a figure, although Mr. Schmidt requested several times to be told what his salary would be.

Mr. Schmidt does not agree with the new salary proposal. He wants 1,000 francs per month. In his opinion there must be something wrong with salary rating in the company if he as a foreman does not receive more than his best worker, who is earning about 910 francs per month. Also, the comparative figures published by the National Foreman's Association are higher than our offer of 900 francs.

Furthermore, Mr. Schmidt expected that Mr. Wohl would talk with him before he took over as foreman, and he regrets that he never did so. In his opinion, the promotion to foreman is not something that happens every day. It marks an important point in his life. During his training he was told that the foreman was one of the most important mainstays of the firm. However, the lack of interest in his career and the handling of the salary question by his own superior indicated to him that this is not true.

I told Mr. Schmidt that I would take up the matter with Mr. Wohl.

Dr. Adam's Reaction

When Dr. Adam had finished reading the preceding memorandum, and a similar one describing the interview with the other trainee, he was disturbed. He considered that, as a consequence of the difficulties outlined in the memorandum, the employee section was caught on the horns of a dilemma.

On one had, he believed that both men could find employment elsewhere as trained foremen if they did not receive the starting salaries they had requested. The employee section, which had proposed the salaries, might then be held responsible for the loss of the two men and the investment of time and money[2] which the company had made in their training.

On the other hand, if the company did meet the men's requests, their salaries would fall above the foreman salary curve, which had been previously approved by the Managing Committee. (As stated in the description of the foreman salary chart in Exhibit 5, the managing Committee of the company reviewed and approved all salary charts yearly.) In that case, Dr. Adam believed that his section would not have fulfilled its responsibilities to the committee in administering the overall policy that it had established.

Dr. Adam's immediate reaction to this dilemma was one of anger. He felt that if his section had been notified at the time Mr. Wohl selected the two men for training, either he or one of his assistants could have discussed the question of salary with the men before they left for foreman training school. A mutual understanding might have been reached, and a contract of employment[3] drawn up.

As he left the plant at lunchtime, Dr. Adam was strongly tempted to ask his immediate superior, Mr. Hoffman, Personnel Manager, to lay the entire problem facing him before the Managing Committee. He felt that some clarification of the relationships between the Personnel Department and the Production Division was clearly needed if the personnel staff were to carry out the responsibilities delegated to it by the Managing Committee.

At the same time, however, the question of why the production executives had been so uncooperative had begun to concern him, and he decided to give both questions some additional thought during the remainder of the afternoon.

The Managing Committee

The top executive body of the company, which made all major decisions, subject to approval by the Board of Directors, was the three-man Managing Committee. This committee was comprised of the president, an acting director, and the sales manager.

The president, age fifty, had traveled widely and was actively interested in

---

[2] Out-of-pocket expenses were estimated at Sfrs. 10,000 for each trainee.

[3] In Switzerland employment contracts specifying salary levels may be concluded that require a man to remain with his company for periods up to a maximum of ten years. Starting foreman contracts at Helveticus usually had a duration of three years.

new trends in personnel administration. In the early 1940s he began to take special interest in personnel administration. In 1944 the employee section was formed as the result of a study initiated by him. In subsequent years the president continued to be an active supporter of increased staff personnel activities in the company.

The senior member of the Managing Committee, age sixty-one, was also a member of the Board of Directors. He was considered by other executives in the company to be less convinced of the value of staff personnel activities than the president. This executive had been appointed acting director by the Board in order to assist the president in operating the company. The Board believed that his greater maturity would help balance the president's more experimental approach to certain problems. He was expected to retire from membership on the Managing Committee in four years' time.

The sales manager, age thirty-nine, had been appointed a member of the managing committee in recent months. Although a specific issue had not yet arisen that would reveal the sales manager's views with respect to staff personnel activities, it was believed that he shared the acting director's position in this regard.

Production Executives

The production manager, Mr. Hans Wohl, age fifty, had been appointed to this position in 1950. He occupied one of the historically most important positions in the company. Over many years, top executives had come to realize that the company's profitability depended in large degree upon the skill with which the production manager operated his division.

The production manager's position was also one that had almost invariably been filled with strong-willed, authoritative executives. Beginning with the founder of the company, the production managers had generally been men who took pride in "running their own show." Their authority in this respect had rarely been questioned.

A graduate engineer, Mr. Wohl had spent over five years as head of the Production Planning Department before taking over as production manager. During this period he had become primarily interested in the technical aspects of the business and a firm believer in various techniques of scientific management, such as methods study, functional plant layouts, and cost control. These interests had begun to take up an increasing amount of his time in recent years.

Members of the personnel staff stated that, unlike the managers of other divisions of the company, Mr. Wohl appeared to regard promotions and certain other personnel matters in his division as being exclusively his concern. They felt that he had deliberately resisted their attempts to help him deal with such matters in the past.

The five production superintendents varied in age from thirty-five to sixty-four years. They had overall responsibility for production quality and unit costs, as well as personnel and other matters in their departments. In fulfilling their duties they worked closely with the staff departments attached to the Production Division, which included production planning, time study, materials handling, and quality control.

With respect to the activities of the personnel department, the three older superintendents took the same position as Mr. Wohl. They tended to resist the attempts of department members to deal with personnel matters within their spheres of influence.

The two younger superintendents, on the other hand, one of whom was a university graduate, had become more cooperative in their dealings with the personnel staff. Staff members were hopeful that they might begin to improve the relationships between their department and the Production Division by first convincing these two younger men of the value of their services and then gradually building greater acceptance of their activities on the part of the other superintendents and Mr. Wohl.

Personnel Staff

The personnel manager of the company, Mr. Hoffman, directed the activities of both sections of the personnel department. His age was forty-eight years. He had been educated in the fields of engineering and psychology.

The fourteen members of the personnel staff were younger men, averaging thirty-two years of age. The majority had been with the company between two and five years. Several, like Dr. Adam, held university degrees in the fields of law and commercial studies.

When he joined the company in 1945, Mr. Hoffman had been appointed head of the employee section. He began at that time slowly to develop the role of the section in the company. Members of the personnel staff attributed his early successes in this regard at least partially to Mr. Hoffman's extensive knowedge of psychology, which he often used skillfully in dealing with other executives.

In 1949 Mr. Hoffman was appointed Personnel Manager of the company. Under his direction, the personnel staff continued to improve and expand its activities. This expansion was carried out in the face of a severe personnel turnover problem, requiring that staff members spend the bulk of their time recruiting and interviewing, which thereby reduced the time available to them for planning and consultation with other executives.

Steps were taken to render more effective the recruiting and interviewing procedures used in the selection process. Merit rating procedures in which the personnel staff actively participated were established for both workers and employees. In addition, salary administration was systematized through a series of company-wide salary curves similar to the one described in Exhibit 5. In 1955 Mr. Hoffman was promoted to the rank of division manager.

In the process of developing the merit rating procedures, the personnel staff stated that they had held several meetings with line supervisors and worker and employee representatives to keep them informed on progress being made. They believed that as a result of these meetings acceptance of the procedures on the part of line supervisors and the personnel had been established from the beginning.

In the case of the salary system, however, staff members believed that some resentment had been created. They recognized that, as a result of the salary curves, the weight of the personnel staff's recommendations in the setting of individual salaries had increased. They had gained the impression that the staff's increased influence in this respect was resented by a number of line executives, especially the production manager. In similar fashion, the department's growing role with regard to hiring decisions, as a result of its expanded recruiting and interviewing activities, was causing some resentment.

With respect to the future, the members of the personnel staff stated that they desired to do a thorough, all-around job of personnel administration. Wherever possible, they were anxious to apply the most recent, advanced techniques to the various personnel problems that they perceived throughout the company. Improving the foreman selection procedure, for example, was one area that they believed required attention. In addition, they were considering the desirability of an executive replacement chart and a management education program, among other possible measures.

Dr. Adam's Proposal

By the end of the afternoon following Mr. Moser's telephone call, Dr. Adam had reached a tentative conclusion. He recalled that problems similar to the one that he was now facing had occurred in several of the years he had been with the company. Now was the moment, he believed, to ask the Managing Committee for clarification of the relationships between the personnel staff and the Production Division.

To this end, he asked his secretary to prepare copies of the two interview memoranda for each of his four assistants, for Mr. Hoffman, and for each of the members of the Managing Committee. He requested his assistants to read over the memoranda carefully that evening and to review in their own minds the background of relationships between the personnel staff and the executives of the Production Division. He proposed to Mr. Hoffman and his assistants that they hold a strategy meeting the following morning to decide what action should be taken.

HELVETICUS COMPANY (B)

After the strategy meeting referred to at the end of Helveticus Company (A) case, Dr. Adam, head of the employee section of the Personnel Department, prepared the following memorandum. This memorandum was reviewed by Mr. Hoffman, Personnel Manager, and sent to the Managing Committee along with the two other memoranda describing the interviews with Schmidt and his fellow trainee (see page 333 of the (A) case for one of these memoranda).

Memorandum

In these two cases (Schmidt and his fellow trainee), the personnel staff was informed that the question of starting salaries would be discussed with the men before they assumed foremen responsibilities on September 1.

In neither case did this happen. Either no discussion at all took place, or the wishes of the two men were heard but not acknowledged.

The present disagreeable situation would not have arisen if an exact and clear agreement had been established <u>before</u> the two men started their training program.

In order to deal with the salary question in a satisfactory manner, the personnel staff must be fully informed in advance, and should know:
1. Who has been chosen.
2. What position he will fill.
3. When he will start his training.
4. What salary is proposed by the Production Division, if any.

We do not, at the present time, get this information in time.

In addition, it seems to us of great importance that
senior production executives increase the number of contacts they have with foremen trainees during the period
in which they are rotated through the various production
departments, prior to leaving for training school. At the
present time it appears that such contact is slight or
nonexistent. It seems to us a mistake to be conserned only
with improving a man's technical competence while at the
same time neglecting his feelings of loyalty toward his
supervisors and the company.

Several days later, members of the personnel staff heard that Mr. Wohl,
Production Manager, had begun to make daily rounds of the plant in order
to talk with the men in his division, especially the foremen and foremen
trainees. It was reported that he asked them questions about their work,
as well as about personal problems, and that he explained that he hoped to
keep in closer contact with them in the future.

Some weeks afterward, however, members of the personnel staff observed
that the number of plant tours that Mr. Wohl was making had decreased
substantially, and was approximately back to its former level.

HARROGATE ASPHALT
PRODUCTS LTD.

Company Background

This case concerns principally the financial and managerial relationships between two companies: British Commercial Investments Ltd. (BCI), an industrial holding company located in London, and Harrogate Asphalt Products Ltd. located in Frampton, a small town in Yorkshire near Harrogate. Before describing these relationships in detail, some information about the overall operation of BCI Ltd. is needed.

BCI Ltd. started life as the Pentiling Rubber Plantations Ltd., a Malayan rubber company. In the fifties the directors decided to diversify out of the politically risky area of their operations and began to acquire a number of small to medium-sized private companies, mainly in the U.K. Twelve years ago, the last of Pentiling's rubber plantations was disposed of, and the company was renamed British Commercial Investments Ltd. The BCI group now comprises some sixteen subsidiary companies, with operations ranging from the manufacture of oil drilling equipment to electrical components and from special steel fabrication to the construction of agricultural buildings.

Mr. Henry Lampton, the Managing Director of BCI, described the group's progress as follows:

> Our decision to get out of the Far East was not easy to make for a number of reasons, chiefly personal to members of the company's Board at that time. The transition was made easier, however, by the success, or, to be honest, the luck, that favored one of our earliest investments, a precision engineering company that we were able to sell to a large international group for several times the price we originally paid for it. This success encouraged the Board to cut out the old Malayan business altogether. Our subsequent growth, due partly to the acquisition of new subsidiaries and partly to internal expansion has been pretty satisfactory. Our gross tangible assets have increased in the last seven years from £9 million to £31 million, and our pretax profits from £900,000 to £3.4 mil-

lion. This large growth has caused us to institute increasingly elaborate systems for forecasting financial requirements and planning to meet them. We have instituted what we call the BCI Three-Year Forecast, which involves much forward thinking-in-detail. This kind of planning is accepted as essential in modern company planning, but even if it wasn't, something very similar would be needed to ensure the continued strength of BCI.

Furthermore, our present investment effort is directed mainly toward internal expansion by existing subsidiaries, and the acquisition of no new subsidiaries, unless they complement technologically those we already have. These two efforts—growth from within and acquisition of *related* companies—is what will produce the kind of profit we are interested in.

We have been trying recently to provide additional help to our subsidiary companies. In today's world, we do not think that they can expand to their full potential without some help from central advisory services provided by BCI central staffs. Until very recently, however, we were rather diffident about providing these services to give specialized advice in particular fields; it would be fatal to try and force them on unwilling subsidiary managements. But recently, the success of our operations research group, the welcome accorded to the monthly economic bulletins of our chief economist, and the demand for the services of our BCI Marketing Adviser all attest the need felt by subsidiary managers. Only in the last three weeks, Mr. J. F. Roberts has joined our staff as Computer Adviser and has begun to familiarize himself with existing EDP installations and projects. We have been too slow in recognizing the part that EDP techniques will play in the future. We hope to provide companies individually too small to justify their own EDP units with access to facilities and to reduce costs for all by organizing a coordinated network available on a BCI-wide basis.

It is, however, a part of our philosophy that our underlying principal subsidiaries (or if you like divisions) should be of a size that they can support their own local functional staff of a high calibre. We are not suffering under the delusion that we can operate a large central services team capable of resolving the local problems of such a diverse organization. Our advisory staff are used as catalysts.

Finally, I would like to say something about the services rendered to subsidiary operating companies by our BCI nominee director. We like to think that the personalities, experience, and sometimes wider contacts that our directors have are an important source of help to managements of BCI subsidiary companies.

In an interview with Mr. E. M. Jackson, another executive of BCI, the case writer was told that

"BCI maintains a (nonexecutive) director on the Board of each of its subsidiaries, usually as Chairman. Although nonexecutive, the BCI nominee normally visits each of his two or three companies about once a week, or twice every three weeks. The BCI nominee typically has had considerable industrial experience before joining our organization, either with a firm of accountants or management consultants or with some other industrial corporation in an executive capacity. Many of them have university education and have also attended advanced management programs such as the Administrative Staff College at Henley, Harvard Business School, Stanford Business School, or IMEDE in Lausanne."

Mr. Lampton continued.

The position of a BCI nominee director involves a rather heavy responsibility. We are not bankers interested only in the financial aspects of the business. We are not there to take a normal dividend and let it go at that. In some financial holding companies, the local managements have the idea that they are entirely self-sufficient, except for dividends. At the same time, the directors nominated by the parent company to the boards of those subsidiaries create the impression that they are banker types—somewhat superior to getting into real operating problems. I personally believe that, in some such holding companies, the subsidiary managers are being supine—they sit there with talent that could add to operations but that they abdicate. Specifically, I am certain that in this day of complex technology and society, the director has a moral responsibility to help his managers—to encourage them to do planning for the future, to aid them in selecting and staffing their operations, and to give advice in areas where the director has talent or knowledge.

I can give you one example. In June, one year ago, BCI acquired the L. M. Trowbridge Company from the Trowbridge family. This company specializes in construction projects using asphalt products —parking lots, tennis courts, large industrial asphalt areas. It is to the benefit of everyone—BCI, Harrogate (which produces asphalt materials) and Trowbridge managers, and employees of both companies—to merge the operations of the two companies. In this way, both will be more profitable, enjoy more growth, and stand a much better chance of survival in the British economy. This autumn we are going to form a company to hold both Harrogate and Trowbridge, in the interest of better all around operations. The move was, inevitably, initiated by the BCI nominee chairman; the managers of Harrogate and Trowbridge don't have the same chance of standing back and taking an overall view of their operations. Without our BCI man the merger would never have come about.

This shows how far we have moved from our position when BCI was still mainly involved in Malayan plantations and when our United Kingdom subsidiaries were regarded merely as diversified investments to be bought and sold, managerial responsibilities resting wholly with the underlying unit. Gradually we have come to acknowledge that this is an untenable position and have taken on full responsibility for the underlying units, while allowing them a very wide degree of local autonomy in the main areas of their businesses.

The Acquisition of Harrogate

Seven years ago, Mr. Jack Stanley, a man of eighty-two and the owner of a number of family companies including Harrogate Asphalt, wanted to put his estate in order so that it could be passed on to his heirs. His brother approached a member of BCI management in London with the idea that BCI might be interested in acquiring Harrogate Asphalt Products Ltd. as part of the BCI group. Mr. Lampton, now managing director of BCI, was then a man of thirty-one years living in Birmingham as the BCI Midlands representative. He was assigned the job of doing a management evaluation of the Harrogate Company for possible acquisition.

Excerpts from Lampton's management and operating appraisal appear as Exhibit 1. It will be seen from that exhibit that his general conclusion was that Harrogate represented an excellent investment. He based this on a thorough analysis of finances, management, marketing, production, and raw material procurement. He also found that the Harrogate management had sold the less profitable coal business fourteen years ago, concentrated on the more profitable asphalt operations, introduced a revolutionary technological process eleven years ago, and expanded production and sales. He found that the Company was in sound financial condition and that profits had increased at a fast pace. As a result of his report, BCI made an offer to Mr. Jack Stanley for his company; this was accepted, and Harrogate became a subsidiary of the London holding company.

At the time of acquisition, Jack Stanley with his wife, daughters, and grandchildren owned 90 percent of Harrogate, and Paul Denham and his wife owned 10 percent. This latter represented an interest that Stanley had permitted Denham to buy. During the first three years of BCI ownership, Denham retained his minority ownership, but this was sold to BCI three years ago on recommendation of his own financial advisor.

In order to compensate Denham, Stanley initiated a suggestion. Because the future of the company's sales and profits looked so good, it was proposed that Denham receive £4,000 net salary per year, and $2\frac{1}{2}$ percent of net profits over £100,000. Previously, he had received a lower salary (£2,000)

Exhibit 1   **Excerpts from Financial and Managerial Appraisal**
Harrogate Asphalt Products Limited
by Mr. Henry V. Lampton[a]

CAPITAL AND SHAREHOLDERS

In this section, Mr. Lampton summarized the ownership of the company, as of August, seven years ago, when this report was written. He showed that present capital is 240,000 shares, but that the directors have voted to increase this to 320,000 shares, effective September 30. The additional shares are to be purchased by current owners, in ratio to their present holdings. If this increase in capital is effected, the resulting £60,000 would presumably be used to expand current operations and facilities. Since Mr. Paul Denham, Managing Director, and his wife own together 10 percent of the business, they would purchase 10 percent of the new stock.

Ninety percent of the company is owned by Mr. Jack Stanley, his wife, daughters, and grandchildren.

HISTORY

The Company was incorporated twenty-three years ago and until eight years ago worked in association with Harrogate Coal Company Limited (owned by Stanley). In that year, the latter company was sold to R. L. James & Co. Ltd., another distributor of coal.

Harrogate Asphalt was a very small unit producing asphalt paving materials by means of one antiquated machine installation, and by hand. It grew slowly until five years ago when a revolutionary new machine was purchased. These machines allowed for vastly increased production, and the company has rapidly expanded since that date to the point where it now has ten of these machines in use. Sales fourteen years ago amounted to £31,000 but have increased to £360,000 last year.

DIRECTORS

Mr. Jack Stanley has provided his financial backing and advice to the company over the past ten years. During the spring and summer he visits the company every three or four weeks from his home in Devon, but 'chases the sun' during the winter. At eighty-two, he is a very spry gentleman, proud and charming; however, he might well prove to be obstinate in negotiations. He would still make a good Chairman and is regarded with great respect by the executives of the company.

---

[a] Written by Mr. Lampton seven years ago, shortly before acquisition of Harrogate.

Exhibit 1 (cont.)

Mrs. Jack Stanley

Mrs. Stanley takes no part in the direction of the company and never visits the concern. She is eighty-four years of age.

Mr. Paul Denham, Managing Director and Secretary

Mr. Denham is forty-eight years old. He has spent the last twenty-five years with Mr. Stanley and has grown up with the business. Originally, he was responsible for the coal distribution concern (sold eight years ago) but has been the prime mover in the expansion of Harrogate Materials over the past ten years.

As will be appreciated later in the report, despite the rapid growth of this company, it is still relatively easy to administer and Denham has a tight personal control over it.

He has a very pleasant personality. He is a strict disciplinarian and is respected for it. As the company is in a rural area and there is a very low labor turnover, Denham regards the employees with Edwardian paternalism.

He has three sons at public school, the eldest (at sixteen) works in the company during vacations. Denham hopes one of the three should join him in the business later.

His remuneration has risen rapidly and it is intended that in the future he should have a basic salary of £4,000 per annum and a commission of two and one-half percent on all net profits over £100,000 per annum.

OTHER TOP PERSONNEL

Peter Jenkins   Age thirty-five, Works Manager, Salary £1,600.

He has spent all his life in the asphalt product industry and joined Harrogate Materials eighteen months ago from Dackman products of Nottingham. Denham has a high regard for his technical ability but believes he is rather weak and immature in his handling of employees (this may well be because Denham himself is "ever present").

He appeared to be rather shy but showed great enthusiasm when explaining production methods and new developments.

K. Warren   Age thirty-two, Transport Manager, Salary £1,600.

Most of the day-to-day problems in this company are not concerned with production but rather with transport of finished goods. Until recently this has

Exhibit 1 (cont.)

been done entirely with hired vehicles, and Warren has been responsible for handling this. To deal with sixty or seventy hired vehicles requires considerable tact, patience, humor, planning ability, and downright strength. Warren appears to have these qualities in full. He was in the Royal Navy prior to joining Harrogate some five years ago.

J. Nixon   Age forty-five, Sales and Production Planning Manager, Salary £1,700.

Nixon was not met, but from the way Denham referred to him he was a weak member of the management team. He evidently does his work well enough in a pedestrian way but has not much strength of personality or many ideas.

*   *   *

All of the above—Jenkins, Warren, and Nixon—are regarded by Stanley and Denham as future Board members, but it would appear that Warren is the only one who is likely to grow to sufficient stature.

OUTSIDE STAFF

In this section, Mr. Lampton pointed out that the workers in the plant earn very good wages compared to general conditions in British industry. The wages are exceptionally high in relation to the surrounding agricultural area. Wages of between £30 and £40 per week were due to the fact that when the new revolutionary production machinery was purchased eleven years ago, neither the manufacturer of the machinery nor the Harrogate management knew that it would be so productive. Piece-rates were established based on what the machines were estimated to produce, but these were "grossly wrong."

The company (in the event wisely) did not change these rates but reserved the undisputed right to trim all production units to a bare minimum of labor. As the company has constantly expanded, no surplus labor has been laid off, but merely transferred to new units.

Needless to say, at these rates competition for jobs at Harrogate is very high. There was an intensely "brisk" air about the whole place. It is nonunion labor. There is no pension scheme. Hours worked are long (normally 07:30 to 18:30), and annual holidays are split, a week in the summer and another in the winter. The work is arduous and in the winter conditions are not good by the very nature of the business. As the rates are all fixed by team output, there is no room for individual slacking. Relations with management appear

Exhibit 1 (cont.)

---

to be good. Total labor force has risen rapidly in the past year to around one hundred.

FINANCE AND OPERATIONS

After presenting a profit and sales summary (which is incorporated in Exhibit 2), Mr. Lampton, among others, made the following points:

1. The increase in gross profits has been due primarily to the introduction of new manufacturing equipment.

2. Management has divided its sales territory into six regions, employs, five salesmen and one agent in its distributive organization, has dealt with 1,560 customers over the past two years. Lancashire, Cheshire, and Yorkshire are the most economic selling areas, but Mr. Denham claims that he has plenty of room to expand in the South as he can compete within a radius of two hundred miles. The reason for this is that all his raw materials are close to hand, while competitors normally have to transport at least some ingredients some distance to their plant.

3. After describing the production process, the machinery, the flow of product, and the number of men necessary on each of the five self-contained production lines, Mr. Lampton stated that the productivity of labor could be still further reduced if one operation were not necessary. "Through the engineering firm of Mason and Grant, secret experiments are taking place with a mechanism that must be changed only once daily, instead of once with each batch of product. This would mean that each large machine could be filled automatically, cutting out one man's work on each of the five lines (at £1,500-plus per annum per line)." Mr. Lampton also made the point that "the finished product is a very strong and high quality job. Harrogate's products withstood the British Standard tests to a very satisfactory degree."

4. In the area of purchasing and supply logistics, Harrogate has a favorable location for securing raw materials economically. Because production is increasing very rapidly (75 percent the past year), one of the company's principal raw material suppliers suggested to Denham that a subsidiary transport company could be set up to pick up raw materials, rather than have them shipped by the vendor. This subsidiary company has been set up with Stanley and Denham as directors, and Harrogate loans five bulk transporters to the subsidiary. Thus, a significant cost saving in raw materials has been achieved. Also, the company has its own electricity substation. "Overall, there is no problem with regard to raw materials."

5. In storage, and in distribution, Harrogate is regarded "as an excellent call" because large amounts of finished product can be handled and loaded in

Exhibit 1 (cont.)

---

a short time. Use of modern materials handling equipment (the company owns, for example, forty fork lift trucks and twenty thousand pallets) has made this possible. Also, the company has bought five flat lorries and intends over the years to build up its own fleet. However, management indicates that they will still use contractors for uneconomic trips and in emergency.

6. Regarding land and buildings, "the production buildings have been built within the last years and have a floor area of eighty thousand square feet. They are principally breeze block sides and metal trussed asbestos roofed. All are in excellent condition. Further additions have been made to shipping platforms and a new building recently erected.

7. Machinery, all heavy duty equipment, "is excellently maintained." Further equipment has been purchased since in the last four months. Most of the repairs to materials handling equipment is done in situ in a small well-equipped workshop.

CURRENT PROGRESS AND FUTURE PROSPECTS

In this section, Mr. Lampton pointed out that productive capacity has increased significantly. He cites the month of June in each of the last four years, showing that production, in tons, had progressed from 5,600 in the first year, to 8,000, 10,100 and 17,700 in the successive three years. A new production line, together with machines, has been set up in the last three months (adding 950 tons to usage of raw materials). Sales for the last ten months have increased to 452,400 as compared with £301,900 in the same period last year.

The reason for the company's success is probably due to its geographical position (both for raw materials and markets), the fact that it invested early in a revolutionary production machinery (outside engineers reckon that Harrogate have more of these than anyone else, but Denham has no proof of this), very efficient management (mainly by Denham), and because it is supplying a material in increasing demand over the past decade."

The future looks good. This is a first-class company and should prove an excellent investment for BCI.

---

plus 5 percent of total net profits. Lampton states that Denham agreed with this and that at the time it meant a total take home of £5,500. His total earnings have risen consistently over the years, reaching about £17,000 for the last year of his employment. This is considered by the case writer to be a relatively high remuneration in British industry.

Exhibit 2   **Selected Financial and Operating Results**
Harrogate Asphalt Products Ltd.

Preceding Fourteen Years

Years Ago	*Sales*[1]	*Profits before Taxes*
14	£ 31,000	n.a.
13	55,000	£ 22,000
12	83,000	28,000
11	110,000	39,000
10	178,000	62,000
9	224,000	87,000
8	361,000	136,000
7	520,000	150,000
6	867,000	260,000
5	1,053,000	310,000
4	1,096,000	300,000
3	1,638,000	450,000
2	1,922,000	595,000
1	2,050,000	600,000
Present	2,500,000	750,000 (estimated)

[1] Figures are rounded to nearest £1000.

The First Five Years of Operation

As of the time this case is written, BCI has owned Harrogate Asphalt for seven years. During the first year, the Board of Directors of Harrogate consisted of Jack Stanley, Paul Denham, and Gerald Kemp, a full-time executive in BCI who was assigned as the parent company representative. More information on these men appears in Exhibit 1.

During those years, Mr. Henry Lampton was serving as BCI representative in the Midlands and as nominee director of two BCI subsidiaries located near Birmingham. Nevertheless, Mr. Lampton recalls certain things that he knew went on during the first five years.

> In that period, the new equipment installed from Mason & Grant gave Harrogate an overwhelming competitive advantage in a business mainly served by fairly small companies, with the result that profits, sales, and return on new capital increased dramatically. Here is a company whose return on net worth was among the highest of any BCI company. Nevertheless, in my judgment, there were definite signs of trouble. Stanley died at the end of the second year. This left the BCI director and Paul Denham. About a year later, these two directors recommended as the third director Roger Sample, a young man who was hired by Denham six years ago (in the second year of our ownership). I'll have more to say about him later, but I acknowledged Roger from the first time I

met him to be a capable chap, though his experience in Harrogate was limited.

The Board meetings of those days consisted of a rather formal, cut and dried reporting of figures, once a month.

The case writer at this point asked "Was Paul Denham making the policy decisions?" Mr. Lampton responded,

If there were any policy decisions being made—though I doubt there were.

Also, in about the second year, Harrogate suddenly found itself with a strike on its hands. Denham was at loggerheads with the union,[1] and he was at a loss as to what to do. The BCI director had to go up there and deal with the union, and a settlement was reached. As I recall, Denham simply gave up and said that he could not deal with them.

Also, Denham operated by turning up at 8 A.M., opening the mail, then sitting in the sales (internal) office for two hours, returning to his own office where he would incarcerate himself and merely look at figures of past performance. He rarely went to see customers off site or saw customers when they came in.

Operations in the Past Two Years

About two and one-half years ago, while some other changes were being made in BCI organization, Mr. Lampton, at age thirty-five, returned from Birmingham to the BCI London head office as a director of BCI; at the same time he was also assigned to the Board of the Harrogate subsidiary. The remainder of this case covers the past two years of his relationships with the latter company. Incidentally, Mr. Lampton, just recently, was named managing director of BCI Industries.

I arrived on the scene of this highly successful company (60 percent on net worth is remarkable by any criteria) full of youthful bounce, and asking why they don't look at the situation in the building products industries for growth. I knew that the company was doing no real forward planning and that with the addition of a lot of hard work along this line the company could do much better. I also had a certain amount of goodwill and ambition—and the knowledge that I would have a delicate time with Paul Denham.

But I soon found that it was an unusual company. I saw a managing director making £15,000 a year, but no other men of

---

[1] In Lampton's appraisal report (Exhibit 1) it is shown that there was no union at the time of acquisition of Harrogate.

responsibility. His four top men, including Roger Sample, were making £3,000 or under. This came as a surprise—here was an outstandingly successful company, profit wise (£600,000), with no staff in depth. In fact, in addition to Roger Sample, the only talent I could see was a good production assistant who had just given notice of his termination.

I'm going to give you a number of facts about what happened during those two years, but first let me say that I am not adverse to local autonomy—I believe it is best—but not for one local autocrat. Let me also say that my relationship with Denham was a good relationship, personally speaking, but when I tried to bring some things up for improvement, around the Board table (I had instituted more frequent Board meetings, and insisted that we discuss company policy problems, rather than just review figures of past performance), he did not want to discuss them. Instead, he would say "this is not a matter for formal board—why don't you come around to my office and lets talk about them informally." Nevertheless, I thought that all three members (including Sample) should be in on important matters, and that there should be formal board meetings, acting responsibility.

Let me give you an example. Our operators in the plant were getting very high piece rates, but it was physically very hard work, fifty-eight hours a week, and two one and a half week holidays that had to be split, one and a half weeks in summer and one and a half in winter: anyone absent without a doctor's note got instant dismissal. When Denham asked me not to bring this up in the Board, but to come to his office, I said "no this is a Board matter." I could see that these conditions would mean trouble, and Roger Sample was telling me—not as a moral issue at all, but as a practical issue—we couldn't keep things this way. For my own part, I regarded it as a practical issue *and* a moral issue. In a way, we were blackmailing the workers with high pay and not providing opportunity for recreation. They were spending money in considerable amounts in gambling and drinking (this seemed to be a problem in the town). So I proposed that we allow them to take their two one and a half weeks together, thus affording more of a real holiday and rest away from the job.

As I persisted in placing this matter before the Board, Denham finally said, "I don't want any part of this discussion. If you want to make Board policy, do it." Notice that he wasn't saying "I am the Managing Director, I will think and be responsible about this." Instead, he was abdicating the managing directorship to us.

I mentioned Roger Sample. Denham had hired him five years ago from a local construction firm, and he subsequently became Production Manager. While he had rather narrow experience working locally up there in Yorkshire, he is a man of talent. He knew I thought highly of him, but he was reticent with me at first, because he didn't know what kind of game I was playing. He did not have much confidence in pushing his ideas, because when Denham resisted, he did not know if I would back him. Gradually, however, we established a relationship of trust. It came about through situations like the following. On my side, I could see great need for looking beyond the narrow confines of present products and processes. The company needed market research and research on new technology. On Roger's side, he had been reading magazines of the industry and had become aware of some new processes which were being developed in Sweden. He wanted to go there to investigate, but had been forbidden by the Managing Director. Later, I raised this at the Board table, but Denham's reaction was "don't let's meddle outside the company now. We have a system which is producing high profit." Why he took this attitude I don't know. I suspect that the real trouble lay in the fact that Denham had been outgrown by the company he managed, and he was afraid that anything new might put him still further out of his depth. Harrogate's very success was against him.

Some time later, the accountant for the plant quit. I think it was because he was mistreated by Denham. At this point, I tried to get Denham to go out and find a really top flight managerial accountant—one who could think and plan rather than simply be an audit clerk. As things proceeded, I could see that Denham just wasn't capable of doing this, so I persuaded him that we should go out and hire an outside firm of consultants to do the recruiting. The consultants presented four candidates for our approval. I was party to interviewing them. We rejected two immediately, and there were two left in my opinion, who were suitable. About this time, I left to attend the thirteen week Advanced Management Program of Harvard University in the U.S. When I returned, I found to my amazement that he had rejected both of them and instead hired a local accountant at £1,800 a year, rather than the £4,000 man I had envisaged.

About this time I recognized that Paul Denham was a man that was going to reject any sort of idea, and any sort of talent, that he was not familiar with. I was utterly disenchanted with what he was doing. When I got back from Harvard, Paul Denham also recognized that I was a chap who was going to stick to his guns. I could see trouble ahead and was determined to do something about it, even though the company's profit record continued to be outstanding.

This last remark reminded the case writer of something said by E. M. Jackson, another BCI executive, who read the first draft of this case at the request of Mr. Lampton. Mr. Jackson said that, during the Harrogate affair,

Lampton knew that Denham must go and yet he was very conscious that the company's success was in some measure due to

the tremendous pace that Denham set for the company in earlier
years. Indeed, the competitive edge that Harrogate had gained
came largely from the fact that the company utilized its machines
so intensively—the credit for which, at any rate initially, was
Denham's.

At the second Board meeting after I returned, Roger Sample
brought up a subject that I had encouraged him to study (I had
encouraged him to look at all facets of the business). Our office
staff had very high turnover. The staff was working on Saturday
mornings, but there was no need, no work, for this. When Roger
proposed it, Paul again said he wanted no part of it. He wasn't
even fighting it. I suspect it was because he knew it was going to be
put into effect anyway.

At any rate, I was intent on pursuing this to some sort of conclusion. The meeting became heated and intense. Denham said
"hell, why do we waste our time on these matters—go out and find
out what the order position is and lets get down to work." At this
point, and in front of Roger, I blew my top. "This is real business,"
I said, " and if we don't pursue it we have a real crisis."

After this incident, which took place about a year ago, Mr. Lampton
came back to London and wrote to Denham the letter that appears as
Exhibit 3 and that requests Denham to come to London for a meeting.

I felt that it was stupid to keep this up and that we must resolve
it somehow. Anyway, Denham had not once been to London in the
six years we owned the company. I always invited him to the

Exhibit 3

```
Mr. Paul Denham, Managing Director
Harrogate Asphalt Products, Ltd.
Frampton, Yorkshire

Dear Paul,

  I have given myself some cooling time since our last
meeting to consider its implications. I believe that it is
most important that you and I meet away from Harrogate to
discuss both the future of the business and the way in which
you and I can operate together constructively for its good.
  Could you come to see me and have lunch on Tuesday 2nd
August, Thursday 4th or Friday 5th. At the moment I have
these days free from outside appointments.

                                        Yours,
```

annual dinner we hold for subsidiary managing directors, but he always accepted and then sent a last minute excuse.

The night before the meeting was to take place here at head office, Paul Denham telephoned to say that he was not feeling well. He had shut himself off and did not realize that someone else owns the company and that he was not, as he thought, master of his own domain. I drove all the way to Yorkshire the next day. He was surprised to see me. I said that it is intolerable to go on this way and that we must cooperate if the company is going to progress. I told him also that we must educate Roger Sample in a wider sphere, that we must move him out of the production manager position and give him experience on the commercial side. He agreed to this, and to promote Roger's assistant to Production Manager.

On the return from Yorkshire, Mr. Lampton also sent to Denham the letter that appears as Exhibit 4. He continues:

During this entire period I had been getting close to Roger Sample, but at this point I got very close. He said "I don't want to be disloyal to the Managing Director. You are moving me from an area where I know the work and feel secure, to an area where I do not. But, I am going to be of no use to anybody if I go on not being allowed to be in contact with customers. I wonder if Paul, who is fifty-four, knows that, at thirty-eight, I am cornered."

Mr. Lampton said that he then offered Sample a service agreement (contract) to insure that he would not be summarily fired. Sample responded, according to Lampton, "No, that is not what I want. I will give you a pledge to stay three years, but I will leave if there aren't some changes in the way the company is running."

Naturally, I did not put it to Denham that way. I told him it would be a good thing to send Roger to a three-week marketing course I knew about at the University of Glasgow. He said that this is not productive for the company but that if Roger wants it and I approve, he would go along.

On the very day that Roger left, Paul Denham took sick, went home, and never reported back to work again. Roger phoned from Glasgow (Paul had phoned him) and wanted to know if he should go back to Frampton. I said no.

I wrote to Denham saying I was sorry he was ill. Then in a month I went to see him. He was obviously a sick man. Outwardly, he was o.k.—he passed his life insurance examination. But he did not want to discuss Harrogate Asphalt at all. Over a period of three months, Roger, the new production manager and I all went to see him. He was perfectly friendly with us, but he was not interested in anything. At one point he told me he wished that he had not

Exhibit 4

Mr. Paul Denham, Managing Director
Harrogate Asphalt Products Company
Frampton, Yorkshire

Dear Paul:

Although I was disappointed that you did not feel fit enough to come down here yesterday, I am glad that we had our discussion about the future, and I hope that you now understand and sympathize with our determination to strengthen the management at Harrogate so that it can be in a position to maintain its leadership in its own field, and to exploit other opportunities in allied fields. I am sure that our decision to put Roger in full charges of sales is sound.

At the same time I hope that you understood that the BCI management is insisting that the individual subsidiaries institute, this year, a formal approach toward three-year planning and forecasting, (the majority of the companies did this last year, of course). This is not an academic exercise but, in our opinion, an essential step both for operating companies and for BCI. The preparation of such a report must essentially be a team effort that has your full backing, and as it is sometimes difficult to start viewing the future in this way, I have, as I told you, arranged for James Kemp, our management accountant and planning specialist, to be free for a week (or more if necessary) at the end of this month or in September to give you any help you may need. I sincerely hope that I have managed to persuade you that one is not just looking for a "figure pledge" that you would consider you had broken were it not achieved. When you look at the framework around which such a report is constructed, you will see that it requires the participation of the whole management team.

Naturally, I am anxious about your health and I do hope that you can soon discover what is wrong with your arm. What you said about overworking and the need for a really worthwhile break of two months or more, seems to me not only desirable but necessary if you are going to be able to maintain your energies in the future. You have our complete backing for this, and I hope you can manage this as soon as possible.

Yours,

sold out his percentage ownership to BCI or changed his service contract. Finally, his doctor advised me that he did not want to see me and that it would not be wise to confront him with any more business.

After much deliberation, I, and then managing director of BCI, decided that it would be best to terminate the relationship with Paul Denham. We considered a number of alternatives—asking ourselves which would be best for Denham himself and which would be best for the company. In May of this year, we sent two letters. One was a letter from me as Chairman of Harrogate Asphalt Products, pointing out that he and I have enjoyed a good personal relationship but that we have radically different attitudes in a business context. I stated how sorry I was to hear of his health developments but that I was glad to hear he was improving enough to consider a long trip overseas. I told him that the corporate view at British Commercial Investments is that we are determined to acknowledge and exercise our responsibility and authority over our subsidiaries, yet we have no intention of dictating the day to day running of our companies. I closed by saying, "the decision we have made has taken into account a genuine desire on our part to help you determine a constructive future for yourself. Initially you may find it hard to accept, but it gives you a wonderful opportunity, granted to very few men, to start a new and meaningful life. You are still a young man with energy, and if you turn your mind to a new enterprise I am sure you will have the backing of your family and friends."

Accompanying Lampton's letter was a more formal one from the managing director of BCI, Ltd. It stated, "This letter should accordingly be treated as formal notice from Harrogate Asphalt Products, Ltd. of the termination of your Service Agreement as Managing Director with effect from 31st March of this year." It offered, in addition to accrued pay and profit commission, £5,000 as compensation for loss of office and a pension of £5,000 per annum for life. It concluded by stating "May I, however, express the sincere wish of myself and my codirectors here that the holiday that you intend to take early next month will complete your return to full health."

POINTE-HOLLAND S.A.

"If I am going to stay with the company there are four conditions that they will have to meet", said Alain Dubois, early in 1970. "First, I will insist that I'll be appointed a member of the new Executive Committee. Second, the president will have to agree to leave the sales force alone, he cannot continue to work with them as he has in the past. Third, we will have to discharge some people regardless of who their friends are in the company. We simply cannot afford to have anything but the most competent people with us now. And finally, I must have the authority to hire the kind of people that I need, both in terms of quality and numbers."

Alain Dubois, thirty-three years old, was the marketing director of the Pointe-Holland Company, a wholly-owned subsidiary in Holland of a large parent company with headquarters in France. The Pointe-Holland Company manufactured and distributed a line of household and food products throughout Europe and was widely known and recognized because of its extensive advertising campaigns. While company headquarters were in France, the parent company had wholly owned subsidiaries in other European countries, each of which was organized as a separate company with separate presidents and administrative staff.

Each president was responsible for the operation of his organization, and each subsidiary was run as a separate profit center. While there were some centralized directions from Pointe headquarters in France, each subsidiary had wide latitude in determining the nature and extent of its activity, especially insofar as promotion and advertising of individual products or product lines were concerned. It was important for each subsidiary to have this freedom and flexibility to accommodate national characterisitcs and demands.

Alain Dubois had been Director of Marketing of Pointe-Holland for two years. He was responsible for all sales promotion, product development, advertising, and sales management activities. He reported directly to the president of Pointe-Holland and had reporting to him all people in the organization involved with marketing activities.

Prior to joining Pointe-Holland, Alain Dubois had been an executive with an advertising agency in France, primarily responsible for preparation of advertising campaigns for organizations active in marketing consumer products. He was widely recognized in Holland for his knowledge of marketing and was considered to be one of the "bright young men" in the field.

Just prior to joining Pointe-Holland he had attended two executive management programs in the U.S. and, as a result of these programs and his own study and experience, was a leader in Europe in utilizing some of the newer concepts of marketing and management. In fact, his expertise in applying new concepts was one of the primary reasons why he was highly sought after by the Pointe headquarters in France for his current job.

In describing the background of this current situation Alain Dubois stated,

> I was really put into Pointe-Holland by headquarters in France to see if something could not be done with our operations here. Up until the time I came we had been losing a great deal of money each year. We are still losing money, but the amount of loss has decreased substantially, and according to my plan we should break-even next year and each year after that make a small profit. My relationship with the president of Pointe-Holland is unique. He is a very fine individual, and he and I get along very well on a social level. However, he is not up-to-date in his methods of management or in his knowledge and understanding of current marketing technique. In fact, while I report to him I really make most major decisions in the Branded-Good Division for the company in Holland, and most of what happens is done at my initiative. The president is still a figure-head, but I really go ahead and do what is necessary without much regard for his opinions or feelings. I have been able to do that because I have had the support of the main office in France. I continue to have this support, but some things have happened recently that make me concerned about being able to continue to make the progress that we have made here in Holland for the last two years.

One of the things that was of concern to Alain Dubois was the formation of the new Executive Committee. An Executive Committee had been formed recently to make and review major policy decisions. The two members of this committee were the president of Pointe-Holland and the vice-president for administration. Alain Dubois was not a member of this committee and thought that he should be. When asked what changes in his status would result if he were appointed a member, he replied that in effect he would be independent of the president's authority. As a member of the Executive Committee he would be on equal status with the president and consequently would not be subject to his control in any way.

A second issue that had been troubling Alain Dubois recently had been the president's actions with regard to some of the sales managers. The president of Pointe-Holland had had a long career as a salesman and still has very close personal relationships with many of the sales managers who had been with the company for some time. Often, perhaps every two months, the president and a few of his friends who were sales managers would meet to discuss the sales situation. Alain Dubois did not attend these meetings. According to Alain Dubois the meetings were primarily gossip sessions at which much information was exchanged but information that had little basis in fact: For example, he described these meetings as one in which the sales managers would report rumors from the trade, would predict how they thought people were going to react based on information acquired during their sales activities, etc. Usually the meetings were held at rather elaborate restaurants and hotels. As the sales force reported directly to Alain Dubois he thought that these meetings were not helpful to the overall selling effort and that they should be discontinued, He stated that he objected to the meetings on two counts: first, that they diluted his authority over the sales managers; and, second, that the kind of information discussed and the results of the meetings were not at all useful to the selling effort.

Alain Dubois reported that the president had a very traditional concept of authority and would occasionally walk through the offices talking to the more junior marketing people (e.g., product managers), much in the way that a general might review an army. But Alain Dubois felt the president had no real understanding of what marketing people were now required to do. The efforts of the salesmen of Pointe-Holland could affect perhaps 40 percent of the potential market. Many of the products were sold directly to large chains of retail outlets and the selling was done at the headquarter's level rather than in the traditional fashion of a salesman calling on an individual customer.

Alain Dubois was especially concerned about a third issue which involved one sales manager in particular, the general sales manager, who he felt was not competent to handle his job. This manager was a long-standing friend of the president, and this made the matter more difficult for Alain Dubois. He stated that:

> I have no personal reasons for wanting to discharge this man. My reasons are entirely professional. He is just not competent to operate in the way that we have to operate now. For example, I am attempting to promote the product manager concept in which we have a great deal of flexibility in our approach for each product depending on the situation. Unfortunately, the manager in question is very traditional in his approach and cannot adapt to this new thinking. He knows my feelings about this but the support from the president on a friendship basis undercuts my efforts to initiate some new concepts and ideas. If we were a very large organization

it might be possible to by-pass this man, but we do not have enough personnel to let us do this. Each of our people has to be a good producer and, in my judgment, this particular sales manager just is not adequate. Many of the people who report to him are more qualified than he and this, of course, causes a problem of morale.

A fourth matter concerning Alain Dubois was that he did not have as complete freedom as he would like in hiring new people. For example, he thought that several additions to the marketing staff were very necessary, but he had not been able to secure the authority to hire additional personnel without discussing his reasons in great detail with the president of Pointe-Holland.

In summing up the current situation Alain Dubois stated:

My relationship with the president of Pointe-Holland has been fine as long as I have been able to ignore him. But with these new developments, especially the formation of the Executive Committee, I am going to have to get my status clarified.

I am going to see the people in France again very soon, but rather than discuss this matter only with the top management of the parent corporation I think that all of us should discuss it at the same time. So I plan to ask the president in France to arrange a meeting between him, the president—Holland—and myself for later this month. I will prepare a written statement of my position and give it to each man before the meeting so that each of them will know exactly how I feel. I hope that this can be resolved, for I'd like to continue the work that I have started. But I feel very strongly that I must have the freedom and the authority to do what I think is right.

Of course, I realize that there are different ways of satisfying the conditions I have established for my own involvement, but I feel very strongly that I must have complete freedom in each of the areas I mentioned. For example, if they would agree to appoint me a member of the Executive Committee but not give me freedom to hire the people I need, this would not be satisfactory. Or if they would give me the authority to hire but not appoint me to the executive committee that would not be satisfactory. In effect, I have to have all four of the conditions satisfied before I feel I can continue to make a contribution at Pointe-Holland.

6

General Management

The course in General Management is designed to provide an opportunity to examine the problems and opportunities in six major aspects of corporate concern: Determining Corporate Strategy; Relating Environment, Resources, and Opportunities; Incorporating Personal Values in Economic Strategies; Integrating Strategies in Multinational Enterprises; Organizing for Implementation; and Developing Standards, Motivation, and Management. The material that follows makes explicit some of the ideas and objectives that may be considered in analyzing the overall progress of an organization from the viewpoint of top management.

An orientation to a philosophy of management is obtained by examination of the fundamental factors involved in organization and management. Major strategy and policy decisions are analyzed so that they may be related to the whole philosophical framework of business. Detailed investigations are made of the effects of policy decisions on marketing, manufacturing, personnel, finance, and other organizational functions.

Environmental factors that influence the strategies and policies of purposeful organizations are considered as matters of great and growing concern to administrators. Major emphasis is given to those factors most directly influencing policies of the firm such as: economic outlook, political climate, industry framework, maturity of the particular firm, personal stature of policy-making executives, and social and technological change.

Development of strategies and policies at various levels of administrative management is analyzed. Stress is placed on policy formulation and evaluation in the light of the interrelationships of major functions of business.

Course Objectives

This course is designed to integrate much of the material developed and learned from experience and the other courses at IMEDE and elsewhere. It is primarily directed toward the development of attitudes on which about 50 percent of the total emphasis is placed. To a lesser degree, it also helps in the development of skills—about 30 percent emphasis—and knowledge—about 15–20 percent emphasis.

THE ATTITUDE OBJECTIVE

The attitudes that, it is hoped, will be developed by participants fall into two general categories:

1. A breadth of curiosity. This includes specific attitudinal objectives as follows:
   a. that there is no single formula or approach for solving complex problems.
   b. that the facts available "on the surface" aren't the only important ones—i.e., "keep looking more deeply."
   c. that important facts outside a problem area must not be overlooked —i.e., "don't discard creative ideas on a hasty, 'customary thinking' basis."
   d. that the basic functions of an organization reflect in large part the feeling of the chief executives of the firm as affected by environment.
2. An appreciation of problem solving per se. This includes specific attitudinal objectives as follows:
   a. that no one, the participant included, can find the *ideal* answer, framework, or method for a complex policy case.
   b. that there is an interesting challenge presented by any problem, even though its solution may not bring tangible reward. The satisfactions in answering strategy and policy questions should stimulate the participants to all kinds of activity in life that involve inherent problem solving satisfactions (particularly in community and social situations).

THE SKILL OBJECTIVE

1. An ability to devise methods of analysis that are applicable in different types of problem situations. The various methods that will be evident

as the course develops imply that there is no one formula for problem solving that is universally applicable.

2. Skill in interviewing, interpreting the meaning of oral and visual expressions or presentations of others, and in questioning others.
3. Skill in oral and written presentation.

THE KNOWLEDGE OBJECTIVE

The knowledge that the course seeks to impact may be viewed as falling in the following broad categories:

1. Knowledge of the various environmental factors that influence policy decisions.
2. Knowledge of business institutions, industries, and functions, and the interrelations of these.
3. Knowledge of the possible effects of policy decisions on marketing, manufacturing, personnel, finance, and other departments or functions.
4. Recognition of the importance of personality problems in business decisions.

The major methods used to achieve the knowledge objective:
1. Individual and small group analysis of cases throughout the course to impart knowledge as well as skill and application.
2. Independent participant research in order to analyze the cases in a practical setting.
3. Integration of the total experience of the class, including the instructor, which often includes insight into the industry or situation under consideration.

ZERSSEN & CO. (A)

On January 1, 1967, Mr. Paul H. Entz, age thirty-seven, became chief executive of Zerssen & Co., of which he and his father were the two proprietors.[1] Zerssen with annual revenues of DM 120 million and employing 1,500 people, was engaged at three different locations in Northern Germany in several wholesaling and service activities, consisting of: ships' agency, chartering, and stevedoring operations; ships' supply; bunkering; shipping; coal and oil wholesaling and retailing; distribution of building materials; collection and sale of metal scrap; sales and service of high rotation diesel engines; and freight forwarding. Exhibit 1 provides financial data on Zerssen's various activities. Upon assuming his new responsibility, Mr. Entz considered his most pressing problem to find and implement the most appropriate organization structure for his 127-year-old company.

Zerssen & Co. had been founded in 1839 in Rendsburg, Germany, a small town (30,000 inhabitants in 1967) one hundred kilometers north of Hamburg and forty kilometers west of the Baltic seaport Kiel. Its first business was that of a shipping agent on the Eider Canal, which connected the North Sea with the Baltic Sea, avoiding the trip around Denmark. During the 1910s, the Eider Canal gave way to the Kiel Canal, which permitted passage of ships up to sixteen thousand tons laden. As a result, it was necessary to locate service activities for the transit ships at the canal locks in Holtenau, about three kilometers from Kiel. A third company location was added in 1923 through the acquisition of Glückauf, a coal wholesaling firm in Kiel (250,000 inhabitants in 1967). Both Holtenau and Kiel operations were constituted as divisions that reported to the chief executive in Rendsburg through their manager and two comanagers respectively. The various departments in both Holtenau and Kiel, in turn, reported to divisional management. Rendsburg departments, on the other hand, reported directly

---

[1] Zerssen & Co. was a Kommanditgesellschaft, a type of partnership provided for by German law. At least one of the partners had unlimited liability while others could have limited liability, in contrast to the regular partnership under which all partners were fully liable for the company debts.

Exhibit 1

Zerssen & Co. (000 DM)

Financial Information, 1965

	Sales	Gross Margin[c]	Department Profits[d]	Profit[e]	Personnel Costs	Fixed	Inventory	Receivables & other
RENDSBURG[b]	26700	4670	1670	800	2105	2300	1270	3460
Water[a]	400	380	140	75	140	200	100	130
Coal (including fuel oil)	11200	970	440	180	240	350	600	1800
Building Materials	15100	3320	1090	545	790	1600	570	1530
Central Services					835	150		
HOLTENAU	25200	9090	1820	690	4190	2250	3150	9780
Ships' agency	1600	1630	440	100	630	350	—	1350
Ships' supply	22700	6550	1200	445	3030	1500	3060	8080
Bunkering[a]	900	910	180	145	530	400	90	350
Local Administrative Services					220			
GLÜCKAUF	39800	7000	1665	810	3540	4510	1440	4950
Coal	8000	1500	260	40	630	1000	350	1100
Oil	1800	350	130	70	90	250	150	500
Building Materials	18500	2500	540	135	920	2000	300	1900
Scrap	5500	1750	530	400	750	700	250	650
Technical	3000	350	160	120	230	230	20	150
Other (largely freight forwarding)	3000	550	45	45	280	330	370	650
Local Administrative Services					640			
SHIPPING	19900	10300	4930	(1340)[f]	7900	33700	220	10490
TOTAL COMPANY	111600	31060	8745	960	17960	42760	6080	28680
							77520	

a Rendsburg water (= Agency, Chartering, and Stevedoring), ships' agency, and Bunkering sales are primarily commission incomes. The excess of Gross Margin over sales in ships' agency and bunkering is due to "other income."

b Rendsburg departments include costs for local administrative services.

c Gross margin = sales — cost of goods sold + other income.

d Departmental profit = gross margin — departmental costs — interest expense incurred directly by the department.

e Profit = Departmental profit — allocated charge for headquarters services and write-offs (including depreciation).

f Depreciation and write-offs.

Reserve for bad debts	245000
Inventory write-offs	75000
Depr. on machinery, equipment + buildings	662000
Depr. on vehicles	707000
Depr. on ships	6057000
TOTAL	7746000

to the chief executive. Exhibit 2 portrays Zerssen's organization as of January 1967.

Ownership of Zerssen was entirely in the hands of the Entz-von Zerssen family, 45 percent being held by Mr. Entz and 55 percent by his father.

Exhibit 1a

Zerssen & Co. (A)

Percentages Calculated on Basis of Exhibit 1[a]

	A	B	C	D	E[b]	F	G	H	I	J	K	L
Rendsburg	23.9	17.5	6.2	2.9	34.8	8.6	4.7	13.0	26.3	9.1	23.8	7.9
Agency, chartering, stevedoring	.4	—	35.0	18.7	3.3	50.0	25.0	32.5	107.5	.8	32.6	35.0
Coal	10.0	8.7	3.9	1.6	7.8	3.1	5.4	16.1	24.6	3.5	16.0	2.1
Building materials	13.5	22.0	7.2	3.6	23.7	10.6	3.8	10.1	24.5	4.8	29.5	5.2
Holtenau	22.6	36.1	7.2	2.7	30.0	8.9	12.5	38.8	60.2	19.6	12.0	16.6
Ships' agency	1.4	—	27.5	6.2	4.3	21.9	—	84.4	106.3	2.2	25.9	39.4
Ships' supply	20.3	28.8	5.3	2.0	19.3	6.6	13.5	35.6	55.7	16.3	9.5	13.3
Bunkering	.9	—	20.0	16.1	6.4	44.4	10.0	38.9	93.3	1.1	21.4	58.9
Glückauf	35.7	17.6	4.2	2.0	35.2	11.3	3.6	12.4	27.3	14.0	15.3	8.9
Coal	7.2	18.7	3.2	.5	1.7	12.5	4.4	13.8	30.7	3.1	10.6	7.9
Oil	1.6	19.4	7.2	3.9	3.1	13.9	8.3	27.8	50.0	1.2	14.5	5.0
Building materials	16.6	13.5	2.9	.7	5.9	10.8	1.6	10.3	22.7	5.4	12.9	5.0
Scrap	4.9	31.8	9.6	7.3	17.4	12.7	4.5	11.8	29.0	2.0	33.1	13.6
Technical	2.7	11.7	5.3	4.0	5.2	7.7	.6	5.0	13.3	.5	40.0	7.7
Other	2.7	18.3	1.5	1.5	1.9	11.0	12.3	21.7	45.0	1.7	3.4	9.3
Shipping	17.8	51.8	24.8	—	—	169.3	1.1	52.7	223.1	57.3	11.1	39.7
Total company	100.0	27.8	7.8	.9	100.0	38.3	5.5	25.7	69.5	100.0	11.3	16.1

a Calculated by case writer
b Calculated on base: 2300 = 100.0, i.e., excluding shipping
A = Sales as percent of company sales
B = Gross margin as percent of departmental (or divisional) sales
C = Departmental profit as percent of sales
D = Net profit as percent of sales
E = Departmental profit as percent of company profit
F = Filed assets
G = Inventory assets
H = Receivables and other assets } as percent of sales
I = Total assets
J = Departmental assets as percent of company assets
K = Departmental profit as percent total (departmental) asset employed
L = Departmental personnel costs as percent of departmental sales.

367

Exhibit 2

Zerssen & Co. (A)
Corporate Organization

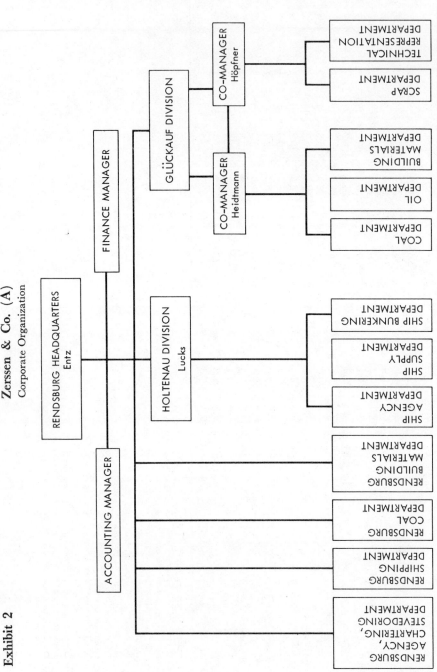

NOTE: This and the following organization charts were drawn by the casewriter based on interview information.

Four successive generations preceding Mr. Entz had guided the company through its 127-year history from Rendsburg, which continually had been both company and family headquarters. Until after World War II, the Zerssen family and offices were housed in the same building near the old locks of the now filled-up Eider Canal. In 1967, upon entering the company conference room, Mr. Entz commented: "This is the room where I was born."

Mr. Entz, born in 1930, began working in a shipyard in 1944 when the war forced him to interrupt his schooling. After the war, he completed a business-apprenticeship[2] and worked and traveled abroad until he joined the family firm in 1956. During the academic year 1961–1962, he was a participant at the IMEDE Management Development Institute in Lausanne, Switzerland. After returning, he assumed progressively more responsibility until it was time for him to head the company.

This case describes the various activities at the Rendsburg, Holtenau and Kiel locations and concludes with a brief description of the organizational issues as seen by Mr. Entz and of his tentative organization plan.

Rendsburg Operations

Rendsburg consisted of four departments: ships' agency, chartering, and stevedoring; shipping; fuel; and building materials. (See Exhibit 3 for their organization structure.) A small corporate staff was also located in Rendsburg, consisting of a finance manager who also doubled as legal and tax expert and an accounting manager who also conducted special studies for Mr. Entz. The finance manager had an assistant and a secretary. The accounting manager had an assistant and a staff varying from fifteen to twenty-five. The managers of the four operating departments, who all had their offices in the company headquarters in Rendsburg, had traditionally reported directly to the chief executive. Thus, from 1936 through 1966, Mr. Entz, Sr. had been closely involved with all four Rendsburg departments, making many of the day-to-day operating decisions. The managers, in turn, had viewed access to the chief executive as a "right" of their position, to which they attached a great deal of prestige.

AGENCY, CHARTERING, AND STEVEDORING   This department was engaged in Zerssen's first activity. Agency operations included (1) canal clearance, involving paper work and payments for canal tolls, pilotage, tying up, etc., (2) port clearance, arranging loading, unloading, and customs clearance; and (3) a dispatching function for the ships, much like

---

2 An apprenticeship is obligatory in Germany in any field. It normally lasts three years.

Exhibit 3

Zerssen & Co. (A)

Organization of Rendsburg Departments

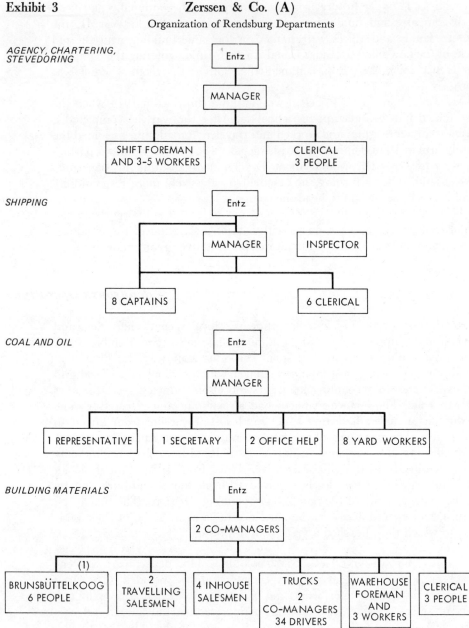

AGENCY, CHARTERING,
STEVEDORING

Entz

MANAGER

SHIFT FOREMAN
AND 3-5 WORKERS

CLERICAL
3 PEOPLE

SHIPPING

Entz

MANAGER

INSPECTOR

8 CAPTAINS

6 CLERICAL

COAL AND OIL

Entz

MANAGER

1 REPRESENTATIVE

1 SECRETARY

2 OFFICE HELP

8 YARD WORKERS

BUILDING MATERIALS

Entz

2 CO-MANAGERS

(1)
BRUNSBÜTTELKOOG
6 PEOPLE

2
TRAVELLING
SALESMEN

4 INHOUSE
SALESMEN

TRUCKS
2
CO-MANAGERS
34 DRIVERS

WAREHOUSE
FOREMAN
AND
3 WORKERS

CLERICAL
3 PEOPLE

(1) Zerssen & Co. operated a small building materials warehouse in Brünsbuttelkoog,
a town on the North Sea.

American Express for tourists, taking care of transport of changed crews, pick up and delivery of mail, delivery of instructions to the Captain from the owner, and preparation of bills of lading for storage or land transport of the ships' cargo. Rendsburg performed these agency operations only for the smaller ships up to 1,500 tons, which were able to dock in Rendsburg, or about six hundred a year. Ships just passing through the canal had to be serviced on the locks at Holtenau, which was done by a separate division of Zerssen. As a result, Rendsburg agency activities were predominantly concerned with port clearance. Zerssen charged a standard commission set by the Canal Authority and based on the ship's tonnage. There was one competitor in Rendsburg with whom Zerssen was on very friendly terms.

Chartering operations involved finding freight for ships or vice-versa for a 5 percent commission. Zerssen, as the only ship charterer in Rendsburg, acted as sole representative for eighteen coastal ships. These ships, ranging from 200 to 1,300 tons, were usually owned by their captains, most of whom lived in Rendsburg and for whom Zerssen also performed bookkeeping functions at a modest charge. Until the early 1950s Zerssen had been able to provide yearly up to forty thousand tons of coal as its own freight for these ships. Subsequently, as coal imports disappeared, Zerssen was forced, in order to fill up the ships, to rely almost entirely on agents representing freight with whom it split the 5 percent commission. Charters were set up by sending out notices looking for ships. The critical element in chartering was timing of the ships' transit and their loads in order to keep them fully booked.

Stevedoring involved the loading and unloading of ships on contract. Zerssen maintained friendly relations with its sole local competitor, reciprocally exchanging workers to meet peak demands. Zerssen had just begun a storage business on a 2,500 m^2 ($= \frac{5}{8}$ acre) lot on the quai, which was previously used by the building materials department.

At the request of insurance companies, Zerssen would also provide estimates, on a fixed-fee basis, on ship's damage.

Agency, chartering, and stevedoring managers had traditionally been located at the Rendsburg head office. Early in 1967, however, they were to move to the company building on the Kiel Canal quai, around which at a two kilometer distance from headquarters, physical operations were conducted.

SHIPPING   Shipping activities dated back to 1873 when Zerssen owned one-sixth of its first ship. As a result of an intensification of shipping activities after World War II, facilitated by special laws designed to rebuild the German merchant fleet, Zerssen had twelve ships in service by the end of 1961. Following the trend in shipping, Zerssen subsequently moved to fewer but larger vessels, owning a fleet of eight by December 1966.

All Zerssen's ships were operating under some form of charter.[3] Five of them ran with the German-Orient Line in an arrangement close to a time charter. These vessels, ranging in size form 3,400 to 8,400 tons brought to Zerssen a monthly payment from which the crewing and ship's maintenance costs were paid. However, at the end of the year, based on an index that related all ships to the average in the line, the year's results were divided among the ships chartered. Revenues for these five ships amounted to DM 8.4 million in 1965.

The two largest ships, 21,600 and 36,200 tons, operated under voyage charters but within the framework of the Fritzen Group, a pool to share risks. The group, through its 600,000 tons of shipping capacity, also negotiated fuel contracts for the ships, although the owner paid for the fuel used. All chartering and rechartering of cargoes was done by the pool secretary, not Zerssen. Both ships together earned DM 6.2 million in 1965.

Finally, the eighth ship, a 19,800 ton tanker, had been chartered to Shell for ten years starting in March 1958. In this case, Zerssen received a fixed rate/ton/month, approximating DM 267,000 per month, during the ten years regardless of the ship's usage. However, since crewing costs still remained to be paid, this type of arrangement could result in higher or extra costs. For instance, when Shell decided to send the ship to a "never come back line" like shuttling between the Persian Gulf and Tokyo, Zerssen had to replace the crew completely once a year at over DM 110,000. Depending upon maintenance costs of shipyards, provisions, health facilities, etc., in those areas, costs could vary greatly without Zerssen's control.

Shipping operations had traditionally received a large share of the chief executive's time. He was assisted by the department manager whose duties included direct contact with the captains of the ships and with numerous charterers throughout the world. The department manager personally controlled the running costs of the ships by making sure, together with an inspector, that maintenance was regularly carried on and that maintenance yards were submitting reasonable bids. Cost control also focused on fuel expenses as well as crewing and provisioning. The department manager commented:

---

[3] In general, a ship's owner had three alternatives for putting his investment to use. Considering all a form of chartering, he might negotiate a *voyage charter*. Under this system the owner received the freight receipts directly and paid all crewing costs, bunker costs, canal fees, harbor dues, and stevedoring on top of the normal costs incurred in maintaining his investment, i.e., maintenance, insurance, and interest. Under a second system, the *time charter*, he would receive either a fixed rate per day or month or a rate/ton/month and would pay only the crewing costs. (All rates per ton refer to the ship's tonnage, not its actual cargo on any one voyage.) Finally, but rarely done, the owner could provide a *"bare boat"* in which case he would give a naked ship to the charterer in return for a negotiated fee. He would have no operating costs to cover, but of course, would still have to maintain his investment.

We need the right numbers of the right people. The captain always wants an extra man, and the cook wants an extra chicken. Before you know it, a ship that should have a crew of ten has fifteen and feeds twenty. However, in spite of all the cost control, the shipping business basically gets down to this. If the market is good, you will earn money. If it is bad, you don't make much. You need good nerves. This is an extremely long-term business.

FUEL   From its agency service function for ships passing through Rendsburg, it was a logical step for Zerssen to also supply the ships with fuel. Hence, a coal bunkering operation was started that was moved to Holtenau in 1914. Once coal was shipped into Rendsburg for bunkering, it was only a small step to extend its distribution to clients on the land. As a result, Zerssen became involved as a coal wholesaler supplying local retailers as well as industrial and agricultural users, such as bakeries and dairies.

In recent years, most coal supplies were obtained from the German mines rather than imports from the U.S.A., England, or Poland. The German coal mines had joined into a sales association thereby stabilizing prices at the mines. The coal companies were also involved in wholesaling operations, and thus direct competitors of Zerssen. According to the department manager, the wholesaling arm of the coal companies would sometimes cut prices and also engage in expensive sales efforts by wining and dining the industrial customers. These efforts had met with only limited success in the Rendsburg area, given the loyalty of his customers and their suspicion toward the sales tactics employed by his competitors.

The major competition for the Rendsburg coal department, of course, came from oil with more and more industrial and agricultural users shifting to this type of fuel. The Rendsburg coal department had added fuel oil to its product line but since fuel oil retailers obtained their supplies directly from the oil companies, Zerssen had to limit its activities to small industrial and agricultural customers, while the larger ones dealt directly with the oil companies.

The department manager, who had his office at headquarters, indicated that personal contact was most important. He stated:

That's why I cannot sit at my desk. Twenty people have as many different needs and wants and they have to be taken care of.

BUILDING MATERIALS   In wholesaling coal, Zerssen was involved in the storage and overland transportation business with a seasonable peak during the winter months and very little activity during the summer. Hence, it was logical to seek a counter seasonal business, and, hence, Zerssen entered into building materials distribution.

The building materials department distributed about one hundred basic articles that the contractor might need for the raw building, such as cement, bricks, eternit, drainage piping, roofing materials, insulating materials, tiles, etc. The variations and sizes of these articles required an inventory of about 2,500 items. Margins ranged from no margin on cement (which was considered a necessary loss leader) to very high margins on such special articles as plastic drainage pipe, sealants, certain finished pieces, and synthetic sidings. Ten years earlier the product line had been smaller and more stable. Recently the number of items stocked had grown in number and heterogeneity, primarily owing to the increase in semifinished and finished pieces as well as many new synthetic materials.

Zerssen purchased its supplies through the Baustoff Union, a group of six building materials companies, among which Zerssen Rendsburg and Kiel counted for two, which had joined for the purpose of securing low prices on high volume purchases.

Zerssen sold about 90 percent of its building materials volume to contractors, mostly on a bid basis. Eighty percent of its sales were shipped directly from its supplier to the building site, largely on Zerssen trucks. The remaining sales were made from the Zerssen warehouse, both to weekend builders and contractors who needed some special or low volume items.

Rendsburg building materials sales had increased yearly in line with the growth of local construction. However, the two managers felt that they faced a buyer's market, although in their rural territory prices had remained firmer than in the large cities. Markets for building materials were localized and Rendsburg covered roughly a twenty kilometer radius within which it held an estimated marketshare of 70 percent with the remainder going to three local competitors. The two managers maintained, together with two salesmen, close contacts with contractors, providing technical knowledge and advice, which they considered as one of their strongest selling assets. Also, architects were regularly contracted to secure their support, even though they did not make buying decisions. Beyond growing with the local market, the managers saw no way to expand sales, either by hiring more salesmen or through advertising.

The department was in the process of moving to completely new office and warehousing facilities across town about three kilometers from the head office building.

Holtenau Operations

Holtenau consisted of three operating departments: ships' agency, ships' supplies, and bunkering. (See Exhibits 4 and 4a for their organization structure.) It was managed by Mr. Egbert Lucks, fifty-six, who had been with the company since he started working under his father, the previous Holtenau division manager, more than thirty years ago. In addition to his division manager's position and as a way of ensuring that Zerssen-Holtenau

Exhibit 4

Zerssen & Co. (A)
Organization of Holtenau Division

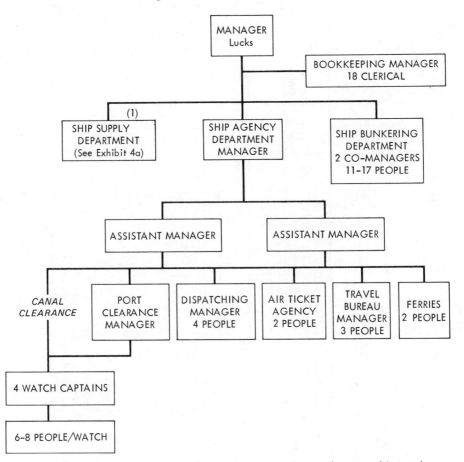

(1) The Ship Supply Department manager also acted as assistant divisional manager (Vertreter).

kept its name before the shipowners and related members of the trade, Mr. Lucks had taken on several highly visible honorary posts, such as ten years as Chairman of the Association of German Ship Suppliers, President of the International Ship Supplier Association in the Hague, and other such positions for various associations of Ships' Agents.

Mr. Lucks, and before him his father, had operated independently from Rendsburg. In 1964, he had effectively resisted an effort to transfer his office to Rendsburg. Reporting and control had been exercised only through the irregular meetings between Mr. Entz, Sr., and Mr. Lucks. For the use of the office building overlooking the locks as well as for the Zerssen central services a charge was levied against Holtenau.

Exhibit 4a

Zerssen & Co. (A)
Organization of Ship Supply Department

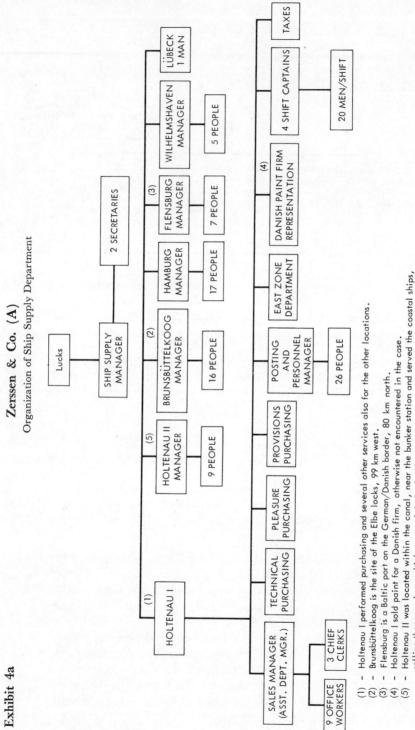

(1) – Holtenau I performed purchasing and several other services also for the other locations.
(2) – Brunsbüttelkoog is the site of the Elbe locks, 99 km west.
(3) – Flensburg is a Baltic port on the German/Danish border, 80 km north.
(4) – Holtenau I sold paint for a Danish firm, otherwise not encountered in the case.
(5) – Holtenau II was located within the canal, near the bunker station and served the coastal ships, selling them goods on which customs' duties had been paid. It was referred to as Supply II.

AGENCY   With the opening of the Kiel Canal it was necessary to move Zerssen agency operations for the transit ships to the new locks at Holtenau, where an office was opened in 1914. Of the three basic agency activities, canal clearance, port clearance, and dispatching, it was canal clearance that accounted for most of the department's income. Dispatching in fact was done without charge as a service, which was considered a competitive necessity.

Zerssen performed agency operations for about 50 percent of the traffic using the Kiel Canal with the remainder about equally shared by four competitors. Fees, set by the Canal Authority, were based on the ship's tonnage. Since it was more profitable to service one 15,000 ton ship rather than ten 1,500 ton vessels, Zerssen was at a disadvantage vis-à-vis its competitors in that about 25 to 30 percent of its business was for East German or Polish ships, almost all of smaller than average size. It was common to give rebates on the standard fees, although these were rarely effective in convincing customers to shift agents. A 10 percent rebate was normal, but it would only reduce the shipowner's total canal bill by 1 percent. Customers, who were regularly visited by the top managers of the Holtenau division, remained typically loyal to their agent as long as he performed canal clearance quickly and without error to permit ship passage with the shortest possible delay.

Traffic on the Kiel Canal was slowly declining. It was influenced by the severity of the winter, which would close several Baltic seaports, by the level of East-West trade, and by the trend toward larger vessels, which were unable to use the canal.

In addition to its prime functions, the ship agency was also running an airticket agency at Holtenau (started because of the need to provide airplane transportation for crews), a regular travel bureau in a nearby town (which relied for about 30 percent of its business on nonairline travel for crews), and an agency that handled ticket sales and customs clearance for two of the three ferries shuttling between Kiel and Denmark.

SHIP SUPPLIES   Established in 1948, ship supplies was in essence a store on the water for ships and their crews. Thus, it was an extension of Zerssen's service activity for vessels using the Kiel Canal, where most of its sales were made, largely at Holtenau but also at two smaller locations. In addition, Zerssen had opened small ship supply offices in Hamburg, Wilhelmshaven, Lübeck, and Flensburg. Ship supplies sold three broad categories of products. Sales were made both to the shipping line and to individual crew members. The major items were stocked by Zerssen, whereas some ten thousand others were simply purchased in Kiel after the order came in.

The product line consisted of provisions (30 percent of sales), technical (15 percent) and pleasure (55 percent). Provisions were taken on board to feed the crew according to standards set by the owner of the line. Technical items covered a wide range of articles, less than half of which were stocked in the Zerssen warehouse, from metal washers to radios or television sets for the crews' private purchases. Pleasure articles were the primary source of private business consisting mainly of beverages, tobacco, and sweets. Several services were also offered such as film developing or minor appliance repairs. Articles stocked by Zerssen were purchased duty-free from suppliers from all over the world, including the Eastern countries. Given the international clientele and its ability to buy supplies in many different ports, purchasing was critical in conducting successful ship supply operations.

Orders arrived mainly by telephone, telex, or telegraph, and rarely by letter. Typically, the ship contacted Zerssen directly and read its order onto a record, in the ship's own language, which later was translated into German and inventory language. The orders would then be put up and delivered to the ships on arrival at the locks. Sales to the shipping line and private crew members were handled in the same way. Sales teams worked around the clock, seven days a week to insure that ships coming at any hour would be properly serviced and supplied. The head of the team was called a "clerk" because of his responsibility for the order forms and handling. Since the ships were only in the locks for twenty minutes, any order received by the clerk at the locks had to be shipped on the Brunsbüttelkoog, at the other end of the canal, if the ships were going into the canal or to another destination if the ships were leaving the canal but wanted forward delivery. Earlier, a bonus system had been in effect that sought to motivate the clerks in making direct sales, but in less than half a year this system was abolished because a study conducted by the managers showed that the clerks rarely sold anything during the twenty minutes except a few cigarettes.

Thus, sales efforts on the locks were ineffective. Rather, regular visits to the shipowners throughout Europe by all three of the Zerssen-Holtenau managers served to develop contacts and offered an opportunity to convince the owners to buy at the Kiel Canal. Contracts were unusual. Normally, the owners gave the captain guidelines within which he could place orders on his own. A "commission" system, universally required of ships' suppliers, was the cornerstone of keeping the captains pleased with both Zerssen quality and service. As a result, sales to owners' accounts required, in the words of one manager, "selling the head office and keeping the Captains as friends." Sales efforts were supported by an annual catalogue that was the main selling tool to crew members, who were largely influenced by price and variety. A significant proportion of all private purchases was made by crews of East Europeans fleets, especially Polish ships.

Inventory losses and bad debts were considered the primary risks. The large inventories carried were expected to be significantly decreased once inventory control had been put on a computer by January 1969, but the extension of credit to 90 and 180 days could not be curbed. Credit sales were typical to shipowners, while sales to the crews were normally, but not always, for cash. Mr. Lucks noted that although canal lists of bad risks were made up, they were not reliable enough to reduce write-offs averaging DM 60,000 a year on private sales and DM 35,000 on owners' sales.

Competition on the locks did not pose a grave problem for Zerssen since there were only two other very small suppliers on the canal. Competition came from suppliers in other harbors and mainly Hamburg, Copenhagen, and Rotterdam.

In an effort to extend its activities beyond the Kiel Canal, Zerssen had experimentally offered a fixed-price provisioning scheme to certain ship-owners. Basically, Zerssen would contract to supply enough provisions with the necessary guiding menus to the ships for a fixed price of, say, DM 4.00 per day. It had not yet been decided whether this plan would be continued, but Mr. Lucks said:

> We are not so happy about it. Fourteen ships, not counting ours, are using it. The owners appear to like it, but, of course, the captains don't, because it goes around them and pretty much eliminates their commissions.

BUNKERING Zerssen had established coal bunkering operations at Holtenau in 1914, almost next door to its office on 500 meters of quai leased from the Canal Authority. In 1952, an oil bunkering agreement was concluded with Shell. The agreement required that Zerssen offer twenty-four-hour service to ships under contract with Shell. In return, Zerssen received a fee for each ton delivered. Also, it was allowed to sell fuel oil for its own account to coastal ships but only at identical prices to those charged by Shell. Pricing, contracts and bookkeeping were handled by Shell, although Zerssen had to keep records of the deliveries for the customs authorities. The tanks and one-half share of the bunkering office belonged to Shell. Zerssen owned the remainder of the facilities, paid the lease, and the workers it employed. The bunkering manager stated that the main requirements for his department were those of quick, competent service and the technical ability to perform preventive maintenance. However, these factors were not considered critical because very few ships were lost as customers due to poor service.

Kiel Operations

In 1923, Zerssen acquired 90 percent of Glückauf (the traditional greet-ing among coalminers in Germany), a coal wholesaling firm in Kiel, whose owner, Mr. Fuhrmann, required additional resources to expand. Mr. Fuhrmann retained his 10 percent until 1955 when, for tax reasons, he sold out entirely. Since 1923, Zerssen had expanded its Kiel operations, largely through acquisitions, to include oil, building materials, freight forwarding, scrap, and a technical representation. The acquired companies retained their names even though they were managed from the Glückauf office. It was planned to bring all companies under the Zerssen name during 1967, save the freight forwarding company, which had to remain separate for legal reasons.

From 1923 through 1965, when he retired at the age of seventy-two, Mr. Fuhrmann had managed the Kiel operations. Since he had been part-owner until 1955, his management of Glückauf had been characterized by its independence from Rendsburg. Strengthened by the later entry in 1936 of Mr. Entz, Sr., and his greater age, Mr. Fuhrmann reported to Rendsburg only informally, for the most part only when Mr. Entz, Sr., met him in Kiel. Furthermore, German law prescribed that only nominal sums could be transferred to headquarters leaving Mr. Fuhrmann almost the entire profits from Glückauf as retained earnings to invest or bank in any manner he chose. Even though Glückauf included charges against its departmental profits for use of the buildings (which were owned by Glückauf) and to cover its own office expenses, this money was not transferred to Rendsburg, as was the case for Holtenau. Throughout his reign, Mr. Fuhrmann issued daily instructions to every manager, hired and fired even the truck drivers and janitors, and kept the only set of figures personally in his own hand.

Mr. Fuhrmann was succeeded by two co-managers. One of them, Mr. Höpfner, an IMEDE participant in 1962–1963, was responsible for the scrap and technical departments; the other co-manager, Dr. Heidtmann, had responsibility for the coal and oil departments as well as building materials. The two co-managers of the Kiel division as well as the department managers had their offices in Haus Glückauf in downtown Kiel, although different yards housing coal, oil, building materials, scrap, the service shop, and the trucks were located in various other parts of the city. Exhibits 5 and 6 show the organization structure of the five Kiel departments.

COAL   Originally, Glückauf sold coal wholesale to retailers, who in turn sold to the public. It also sold directly to small businesses. Through acquisition it became involved in retailing and, faced with a market declining by 7 percent a year, the department expanded its coal activities by taking on the inventory responsibility for small, elderly retailers, whose children were unwilling to continue the business. Instead of taking a wagonload and storing and sacking it himself, as in the past, the retailer who sacking it himself, as in the past, the retailer who used this service would call Glückauf, give a specific order, which would then be sacked for him, and he would pick it up and distribute it to his customers. This policy had arrested Glückauf's sales decline.

Prices were stable at retail with everybody charging the same and competing solely on the basis of service. Wholesale prices, on the other hand, were subject to downward pressures as a result of aggressive sales tactics by the

Exhibit 5

Zerssen & Co. (A)

Glückauf Division
Organization of Departments
under Co-manager Heidtmann

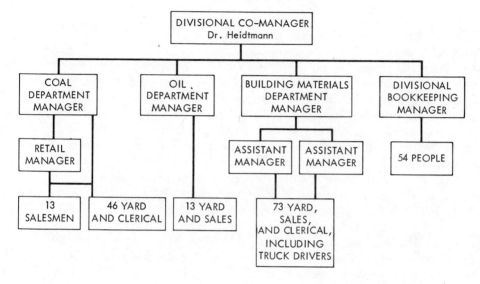

Exhibit 6

Zerssen & Co. (A)

Glückauf Division
Organization of Departments
under Co-manager Höpfner

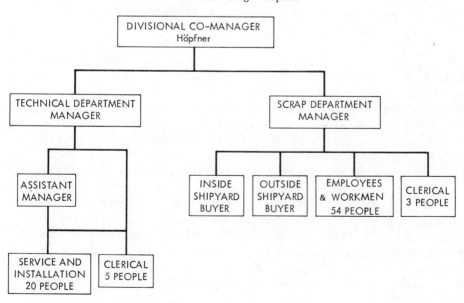

captive wholesale arms of the coal mines, especially with large users. Like Rendsburg, Glückauf depended largely on the German coal mines for its supplies.

Oɪʟ   With the decline of coal markets, Glückauf had entered fuel oil distribution. Most of its sales were retail to individuals or apartmentblocks. Most industrial customers, on the other hand, and particularly the larger ones, purchased directly from the oil companies. Competing oil retailers, some of which were tied to the oil companies, also obtained their supplies directly from the refineries. Thus, there was no opportunity for Zerssen to act as a wholesaler for oil. Oil operations differed from coal in one other significant respect. Whereas retail prices for coal were stable and customers not price-sensitive, oil prices fluctuated widely and customers were influenced by even the smallest price difference. As a result, Glückauf had lost orders when its prices were 20 pfennig (5 cents) higher per 100 liters (26.4 gallons), which ordinarily retailed around DM 8.60 ($2.15). One of the reasons for this price sensitivity was the government requirement that every transaction be recorded and filed, thus allowing everyone to see the price of oil at each of the steps in reaching the ultimate consumer. This information, from which the price of bulk oil was quoted daily in the newspapers, was required for tax reasons. The same oil could be used for running a diesel engine, in which case it was taxed, or for heating, for which purpose it was tax free.

Glückauf purchased its supplies directly from the refineries, shopping around for the lowest quote. To the refinery price a standard markup would be added. In view of the severe fluctuations in refinery prices, Glückauf minimized its inventories, having only 1,000 m^3 (264,000 gallons) of oil storage capacity.

Bᴜɪʟᴅɪɴɢ Mᴀᴛᴇʀɪᴀʟs   Glückauf's building materials department was similar to Rendsburg in terms of its origin, product line, purchasing, customers, and pricing. Five aspects, however, were different in Kiel. First of all, Glückauf relied for the bulk of its sales on few contractors, with five of them accounting for 50 percent of sales. Second, some large contractors in the Kiel area, particularly those who specialized in building between fifty to one hundred prefab houses a year, had started their own building material companies for captive use. Dr. Heidtmann felt that Glückauf was powerless to counter this trend since it was more acceptable in Germany to compete with one's suppliers than with one's customers. Third, in terms of competition, two Hamburg companies had invaded the Kiel market by cutting prices. Glückauf at first did not go down, and consequently its market share dropped from 70 percent to 45 percent. Glückauf, the two Hamburg companies, and one other major Kiel competitor accounted for 95 percent of the market. Fourth, the nature of construction in Kiel had changed toward larger projects for which supply contracts were let only on a bid basis. This reduced the department's price maneuverability. Fifth, the trend toward a broader product line was even more pronounced in Kiel. This permitted expansion into higher margin but lower volume items as a potentially more profitable strategy, of course, requiring higher inventory investnents. When asked about the advisability of such a move, Dr. Heidtmann replied:

> No, I don't think building materials in Kiel is a good investment any more. Not even in the high margin items.

Like Rendsburg, Glückauf delivered about 80 percent of its sales, mostly with its own trucks, directly from its supplier to the building site. Management considered this its strongest competitive tool, thereby also averting excess handling costs. For legal reasons, this activity was handled by a technically separate freight forwarding company. However, with exception of separate accounts, the freight forwarding activities were organizationally part of the building department.

SCRAP   This activity became part of Glückauf in 1942 when a local coal wholesaling and retailing company was acquired that also engaged in scrap. Operations consisted of buying scrap from metal fabricating shops and businesses or by acquiring junked cars, rails, etc., sorting it and arranging it according to different mixtures, and finally selling it, largely to the purchasing arms of the steel companies.

The major scrap supplier in the Kiel market was the shipbuilding yard of the Kieler Howaldtswerke, which accounted for 50 percent of its volume in weight and 70 percent in value. The purchasing arrangement with the Howaldtswerke was a rather special one. Glückauf and two other Kiel firms were allowed to work inside the shipyard on a coordinated schedule. Since Glückauf had been in the yard before either of its competitors, it was allowed to stay permanently in the old shipyard—where few ships were being built anymore, the biggest of which would be 3,500 tons. The rest of the yard was divided into two areas. In area I, the three firms alternated by month. In area II, usually the heaviest, they alternated by week. Thus, in the months when Glückauf was in the old shipyard, area I, and area II for two weeks, it might be able to purchase 1,500 tons. In the months when Glückauf was only in the old shipyard and area II for one week, it might have difficulty purchasing 500 tons. This widely fluctuating purchasing tonnage was complicated by the internal fluctuations of the individual area's scrap productions, caused by the number and stages of ships under construction. To counter this problem, good relationships with the yard's foremen were essential as a means of influencing scrap availability.

Once faced with a pile of scrap, the shipyard buyer, armed with a walkie-talkie, made his purchases without any reference to price. He radioed the

Howaldt control for permission to have a truck take (a) a specific pile (location) (b) an estimated size (tonnage) of (c) class 2 though 6 scrap. Since class 1 through 5 scrap was priced at the end of the month in a percentage of the class 6 scrap purchasing price, the buyer had to be trained in identifying the correct classification. As one manager discreetly commented:

> The buyers have to have the cooperation and trust of the inspectors at Howaldt.

Once the scrap had been purchased, Glückauf sought out potential buyers. Price quotations were based on the prices quoted each day at noon in London. These prices varied widely, and in an effort to stay out of speculation, Glückauf had chosen to keep small inventories. Also, in addition to the fluctuations, the London scrap prices were moving downward, thus reducing Glückauf margins. Glückauf's major customer to whom it sold over five hundred tons a month, was Deu Mu, the ore buying company for Salzgitter, the owner of the Kieler Howaldtswerke. In view of the fact that Glückauf both bought from and sold to the same corporate family, a special arrangement had been developed. Deu Mu, which took about one-half to one-third of the scrap obtained from the Kieler Howaldtswerke, would meet once a month with the scrap companies that had access to the shipyard to set a price for that entire period. This base price, which was established for the top scrap classification, determined through a fixed formula both the selling price of the other five classifications as well as the purchase prices that scrap companies would pay to the Kieler Howaldtswerke.

In addition to the two scrap companies having access to the shipyard, there was still a third competitor who, according to the scrap manager, was probably the most profitable. Glückauf's share of the Kieler scrap market amounted to roughly 50 percent.

TECHNICAL DEPARTMENT   The technical department was acquired at the same time and in the same way as the scrap department. It acted primarily as sales and service representative for Daimler-Benz, being limited to fast diesel engines, capable of 4000 rpm. These high-rotation diesel engines were used largely for generating electricity on ships. To a lesser extent, they were used to propel small fishing boats. Finally, the technical department used these diesel engines for putting together auxiliary generators for hospitals.

Although serving only a specialized, local market, Glückauf had upwards of one thousand potential customers who were easily identifiable, aside from the small number of hospitals involved, through Zerssen's contacts in the shipping industry and through the technical manager's assiduous

444444

444

cultivation of the Bureau of Fisheries in Kiel, an agency that aided small fishermen in finding the best ways to outfit their boats. Sales were made on a commission basis, with prices set by Daimler-Benz. A large portion of the department's income derived from servicing Daimler-Benz and other diesel engines as well as from making modifications and installations.

During a period when Daimler-Benz had taken over two other representatives in Kiel, it was Glückauf's service organization that had allowed the technical department to retain its Daimler-Benz representation. This department was seen as one of the few areas of present Zerssen involvement where future growth might be strong. With Daimler-Benz' captive outlets as its primary competition, the technical department had secured a toe-hold, in the words of its manager, in Hamburg and had plans for expanding into a North German-wide sales and service organization.

ORGANIZATION ISSUE

My most pressing problem—commented Mr. Entz in 1967—is to find and implement the most appropriate organization structure for our company. I am inheriting an organization rooted in both German and family traditions, resulting in many unwritten guidelines on how things should be done. Many of our employees have been with Zerssen between twenty-five to forty years and a number of these men are the second or third generation with the company. The leadership by my ancestors, including my father, has been very patriarchal. My father in Rendsburg, Mr. Lucks in Holtenau, and Mr. Fuhrmann in Kiel used to run their respective location authoritatively, getting directly involved in all, including even the most trivial, operating decisions. They obtained their information and exercised their control informally through their day-to-day contracts. In contrast, there was little coordination or control between locations, with each of the three men running his domain independently. This held true both at top and operating levels. For example, my father as Chief Executive made few visits to the other locations with most contacts being of a social nature. On the operating level, in building materials or coal, for instance, Rendsburg and Kiel acted independently in the market place. One of the managers in our organization referred recently to Zerssen as "a company with no central focal point, but three loosely connected operating centers." Finally, the three men running their geographic units have been in charge for many years: my father since 1936, Fuhrmann since the early '20s, and Lucks has been in Holtenau for over thirty years when he started to work for his father whom he succeeded in 1947.

Mr. Entz continued: As a newcomer I do not feel that I can continue with the previous organization setup. First of all, my father is gradually withdrawing from all business activities while Mr. Fuhrmann retired last year. Thus, two of the three strong men have withdrawn from the business. Second, we have now reached a size that makes the authoritative and informal organization of the past both difficult and inefficient. It was not uncommon for my father to receive a telephone call from one of our truck-drivers to ask him if certain necessary repairs could be made. If I were to deal with all these small day-to-day operating decisions, there would be no time left for planning. This leads to the third reason as to why we cannot continue the traditional organization. Many of our hitherto secure and stable businesses have come under attack. Coal is an obvious example given its declining market. But, this is not the only instance of Zerssen being faced with stagnating demand. Traffic through the Kiel Canal, for example, is slowly declining, which has implications for a number of our activities. As if this is not enough, we are also encountering stiffer competition, for example, in building materials. Finally, capital requirements have increased in recent years, such as the inventories that we must carry in building materials and particularly the investments required in shipping given the trend toward larger and larger ships.

In view of the above factors, I am inclined to change the organization by centralizing planning and by decentralizing and by pushing further down the line the operating decisions. However, I am by no means committed to this approach. If I were to proceed on this basis, I am thinking of four divisions: shipping, water, land, and finance, each with a top operating manager. I would double as chief executive and the man in charge of shipping and with the three other managers we would constitute the top planning and coordination team for the company. This may allow us to decentralize operations ensuring that day-to-day decisions are made as close to the firing line as possible. For example, both the building materials department in Rendsburg and in Kiel would have more operating freedom than before. Both departments would report to the manager of the land division, rather than have one report to the chief executive in Rendsburg and the other to the top man in Kiel, who in turn reports to the boss in Rendsburg. If we proceed this way, we can abandon the office in Kiel and move all the department managers out to the location where physical operations take place such as the building materials warehouse, the scrap yard, the coal yard, etc.

I have not yet talked to my managers about this plan, and I must admit that one of my real problems is manpower. I am not sure that we have enough management depth to fill these various positions satisfactorily. Also, it is important in a company like ours, to remember the psychological impact of organizational change.

The longer I think about my organization problem, the more difficult it becomes. It must have been sort of comfortable to be guided by tradition as were my ancestors. On the other hand, it was fun at IMEDE to develop ideal organizational structures for the companies in our cases, specifying the management talent required, their cost, the necessary reporting and control systems, and the timetable to implement organizational changes. However, if you are forced to combine our 127-year-old tradition with the rational but somewhat abstract classroom analysis, life suddenly becomes a lot more complicated. And don't forget, departing from tradition is painful for those concerned, and, as a result, I feel that I will not have much room for experimenting. My first try has to be right because I am afraid that I will not have a second chance. Zerssen with its traditions and its people may be able to digest only one organizational change in a generation.

ZERSSEN & CO. (B)

The Intervening Ten Months

The events of the almost ten months between Mr. Entz's takeover in January 1967 and mid-October 1967 had pointed up several issues that would have to be resolved on the way to making the major organizational changes that were discussed in Zerssen & Co. (A). So far as most managers could tell, it had been "business as usual" with roughly the same sales as before, the same competitive threats, and the same routine of day-to-day operations. But to Mr. Entz it had been a somewhat frustrating first year with only the accomplishment of minor changes in accord with his overall organization plan.

In terms of decentralizing the department managers from their division headquarters, the Rendsburg Building Materials Department had completed its move to new quarters across town; the Rendsburg Agency, Chartering, and Stevedoring Department had been moved to the canal quai, and its name changed internally to Rendsburg Water; the Glückauf complex had come under the Zerssen corporate name in Kiel, and its building materials, coal, and scrap managers had moved their offices to their respective warehouses and yards; and the Glückauf Division's comanagers had developed and instituted a year-end bonus system for the department managers based primarily on departmental performance. Although the future status of the Glückauf comanagers had not yet been resolved, Haus Glückauf had been sold thereby simultaneously signaling the end of an era and stilling a debate over the best location for Zerssen & Co. headquarters. Zerssen & Co. would remain in Rendsburg.

In a first step toward centralizing financial information and creating adequate reporting and control systems, a staff group had researched and chosen a computer that Mr. Entz decided to install and expected to be in operation by early 1969. Further, a tentative step toward long-range planning had been taken with the beginning of a three-year planning system to originate at the department level and work upward to top management decision. Unfortunately, the finance director had a serious heart attack in February, requiring a six-month convalescence, with the dual result that he was apparently not intimately involved with this decision and that the year-end statements for 1966 were not completed until October 1967. The delay of these statements, in the opinions of some managers, impeded the development of an overall understanding of the company among those managers who had long been used to detailed operating instructions without any knowledge of financial data.

In view of these minor changes and the frustrations involved in making any changes at all, the case writer interviewed the managers and Mr. Entz with the intent of learning what they felt should be done now. Four issues seemed to be imminently at hand: (1) what form of reporting and control should be installed; (2) the use and adequacy of financial planning; (3) the correct relationship between staff groups and operating managers; and (4) the changing role of the chief executive in Zerssen & Co.

REPORTING AND CONTROL SYSTEMS   *Rendsburg* managers reported directly to Mr. Entz in two ways—both oral. First, it had been traditional, and Mr. Entz continued with this tradition, on the first Tuesday of every month, at 5:30, to hold a meeting of all the department managers to "talk over all the problems as a group." These meetings lasted two to three hours and were run with an open format. Second, the managers also continued to call up Mr. Entz to ask for information, request for decisions, or inform him of problems that had come up. To a certain extent, Mr. Entz as well called these managers to ask for explanations of decisions or information. Managers in departments outside Rendsburg expressed displeasure at what they called this "Rendsburg viewpoint." When asked about this, Mr. Entz replied that he tried to rely on reports, but the only reports he received were balance sheets and income statements, and his Rendsburg managers simply ignored the medium of written reports or reporting through the finance director. He felt he might be able to change this direct information exchange if he were able to change the organization structure. At the very least, he looked forward to the date when the computer would give him three monthly reports.

The Rendsburg managers allowed that reporting to someone else would be possible but were confused as to what reporting meant in terms of the businesses in which they were involved. For instance, the coal manager noted that he did not worry about sales volume in Deutsche Marks, but that his tonnage was running at 150,000 a year, which was a profitable level. A second manager said that he looked to see if he had made more money that day than the day before. Still a third said that he wanted to know earning in relations to sales, and for his business a gross margin of 4 to 7 percent would be fine because that was his markup.

Furthermore, the use of reports in helping a manager to evaluate his subordinates or in helping Mr. Entz to evaluate him remained a totally alien concept. One manager replied:

> I can't tell whether my subordinates are doing a good job by looking at figures. I watch—I can see what they do and how they handle a customer. The rest is feel. If something is wrong, I can feel it. If Mr. Entz were to ask for a report on one of my men, I would give it based on what I know of his personal characteristics. I can't measure his talent, but I can say whether he works hard and keeps his nose clean.

During his convalescence, the finance director had developed a set of reports that showed for each department (1) an overview of the department's yearly results in terms of total sales, gross margin, and costs by account, and (2) a profitability statement, in percentages, of the department's performance in terms of (a) gross margin as a percent of departmental costs, (b) gross margin as a percent of departmental costs + interest charges, and (c) gross margin as a percent of departmental costs + interest charges + allocation of headquarters expenses. In explaining these reports, the finance director commented:

> We do not want to give the figures to the department managers except for their own department because people talk too much.

Holtenau still reported to Rendsburg orally, but Mr. Entz felt that this method was becoming more regular in its application. Owing to their location within the same building and the nature of the businesses involved, the Holtenau department managers felt that their system of oral reporting within Holtenau was adequate.

Mr. Lucks, the manager of the Holtenau division, stated that more than 80 percent of the reports that he received in the course of managing his division were made to him orally through the direct intercom, which sat at his elbow on his desk. He also received monthly reports that were simple listings of: (1) all the ships that came through the locks; (2) the ships that used Zerssen as agents; and (3) the general sales figures of the Ships' Supply Department and the bunker. Other written reports he received dealt with such subjects as the use of the automobiles and trucks in the Supply Department and general travel reports detailing where his managers were traveling and for what purpose. He received, periodically, a photocopy of all the clearances on the canal. From this copy he could discern which of his clients had changed to other agents. He then asked them why they changed, specifically to find out if it was due to a mistake or due to some service that the other agent had offered. In trying to keep a finger on the pulse of his division, he looked periodically at the accounts for salaries, wages, overtime, and employment of new personnel. He felt that any other reports that might help would come with the use of the new computer. He commented:

> This computer will tell us what products move, how, and then give us an ability to sort out the inventory. It will also show us which client provides us with the most profit on the sales we make to them.

When asked how he used these reports, Mr. Lucks said:

> I watch the development of our clients in terms of sales to them, the number of ships having used us for canal clearance, and, of course, the year-end result. I look for the return and compare it to the year before. I check to see how the individual accounts have changed. I try to spot bad relationships and figure out how they might develop. There are other accounts that I check, such as commissions to the captains or rebates to the owners, both of which have a tendency of getting out of line and thus need to be watched. This division can be handled from my office with oral reports because I know what is going on. Besides, I am director of the firm, and this gives me the opportunity to know what is happening in the other parts of the company.

Mr. Lucks also made his orders, requests, and questions mostly orally. Whenever a subject was of importance to all the departments, he would send a memorandum; when it dealt with only one department, he would merely call in the department manager and talk with him.

The manager of the Ships' Supply Department had the same fourteen men reporting to him as one year earlier and considered such reporting relationships necessary due to the specialized nature of the work in each man's area. He received daily reports on a standard form showing for the previous day (1) how many ships had passed through the locks and (2) the total deliveries. He also received a monthly sales report. Beyond that, he felt he was close enough in touch with his subordinates to know what was going on, and stated: "I can always ask questions." Reporting upward by the Ships' Supply Department manager to Mr. Lucks was completely oral, through the medium of a "mail meeting" the two had each morning.

The Ships' Agency Department manager also received about 80 percent oral reports, and considered written reports as special, serious problem reports. Sales reports were considered superfluous because every ship was lined up with an agent before it reached the locks. The fixed canal fees made profitability reports, in his mind, a matter of manpower accounting. When asked if he did not think more formal reporting would help him in managing his department, he said:

Look at these offices. My door is closed now and you can hear my assistant manager on the telephone. See his back is right to my window and even without trying I can hear what he is doing and saying. We are so close that it is very easy to know how my people are working. I know what he gives for orders; I know how he makes decisions; I can see the results of his work.

Finally, the manager of Holtenau bookkeeping said:

Structured reports aren't of any help. We talk about the problems here on a regular basis whenever problems come up. But we do not have any particular month-end discussion, because what good would it do? With a longer time span, it may help, so we have semiannual meetings. We just could not gain any benefits from monthly reports. Sure, with a new type of business, we make intermittent balances to see how the business is doing; or with something like Supply II, which has lost money for five years. We want to figure out ways of changing the losses. We know when sales will drop because we can see the ships passing through the locks. Before you start making lots of reports, you have to look at the requirements of the situation. We don't have reports as you understand them, but we do have a reporting system.

Glückauf had used a formal reporting system for more than a year. The two co-managers, upon Mr. Fuhrmann's retirement, had initiated these reports, feeling that formal reports were necessary both for the education of their department managers and as a management tool for the better direction of their division after its decentralization. However, one manager felt that the reports could be improved both in their usefulness to management (they were cumulative, forcing him to look up last month's report and subtract it to get the month's result) and in their timing (they came out of bookkeeping on average six weeks after month's end).

The main issue, however, lay in how to use these reports that each co-manager received only for the departments reporting to him; he passed these figures on to the respective department managers; and there they were regarded, by some managers, in awe as documents of complete mystery. The simultaneous installation of a department performance-based bonus system, based on these reports, had brought the managers closer to an awareness of the elements of profitability in their departments. The adequacy of the report was considered by the same co-manager, as perhaps, completely in doubt since they did not differentiate between tax accounting and management accounting. Finally, there were no regular meetings of all the managers to discuss these reports; although a weekly meeting was held to discuss general problems in the division.

PLANNING   The nature and requirements of financial planning had become an issue during the last ten months because of the institution of a three-year financial plan. The formulation of the financial plan began with the managers' estimates of what would be required in the departments over the next three years. These were refined within the divisions, where also a half-year plan with specific requests and backup arguments would be developed. Mr. Entz would then meet in Rendsburg with each division separately and discuss the stated half-year needs, particularly within the framework of the overall three-year plan, culminating in the allocations that Mr. Entz thought necessary. Most of the managers seemed to be very happy about using such a plan and thought of it as a first, tentative step toward planning for their areas as a part of the total company.

The finance director, however, felt that most of this planning activity was wasted motion. Some other managers had the same concern based on a feeling that Mr. Entz had not yet established sufficient financial guidelines within which they should work, although they felt they could learn whatever remained to be learned in order to use financial planning as a tool; however, the finance director felt it simply would not work for a company like Zerssen. He listed three reasons for this pessimism: (1) the problem of liquidity; (2) the bureaucratic mentality of managers; and, (3) heterogeneous nature of Zerssen's business. He stated:

> Liquidity may vary from one year to the next by 2.5 to 3 million marks, mostly because of the Shipping Department. Look, one has to work with these figures:

	Year End Liquidity (DM)
1961	1,900,000
1962	(400,000)
1963	2,300,000
1964	6,100,000
1965	2,800,000

> I don't know what liquidity we'll have over the next six months, let alone two or three years. The liquidity balance is my planning figure and that's how I decide what we have to invest. Also, if these plans are merely to show us what the managers would like to see happen, then good, we will take it into consideration and see if we can fulfill their wishes. Beyond that, most managers have a somewhat bureaucratic attitude. They say, "I will take what I can get if it is in the plan." In other words, if they don't need the money but they have had their plan accepted, they will use the money anyway. Finally, we are in so many different businesses that a department manager cannot tell whether or not his request is best for the overall company. We might spread our limited re-

sources too thin by planning investments in every area. Thus, for these reasons, almost all of our investments have been made with an eye to the short-term movements, except maybe examples like the new building materials building in Rendsburg where we got involved with that project seven years before it was completed. We rarely can see very far ahead in terms of the need for an investment. For example, we knew about the need to invest in one of our ships to improve its performance, but we studied that for years and ultimately decided not to invest. Then, one-half year later, we got better conditions and decided within a week to invest one-half million. Or, take the scrap yard in Kiel. We found out that the city planned to lease that land to someone else, and send us elsewhere. We wanted to stay, so we bought the land within two months. No one could have foreseen that or put it down in the financial plan. There are many more examples of decisions that came up and had to be made and financed within six months. You see we are not a manufacturer but a trader, if you will. We are more dependent on the outside world than a manufacturer. Therefore, we must keep a reserve for moving fast. Of course, there are long-turn trends to watch, like the ones in coal and oil, and we have to work with them, but these can be seen and planned for. I wouldn't say to a department manager to plan on a certain new investment as long as I do not know how much money we will have available when that investment is needed.

RELATIONS BETWEEN STAFF AND OPERATING UNITS   Two specific decision problems exemplified the frustrations that operating managers had felt in trying to work with newly established staff groups. Although some managers appeared oblivious to any such conflicts, the younger, more aggressive managers seemed the ones who were pushing hardest to help Mr. Entz reorganize and systematize the management of Zerssen and who chafed in these relations. Since Mr. Entz saw a certain amount of central staff support essential in an organization the size of Zerssen, he also was interested in what the correct relationship should be, within the broader question of what should be kept in the operating units and what should be centralized.

The first of these problems related to a 10 percent special write-off, which was given by the German government, as a counterrecessionary tool on all vehicles purchased by midnight, October 31, 1967. One operating manager said:

> I actually had to call the finance director, on October 30, to see whether or not we should take advantage of this 10 percent write-off. He did not know. I can't honestly say whether he did not know if our division should take advantage of the write-off, or if he even knew about the 10 percent. I doubt he even knew about it. He should have known, both about the opportunity and its

effect on our operations, and reported to us the policy that had been established in Rendsburg. We should simply have been told whether or not we were allowed to take advantage of this write-off if we needed to.

The finance director, on the other hand, commented:

> The 10 percent special write-off was no special thing because we had pretty much invested what we need already. But we did take advantage of it with a contract of 600,000 marks on trucks, which we can buy later if we want them. A very simple proposition, we merely put 2 percent down to seal the contract and then, if delivery is needed, we can take as few or as many trucks as we want up to the 600,000 marks any time within the next year.

On the question of how he made this decision, he replied:

> I asked the department managers what they needed, that is the Rendsburg managers of building material and coal and the agency. One other division called us up to ask what they should do, and I told them they could order but only if they had a cancellation clause. There was nothing needed in the third division so I didn't even ask them, but if something does come up we can cover it with our 600,000 mark contract.

The second of these problems concerned the selection of a computer. Two study groups were formed, one, called the inner group, had Mr. Entz, the bookkeeping managers from Glückauf and Holtenau, the company's manager of accounting, and a computer specialist; another, called the outer group, was formed of the managers of the divisions and their major departments. Immediately upon formation of these groups, confusion arose. One operating manager believed that the inner group had been formed to "study the problem," and outer group had been formed to "consider the problem and help make the decision." With this in mind, he said:

> At the general meeting in which all the information was to be discussed, Mr. Entz opened the meeting giving his reasons for why the Univac 9300 would be a better computer. So there wasn't actually any opportunity to participate in that decision as a group. The meeting started off with a clear statement that the Univac would be the computer we were going to use.

Zerssen's manager of accounting, who had led the inner group study team, said that the the inner group's mandate was clear—it was to study Zerssen's needs and find an adequate machine, given Zerssen's lack of computer skills, from among several alternatives. The bulk of the work was done by the manager of accounting and the computer specialist; and they prepared recommendations for Mr. Entz that he accepted. Mr. Entz then called the general meeting of all the managers involved. According to the manager of accounting:

> The meeting concerning the computer, which all of the managers attended, was not conceived of as a decision-making meeting but rather as a meeting to transmit the decision that Mr. Entz had already made, based on the recommendation of his appointed staff group.

Without any reference to the above discussions, Mr. Entz was asked about the computer decision. He replied:

> A year of intensive work led us to what we chose. We had an inner group who made the decision and they showed me what they thought was needed. I worked partially in the group and then made the decision and we communicated back to the broader group. That was done without my direct involvement, yet I am quite sure it was done thoroughly and with the best possible result.

Entz in the Changing Role of Chief Executive

> When the owner grows up as ruler of a company, how can he possibly begin to see himself as a general manager, who also by accident owns the shares.
> —a division manager

> I'd want him to evaluate me by judging whether or not I'm handling his money as if it were my own.
> —a department manager

> I don't want to create another group of little kingdoms, but I have to develop a manageable organization so that I can get away from detail and concentrate on planning the future of this business.
> —Mr. Entz

These comments exemplify the multifaceted dilemma that faced Mr. Entz in implementing changes in Zerssen & Co. His talented managers wanted him to act like a manager but still saw him acting like an owner who did not manage, but meddled, while his lower level managers thought of him as an owner and did not understand what being a manager was all about. Mr. Entz, in turn, saw the need for breaking the tradition of the company so that it could be managed. His efforts to bring about organizational changes were complicated not only by this tradition behind his position and associated with his family, but also by the memory of a disastrous experience of his father, who, seven years earlier, when trying to bring about organizational change through the medium of two consultants, had met passive but effective resistance. One manager felt that rather let this problem arise again, Mr. Entz had sometimes made decisions for no other reason than to show who was the boss. But he further felt that new starts could not be made cyclical or they would be guaranteed of failure. In other words, Mr. Entz had only one chance, in this manager's opinion, to begin to bring about the changes he desired.

Mr. Entz heartily agreed that he had to establish his own leadership early, but he felt that his main problem lay in overcoming a tradition he had not made. He pointed out Zerssen's history of three autonomous units each managed by a man who centralized everything by making the decisions himself. Supporting this "decentralized centralization," as he called it, the units did the same things year-in, year-out. He thought the company and its units were now too large for such management; and such management would not allow Zerssen to meet the environmental threats that they faced. He thus felt it necessary to centralize policy making, but not in his hands alone, and simultaneously to decentralize operating decisions: "centralized decentralization."

However, his current plans and actions, when placed against the backdrop of the old tradition, resulted in conflicting messages being received by his managers at every level. To some, the idea of decentraliation of operating decisions smacked of a weakness not to be found in the previous chief executives—and perhaps a signal to reach for more autonomy. To others, the centralization of policy making meant that he was "not at all serious about all this decentralization talk." Aside from the computer, special write-off, and the financial planning decisions already mentioned, two other examples illustrate this dilemma. One Glückauf co-manager expressed grave concern over the meaning of his job because of this decentralization:

> I don't see how we can scatter the Glückauf division into five parts without destroying it and creating in its place separate scrap, technical, coal, oil, and building materials departments linked directly to Rendsburg. In all honesty, this means my job and my colleague's job will be absolutely unnecessary.

The other example came up in reference to a meeting called by Mr. Entz about a year before becoming chief executive in order to solicit ideas concerning Zerssen's future. To this meeting, which was held in a North German retreat area, all division, department, and accounting managers were invited. Everybody attended, except Mr. Fuhrmann and Mr. Lucks Late in 1967, three managers identified this meeting as a good start but apparently only another plan that had been shelved, as no further such meetings had been held. Mr. Entz, however, felt that it had been designed as a long-term policy meeting and that it would only be necessary to hold such a meeting once every two or three years. The top management group that he planned for was designed to meet regularly on policy, so department managers only had to be briefed and intermittently included.

COMPAGNIE CHILLON
ELECTRONIQUE

On January 19, 1962, Professor Harold Stevenson and Research Associate Joseph Wagner first met M. Michel Vallotton, founder and owner of the Compagnie Chillon Electronique. From M. Valloton's opening remarks, it soon became clear that Chillon El, as the company was known in trade circles, had experienced remarkable growth during its ten years of existence.

It also soon became apparent to Professor Stevenson and Mr. Wagner that M. Vallotton was facing a serious hurdle in the development of his company. As M. Vallotton remarked:

> So far, we have been a development engineering company specializing in electro-mechanical devices. We have traditionally been involved in contract development work, the production of prototype models, and, in recent years, even the manufacture of equipment on a small scale. But I am finding that production problems and odd jobs, such as customer service, are taking up more and more of my time.
>
> M. Lang, my sales agent in Zürich, tells me that standard production and repeat sales are where the money is to be made. I quite agree, but my heart is not really in this area. My interest lies in solving technical problems and in creating electronic devices.
>
> I often wonder if there really is a future for a small company like this. I think it is uncommon in Continental Europe to find companies as small as Chillon El that have been able to succeed in the electronics industry all by themselves.

Case Organization

In discussing their reactions to the meeting that had just taken place, Professor Stevenson and Mr. Wagner both felt that this situation was most interesting and one that might warrant unorthodox treatment.

The situation—the development of a commercial organization from a small technical embryo—was particularly appealing because it was comparable to the emergence of Electronic and other technically based, companies in the United States since World War II. Both men had been personally involved in the management of small technical companies in the United States, and this former experience contributed to their interest in Chillon El. As Professor Stevenson remarked, "I see in M. Vallotton a man who has succeeded in building the foundations of a growing company but who is no longer sure of where to go next. He is a manager who knows that he has a need but cannot define it. In view of his genuine interest in talking with us about his problems, why don't we do what we can to help him?"

For three reasons the researchers decided to deviate from their normal passive role as observers. First, the company faced a problem that was both critical and urgent. Second, M. Vallotton clearly indicated that he would appreciate any objective advice that could be given. Third, the researchers believed that they might be able to offer some constructive suggestions in view of their interests and experiences.

The format of the case attempts to reflect the unusual situation and case research approach. First, the data has been organized in chronological order, rather than by topical areas, in an effort to capture the evolution of the events. Second, the actions of the researchers are contained in the case because of the active roles that they played.

A First Meeting with M. Vallotton, January 19, 1962

The initial meeting—attended by M. Vallotton, Professor Stevenson, and Mr. Wagner—was held in the company's offices and lasted about one hour. Professor Stevenson started the discussion by describing IMEDE and explaining the purposes and mechanics of case research. To this, M. Vallotton replied, "I find your work very interesting, but I think you will find Chillon El much too small a company to merit a case study."

Professor Stevenson quickly assured M. Vallotton that big lessons could be learned from small companies and that Chillon El might well provide valuable case material. M. Vallotton accepted the comment and stated that he and his organization would be completely at the researchers' disposal if they should wish to make such a study. He then continued with a brief sketch of Chillon El's background.

THE COMPANY AND ITS HISTORY   M. Vallotton remarked:

> I started the company in 1953 with the help of my wife, a small income from royalties, a few contacts in industry, and some ideas that I wanted to explore further. I expect that our sales have reached more than 700,000 Swiss Francs (Sfr.) this past year, and we are receiving more inquiries for our work and services than we can handle. Our major customers are the watchmaking and machine tool industries. We now have about twenty-five or thirty employees.

I was educated in physics and mathematics at the College of Geneva and later received a M.S. degree in Physics in the United States. My industrial career began in 1946 with the Switch and Signal Union, Pittsburgh. In 1948, I became an engineering consultant for Westinghouse Airbrake Company in Europe. At this time, I also set up a little company to handle royalties received from a number of patents that I held. In 1952, I went to the U.S. to work in the Westinghouse engineering laboratories. After a year, I returned to Switzerland to start Chillon El. I might mention that Westinghouse Airbrake was one of my best customers in those early years.

I have enjoyed these past years because I have had a chance to be creative and to work with interesting technical problems. But lately there has been more and more need to become involved in the manufacturing of some products we have developed, to meet with customers, to service machines in the field, and to deal with many other commercial tasks, all of which are detracting from my engineering work.

I guess what I need is a man who can help me with manufacturing problems and business details, I am just not a businessman. I think it is more difficult to find a good businessman than a good engineer. Excuse me, but perhaps you would like to see the plant before the employees leave for the day?

Chillon El was housed in a modern two-story brick building located near Villeneuve, Switzerland. The upper floor was all one room with work benches containing electronic test apparati and tools conveniently placed. The main floor contained a number of rooms that served for special testing, display purposes, and office space. The total floor space of the plant was about 760 square meters. The plant appeared to the researchers to be exceptionally neat and clean. M. Vallotton's home was located next to the plant, the two buildings being complementary in architectural appearance; they were located on a 9,000 square meter plot of ground.

At the end of the tour, M. Vallotton added:

I am very sorry that our meeting must be so short, but, as you know, I am just about to leave on a three-week trip around the world. The main reason for this trip is to meet with our new Japanese agents in order to teach them how to service our equipment. They became our agents as a result of M. Lang's efforts and have already begun to sell our equipment. From there, I will go to the United States to look over my American competitors' products.

If you should have any questions during my absence or wish to see anything, please get in touch with my wife. She will be in change of the company while I am gone and will be glad to help you in any way she can.

A Second Meeting with M. Vallotton, February 27, 1962

A second meeting of Messrs. Vallotton and Wagner was held in the company's offices and lasted about two hours. During this time, M. Vallotton reviewed the functional areas of Chillon El in detail. He commented on the products, sales, finances, organization, his own job, an important personnel problem, and finally the search for a commercial director.

PRODUCTS   M. Vallotton began by giving Mr. Wagner sales pamphlets for each of the products currently in production. As he explained:

> It is no use to give you the catalogue because, although it was printed only last year, it is already out of date. I have not bothered to have it revised, because one can scarcely keep up with the product changes.
> In general, the products can be classified into three groups:

1. Products for the watchmaking and small precision machines industries;
2. Products for the machine tool industry; and
3. Miscellaneous products.

Here are some sheets that list our complete product line in each group.

Exhibit 1 lists the Chillon El products as of 1962.

Exhibit 1   **Compagnie Chillon Electronique**
The Company's Products in Production and Development February, 1962

GROUP I: Products for the Watchmaking and Small Precision Machines Industries

a. Automatic counter-distributor-packager, transistorized (for the counting distribution, and packaging of small parts)
b. Automatic counter-distributor, transistorized
c. Industrial ultrasonic generator, high power (for cleaning small parts)
d. Ultrasonic generator, high power (for ultrasonic welding)
e. Ultrasonic generator, low power, (for ultrasonic cleaning)
f. Photoelectric relay
g. Magnetic field generator (to control clocks)

GROUP II: Products for the Machine Tool Industry

a. Electronic speed control, transistorized (to ensure the constant speed of direct current [DC] motors)

b. A triple-phase variable frequency powersupply, transistorized (for three-phase motors where the speed must be variable over a fivefold range)
c. Command logic circuit—in development (electronic control of machine tools)
d. Numeric command control of machine tools by magnetic tape (in development)

GROUP III: Miscellaneous Products

a. Teaching machine (in development)
b. Electronic relay
c. Photoelectric relay
d. Vibrating distributor
e. Adjustable variator, transistorized (to control intensity of fluorescent bulbs)
f. Electronic chronometer
g. Road signals (electronic control mechanism for traffic lighting)

Source: Company product lists.

SALES   M. Vallotton continued:

Of the products that you see on those sheets the automatic counters and ultrasonic units have accounted for the major part of the product sales. In addition to product sales, as you know, we do contract engineering and also get some income from our service work. I mentioned last time that I expected our 1961 sales to exceed 700,000 Sfr. Well, they actually totaled 784,000 Sfr. Here is a list of our annual sales figures, which I have had prepared for you (see Table 1).

Mr. Wagner asked if he could also have a breakdown of recent sales figures by product groups or by the different sources of revenue activity, i.e., contract engineering, product sales, and service work. M. Vallotton replied

Table 1   Annual Sales for Compagnie Chillon Electronique and Predecessor Company, 1948—1961

Year	Annual Sales Sfr.	Year	Annual Sales Sfr.
1948	390	1955	78,831
1949	20,734	1956	120,067
1950	4,304	1957	220,128
1951	17,419	1958	291,540
1952	32,787	1959	280,476
1953	32,236	1960	412,264
1954	87,982	1961	784,687

Source: Company records.

that the company did not keep any sales statistics other than monthly aggregate amounts. He added that he would ask his secretary to compile these figures from the invoice copies, inasmuch as he himself would be interested in knowing this information. Exhibit 2 contains these data for 1957 and 1961.

Exhibit 2   **Compagnie Chillon Electronique**

Sales Breakdown by Market and Activity, 1957 and 1961
(in Swiss Francs)

1957

Activity \ Market	Watchmaking Industry	Machine Tool Industry	Miscellaneous	Total	Percent of total
Contract engineering	151,248	—	6,096	157,344	71.5
Products	7,704	—	51,168	58,872	26.7
Service and repairs	938	—	2,974	3,912	1.8
Total	159,890	—	60,238	220,128	
Percent of total	72.6	—	27.4		100.0

1961

Activity \ Market	Watchmaking Industry	Machine Tool Industry	Miscellaneous	Total	Percent of total
Contract engineering	109,176	9,600	33,000	151,776	19.3
Products	550,459	—	66,120	616,579	78.6
Service and repairs	7,848	144	8,340	16,332	2.1
Total	667,483	9,744	107,460	784,687	
Percent of total	85.1	1.2	13.7		100.0

Source: Company sales invoices.

FINANCIAL ASPECTS   Continuing his review, M. Vallotton said:

Despite the substantial growth of sales and activities over the past few years I cannot say that we have had any financial strain so far. As a matter of fact, I am forever receiving bankers here who want to loan me money. The company has had little or no need for external financing to date. Of course, we are talking about my need to borrow since the company is a proprietorship, and its resources are really my own personal resources. I have actually borrowed quite a bit of money to finance these buildings, but I did this mainly because it is advantageous under Swiss tax laws to use borrowed money for this purpose. You will have to speak to the people at the fiduciary company that handles our account, because they take care of all the tax matters. We just give them the operating figures, and they do the rest.

You can also get the financial statements that you were asking for from them. They can supply you with the information much better than we can, but you must be careful how you interpret those figures. The accounting has been done so as to assume a most favorable position with regard to taxation.

Exhibit 3 contains comparative balance sheets for the company for the period 1955–1960. Exhibit 4 contains comparative profit and loss statements for the period 1956–1960.

Exhibit 3   **Compagnie Chillon Electronique**

Balance Sheets as of December 31, 1955–1960

(in Swiss Francs)

	1955	1956	1957	1958	1959	1960
Current Assets						
Cash	9,234	6,222	1,198	77,063	5,588	3,604
Accounts receivable	11,400	20,542	12,948	4,680	42,012	76,188
Loan, M. Vallotton						8,935
Inventory			8,400	6,000	3,600	2,400
Deposits and retainers	1,200	1,200	1,200	1,200	1,200	1,200
Fixed Assets						
Vehicles	}4,800	}13,200	}9,600	15,600	10,800	10,800
Furniture and fixtures				3,840	4,800	3,600
Machines and						
equipment			1,800	7,800	16,800	15,600
Buildings and land			45,827	288,000	435,816	561,600
Total Assets	26,634	41,164	80,973	404,183	520,616	683,927
Current Liabilities						
Accounts payable	9,415	6,896	10,739	48,883	19,701	21,818
Customer advances			6,000	3,410	61,200	102,000
Bank loan			16,762	221,811	172,369	78,986
Loan, M. Vallotton	16,619	33,668	46,872	50,425	58,121	
Fixed Liabilities						
Deferable payment				79,054	22,721	32,604
for construction						
Bank loan					181,104	435,799
Reserves and Proprietorship						
Reserve for bad debt					4,800	6,120
Employee fund						6,000
Proprietorship						
(legal reserve)	600	600	600	600	600	600
Total Credits	26,634	41,164	80,973	404,183	520,616	683,927

Source: Company records.

As far as investments are concerned, I am sorry to say that we have no budget for this purpose. I have no real idea of how much money should or will be spent for tooling and equipment for the following year. I know that I should have some kind of budget for capital expenditure, but we just have not had the time to do this sort of planning.

Exhibit 4   **Compagnie Chillon Electronique**
Profit and Loss Statements, 1955–1960
(in Swiss Francs)

Year	1956	1957	1958	1959	1960
Credit					
Sales	120,067	220,128	291,540	280,476	412,264
Debit					
Salaries	31,341	54,590	60,760	64,489	106,518
Materials	c	c	130,214	102,700	150,545
Change in inventory	c	c	2,400	2,400	1,200
Cost of goods sold	n.a.	n.a.	193,374	169,589	258,263
Improvements	61,149	109,915	10,435	13,335	19,544
General expenses	20,583	38,328	62,453	65,422[a]	97,590[b]
Depreciation	3,736	4,781	22,425	29,706	33,531
Total expenses	116,809	207,614	288,687	278,052	408,928
Net benefit to Company	3,258	12,514	2,853	2,420	3,336
Total debit	120,067	220,128	291,540	280,472	412,264

a Includes an allocation of Sfr. 4,800 for reserve for bad debt.
b Includes allocations of Sfr. 1,320 for reserve for bad debt and Sfr. 6,000 for an employee fund.
c Contained in improvements.
n.a. = not applicable.
Source: Company records.

COMPANY ORGANIZATION AND JOB DESCRIPTIONS

The company's operating staff is more or less divided into different product-line and supporting groups, explained M. Vallotton, as he sketched an organization plan. We have an ultrasonic section, a counting machine section, and a miscellaneous product section. They perform the development and supervise the production of their products. To support these three groups, we have an electronic section, a mechanical section, and a technical section. Every section, except for the technical section, is headed by an engineer. (Exhibit 5 shows an organization chart of Compagnie Chillon Electronique for February 1962.)

As I mentioned, my wife is in charge of the office force and handles all the bookkeeping and accounting. We might also con-

Exhibit 5

Chillon Electronique
Company Organization Chart

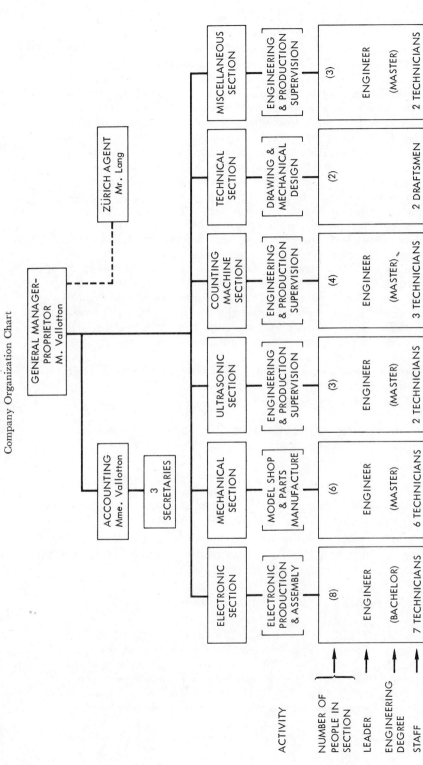

sider M. Lang, our Zürich sales agent, as part of the organization since he executes much of Chillon El's sales efforts.

As General Manager and sole proprietor of this company, I get involved in a lot of different jobs. I try to limit my activity in the company to a ten-hour day, five days per week. The employees work nine hours and fifteen minutes each day, excluding lunch, which comes to a 46¼ hour week. If I were to try to estimate how I spent my time, I would say that I use about fifteen minutes of each hour in which I am on the company premises controlling and administering the operations, and forty-five minutes studying the new technologies and keeping abreast of the electronics industry.

I make it a habit to tour the plant quickly every quarter of an hour to see what is going on, to control operations, and to give assistance whenever needed. This task really keeps me a captive in Villeneuve, but I have no doubt that it is one of my most important jobs. You may be interested to know that it cost me more money during my absence because I was not here to control the operations than the expense of the trip itself. It is not really a matter of trying to keep the engineers alert and working, but rather one of providing technical initiative and of helping them over trouble areas.

Looking at a full week's activity, I would say that on the average my week can be broken down as follows:

1.	Technical study and development engineering	28 hours
2.	Technical and personnel control	10 hours
3.	Business administration (e.g., correspondence)	7 hours
4.	Selling	5 hours
	Total	50 hours

Mr. Wagner remarked about the relatively small amount of time spend by M. Vallotton in selling Chillon El's products and services. M. Vallotton responded, "The company is already receiving more orders for products and engineering than it can handle. As a consequence I do not think that there is any need to spend more time on this function."

PERSONNEL PROBLEMS   M. Vallotton continued:

One of the difficult problems that I face is trying to get and keep good engineers. This company is in great need of engineers having the equivalent of a Masters Degree in education, about five years of experience, and specialization in a knowledge of semi-conductors and solid-state circuitry. The problem is that it is almost impossible to compete with American firms for engineers because of the very much higher salaries that they offer, even for work in Europe. An American company might pay three to four times as much in the U.S. as is normally paid in Switzerland. Just last month I lost one of my better engineers to an American firm in the United States. I had even offered to help this fellow finance a new home and a new boat that he could use on the lake, but the offer from the American firm was just too attractive.

So far, I have found engineers either through personal contact or through the engineer's own initiative in contacting Chillon El. After all, one of the main attractions of the company is its location in Villeneuve. Since there are only about ten electronic companies in Switzerland that do any significant amount of development work, those Swiss engineers who are looking for jobs in electronics will probably be aware of this company's existence, and if they are interested in coming to this area, they will probably contact us on their own.

The company cannot use inexperienced engineers, and so I have not done any recruiting among students. I am planning some day to send a student to the United States for engineering studies with the hope that he will return to the company, but I have not yet made any definite arrangements in this respect.

COMMERCIAL DIRECTOR   Toward the end of the interview, M. Vallotton remarked:

You know, I have been doing a lot of thinking about our previous discussion concerning the need for a commercial man in the company. Since then, the matter has become more urgent then ever.

If you remember, I mentioned that my wife was in charge of the office force and also took care of the bookkeeping. During my absence, she took full charge of the operations as best as she could. Unfortunately, the responsibilities and pressures were much more than should have been thrust upon her, and as a result she became seriously ill and has had to be sent to a hospital. Now, not only do I have the pressures of which I spoke to you during our last meeting, but I also have to worry about all those areas that my wife so ably supervised. I do not think she will be able to resume those jobs again.

Since my return, I have spoken with my brother-in-law about the problem, and he has put me in touch with a woman who might possibly be able to help me with the business. She is managing one of the sanatoriums above Montreux and is supposed to be a very good administrator. She was just here this morning to look over the office. Maybe she would be good for the commercial post in the company.

In view of these comments, Mr. Wagner felt that M. Vallotton was failing to distinguish between two different needs of the company. In Mr.

Wagner's opinion, the company had a long-term need for a commercial director who could carry the company further into the business of product manufacture and sales, and a short-term need for a special administrative assistant for M. Vallotton to replace his wife.

In order to make this distinction clear to M. Vallotton, Mr. Wagner asked a number of questions. He hoped that the questions would help M. Vallotton think out for himself what it was he was really bargaining for.

> Q. *What do you think that the commercial director will have to do for the company?*
>
> A. I expect that he would start by handling the bookkeeping for the company. From this point, he would assume more and more responsibility until he finally operated as a commercial director.
>
> The commercial director would advise me what we should do concerning the commercial aspects of the business. He would make up a budget for capital expenditures and other important expenses. He would control the business while I was away. He would also be able to meet and take care of visiting customers and other visitors whom I did not have to see for any special reason.
>
> Q. *What would be the qualifications that you require of this man?*
>
> A. I really do not know!
>
> I would expect that the man should be about forty years of age, and he should be able to speak French perfectly and also English and German well. It is very difficult for me to know exactly what kind of experience a commercial director should have. When it comes to engineers and technical people, I know exactly what kind of people we need in this company. I am afraid that my knowledge and experience is not such that I can make any equivalent kind of evaluation of a commercial man.
>
> Q. *What are you doing to locate this man?*
>
> A. I have been looking in the newspapers, and this is about all so far.
>
> Q. *What are you willing to offer such a man as regards pay, responsibility and authority?*
>
> A. It is hard for me to think clearly about what salary such a man should earn, because it would not be a productive salary,

such as is paid an engineer. Perhaps it would be between Sfr. 1,000 and Sfr. 1,500 per month. A very good engineer, one with five years' experience, is paid Sfr. 2,000 per month. This is pretty much the ceiling because the maximum charge that we can invoice for development engineering is approximately this amount.

Mr. Wagner went on to query in general terms what other forms of remuneration might be considered to get a good man. Although it was not possible to determine any definite limits, M. Vallotton expressed a recognition that it might be necessary and even advisable to include a percentage of the company's sales as part of this pay, or even a stake in the ownership of the business.

A Third Meeting with M. Vallotton, March 29, 1962

A third meeting of Messrs. Vallotton and Wagner was held at the company offices and lasted about two hours. During this time discussions were held about the selection of a commercial director, about M. Vallotton's personal values, and also about the contract engineering activity of the company. During the meeting, the researcher accompanied M. Vallotton during one of his normal "control-tours."

COMMERCIAL DIRECTOR

I have been giving a lot more thought to our conversation concerning a commercial director for the company, commented M. Vallotton in opening the meeting, and I would like to let you know what I have done since we last met. Over the years I have received a number of inquiries and even offers for association or merger from some of my watchmaking customers who were anxious to diversify into other fields. I had never really seriously considered taking such a step before, but under the present circumstances I wonder if such a move might not be a way to solve my problems. What I think would be very good would be to merge with some company that could take over the administrative and commercial operations of Chillon El, leaving me free to conduct the development engineering part of the business. Perhaps we could form a joint company where I could keep a majority, of let us say 51 percent. I would consider such a merger with a British company, an American company, or any other electronics company for that matter.

With this in mind, I recently paid a visit to the Office Vaudois Pour le Développement de l'Industrie et du Commerce to see if they could help me locate a company that would wish to enter into such arrangements with me. I spoke with M. Breband, the Director of the Office, and explained the situation. As soon as I finished telling M. Breband about my thoughts, he began to discourage me from seeking to merge. He said that it would be a shame to let others into the company at this time. He recommended instead that I find a man who could assume the commercial responsibility of the company and then suggested that I contact a M. Durret who might qualify for the job.

I first telephoned M. Durret and discussed the possible job opportunity with him. He expressed an interest, and we consequently met here. During our first meeting we agreed that he examine the company closely to see if he would like to take the job. He then spent a period of about fifteen days, four to six hours each day, examining the company from top to bottom. I think it would be advisable if you would speak with M. Durret since it might be valuable for you to see the company through someone else's eyes. Furthermore, after his careful examination of our records, he can probably tell you more about the commercial side of the company than I can. I also would like very much to have your opinion about M. Durret's qualifications for the job.

Mr. Wagner agreed to meet with M. Durret as suggested. The only information about the candidate that M. Vallotton could provide was that M. Durret was a fifty-seven-year-old Swiss who had been a manager of an oil refinery in Argentina.

When Mr. Wagner asked about the woman who had been interviewed for the position, M. Vallotton replied that she had decided against it because she felt the job would be to much for her.

One example of how the company is suffering from my inability to take on more responsibility, continued M. Vallotton, "can perhaps be seen from the way manufacturing and service activities are stealing men who are better qualified to carry on development work. Just today, two very good engineers are away from the company in order to service some counting machines in Neuchâtel. This is always happening, and the interruptions are hurting our engineering work. I know that I should take on more engineers specifically for the jobs of production and service engineering. But I cannot take this step, because I cannot run a larger organization than I already have. The first step, I believe, is to get this commercial man we have been talking about, and then we can add to the staff as necessary.

PERSONAL VALUES   Following M. Vallotton's comments of his search for a commercial director, Mr. Wagner directed the conversation to a discussion of the personal values that M. Vallotton held concerning his interest in Chillon El.

I think that I would list my personal business objectives in the following order of importance to myself:

1. To conduct the business in such a way that it would only place a reasonable workload on me, so that I can also have time for personal interests and my family life;
2. To be able to devote a large part of my working time to technical exploration and creativity;
3. To earn enough money to allow my family and me to live comfortably and to remain free from financial worry.

I might add that I am a little concerned about the possible effects of the workload on my own physical health. Now that I have to deal with the whole operation without my wife's help, I am a little worried that the total workload could be as overwhelming and damaging to my health, as it was to my wife's while I was abroad. I find that I am already becoming irritable and nervous and tend to snap at people for little things; this is not good for the people here.

What I would like to do is get a man in the company who could take care of the commercial problems. Then I would like to get a man in who could be in charge of the technical side of the business. This would allow me to think more about the business as a whole and also permit me to work on those technical problems that really interest me. But it will be some time before this arrangement will be settled.

Product Activity

The fountain of our growth has been and will continue to be our contract development engineering work. All of our present products have stemmed from this work, and we will continue to broaden our product line from new developments.

I would say that, on the average, about 80 percent of the development work is supported by customer contracts and the remaining 20 percent is "in-house" (at company expense). The rights for patents on all development work sponsored by customers of course goes to the customers. Chillon El, however, is fortunate in that most of the customers limit their demands for patent rights to cover their own specific application or field of interest. We are normally free to develop good prospects further for other applications. Most of our "in-house" development work has originated as an extension of the more promising contract work.

In those cases where our "in-house" development work grows too big for us to support alone, we would go to some large company for help or financial support. As an example, we are now looking for someone to support Chillon El in its development work of a digital position controller for certain machine tools. This position controller had originally been developed under contract for a machine tool company who used the product for lathes. We were permitted to extend the process for other machines at our pleasure, so now we are trying to develop this product for grinders. The project seems promising, but we would like financial backing from a grinder manufacturer to obtain funds for its development and to have a ready customer who will then use and market our controller. I intend to visit the industrial fair at Basel next week to talk with various prospects there, and as another step I might write various U.S. manufacturers to see if they would be interested.

CONTROL TOUR OF PLANT   The researcher accompanied M. Vallotton on one of his normal control tours of the plant. During this walk, M. Vallotton only stopped to speak with two of his engineers concerning some technical point of their projects. The whole tour took about four minutes. M. Vallotton said that this tour was typical.

A Fourth Meeting with M. Vallotton, April 9, 1962

The fourth meeting of Messrs. Vallotton and Wagner was held in the company offices and lasted about two hours. The major part of the discussion centered on the problem of selecting a commercial director. M. Vallotton also commented on a special project with which he had been concerned during the past week.

COMMERCIAL DIRECTOR   Prior to this meeting, Mr. Wagner had prepared a preliminary outline of a job description for the position of a commercial director of Chillon El. A copy of this outline was given to M. Vallotton, and the two reviewed the outline together, Mr. Wagner making explanatory comments as appropriate. During the discussion, M. Vallotton did not ask any questions. At the conclusion, M. Vallotton remarked, "For the first time I am beginning to see what a big job the position of commercial director could be. There is really so much to be done."

After the outlines had been reviewed, Mr. Wagner mentioned that he had not yet heard from M. Durret. M. Vallotton answered that he had not been in touch with M. Durret since the last meeting because the latter had been traveling. M. Vallotton then added, "Perhaps M. Durret is not the right man for the job because of his advanced age. You know, M. Durret wants to work only six hours per day, and he would like to receive Sfr. 1,500 per month. But don't you think I could hire him for a trial period until December?"

OTHER CONCERNS   M. Vallotton then brought up a new subject:

You might be interested to know that I have just bought a large plot of land next to our present property. I have had my eye on this property for some time and finally took advantage of an option that I held, although it was very expensive. The main reason I bought it was to prevent others from coming in and erecting a tall building that would obstruct the view from my home and the plant. To cover the cost of maintaining it, I shall have a gas station erected on the property. I have been in touch with a number of oil companies, all of whom are anxious to put a gas station on the spot. At least we can keep the profile of a gas station quite low. My only real worry is to clear any zoning regulations that the city authorities may cite.

A Fifth Meeting with M. Vallotton, April 25, 1962

The meeting of Messrs. Vallotton and Wagner was held in the company offices for about one and a half hours. During this time the men discussed engineering personnel and the selection of a commercial director.

PERSONNEL PROBLEMS

I am sorry to keep you waiting Mr. Wagner, said M. Vallotton as the two men met, but just twenty minutes ago one of my engineers came into the office to tell me that he would be leaving the company. Fortunately, this man is not one of my better engineers, and he will not be any great loss to the company. However, I will have to find another engineer to replace this man.

When asked as to the reason why this man had resigned, M. Vallotton answered that he had had on many occasions to correct this man's performance and that it was probably these reprimands that had caused this man to seek other employment.

M. Vallotton continued:

You may be interested to know that I have just recently made an offer to my two best engineers of a one percent share of all sales of their own department's instruments. I think this might give them an incentive to become real leaders of their departments. This is not to say that these men will necessarily become department heads, because I would still like to find a top-notch man who can be placed in charge of both departments. I am not sure, at this time, in which direction I will move. This will depend largely on the results I receive from these two engineers.

The two departments concerned were the Counting Machines and the Ultrasonic Equipment Departments, and the two engineers were aged thirty-four and twenty-two respectively. As a result of questioning, Mr.

Wagner learned that there were no titled or responsible heads in the company other than M. Vallotton himself.

COMMERCIAL DIRECTOR   M. Vallotton continued:

> As for M. Durret, I have just about decided that he is not the man for the position. I have spoken with M. Lang (Zürich agent) about M. Durret, and he completely agreed that the man for the position of commercial director should be relatively young and certainly dynamic. M. Durret does not seem to meet this need when you consider his desire to work only thirty hours per week.
>
> Nevertheless, I did ask M. Durret to meet you but he said he did not care to. He said something about "I know about IMEDE, and I do not wish to see those people." He did, however, make a tentative appointment to see M. Lang. I think that M. Durret did not wish to meet you because he was afraid that you might tell him that he was not qualified for the job.

M. Vallotton went on to say that he had heard that it was possible to get a good man straight from the university for about Sfr. 20,000 per annum plus some percentage of the company sales. He then asked Mr. Wagner whether he thought such a man might not be good for the job.

After these discussions, Mr. Wagner presented M. Vallotton with a finished set of outlines that described the job of Commercial Director of Compagnie Chillon Electronique and also listed criteria that might be used in evaluating candidates for this position. This set of outlines was slightly changed by Mr. Wagner from the preliminary set as a result of the previous discussion with M. Vallotton and a review with Professor Stevenson. Mr. Wagner suggested that a full discussion of the documents be postponed until M. Vallotton had had an opportunity to review them thoroughly. A copy of the outlines and a covering letter is contained in Exhibit 6.

M. Vallotton finally remarked:

> I would guess that I could hold out for about two years, if I had to, in order to find the right man for this job. I do not believe that I could carry the load any longer than that. If I cannot find a good commercial director in that time, I will either have to merge with a larger company who could provide the administrative assistance that I need, or sell my company. I have another alternative of just continuing operations at a reduced level, but I do not think this is a good way to do business.

Exhibit 6   **Compagnie Chillon Electronique**
                            Documents Relating to the Selection of
                                a Commercial Director for
                            Compagnie Chillon Electronique

Monsieur M. Vallotton,
General Manager,
Compagnie Chillon Electronique,
Villeneuve
Switzerland

                        JFW/VT   April 25, 1962

Dear Monsieur Vallotton:

  The first of the two attachments under cover of this
letter is submitted to you to help you better understand
with which managerial functions a new commercial executive may become concerned in Compagnie Chillon Electronique. The second attachment attempts to indicate some
of the abilities and characteristics that you should
consider in your evaluation of candidates for this position. Although we have already discussed preliminary
versions of these documents for some hours, I should,
however, like to elaborate on certain aspects of these
present versions.
  Basically, the job of commercial director has been
specified in view of the needs of the company as a whole,
and my understanding of your personal objectives and
capabilities. I believe that it is important not to
limit our thinking to your own currently pressing administrative problem; that is, your urgent need for assistance in bookkeeping and administrative work. This
problem, too, is important, but it should not be confused
with the broader needs of the company.
  I should like to emphasize that not only has the job
description been designed specifically for Compagnie
Chillon Electronique but that, moreover, it should be
considered valid only for this one point of the company's
development. It is not to be viewed as a general criteria
for a commercial director of an average European company
or even for your company at some later stage of organization. The most striking example of the special nature
of this job specification is the inclusion of production

Exhibit 6 (cont.)

management within its scope. This inclusion was made, as you may well understand, because of your personal interests and desires. As the organization grows and is better able to support a broader management team, such functions as production supervisor and accounting chief will be placed under the authority of new men.

Attachment I is organized in the following manner. In the left-hand column, the business functional areas in which the commercial director will be involved have been listed. These comprise general management, marketing (sales), finance, production, and a limited aspect of personnel. Especially and totally excluded are the important areas of technical research and development, which will remain initially under your direction, as well as legal and other specialist activities. In the right-hand column, the more important duties have been outlined in some detail. Finally, in order to assist in the definition of the many duties listed, the post of commercial director has been subdivided in the center column into a number of managerial posts equivalent to those performed in large companies.

Attachment II, listing the most important experiences and characteristics that the new commercial director should possess, can only be used as a check-off list. Of course, certain items are much more important than others. We have already discussed this point to some extent. Eventually, we should try to decide which attributes or combination of attributes you would be more willing to overlook, since it is unlikely that any one candidate will meet all the requirements.

I hope that these outlines will help you with the problem we have been considering. Certainly, they are not to be taken as the last or best words on the subject.

Please call me as soon as you are prepared to review these documents.

Very truly yours,

Joseph F Wagner

Joseph F. Wagner
Research Associate

Exhibit 6 (cont.)   **Attachment I**
                           Compagnie Chillon Electronique
                         Job Description of the Commercial Director

Business Function	*Equivalent Position*	*Duties*

General Management		1. To help the managing director (M. Vallotton) set the general policies, objectives, and goals of the company. This duty involves answering questions such as:
		  a. What kind of company do we want in five, ten, twenty years?
		  b. What business activity is most consistent with our personal values, business experience, and the company's past accomplishments?
		  c. What kind of professional people, workers, products services and so forth, should the growth of the company be based on?
		2. To inform the managing director of the impact on the financial, marketing and production activities, and resources in the company for courses of action under consideration.
		3. To conduct special studies, as required.

Marketing (Sales)	Marketing Officer	1. To make major marketing decisions, in consultation with the managing director, regarding such matters as:
		  a. The relative marketing emphasis among various products and market areas;
		  b. The proper methods of selling the product (such as agents versus company's salesmen);
		  c. The proper channels of distribution, and even the selection of markets for new products;
		  d. The extent of employing various marketing activities such as advertising, trade shows, and special promotions.
		2. To execute advanced product planning based on market considerations, pointing out:
		  a. New product areas for development;
		  b. Desirable revisions of existing products.
		3. To provide the managing director with timely records of sales performance and marketing costs.

Exhibit 6 (cont.)   **Attachment I (cont.)**

Business Function	Equivalent Position	Duties

Marketing (Sales)	Sales Director	1. To conduct sales planning:
		  a. Sales estimates;
		  b. Sales expenditure budgets.
		2. To supervise the sales force:
		  a. Agents;
		  b. Company salesmen;
		  c. Technical service representatives.
		3. To sell the products:
		  a. Calls on customers;
		  b. Meetings with customers in Villeneuve;
		  c. Attendance at fairs and exhibitions.
		4. To supervise field customers' service activities:
		  a. Service and maintenance of equipment by Chillon El engineers;
		  b. Service and maintenance by independent agencies.
		5. To supervise field market research conducted by the sales force.

	Marketing Services Director	1. To conduct and present market research:
		  a. Library research;
		  b. Special field research;
		  c. Research report.
		2. To display products at exhibitions.
		3. To plan and conduct general promotion activities including advertising.

Finance	Financial Officer and Controller	1. To make major financial decisions, in consultation with the managing director, regarding such matters as:
		  a. Major investments;
		  b. Borrowing policies and procedures;
		  c. The capital structure of the company.
		2. To conduct financial planning and control, for example:
		  a. To devise a capital budget;
		  b. To evaluate major capital equipment purchase proposals;
		  c. To project fund-flows, and to make up pro

Exhibit 6 (cont.)   **Attachment I** (cont.)

Business Function	*Equivalent Position*	*Duties*
Finance	Financial Officer and Controller	forma (future) financial statements and statistics. 3. To maintain a contact with financial sources: a. To maintain contact and perform negotiations with banks, stock shareholders, debtors, and so forth; b. To keep informed on special financial arrangements available for exporters. 4. To maintain control over all corporate funds.
	Chief Accountant	1. To evaluate and design the accounting and control systems—as the company grows and changes form, to introduce the necessary changes in accounting and control. This will involve significant effort when the possible new production center or corporate structure is set up. 2. To supervise bookkeeping and accounting clerical work—this includes the accounting of billing, purchasing, employees' salary, and so forth. 3. To work with the external accountant and to check his work and advice.
	Purchasing Officer	1. To devise purchasing procedures and policies. 2. To conduct negotiations concerning important purchases or source relationships. 3. To supervise the regular purchasing of expendable items.
Production	Production Manager	1. To advise the managing director concerning major decisions on production and capital equipment purchasing.
	Production Supervisor (temporary)	2. To supervise production work and to control manufacturing materials.
	Customers' Services Department Head	3. To supervise service and maintenance of customers' equipment sent in to Villeneuve.

Exhibit 6 (cont.)   **Attachment I (cont.)**

Business Function	*Equivalent Position*	*Duties*
Personnel	This job is an integral part of the jobs listed above.	1. To supervise clerical and commercial personnel in finance, sales, and accounting. 2. To supervise production personnel (possibly temporarily). 3. To train personnel for supervisory positions, such as chief accountant and production supervisor. 4. To recruit clerical and commercial personnel and initially production laborers (a production supervisor may perform this job in the future; production and service engineers should be recruited by M. Vallotton). 5. To advise the managing director in regard to salaries, raises, promotions, and disciplinary actions concerning all personnel under his organization.

Exhibit 6 (cont.)   **Attachment II**

Desirable Attributes of the Commercial Director

A. *Experience and Understanding*
   1. General business experience:
      a. A familiarity with the modern techniques of the various business functions, for example:
         i. *in finance*—to be familiar with cost accounting, return-on-investment calculations, and capital budgeting;
         ii. *in marketing*—to be familiar with sales planning, market research, and selling techniques.
   2. Small business experience:
      a. An understanding of the special dangers involved in operating a small business.
      b. An appreciation of the special strengths of a small business.
      c. An awareness of the required versatility of organization and of management in operating a small business.
   3. Experience with a research and development business:
      a. An appreciation of technical problems and the timing involved.
      b. Some experience in conducting a business that has a high proportion of engineers and that is technically oriented.
   4. Familiarity with and contacts in the electronics, machine-tool, and

watchmaking industries, especially in Switzerland, the United States, and Continental Europe. (The United States and certain Western Hemisphere countries represent the area of potential growth for this company.)

5. Experience in conducting, supervising, and analyzing market research for technical products.
6. An understanding of electronics and of electro-mechanical technology.

B. *Personal Characteristics*
1. A broad business background and an ability to be flexible in his work.
2. Ability with languages—French, English, and German.
3. A fairly young man (thirty to forty-five years of age) so as to be able to grow with the company and to tie in his career for the long-term.
4. "Self-starter" who can work without supervision or guidance. (This is important since the managing director would not be knowledgeable about a number of his activities.)
5. A man of high integrity and character.
6. A personable individual who can work well with all people.
7. A healthy and energetic man.

C. *Educational Qualifications*
A degree in commerce and/or electronics, or equivalent experience.

A Meeting with M. Lang, April 27, 1962

Messrs. Lang and Wagner met in the office of Lang S.A. in Zürich for about two and a half hours. During that time, Mr. Lang described his relations with Chillon El and commented on various aspects of sales and products. Mr. Lang also expressed his views concerning a possible commercial director for Chillon El.

Lang S.A. had been organized for the purpose of representing a number of small noncompeting manufacturing firms in Switzerland who were dealing or were interested in the export market but were not large enough to exploit it by themselves. In 1962 the company represented more than ten clients, most of whom manufactured equipment relating to some aspect of the watchmaking and machine tool industries. The company's turnover in 1962 was about Sfr. 6,000,000, of which Chillon El accounted for Sfr. 300,000 or about 5 percent. Mr. Lang himself was a young man of about thirty-eight years of age, who appeared to Mr. Wagner as being very dynamic and competent.

In reviewing the relationship between Lang S.A. and Chillon El, Mr. Lang commented:

> In 1958 I was looking for electronic counting and packing apparati because of requests from some of my foreign contacts.

As a result of this search, I ran across Chillon El, which was then only a small laboratory producing a few prototype models of counting machines that were excellent for my limited purpose.

After several meetings we agreed that I would handle the full line of Chillon El products, as a general sales agent. I made an exception and also represented the company in Switzerland because of my many contacts in the watchmaking industry that would, and did, result in substantial sales within a short time. As part of my service to Chillon El, I have begun to develop a line of product pamphlets (Exhibit 2) and other sales literature.

SALES

The contractual agreements between us have always been based on straight commission. The commissions range between 10 percent and 20 percent of sales. The spread above 10 percent is related to any special arrangements and servicing that the agencies have to handle. For example, the commission for products sold in Japan is 20 percent, because our collaborating agency in Japan handles all service and maintenance. Likewise, a premium above 10 percent has to be paid for sales in France, because we are obliged to carry accounts for three months on all sales. On the other hand, the charge is normally 10 percent for sales in Switzerland, because Chillon El's engineers conduct all service and maintenance.

I would estimate that the geographical distribution of my company's sales for Chillon El was as follows:

Switzerland	20%
Germany, France, U.K., Sweden	40
Japan, U.S.A.	20
Other areas	20
Total	100%

Automatic counting machines accounted for 75 percent of these sales and ultrasonic apparati accounted for the remaining 25 percent. The distribution sales breakdown was similar for both machines.

As far as real growth potential, I believe, that the greatest opportunity will be in the four European countries now accounting for 40 percent. I consider the U.S.A. a difficult market, first because the technology is so advanced in electronics there and, second, because of tariff problems.

PRODUCTS

There are five products that would be significant in our discussion of the Chillon El line. This list would include the automatic counting machines, the ultrasonic cleaners, the automatic speed control for DC motors, the command logic circuit for machine tools, and a machine tool control by magnetic tape programming.

The main product of the company is the automatic counting machine. An unfortunate problem is that the market for this product, as it now is, is severely limited. We expect to sell about twenty in 1962, but I would estimate a total market potential, and I do not mean per annum, of only one hundred machines. The reason that the market is so restricted is that such an expensive machine is only worthwhile when the parts to be counted are of high value; otherwise, a simple measurement by weight is more practical. Furthermore, this machine will only allow parts that are not too large or that are not intricate to be counted. If the parts are intricate they might hook or stick together, and then the conglomeration of pieces would be counted as one. These limitations of the machine pretty much restrict its application to the watchmaking industry. It would be wonderful if there were some way to improve the capabilities of the machine. As it now stands, the selling price of this machine is approximately Sfr. 25,000.

The ultrasonic cleaning apparatus is the other product that we are currently selling. We expect to sell about fifteen to twenty of these machines in 1962. This machine, however, has a much greater market potential than that of the counting machine, and I would estimate a future potential of one hundred machines per year. The reason for this enlarged sales potential is that these units are not limited to the watchmaking industry. It is a very reliable machine with a high capacity and also a relatively low price. It is probably one of the best machines of its class in Europe. The selling price is about Sfr. 9,000.

Another product that is of interest is the automatic speed control for DC motors.[1] It is now in an advanced stage of development, and we are planning to conduct some test sales and market research on this item soon. Such a testing period will last six to twelve months and may result in requirements for further product design. When we know that we have a good product, we will then support a full sales effort in Switzerland for one year. We limit our initial efforts to Switzerland so that we can easily take corrective action, should that be required. I expect the future market might range between three hundred and one thousand units per year when sales are developed. The selling price might be about Sfr. 1,200 per unit.

The other two products in development that show promise are the command logic circuit for machine tools and a machine tool control by magnetic tape programming.[2] Both of these products have a high market potential because they will apply to the vast machine tool industry.

---

[1] Item II. a in Exhibit 1.
[2] Item II. c and II. d in Exhibit 1.

I am very pleased with these new products because they are Chillon El's first step away from complete dependence on the watchmaking industry, which after all is a rather limited market. I think it is important for the company to develop products that will be directed toward markets such as the general machine tool industry with much higher potential requirements than is available from the watchmaking industry. It is difficult to say for which markets new products will be developed. There is no telling what new inspirations will result from the laboratory work, and with electronics, there are really no restrictions.

COMMERCIAL DIRECTOR   As the conversation came around to the subject of the company itself and some of its more general problems, Mr. Lang remarked:

As I see it, there are two jobs to be done at Chillon El: the first is to guide the electronic engineers in their work, and this M. Vallotton is well qualified to do; the second is to direct the commercial activity of the company, and for this he needs someone else. He simply does not have the time to conduct both the technical and the commercial side of the business nor is he really interested in the commercial work.

Mr. Wagner then asked Mr. Lang in what areas of activity he thought the commercial director should be involved. Mr. Lang answered:

It is difficult to pin down all of the many duties such a man will have to do without carefully reviewing the situation. However, I think that the man would be occupied in the following ways: (1) leader of the commercial staff; (2) supervisor of the Sales Department; (3) supervisor of the Purchasing Department; (4) head of Accounting; and (5) involved with the general administrative work. The man must, of course, be supported in these activities by adequate staff.

I do think it is very important to add that such a man must be capable of working on his own initiative and not be the type that would go to M. Vallotton for every decision. After all, what M. Vallotton needs is a man who will relieve him of worries, not bring additional ones.

*   *   *

Having completed the case, Mr. Wagner planned to see M. Vallotton once more. The purpose of this meeting was to answer any questions M. Vallotton might have and to make any suggestions that might be of help.

Mr. Wagner realized that M. Vallotton and he had explored only one problem area to any depth during their past meetings, that of the need for and selection of a commercial director; and even here, the process of analysis had only been started. Mr. Wagner wondered whether it would not be of greater value to review some of the other problem areas that they had only touched upon in their discussions. He remembered M. Vallotton's concern about the problem of getting and keeping good engineers and whether to set up a manufacturing organization separate from the development company. Mr. Wagner also thought of other possible problem areas that should be brought to M. Vallotton's attention, such as the financial impact of setting up manufacturing facilities and that of advanced product planning.

Mr. Wagner believed that not only would it be appropriate to extend their discussion to these topics, but he also felt that they ought to move beyond general analytical evaluations and begin outlining some specific actions and programs.

SOLARTRON ELECTRONIC
GROUP LTD.

"I do not think we could have expanded as we have if it had not been for forward planning," said Mr. John Bolton, chairman and managing director of the Solartron Electronic Group Ltd. in November 1958. "Nor would I have the same degree of confidence in our future as I do if we were not continuing to plan ahead."

The Solartron Electronic Group, with headquarters in Thames Ditton, Surrey, England, designed and manufactured two main types of electronic equipment: (1) A range of approximately eighty laboratory and other precision test instruments ranging in price from £50 to £700, such as oscilloscopes, power supplies, amplifiers, and servo test equipment. In the operating year ending June 30, 1958, sales of such instruments comprised 66 percent of total company sales. (2) A variety of higher unit price "systems engineered" products, which were broadly defined as electronic systems designed to perform a series of operations comprising a definable task. In a majority of cases these systems were designed, constructed, installed, and serviced by Solartron for customers relatively unfamiliar with electronic equipment. They comprised single products or families of products each one of which was so chosen that it could constitute an important field of activity for companies in the group. They included: (a) *An electronic reading machine* designed to read digits zero to nine, eight alphabetical letters, and four accounting symbols at speeds up to three hundred characters per second. The first production model of this machine had been sold to Boots Chemists (a chain of pharmacies) at a price of £23,000 and was scheduled for delivery in November 1959. It was to be used in connection with a digital computer to analyze daily the sales registered on tapes from approximately two thousand cash registers. During the 1958/59 year six additional orders to large firms were expected to bring the total to seven. (b) *Radar simulator devices* that reproduced the radar image of single or formations of aircraft or missiles for defense planning and training purposes. By November 1958 £400,000 worth of orders, varying from £60,000 to £180,000 per system had been received from defense and military authorities of various NATO and other European countries including Germany, Italy, and Sweden. (c) *High speed electronic checkweighers* designed to checkweigh packaged products, after filling, as they moved on a production line at a speed of up to 120 packages per minute and at an accuracy of 0.2 percent; to deflect and count underweight and overweight packages; and to signal continuously to the packing mechanism any correction required to keep the delivered weight constantly correct. Thirty-two production units at £1,500 each were planned for 1958/59 for sale largely to food and other consumer goods manufacturers. (d) *An X-ray spectrometer* that provided an automatic, nondestructive method for the quantitative analysis of crystalline materials, such as metals and chemicals. Six units at approximately £10,000 each were planned for 1958/59 for sale to scientific and engineering organizations. (e) *Cybernetic teaching machines,* the first of a planned series of inductive logic computing devices that were designed to teach punch-card operators the manual skills needed for punch-card preparation by giving a series of exercises, evaluating progress and mistakes, and automatically varying the speed of the exercise while concentrating on those parts in which errors were made. Ten to twelve units at £500 each were planned for 1958/59 for sale to companies employing punch-card equipment. (f) *A range of analogue computer "building blocks"* from which a custom built analogue computer chiefly for use in solving complex mathematical problems could be assembled.

The Group also performed precision engineering and design and development work on a contract basis, and it sold electronic equipment made by other firms through its domestic and foreign sales organizations.

Exhibits 1, 2, and 3 show actual and forecast sales by product group, balance sheets, and profit and loss statements for recent and forthcoming years. The table below indicates the rate of growth of Solartron through June 30, 1958.

Statistics Indicative of Solartron Growth
Years Ending June 30

	1950	1951	1952	1953	1954	1955	1956	1957	1958
Personnel	18	22	66	110	240	400	550	600	83
Floor space in sq. ft. (000)	4	4	6	8	30	35	65	70	8
Assets £(000)	8	12	34	74	226	420	654	902	134
Deliveries £(000)	13	20	34	90	152	399	758	1005	143
of which exports (000)	—	—	—	—	10	20	80	186	33
Development write-off (000) (specific products)	n.a.	n.a.	n.a.	n.a.	n.a.	24	38	76	7
Net profits after taxes and development write-off (000)	—	1	1	3	5	4	23	10	3
Nonspecific development expenditure[a]	—	—	—	—	10	25	50	75	12

a Written-off in overheads, e.g., market research, planning new factories, etc.

Exhibit 1   The Solartron Electronic Group Limited

Schedule of Deliveries 1954/55 to 1957/58 and Targets through 1962/63

Product Group (in £000's)	Actual				Possible Targets for Next 5 Years				
	1954/55	1955/56	1956/57	1957/58	1958/59	1959/60 Max.	1960/61 Max.	1961/62 Max.	1962/3 Max.
	£	£	£	£	£	£	£	£	£
Solartron Laboratory Instruments Limited									
Standard Instruments	300	589	741	945	1,400	2,000	2,750	3,500	4,500
Government & outside contracts	42	63	37	57	60	100	150	250	250
Solartron Engineering Limited									
Government & outside contracts	35	87	115	96	60	100	125	150	200
Solartron Research & Development Limited Government & outside contracts	5	10	44	75	100	100	125	125	150
Data processing	—	—	—	32	130	250	300	400	500
Radar Simulators Limited	—	—	6	111	250	400	500	600	750
Solartron Industrial Controls Limited	—	—	6	12	60	150	250	300	350
Solartron Electronic Business Limited	—	—	2	10	50	200	300	400	500
Merchanting & sundries	16	9	54	96	140	200	250	275	300
Total Deliveries	398	758	1,005	1,434	2,250	3,500	4,750	6,000	7,500
Export content included in above figures	20	80	186	335	600	1,000	1,500	2,250	3,500
Total orders	400	800	1,250	1,900	2,750	4,000	5,500	7,000	8,500
Total personnel at year end	400	550	600	830	1,250	1,750	2,250	2,750	3,500

Note: It was apparent in March 1959 that it would probably be necessary to extend the 1962/63 targets to 1963/64, that is to spread the five-year program over six years.

Exhibit 2

The Solartron Electronic Group Limited

Outline Profit and Loss Accounts for the Years Ended June 30, 1955/58 and Targets through 1962/63

(In £000's)	Actual				Possible Targets for Next 5 Years				
	1954/55	1955/56	1956/57	1957/58	1958/59	1959/60	1960/61	1961/62	1962/63
Deliveries	398	758	1,005	1,434	2,250	3,500	4,750	6,000	7,500
Less: Direct labor	75	119	141	192	270	420	560	720	900
Materials	134	226	289	468	750	1,180	1,590	2,000	2,500
Gross margin on deliveries	189	413	575	774	1,230	1,900	2,600	3,280	4,100
Add: Overheads in development & W.I.P. increase	30	60	60	48	70	100	100	100	100
Gross margin on trading	219	473	635	822	1,300	2,000	2,700	3,380	4,200
Less: Manufacturing overheads	105	214	258	356	480	730	950	1,150	1,400
Administration overheads	20	50	63	66	90	120	160	200	250
Commercial overheads	53	123	197	226	320	480	620	720	900
	178	387	518	648	890	1,330	1,730	2,070	2,550
Net profit before dev. write-off	41	86	117	174	410	670	970	1,310	1,650
Development write-off (specific products)	24	38	76	72	125	175	225	300	400
Net profit before appropriations	17	48	41	102	285	495	745	1,010	1,250
Loan interest & pref. divs. (gross)	9	21	31	45	48	50	50	50	50
Ordinary dividends (gross)	4	—	—	—	22	44	88	132	220
Sundry appropriations	—	—	—	2	—	—	—	—	—
Taxation	4	15	4	34	120	220	320	433	517
Retained profits	—	12	6	21	95	181	287	395	463

Exhibit 3

The Solartron Electronic Group Limited
Balance Sheets

(In £000's)	Actual						Forecast		
	30/6/55	30/6/56	30/6/57	30/6/58	30/6/59	30/6/60	30/6/61	30/6/62	30/6/63
Monthly sales volume	55	70	125	200	250	400	500	600	750
Cash at bank	77	1	3	7	5	—	—	175	283
Trade & sundry debtors	99	154	259	400	475	750	1,000	1,200	1,500
Stock-in-hand & materials, etc.	85	89	121	158	200	270	350	450	560
Finished instruments	29	96	105	118	150	180	200	225	250
W.I.P. production	59	62	72	233	270	350	440	540	650
W.I.P. development	40	72	103	90	75	50	25	—	—
Associated companies	—	—	—	109	150	150	175	200	225
Total Current Assets	389	474	663	1,115	1,325	1,750	2,190	2,790	3,468
Freehold land & buildings	40	74	118	88	96	100	110	120	130
Improvements to leasehold factories	2	3	5	7	75	100	125	150	175
Equipment plant & machinery	22	36	35	46	125	175	225	275	325
Furniture, fixtures & fittings	11	26	31	34	80	110	130	160	200
Motor vehicles	13	23	33	37	17	15	20	20	25
Goodwill	18	18	17	17	17	—	—	—	—
Total Fixed Assets	106	180	239	229	410	500	610	725	855
Total All Assets	495	654	902	1,344	1,735	2,250	2,800	3,515	4,323
Bank overdraft	75	139	173	58	118	77	20	—	—
Progress payments	—	—	21	109	75	—	—	—	—
Trade & sundry creditors	104	117	166	410	410	600	700	800	900
Hire purchase commitments	10	18	18	18	40	75	70	65	60
Current taxation	8	18	21	30	20	150	260	375	505
Total Current Liabilities	197	292	399	625	663	902	1,050	1,240	1,465
Future tax	6	18	20	51	150	260	375	505	625
Unsecured loans	53	85	218	364	365	350	350	350	350
6% pref. shares (£1 each)	97	100	100	100	100	100	100	100	100
7½% pref. shares (£1 each)	95	100	100	100	100	100	100	100	100
Ordinary shares (10/- each)	47	47	47	47	220	220	220	220	220
P. & L. A/c & Reserves	—	12	18	57	137	318	605	1,000	1,463
Total All Liabilities	495	654	902	1,344	1,735	2,250	2,800	3,515	4,323

Organization

In November 1958 Solartron was comprised of the Solartron Electronic Group Ltd. (the parent company), seven domestic, and three overseas subsidiaries. The parent company was owned largely by members of management and their families. A number of employees were also shareholders. From 1951 to 1958 a majority of the common shares had been held by Mr. Bolton. (See Figure 1, pp. 436–37.)

Solartron's senior executive group was the eight-man Group Board of Directors, which met monthly and included two men for each of the following major functions: general management (including personnel administration), production, and finance, and one each for marketing and research and development. The average age of these men in November 1958 was thirty-eight years. As indicated in the company letterhead they held the degrees shown below. They held other positions in addition, as follows:

J. E. Bolton, D.S.C., M.A. (Cantab), M.B.A. (Harvard), M.B.I.M.
Chairman and Group Managing Director (temporarily holding Chairmanship of Solartron Industrial Controls and Solartron Radar Simulators).

L. B. Copestick, A.M. Inst. E., A.M., Brit. I.R.E.
Chairman and Managing Director, Solartron Research and Development Ltd.

J. E. Crosse
Chairman and Managing Director, Solartron Engineering Ltd.

R. A. Henderson
Director of Robert Benson Lonsdale, Merchant Bankers.[1]

Eric E. Jones, M.S.M.A.
Group Marketing Director (Managing Director of Solartron-Rheem Ltd.)

E. R. T. Ponsford
Chairman and Managing Director, Solartron Laboratory Instruments Ltd.

Bowman Scott, M.B.E., M.B.A. (Harvard), B.S. (Eng.), A.C.G.I., A.M.I.E.E.
Group Personnel Director and Managing Director of Solartron Electronic Business Machines Ltd.

J. L. E. Smith, M.A.
Director of Coutts & Co., Bankers[2]
Chairman of Industrial Automation Developments Ltd.

The purpose of Board meetings was described as follows in a memorandum written by Mr. Bolton to explain and defend his practice (once

---

1 Robert Benson Lonsdale was an investment banking firm.
2 Coutts and Co. was a commercial bank.

criticized by the outside members) of allowing Board meetings to "wander away" from a strict interpretation of the agenda.

> ...they are not, in these days, intended for transmission of information because this can be done effectively via detailed management data in the form of monthly reports....
>
> It seems to me that (their) main purpose lies in the area of creative discussion in order to achieve not only a better understanding of each other but also of the human and technical factors that govern the job we are doing. These factors of course change almost continuously. This in my view is how an effective and flexible policy (whether it be at board level or at research level) is rough hewn from the range of opinions that a balanced team should have. As you may have seen, I usually endeavor to bring out something controversial so that at least one member of the board will get hot under the collar about it. It we can each of us do this without fear then I think we are creating a very powerful team relationship that will insure that we are approaching the various new problems that we shall continuously face in a coordinated and constructive way....

In addition to the general management functions performed by the Board, the parent company also provided a number of services to the Group, including purchasing, personnel, Group Commercial activity (such as overseas selling effort), publicity, secretarial, accounting, and internal consulting (Group Productivity Services Department).

The Boards of Directors of certain of the subsidiary companies did not actually meet; management responsibility rested with the managing directors and other senior executives concerned. The relative size and functions of the various subsidiary companies is indicated in the chart below (Companies of the Solartron Electronic Group Ltd.) (subsidiaries wholly owned except where otherwise indicated). Exhibit 4 shows operating profits of the various subsidiaries for the nine months ended March 31, 1958.

Exhibit 4

The Solartron Electronic Group Limited and Its Subsidiary Companies

Abridged Manufacturing, Trading, and Profit and Loss Accounts
for the Nine Months Ended March 31, 1958

	S.E.G.	S.L.I.	S.E.	S.R. & D.	S.E.B.M.	S.I.C.	R.S.	Total
Subsidiaries:								
Sales		£365,996	£221,473	£114,389	£ 9,798	—	£15,226	£726,882
Increase/decrease in W.I.P.		64,775	(5,850)	30,589	4,667	30,874	—	125,055
Net Output		430,771	215,623	144,978	14,465	30,874	15,226	851,937
Materials consumed		272,995	75,189	60,977	2,596	16,964	4,069	432,790
Direct wages		47,318	38,507	29,213	5,275	6,182	4,959	131,454
Manufacturing overheads		99,145	79,302	39,028	10,713	13,326	6,157	247,671
Works cost		419,458	192,998	129,218	18,584	36,472	15,185	811,915
Net Profit (Loss) of Subsidiaries		11,313	22,625	15,760	(4,119)	(5,598)	41	40,022
		430,771	215,623	144,978	14,465	30,874	15,226	
Holding Company								
Sales	917,756							
Cost of sales	636,742							
Gross profit	281,014							
Commercial overheads	157,779							
Admin: overheads	46,412							
Net Profit of Holding Company	76,823							76,823
								116,845
APPROPRIATIONS: Unsecured loan & loan stock interest gross							21,734	
Dividends gross							10,103	31,837
PROFIT OF GROUP BEFORE DEVELOPMENT WRITE-OFF, TAXATION AND PARTICIPATING DIVIDEND =								£ 85,008

435

Figure 1   Companies of the Solartron Electronic Group Ltd.

	Date of Incorporation	Personnel Strength in Nov. 1958	External Deliveries in year ending June 30, 1958 (000)	Deliveries as a Percentage of Total	Functions
United Kingdom: Solartron Laboratory Instruments Ltd (SLI)	1948	375	£1002	69.9%	Manufactured approximately eighty standard and laboratory and precision instruments at Thames Ditton plant in production lots of batch size (0–50 per month). Sales were made largely to scientific and engineering organizations in the U.K. through a sales force of approximately 20 technical service representatives (T.S.E.S).
Solartron Engineering Ltd (SE)	1951	194	£ 96	6.7	Supplied the mechanical engineering requirements of the individual companies within the group. Also undertook a selected amount of outside work to insure competitiveness and to utilize fully its capacity. Located at recently built Farnborough plant.
Solartron Electronic Group Ltd (parent company)	1954	280	£ 96	6.7	General management and staff activities, including export sales, as described in the foregoing section.
Solartron Research and Development Ltd. (SR & D)	1954	144	£ 107	7.5	Performed outside contract R&D work; all research and development on standard electronic instruments; plus a portion of the work on "systems engineered" products (chiefly data handling and analogue computers). Also produced prototypes and initial production runs of instruments and other equipment (such as magnetic data tape recorder). Located in Dorking, Surrey.

Company	Year				
Solartron Electronic Business Machines Ltd (SEBM)	1955	20	£ 10	0.7	One of three "development" companies at the Farnborough plant. Responsible for developing, manufacturing, and marketing (in cooperation with Group Commercial department) electronic business machines primarily for office use. Principal product in 1958 was the reading machine.
Industrial Automation Developments Ltd. (jointly owned with Scribbans-Kemp Ltd)	1956	—	—	—	Responsible for developing under contract hydraulic programmed actuator for industrial packaging use. Work actually being carried out by SIC.
Solartron Industrial Controls Ltd (SIC)	1956	29	£ 12	0.8	Responsible for developing, manufacturing, and marketing industrial controls[a] under "quasiconsulting assignments." Principal products checkweigher, X-ray spectrometer, and punch card teaching machine.
Solartron Radar Simulators Ltd. (SRS)	1957	58	£ 111	7.7	Responsible for developing, manufacturing, and marketing radar simulator devices for defense and training purposes. Principal product aircraft simulator sold to NATO countries.
Solartron Rheem Ltd. (Jointly owned with Rheem Co.) of New York	1958	—	—	—	Responsible for developing products of joint interest to Solartron & Rheem.
Totals		1100	£1434 of which £335 was export	100% of which 23.4% was export	

Overseas:

Solartron Inc. (Associated Company in U.S.A.)	1956	6
Solartron SRL (Italy)	1957	3
Solartron GMBH (West Germany)	1958	12

Associated Companies in India, France & Sweden and a subsidiary in Holland were in process of formation.

[a] An industrial control was broadly defined as a device to improve the quality of an industrial process by sensing some property of the product, processing the data thus obtained, and actuating the controls of the plant or machine involved to achieve a desired end. The variety of sensing effects that might be used ranged from simple weighing to spectroscopic examination by X-ray.

A number of Solartron's objectives had been stated explicity in recent years either in the firm's Annual Reports or in other written documents as quoted below. Others were expressed orally by company executives as quoted or paraphrased below:

For the long run: Expansion into rapidly growing sections of the electronics industry as fast as "balanced attention" to the various factors of production would allow, taking into consideration: (1) rate of development of the existing staff; (2) rate of integration of new personnel; (3) rate of development of the company's markets; (4) pace of R&D activity, as influenced by human and financial considerations.

For the next five to ten years: (1) Achieving more intensive effort in the major fields already chosen, in order to build "strong, viable, subsidiary units in those areas." There were to be fewer radically new products developed than in recent years, and emphasis was to be placed instead on perfecting and increasing the applications of equipment already developed. (2) Increasing export sales of Solartron products in order to broaden the company's customer base and spread development costs over an increased number of production units. (3) Making more effective use of the relatively large organizational structure created for the purpose of preparing for future expansion.

With respect to people:

> Our emergent philosophy of life lays great stress not only on the importance of the individual as a person, but on the essential need to devise a "permissive" system in which individual initiative is nurtured and encouraged to make its maximum possible contribution to the whole.... We recognize that in selecting a team of potentially outstanding young men and women at all levels and in training them to carry increasing responsibility, the natural corollary is that they should want to make a personal contribution to decisions affecting their particular working group or company's future, in an atmosphere that is as free as possible of status barriers and prejudice. Furthermore that they should want to know that those who demonstrate outstanding qualities of leadership and judgment can progress to Board level.

In line with this objective the following policies had been adopted: (a) Whenever possible promotions to senior positions were made from within the organization. The principal exceptions to this rule were senior specialists such as Mr. Christopher Bailey, designer of the reading machine, and Mr. George Sanders, head of the Group Productivity Services Department. (b) To the extent possible, managers at all levels of the company were given the opportunity to discharge their responsibilities as they thought best within the broad framework of agreed objectives. In this regard, Mr. Gordon Bates, who was leaving Solartron to do management consulting in the consumer marketing field, said that he and many of his colleagues felt themselves to be "part of an experiment in British industry." He contrasted Solartron with a number of older, larger firms that he and his friends had worked for, saying that "the standard form in many of these firms is to treat the younger men like useless appendages during the first fifteen years or so, and then gradually let them in on one aspect of operations. Here the form is to give a man a little more than he thinks he can handle as soon as possible." (c) To encourage personnel to increase their potential the company paid the fees of suitable training courses and conferences, while "Training Within Industry" classes were held during working hours. There was also a library of technical and management books. (d) An attempt was made to keep executives throughout the company informed on current developments. In this regard, Mr. P. B. H. Cuff, Group Purchasing Director, said that in his early years with the company Mr. Bolton had on several occasions stopped him to tell him of recent events that had no immediate bearing on his work but were of great interest to him in understanding the company's position. By 1958 annual management conferences were being held for all senior and junior executives in which board members described the current state of affairs and plans for the future in their areas. (e) To avoid unnecessary status barriers reserved spaces in the parking lot had been eliminated; on most memoranda the names of executives were alphabetized; the use of first names was encouraged; and all personnel regardless of position and function were expected to "clock in" at the same time. (f) Since 1954 the personnel selection and training functions had been entrusted to a director, Mr. Bowman Scott. (g) To assure attractive working conditions there was also a pension scheme, employee restaurant, Health Center, Sports and Cricket Club, and a trend toward yearly or longer term employment contracts.

With respect to formal organization:

> Our policy is to develop a number of virtually independent company units within the Group, each concentrating on either a specialized function such as research, or a logically grouped sales and production activity such as test instrumentation. . . . We envisage each individual company unit growing to a size of perhaps five to seven hundred personnel—a size that we believe will meet on the one hand the need to maximize personal satisfactions, and on the other to operate near to the optimum unit size for the technical requirements of our particular industry. The dangers of growing apart are apparent, but we are confident that through our group structure and because of the experience our senior executives have gained in working as a very closely knit team, we

shall be able to achieve the principal benefits, of centralized policy-making and the economics of joint services, without hampering the exercise of individual initiative in the separate companies.

Mr. Bolton was particularly desirous of avoiding what he termed a "peaky" organization, in which management thinking would be dominated by his personal views. In this regard he said he had found that people in an organization tended to create a pinnacle, even when the managing director was anxious not to become an all-powerful father-figure. People had come to him, for example, and suggested that he ought to buy a new car, since his Jaguar was not as new as it might be and therefore not fully appropriate to his position. He said that one of a number of problems that could arise in a peaky organization was the difficulty of hiring number two men who were intimidated by the individual brilliance of their prospective bosses and feared being completely submerged by them.

In contrast with the "peaky" organization, "great-man" approach to management, Mr. Bolton believed rather in what might be termed a "natural" approach. He expressed the opinion that managerial needs were, like vacuums, abhorred by nature and ultimately filled of their own accord. For example, he considered that if he and Mr. Eric Jones, Group Commercial Director, had not pushed product diversification "two other chaps would have, and the result would have been the same." Similarly, he believed that if Solartron had not developed the reading machine or the radar simulator, some other firm would have.

With respect to finance: (1) To increase borrowed in relation to equity and preference funds on a 2:1 ratio. (2) to use company funds principally for working capital; and other sources, such as leaseback arrangements, for the plant and fixed assets. (3) starting in 1958/59, to establish a progressive common stock dividend record against the possibility that in three to five years there might be opportunities for greater expansion than visualized in 1958. (Although profits had been sacrificed for balanced and rapid growth in the first ten years increasing dividend payments were believed to be important ultimately because company executives considered that English companies were judged on a dividend rather than earnings yield basis). (4) To achieve gross margins[3] on products in full production (beyond the initial progress payment or pilot production stage) of 60 percent or more. (5) To progressively reduce overhead spending to approximately 33 percent of projected gross sales.

With respect to R&D:

(1) ...we have established a prime objective of achieving entirely new developments which show substantial improvements

---

3 Sales price less bought out materials and direct wages.

in contemporary design practice. As a rough rule of thumb we have endeavored to produce new designs that will be some three to five years ahead of the existing "state of the art" in other countries, and in this way we hope to achieve a breathing space in which our new products can become fully established before the pressure of competition might catch up with them. (2) In contrast with many military organizations, where research funds are all too often taken as a symbol of power, and prevailing sentiment is to get as much as you can and to hell with the whole, we are attempting to build the feeling instead that R&D funds are a means by which a subsidiary or research team can make a contribution to the Group and that this contribution, rather than the power involved, is the important thing. (3) Eventually we are aiming for more and more new projects at SR&D—tending more toward research and away from development—and we intend to have the development work done by the individual manufacturing subsidiaries.

Product Planning

EARLY PRODUCT HISTORY   The initial development of Solartron's product line has been described as follows:[4]

> The start and growth of the enterprise has followed a familiar pattern; at first a handful of men in a shed, and then a leapfrogging into larger and larger premises as the work prospered. In 1947 two young engineers, Mr. E. R. Ponsford and Mr. L. B. Copestick, scraped together a few hundred pounds, hired a disused stable and set up as makers of electronic test instruments. Both had been apprenticed in the electronic industry and were aware of shortcomings in the available equipment. In 1948 they registered the name Solartron, but eighteen months were to pass before they were in a position to produce an electronic instrument of their own —the first proprietary laboratory amplifier on the British market. The main activity of the two directors and their three employees at first was the development, manufacture and repair of equipment under government contract. This steady work enabled them to lease a small factory in Kingston, and additions to the Board brought enough working capital to proceed with more ambitious plans. Two years after the introduction of their first instrument the company was invited to exhibit at the Physical Society's Exhibition, and this they regarded as a mark of acceptance in the sphere of electronics.

---

[4] From a paper presented by a company executive on May 27, 1958 before a meeting of the Seminar on Problems in Industrial Administration at the London School of Economics and Political Science.

The early years were hard but rewarding in every sense except the material. Many of the founders' old associates and trainees were anxious to join the company, even at reduced wages, for the sake of opportunities to come.

Ploughing back of all profits was never adequate to finance the rapidly growing production and development, and substantial additional capital was introduced when Mr. John Bolton and Mr. John Crosse joined the company in 1951 and 1952 respectively.

Thus, by June 30, 1953, at the end of the first five years of its corporate life, Solartron had become established with 110 personnel, 7,500 square feet of factory space, and a turnover of approximately £100,000 per annum. There were then two companies, Solartron Laboratory Instruments Ltd., with a growing product line of electronic test instruments, and Solartron Engineering Limited, which was responsible for the precision mechanical engineering and metalwork aspects of Solartron products. The stage was set for the broadening of the organizational and products base and substantial increase in sales volume during the second five years 1953/58.

DIVERSIFICATION   During its second five years Solartron diversified into "systems engineered" products. The initial decision to do so was made in 1952/53. It was based on what were considered to be the limitations of laboratory instruments as a product line on which to base future growth. The reasoning as reported in 1958 was as follows (paraphrased):

On one hand, delivery periods must be kept short. For once a customer has ordered an instrument he expects rapid delivery (a month or less) or will seek an alternative source of supply. On the other hand, inventories must be kept at a minimum, because as a rapidly growing company our finances will be limited. Operations will therefore be continuously balanced between the risk of an inventory buildup if sales decrease, and a scramble to increase production if sales increase.

Solartron could safely base its expansion on laboratory instruments only if it specializes intensely in one type of instrument, such as certain firms have done in the United States. Because of the size of the U.K. market, however, this will not be feasible.

Our wisest move would be to seek additional "systems engineered" products with higher unit prices and longer delivery requirements. Such products would broaden our customer base and reduce the complexity of current operations. Because they would lengthen our order book it would also be easier to obtain outside finance.

In order that we can make the maximum contribution and utilize our resources to the fullest, these new products should be in rapidly expanding sectors of the electronics industry where it will not be necessary to design somebody else out of the market.

CHOOSING NEW PRODUCT AREAS   In connection with this analysis, Mr. Bolton prepared a rough evaluation of the industry's future growth along the lines of Figure 2, p. 444. This was based on the assumption that already developed sectors of the industry would remain a constant or decreasing proportion of the total, while undeveloped and as yet unknown sectors would become larger. An overall fivefold increase over twenty years was estimated.

ENTERING THE NEW FIELDS   As a consequence of this analysis, Solartron began slowly to diversify its product line during the second five years of its existence. Impetus to enter the new fields came from various sources. In 1953 and 1954, a study was made by the company of the business machine field, and the conclusion drawn was that the most important undeveloped requirements were: (1) fast input devices for computers; (2) memories with large storage capacity and quick access; (3) equipment for sorting information. Of these the first was selected for development, and work was started on the reading machine. In 1954 a decision to develop the check-weigher was made, based on the belief that this was a fundamental requirement and work started in the field of industrial controls. In 1955 evidence of strong interest by the Swedish Air Ministry touched off development of the company's radar simulator device. In 1957 "Anglicization" (adaptation to British components) of an American designed "data-tape" recording machine was begun under license from the Consolidated Electrodynamics Corporation. During this same period Group sponsored research and development carried out in the field of data processing (chiefly analogue computers).

In speaking of the company's diversification, Mr. Eric Jones, Group Commercial Director, said, "Not everyone was agreed that we should go into systems, perhaps partly because when you look two or three years ahead in a new field it looks more like science fiction than commercial reality.[5] I think even J. B. (Mr. Bolton) thought that diversification might be premature. But I pushed radar simulators, he pushed business machines, we got agreement to develop the checkweigher, and here we are today."

ALLOCATING R&D FUNDS   "We are compromising between forward research and spending on present products," said Mr. Bolton, "and we are doing it by eye." Mr. Bolton stated that this involved making choices between "picking up basic principles at an early stage, or applying more

5 Exhibit 5 contains an article from *The Economist* on the commercial applications of data processing equipment like the reading machine.

Figure 2   Solartron Estimates of Future Growth
                                    of Electronics Industry

Market Sector	Solartron rough estimates of Sales of Sector as a % of the total electronics industry	
	1953	1973
1. *Domestic Radio and TV* Comments: Few export sales; domestic market will probably reach a plateau as in the U.S. Would have to compete with large, well-established firms. Not for us.	25%	10%
2. *Communications* Comments: Major European networks already installed. Sales will be for improvement and replacement purposes. Industry cartelized; suppliers often affiliated with communications firms. Not our cup of tea.	20%	8%
3. *Radar and Navigational Aids* Comments: A growing field that should have possibilities for us. Assume market percentage will remain the same. Total increase will thus be fivefold.	5%	5%
4. *Military Requirements* Comments: Assume total static even though electronic share will increase, therefore ultimate percentage of the market down. Not so interesting as some other sectors.	35%	15%
5. *Data Processing* Comments: Increasing use for computation as well as to reduce paper work. Digital computers have already been extensively developed by several large firms but analogue techniques and a number of other problems remain. An interesting field for us.	negligible	20%
6. *Industrial Controls* Comments: Ultimately will be larger than data processing. Since automation of production operations will come after the automation of paper work, however, this sector will develop more slowly. This deserves our attention.	negligible	15%
7. *Scientific Education* Comments: May never loom too large but relatively untouched. Has possibilities.	negligible	5%
8. *Atomic Energy* Comments: Insignificant at present but will grow.	negligible	5%
9. *Miscellaneous*	15%	17%

intensive effort to remaining problems in already developed areas—such as increasing the reliability of a particular kind of oscilloscope." He explained that in the most recent operating year (1957/58) this choice had been made by allocating Group R&D funds to the various product groups in proportion to their estimated growth in sales over the subsequent five-year period. Mr. Bolton added that "to some extent we are still a little paternalistic in this regard, in that I am still doling the money out, as from a family kitty, basing individual allocations on the individual family members' estimates of their needs scaled down to fit the total budget."

PICKING INDIVIDUAL PROJECTS   According to Mr. James Rothman, administrative assistant for SR&D, the principal sources of ideas for new projects were as follows: (1) logical extensions of existing products, either by simple adaptation, such as redesigning a machine to read in polar as well as x and y coordinates; or by using new principles or components. Interest for such extensions came mainly from the existing staff, and they were the source of the largest number of new projects. (2) Outsiders who joined Solartron and brought new ideas with them. This was the main source of radically new developments. (3) Outside requests of the "we need help badly" variety. In this respect senior engineers were encouraged to visit with and discuss customer problems. As many as two thousand visit reports were also received each month from the Technical Service Engineers in which they reported on unresolved difficulties they had encountered in the field.

Exhibit 5   **Solartron Electronic Group Ltd.**

Computers or Clerks[a]

The electronic computer is ten years old, a teen-ager among industrial machinery with a teen-ager's problems of adjustment to society. During its first decade, when it was being used largely as a research tool for resolving equations beyond the capacity of mathematicians, the decision to buy a computer or not depended on the straightforward point whether a company or a government research department had enough work of this kind to justify the investment of upwards of £150,000 in a single computer. There was no question of doing the work by other means. Such abstruse scientific, aerodynamic and even economic calculations were either done on a computer or not done at all. But now computers are being offered to a wider market as machines that will mechanise clerical work and control production processes, and they are being judged by different standards. Here a company does have a choice between two alternatives—it can choose between electronic computers and human clerks, or laborers.

---

a From *The Economist*, December 6, 1958, pp. 915–16. Reproduced with permission.

Exhibit 5 (cont.)

The saving of labor by a computer can be exaggerated. The real gift it brings to management is the opportunity to cut through the red tape and the paper work that assumes alarming proportions once a company's operations reach a certain size. Much of this routine could now be transferred to computers, inside which it would be promptly assimilated, sorted, added to, subtracted from, pigeonholed, filed for future reference, while a neat printed record appeared at the other end. But is this worth doing?

The answer varies from company to company, depending on how vital it is to the sound management of the business to have quick access to day-to-day information. Boots, which is making a big changeover to electronic accounting, obviously sets great store by prompt reports on the changing level of sales and stocks for the sixty thousand different items sold by the company's retail shops. Bibby's manufacturing animal feeding stuffs, uses a computer to keep watch on rapidly changing raw material prices, so that the feeding-stuff formula can be varied to make allowance for them—a job that requires an unexpectedly large number of weekly calculations. Tube Investments, selling products that vary from order to order, uses a computer to sort the orders, stipulate the most economical raw material, give manufacturing instructions and prepare cost figures, spending thirty seconds on planning and printing instructions about each order, against thirty-five minutes by ordinary methods. The Banco di Roma has just installed a computer to handle all the accounts of its two hundred–three hundred branches. Many other examples can be found among the one hundred-odd computers now in use in this country where resort to a fast-thinking computer has probably improved a company's efficiency. But users are noticeably reluctant to quote any estimate of the amount of money saved by electronic accounting. Boots calculate that the company's change to electronic bookkeeping will stop the annual 10 percent rise in clerical staff that has gone on now for several years. But even this type of saving is difficult to assess.

Computers still have obvious limitations; skillful handling is needed to make them earn their keep. Initial cost is the biggest single factor. At the first exhibition in the world devoted entirely to electronic computers, which has been open in London during the past ten days, the price of the twenty-seven different models on sale ranged all the way from £20,000 to £800,000, the cheapest being made by Elliott and the dearest by IBM. A computer consists of two basic parts; one that does the arithmetic and is relatively cheap to make, and the other that acts as a "memory" and stores all the relevant data and instructions upon which the computer operates. There are several ways of building a "memory"; some of them are cheaper than others but unfortunately they are also slower-working. If the "memory" is slow, this tends to hold up the rate at which the computer works.

Exhibit 5 (cont.)

As a rough rule of thumb, the cheaper computers have small "memories"; the more expensive the machine, the bigger its memory and the faster it can get at the facts. In scientific calculations, calculating ability is frequently more important than capacious memory, so the small computers, many of which are only just on the market, are ideally suited for research purposes, providing the maximum computing ability for the minimum cost. For business accounting, however, a big "memory" is more important than calculating ability; the machine is required to hold data about stocks, or invoices, or temperature levels, or railway schedules, or insurance policies, and carry out one or two simple calculations on them when the need arises. The ideal computer for business accounting therefore tends to come in the £100,000 to £300,000 range.

It would be unfair, however, to blame the high cost of computers entirely on the electronics engineer. The computer itself frequently costs less than the mechanical equipment that goes with it. The second big limitation on the use of computers is in the design of this equipment. A computer cannot read—yet. Data have to be fed into it in a form it can understand, from punched cards, punched tape or managetic tape, and fed out again in a form that the operator can understand. This requires tape readers, mechanical feeds, and printing equipment, all of which operates at unnaturally high speeds. The purely mechanical difficulties created by these high speeds make all this ancillary equipment extremely expensive, considering the basic simplicity of its design. Some steps have been taken towards the development of electronic "readers" that could read type faces and transmit the results directly to the computer; the specification put out by the banks for a machine that would "read" magnetic characters printed on cheques has given a marked fillip to this type of research.

The first two "reading" machines of their kind were exhibited at the computer exhibition, one of them being Solartron's complex reader, which is now said to be able to decipher not only carbon copies but even handwritten characters. The cost is £25,000 for a machine "reading" three reasonably similar type faces; the much simpler apparatus developed by Electric and Musical Industries solely for "reading" a specially designed type printed in magnetic ink, and intended primarily for cheque sorting, might cost one-tenth of this amount when in production. These figures give some indication of the cost of the trimmings that go with a computer. Ferranti, the first company to make computers in this country, designing machines used mainly by laboratories for vast calculations, sells one basic computer for £50,000, but the full installation costs £160,000.

The third big limitation on the use of computers lies with the customer rather than the machine. Production engineering must be fairly well understood in

Exhibit 5 (cont.)

industry by now, but the application of the same technique to office work is not. In most cases, wholesale changes in routine are needed to fit the job to the computer, and it is doubtful whether this is always appreciated by the buyer. Commercial computers have a vast appetite for work, but they are not the "thinking machines" that scientists were discussing at the National Physical Laboratory a week ago. They cannot plan the way a job ought to be done; they can act only on data and instructions fed to them by human operators; and if the work is badly planned, the computer can do nothing to correct it.

Some experts have a shrewd suspicion that managements have found it more difficult to adjust their methods to computers than they had expected, rather in the way of those housewives whose pressure cookers sit unused on the top shelf. Their evidence is the large number of commercial computers used—on the admission of the owners—mainly for calculating wage packets. To put a computer to this work is like taking a steamroller to crack a nut—a useful way of filling odd moments but a sad under-employment of the machine's great capabilities. But wage calculation happens to be one of the easiet jobs to tailor for a computer—this is why manufacturers frequently use it for demonstration purposes—and it gives both computer operators and management a breathing space to learn how to use their new toy.

Although manufacturers can supply computers with a plan of work built into them, this is essentially a job that can be carried out only by men who know and have worked in the company buying the machine and who understand its business. The planning of work for a computer goes far beyond the mere mathematics of working out a code of instructions telling the machine how to do the job. It calls for a certain amount of imagination to grasp the computer's potentialities for helping the company, and, although the manufacturer's staff can give advice on what is or is not technically possible, they cannot be expected to understand how each business works or the best way that it should be run. Management must be prepared to spend some time learning the job itself. It may take months, or even years, to learn how to get maximum value from a computer. In some cases, it is still going to be cheaper and less troublesome to do the job with clerks.

Over one hundred possibilities for new projects were generated by these various sources in the course of a year: Of these approximately 10 percent were chosen to be worked on, and the remainder were either rejected or held in abeyance. In the case of SR&D, decisions were made by Mr. L. Copestick, Managing Director, and Mr. R. Catherall, Research Director, and in the case of SEBM, SIC, and Radar Simulators by the senior executives involved. Decisions were made on a basis of these criteria: The estimated sales and gross profits that would result from making a given investment; and the interest of the engineers involved in carrying out the project.

Although formal calculations were not always prepared in selecting projects, a work order stating the estimated completion date and cost was issued at the time a project was begun. During the course of the project monthly comparisons of work-in-progress (labor, materials, and overhead) were made with the budgeted cost by the senior executives and project engineers involved.

In late 1957 Mr. Rothman had been asked to devise a formula so that the decision whether a proposed project should be financed with Group funds could be made by a representative committee on the basis of the project's profitability ratio (the ratio of present value of profits over three years to the initial investment). Efforts to formalize the research and development program had been under way for over five years. This formula was enthusiastically received by Mr. Bolton, but it had not been implemented because it had been viewed more coolly by senior SR&D executives, on the grounds that the present system worked well and that the estimates needed to calculate the profitability ratio would be too sketchy to be of real value. Excerpts from the summary of Mr. Rothman's proposal follow:

NEW PRODUCTS ASSESSMENT
SUMMARY

It is suggested that the decision whether a proposed development project should be financed by Group should be based very largely on its profitability ratio....

In order to obtain a fair assessment of the profitability ratios, a representative committee would be formed to collate and agree the individual forecasts from which the profitability ratios would be calculated.... This committee would also draw attention to other intangible factors that might affect a decision on a particular product.

The managing directors of the development companies concerned could start development on any project approved by the committee. However, in order to insure that the Group's financial resources are not overstrained at any one time, a subcommittee of the Group Board will decide at three-month intervals the amount to be spent on development by each company in the next but two three-month periods. This decision would be based on a consideration of projects under way and of projects approved by the New Products Committee.

It would then be the responsibility of the managing directors concerned to insure that they did not overspend their budgeted allocation.

The aim has been to provide an agreed selection process and while providing short-term stability in development budgets, it is designed to give long-term flexibility in allocation of funds for S.E.G. sponsored development.

INSTRUMENTAL CONTROLS INC. (VIENNA)

Mr. Paul R. Thompson sketched the story of Instrumental Controls Inc. (ICI) before the plant tour with the IMEDE researcher was started. The parent company was founded about thirty-five years ago in Boston by Dr. Jonathan Trumbull who had been associated with Massachussetts Institute of Technology. Dr. Trumbull developed instruments using spectroscopic techniques that enabled the user to measure quantitatively what a sample of metal or other material contained by direct reading. Major users included the steel industry and other large companies in the basic materials industry. The successful application of these techniques was widely publicized among metallurgical laboratories and, in the early 1950s, a sales branch was founded in Vienna, Austria. As the servicing needs increased in Europe, repairing and some assembly was started in Vienna. Gradually, the sales branch began to "meet market needs" by developing special adaptations that required engineering. The "adaptations" eventually became so differentiated that some of the Vienna manufactured instruments are being imported into the United States.

When Consolidated Technical Research Inc., a major factor in the instrumentation industry in the United States, purchased ICI in 1962, the pattern of development of the European branches was continued, and subsidiaries in England and Belgium were given geographic areas in which their products could be sold. In 1970, Belgium covered France, the Benelux countries, and Spain while England handled business in the United Kingdom, Australia, and India. The Austrian company had a sales volume in 1969 somewhat larger than the volume of the other two European subsidiaries.

During the four years ending in 1969, the "technically dynamic" product line of the Austrian company had been vigorously developed under the leadership of Paul R. Thompson. Technical instruments measuring trace elements as small as a few parts per million, and other techniques accurately measuring large concentrations of elements, were used for quality control originally. More recently, instrumentation was being developed into a closed loop system that has been installed as a process control device in a major

European cement plant. Systems engineering, to which ICI contributes certain segments, is increasingly important as a potential market for ICI instrumentation.

Sales volume increased over 400 percent during the decade ending in 1969. The manufacturing and display space spilled out of the original building into rented quarters nearby so that the operations were being carried out, in 1969, under severe handicaps because of crowding and frequent handling of various elements that were being assembled or manufactured. Early in 1967, projections had been made that seemed to indicate the need for additional manufacturing and other space. The return on investment was developed based upon building a new plant since no suitable rental property could be found. Management at Vienna submitted its ROI to ICI headquarters in Boston. ICI (Boston) figures, differing slightly, were submitted to CTR headquarters in Houston. When the report was returned to Vienna, the assumptions of the three groups that had developed ROI figures were found to be all different with resultant communications problems over what the ROI would be. Despite differences the decision was finally made to proceed with a new plant that was completed near Vienna, in the spring of 1970.

The new plant provides adequate facilities but is sufficiently far from eating places that even the traditional Austrian two-hour lunch period would be insufficient for the workers. For this reason and because of a desire to reduce the customary shutdown for a "lunch break," management was developing plans for in-plant feeding. Experiences of manufacturers in the Vienna area indicated that the company would have to hire its own chef and arrange the menus since "contract caterers" had been notably unsuccessful in helping managements to hold skilled labor. The solution of this potential problem is of considerable concern to management.

As indicated above, the Austrian subsidiary was restricted in its European marketing to an area east of the Rhine river but including Italy by the presence of the two other subsidiaries. Major markets developed where heavy industry was concentrated although laboratories in research organizations were also a good potential market. In Germany, a direct sales organization in the form of a subsidiary company was set up. The same is true in Scandinavia. Other areas were covered by a combination of sales representatives backed up with direct support from Vienna. Although some instruments were almost ten years old, the replacement market was just beginning to develop as computer attachments—both analog and digital type—were being included in the newer instruments. Average prices were trending upwards as the basic models of the original instruments were supplied with more sophisticated readouts and printouts. Instrument sales prices ranged from £20,000 to £75,000.

Opportunities in combining with process-control systems engineering appear great, but this is a relatively new market and one that the other subsidiaries are not developing; so Vienna must take the risk of innovation alone. Skills are available, and the market is exploding as automation becomes more widely accepted in the labor-short industrialized European heavy goods industries.

The development of ICI Vienna has been accomplished with relatively little guidance or control from the parent company, ICI Boston, or its parent Consolidated Technical Research. Although ICI Vienna was originally simply a sales organization, it has become a fully independent manufacturer of instruments. Some Vienna products are being exported to the U.S., and characteristics of instruments manufactured in Boston, Belgium, and England differ slightly from those manufactured in Vienna.

These differences are posing problems in supplying multinational organizations. A multiplant international organization may not have duplicate instruments, although all are manufactured by ICI, if the instruments are purchased, according to the controlled territories, from more than one of the ICI group. In particular, there is a difference between Vienna where instruments are manufactured with identical basic units of modern modular design and the products of Belgium and England.

As production runs have increased, reflecting increasing sales volume forecasts and some standardization, the opportunity for economies of scale on some product elements are great, but the subsidiaries have independent reasons for not desiring to allow one plant to manufacture for more than its own organization. Part of the reluctance of any of the subsidiaries to "buy" from another may be the tight labor market. Part may be the desire to grow in importance. Another deterrent to cooperation may be relatively subconscious competition for reputation in the country where the plant is located.

On the other hand, the efficiencies of large-scale manufacturing are not being secured because of the decentralized managerial organization. Transfers of product knowledge, technical know-how, and personnel are hampered by the extreme independence of the ICI units. It was pointed out that in 1970 one demonstration engineer, originally with the Belgian company, is the sole example of employee interchange in ICI Vienna or any other ICI unit.

Although general performance and profits of ICI Vienna have been good, there are indications that warrant serious consideration of a change or modification of the decentralization of subsidiaries with respect to manufacturing and marketing. Some of these indications are:

1. With three main product lines to support, it is doubtful that normal engineering development budgets can be sufficient to maintain product superiority. In the case of the U.S. subsidiary, the only one to manufacture products in all three lines, the effect has been a reduction in development support for the older lines and a consequent loss of market position.

The Vienna subsidiary has emerged as the technical leader in development of the original instruments, and, as a result, the newer Vienna manufactured instruments are being imported to the U.S. for sale. For each subsidiary to maintain an engineering or development capability for each product line will probably not be economical in the long run, and, as further lines are adopted, this will become even more true.

2. Divergencies within main product lines have led to occasional difficulties between subsidiaries, in spite of territorial exclusivity. Customers with branches in many countries may be unwilling to observe territorial exclusivity. International meetings and shows in one territory certainly attract potential customers from all territories. Intracompany competition can result, and frequently has resulted, in enough "cross border" cases to be a problem, and this is particularly of concern in the original instrument line where all four subsidiaries manufacture equipment.

3. One of the original reasons for multiple manufacturing locations was to minimize import duty charges to the customer for the same item. In 1970, ten years after this decision was made, the variations in import duties do not seem as important. With an import duty of approximately 10 percent on most instruments, increased volume of production in one item in one place might well result in an increase of overall company profits *even after* paying duty. Import duties are likely to become even less important in the future.

4. A proliferation of product lines puts the individual independent subsidiary general manager in a difficult spot in deciding whether to make, buy, or develop. Although there has been some attempt to minimize duplication of effort at the development level by "coordination," it has been only partially successful. The decision made on the basis of "what is good for the subsidiary is good for the company" is not as likely to be valid today as it was ten years ago when the business was less complex and when there was only one product line.

5. In the future, if still more product lines materialize, it will be virtually impossible to maintain technical or development proficiency in all. That is to say, what is now a suspicion will become a certainty.

Several possibilities for change were being considered that could help solve the problems described above. These changes might be advantageously adopted separately, all together, or in many combinations. Each possibility considered entails some specific potential difficulties.

1. *"Specialist" Product Line Engineering and Manufacturing*

By new company policy, each subsidiary could be restricted to technical or development work in one product line area. That engineering and manufacturing unit becomes the "specialist" for that product line and manufactures it for worldwide distribution. Other units manufacture the product line only when economic factors clearly indicate this to be necessary. When another unit manufactures, its product is identical, in terms of interchangeability, which that of the "specialist." If adopted, this change would probably have had effects on certain technical "experts" who see their area of technical expertise assigned exclusively to another plant. This might be counteracted by transferring personnel to the subsidiary where the technical ability is best utilized, but this also has difficulties.

2. *Joint Marketing Effort*

The sales departments of all subsidiaries could be combined under a sales manager reporting to the president. This would have the effect of rapidly eliminating the less competitive models of similar but not identical, instruments manufactured at different plants. Marketing would remain with the individual plants. If adopted, this change would certainly disappoint many of the present sales managers who would become essentially area or product sales managers. More important, the independence of the subsidiary managers would be seriously changed, and his profit responsibility clearly different.

3. *Centralized Marketing and Technical Development*

The marketing and technical development organizations might be centralized administratively (although probably not geographically) and the subsidiaries become essentially manufacturing plants being assigned work according to overall strategy set by the centralized organization. This would most likely be unacceptable to the present general managers of the present subsidiaries because only one real general manager can exist. Although other, new, high-level positions might be created in the company, someone accustomed to general management is not likely to relish reverting to a department manager's position. This is also an extremely profound reorganization with attendant dangers of losing flexibility, motivation, and devolution of managerial skills.

4. *Coordinating Committees*

Increasing the depth of coordination at the top level might achieve the same ends as the more drastic measures described earlier. For instance an "executive committee" consisting of the president, the general managers of each subsidiary, including the U.S. company, could be established to meet frequently and create policies and take actions that would deal with the foreseeable difficulties. Within this committee, for example, company-wide staff authority for a functional area such as finance, marketing, etc., could be assigned in addition to line responsibility. This plan infringes on the present independence of the general managers but in a way they have a possibility of participating in policy decisions. The main difficulty in this suggestion is that it requires a very skillful president who can truly take an international viewpoint and really satisfy the often divergent viewpoints of the general managers. Gradually, under this plan, the autonomy and flexibility of the present four separate organizations would be lessened.

In reviewing these ideas, Mr. Thompson commented that the problem posed and its suggested solutions seemed to revolve around two conflicting managements precepts:

1. Good management is synonymous with forward planning and change to meet the future.
2. Profit-making arrangements are hard enough to come by that they should be strengthened, not destroyed; or put another way, "don't rock the boat," if it seems to be going well.

At a later date, while reviewing the case material, Mr. Thompson commented further:

> Since in most cases, particularly with smaller high technology companies like ICI, the individuals in the company are its greatest assets, any move that might alienate a large number of individuals or in any way affect their contribution must be very seriously considered from just this point of view.

Index of Cases